MARKED WOMEN

Patrick McGilligan | Series Editor

MARKED WOMEN

PROSTITUTES AND PROSTITUTION IN THE CINEMA

Russell Campbell

THE UNIVERSITY OF WISCONSIN PRESS

This book was published with the support of the Community Media Trust of Wellington, New Zealand, and a research grant from the Faculty of Humanities and Social Sciences at the Victoria University of Wellington.

The University of Wisconsin Press
1930 Monroe Street
Madison, Wisconsin 53711

www.wisc.edu/wisconsinpress/

3 Henrietta Street
London WC2E 8LU, England

5   4   3   2   1

Printed in the United States of America

Library of Congress Cataloging-in-Publication Data
Campbell, Russell.
Marked women : prostitutes and prostitution in the cinema / Russell Campbell.
p.   cm. — (Wisconsin film studies)
Includes bibliographical references and index.
ISBN 0-299-21250-5 (hardcover : alk. paper)
ISBN 0-299-21254-8 (pbk. : alk. paper)
1. Prostitutes in motion pictures. I. Title. II. Series.
PN1995.9.P76C36 2005
791.43'6692—dc22
2005008259

CONTENTS

ILLUSTRATIONS

ACKNOWLEDGMENTS

This project turned out to be more massive than I ever imagined. It has taken a long time, and I've accumulated many debts of gratitude along the way.

The research and writing were principally facilitated by two periods of Research and Study Leave granted by Victoria University of Wellington, New Zealand, the second through the Faculty of Humanities and Social Sciences. I'm also grateful to VUW for research grants from the Internal Grants Committee and the FHSS Research Committee, one of which assisted publication. Assistance from the Community Media Trust, Wellington, is also much appreciated.

Research many miles from home was made a pleasurable experience by the hospitality of those I stayed with, including Gerd Pohlmann and Rod Prosser, Peter and Win Campbell, Stephen Whitehouse, Julie Boddy, and Anthony Slide.

I'm enormously grateful for the assistance of staff at the Stiftung Deutsche Kinemathek, the Bundesarchiv Filmarchiv, the Freunde der Deutsche Kinemathek, the Deutsche Institut für Filmkunde, Det Danske Filmmuseum, the Centre National de la Cinématographie, the Cinémathèque Française, the Vidéothèque de Paris, the Centre Audiovisuel Simone de Beauvoir, the National Film Archive and British Film Institute, the Library of Congress, the Museum of Modern Art (New York), the Wisconsin Center for Film and Theater Research, the Margaret Herrick Library of the Academy of Motion Picture Arts and Sciences, and the New Zealand Film Archive. The Film Department of Pro Helvetia (Arts Council of Switzerland) generously helped with loaning tapes. In Wellington, the Aro St. Video Shop was indispensable.

For discussing their film work with me I'd like to express special thanks to Dagmar Beiersdorf, Lothar Lambert, Klaus Tuschen, and Louise Smith. Thanks, too, to those who helped with translation, especially Gerd Pohlmann, Rachel Juniot, Catherine Juniot, Giovanni Tiso, and Robèrt Franken. Others who assisted the project and offered encouragement in diverse ways, all greatly appreciated, were Emilie Dear, Sarah Davy, Karyn Kay, Andrew Horton, Barry Grant, Libby Hogg, Phil Mann, Kim Worthington, Diane Kearns, Pat McGilligan, Jane Wrightson, and Alister Barry. Finally, I'm grateful for the opportunity to discuss questions raised by my research with Catherine Healy of the New Zealand Prostitutes' Collective.

EPIGRAPH CREDITS

Chapter 2: excerpt from Sheila Rowbotham, *Woman's Consciousness, Man's World* (Harmondsworth: Pelican, 1973), p 43, copyright © 1973 by Sheila Rowbotham, reproduced by permission of Penguin Books Ltd.

Chapter 7: excerpt from "The Harlot" by James K. Baxter, from *Collected Poems of James K. Baxter* edited by J. E. Weir (Wellington: Oxford University Press, 1979), reproduced by permission of J. C. Baxter.

Chapter 7: excerpt from "The Detonated Man" by Blaise Cendrars, from *Selected Writings*, copyright © 1966 by Walter Albert, reproduced by permission of New Directions Publishing Corp.

Chapter 8: excerpt from *The Poems of Catullus* translated by Peter Whigham (Harmondsworth: Penguin Classics, 1966), p 222, copyright © 1966 by Penguin Books Ltd, reproduced by permission of Penguin Books Ltd.

Chapter 10: excerpt from Nuj, in Siriporn Skrobanek, Nataya Boonpakdee and Chutima Jantateero, *The Traffic in Women: Human Realities of the International Sex Trade* (London and New York: Zed Books Ltd., 1997), p 2, reproduced by permission of Zed Books.

Chapter 11: excerpt from Barbara Sherman Heyl, *The Madam as Entrepreneur: Career Management in House Prostitution* (New Brunswick, NJ: Transaction, 1979), p 104, reproduced by permission of Transaction Publishers.

Chapter 12: excerpt from *Gilgamesh: Translated from the Sîn-leqi-unninnī Version* by John Gardner and John Maier, copyright © 1984 by Estate of John Gardner and John Maier, reproduced by permission of Georges Borchardt, Inc., Literary Agency and Alfred A. Knopf, a division of Random House, Inc.

Chapter 13: excerpt from Estela V. Welldon, *Mother, Madonna, Whore: The Idealization and Denigration of Motherhood* (New York: Guilford Press, 1991), reproduced by permission of Guilford Press.

Chapter 14: excerpt from "M," in Kate Millett, "Prostitution: A Quartet for Female Voices" in Vivian Gornick and Barbara K. Moran, eds., *Woman in Sexist Society: Studies in Power and Powerlessness* (New York: Basic Books, 1971), p 29, reproduced by permission of Perseus Books Group.

Chapter 15: excerpt from Nick Davies, *Dark Heart: The Shocking Truth about Hidden Britain* (London: Chatto & Windus, 1997), copyright © 1997 by Nick Davies, reproduced by permission of The Random House Group Ltd. and the author c/o Rogers, Coleridge & White Ltd.

Chapter 16: excerpt from Hilary, in Jan Jordan, *Working Girls* (Auckland: Penguin Books [NZ], 1991), p 112, reproduced by permission of Penguin Books (NZ).

Chapter 17: excerpt from Xaviera Hollander, with Robin Moore and Yvonne Dunleavy, *The Happy Hooker* (New York: Dell, 1972), p 189, reproduced by permission of Xaviera Hollander.

Chapter 19: excerpt from Sam Rohdie, *Rocco and His Brothers (Rocco e i suoi fratelli)* (London: BFI, 1992), p 30, reproduced by permission of bfi Publishing.

Chapter 20: excerpt from Michelle Citron, in "Women and Film: A Discussion of Feminist Aesthetics," *New German Critique* No 13 (Winter 1978), p 104, reproduced by permission of Telos Press Ltd.

MARKED WOMEN

1

The Sex Trade and the Cinema

If people arrange the world that way for women, there's no good
pretending it's arranged the other way.
—GEORGE BERNARD SHAW, *Mrs. Warren's Profession*[1]

In *The Creation of Patriarchy*, Gerda Lerner writes: "The division of women
into 'respectable women,' who are protected by their men, and 'disreputable women,' who are out on the street unprotected by men and free
to sell their services, has been the basic class division for women."[2] Patriarchy has thus created the institutions of marriage—to provide for a
man's nurturing and companionship and for the orderly production of
his offspring, and of prostitution—to supply the sexual pleasures he
might otherwise miss out on. They are complementary institutions, but
they form an odd couple, a mismatched pair. While marriage is upheld,
celebrated—especially idealized whenever social forces threaten to undermine it, as in the current phase of late capitalism—prostitution is
swept under the carpet, hidden away out of sight or quarantined in red-
light districts. The woman who attaches herself to one man is accepted
as a respectable member of society; the woman who offers herself to all
is stigmatized and ostracized—in order to proclaim, as Engels argues,
"the absolute domination of the male over the female sex as the fundamental law of society."[3] The married woman, under the sign of Western
individualism and at the cost of rigidly curtailing her sexual activity, has
been able to claim something approaching legal equality with her husband; the prostitute battles always against discrimination, against laws
that hedge and confine her.

As sexual *object*, fucking machine, the prostitute is created and sustained by patriarchal society to service men's desires: she is required to
make her body available to men on demand, and then condemned for
doing so.[4] As *subject*, the independent woman contemptuous of the
hypocrisy of the system, she poses a threat to that society. Male anxiety

over this class of person who is assigned a place but stubbornly resists her subordination, constantly threatening to step outside the defined limits, is at the root of the repressive measures against her profession, which have returned in waves throughout the centuries. The tendency to legalize brothels when they are firmly in the hands of men, and outlaw them when they are run cooperatively by women, is but one example of this patriarchal regime; and the inveterate preference the prostitute shows for working illegally rather than submitting to a male-supervised system of tolerance is indicative of her defiance of it.

Although, of course, details of the practice vary between societies and over time, sociological studies and firsthand accounts concur, in general terms, in describing the social reality of female prostitution.[5] Financial need is overwhelmingly identified as the motivating factor for women to enter the profession. Depending on the setting in which the prostitution takes place, there may be an element of coercion. The work in itself is not normally experienced as pleasant (though the money rewards may compensate): Xaviera Hollander notwithstanding, prostitutes report that they seldom enjoy sex with their clients. The job takes its toll in terms of psychological well-being, especially on those who engage full-time in the profession for sustained periods; and it is hard for prostitutes, especially heterosexual ones, to maintain affectionate relationships while they are working. There is a high incidence of a history of sexual abuse in childhood, and of drug and alcohol addiction. Women who engage in mercantile sex are frequently denied civil rights and subjected to laws that curtail their freedom, making them liable for fines or imprisonment for exercising their profession; and their stigmatized condition and marginal legal status make them vulnerable to violence and exploitation by pimps, police, landlords, and clients.

This is the background in reality for the figure at the margins of society, oppressed but often insubordinate, who has attained a potent symbolic value for creative artists, haunting the imagination of filmmakers throughout the twentieth century and beyond, as she did that of writers and painters in the nineteenth. In *Femmes Fatales*, Mary Ann Doane argues that in the cinema the representation of the prostitute "is nowhere near as pervasive and insistent as in literature and art" and that after the 1920s such fascination as there had been (in films such as *Traffic in Souls* and *Pandora's Box*) fell away.[6] A study of the subject does not support this hypothesis. True, rigid censorship all but banished the prostitute from American screens when the Hays Code was enforced between 1934 and the early 1960s, and similarly constrained filmic expression in countries such as Britain, Nazi Germany, and the Soviet Union. In other major centers of filmmaking, notably France and Japan, a taboo against the representation of prostitution never applied, while the loosening grip of censorship internationally from the late 1960s brought a flood of prostitute stories to the cinema.

James L. Limbacher's 1983 filmography *Sexuality in World Cinema* (which is largely confined to films reviewed and/or released in the United States), lists some fourteen hundred titles dealing with prostitutes and prostitution, and since its publication the tide shows little sign of abating.[7] The roll call of female actors who at one time or another in their careers have played prostitutes includes nearly every major star, from Lillian Gish to Greta Garbo, Brigitte Bardot to Sophia Loren, Jodie Foster to Julia Roberts, and scores more; a few — such as Simone Signoret, Anna Magnani, and Shirley MacLaine — have made the prostitute character their specialty.

Predominantly, and unsurprisingly given that the film industry internationally has been male-dominated, prostitute characters in film are creatures of the male imagination. That is, though the characters are of course portrayed by women, the roles are usually written and the performances directed by men. In chapter 2, drawing on the psychoanalytic studies of Nancy Chodorow and Dorothy Dinnerstein, I suggest that men's fascination with the figure of the prostitute may be traced to the troubled process of attaining masculine identity that males undergo when growing up in a patriarchal society, particularly one structured on the nuclear family in which the primary caregiver is female.

Disturbed by woman and what she represents as the sexual other, men have found the fictional prostitute uniquely suited to embodying fantasies in which their acute desires and anxieties find expression. Because of the contradictory emotions she generates, she has come to occupy an equivocal position in the male imagination, both valued and vilified. A symbol of eroticism in a sexually repressive society, or of endurance in the face of intense humiliation and suffering, she attains a positive coloring; but as a symbol of flesh against the spirit, of the polluted against the pure, of the commercial against the freely offered, or of the depths of social life against its heights, she is negative. She incarnates much of patriarchal culture's ambivalent attitude to sex, but in a specific way; it is sex per se that she offers, sex severed from both legal and affectionate ties, sex as a momentary act as against sex as the intimate heart of a sustained relationship.

Male-fantasy representations of the prostitute in the cinema are however not (except in the low-budget pornographic underground) given free reign: they are shaped not only by the need to create a plausible fictional world but also by the demands of patriarchal ideology. Men have much invested in upholding and sustaining their system of control in society, which means that depictions of prostitution may need to be modified to minimize any damage they might cause to the prestige of the existing social structure. (The prostitute is in fact such a troublesome figure that ideally the patriarchy would like to erase all traces of her, and at times, as under the Hays Code, it has succeeded in creating the censorship mechanism to enable it to do so.)[8] The killing of a prostitute on screen, for example, may serve to assuage male fears: for a time at least the anxieties that the female as sexual being provokes can be stilled. Commission of the act itself, however, may be displaced from the male protagonist onto a surrogate figure, such as a pimp or a serial killer, so that the murder may be simultaneously enjoyed and disavowed: the existence of violence against women in society is thus acknowledged but attributed to bad elements who will themselves, very likely, be obliterated.

Interaction between the impulses of male fantasy with the (sometimes contradictory) demands of patriarchal ideology, moderated by changing social practices and attitudes, has generated a wide variety of prostitute representations on screen, which do, however, tend to fall into recurrent patterns. More recently feminist interventions have complicated the picture, in particular by de-romanticizing the prostitute and bringing her representation back closer to the social reality described above. In *Marked Women* I have attempted a form of classification of these diverse depictions, identifying a number of distinctive character types and narrative structures. In some respects it is helpful to think of these categories as "archetypal," but I use the word not in the specialized Jungian sense but in the broader meaning of pertaining to (as the *Oxford English Dictionary* puts it) "any pervasive symbolic representation." I explore the character types in chapters 3–16, and the narratives in chapters 17–19.[9] In the structure of the book, the archetypes are ordered according to when (to the best of my knowledge) films featuring them first made a definitive entrance on the scene, while each chapter is organized chronologically.

If in life it is sometimes difficult to define just what constitutes a "prostitute," it is even more so in the cinema, which often thrives on a tantalizing ambiguity. To keep the scope of this study somewhat manageable, I have striven to confine it (not always successfully) to characters who one can fairly assume, on the strength of the evidence presented, make cash transactions for sexual services with multiple clients. Gangster's molls, mistresses, courtesans,[10] and high-class geisha are thus excluded, along with sluts who do not charge and "furniture" in the year 2022 (*Soylent Green*).

The field covered in *Marked Women* is that of fictional feature films, together with a few shorts, particularly from the silent period; television dramas and series have by and large been omitted, as have documentaries. Geographically the scope is as broad as I have been able to make it, but most of the examples come from European and North American cinema, while the coverage of the cinemas of Asia, Latin America and Africa is much less extensive, through lack of familiarity. Any claim to universal validity is therefore tentative and suspect, though such research as I have been able to conduct into films from outside Europe and the United States tends to confirm the impression that cross-cultural differences in the representation of prostitution are not as great as one might expect. This is possibly because patriarchy is universal, and its effects in shaping male consciousness and imposing ideological constraints on expression are very likely similar from society to society.

In terms of timeframe, the concentration of this study is on sound film, and particularly movies from the post–World War II period. I have however included some consideration of silent cinema, recognizing that it was in the early years of motion pictures that the representation of prostitutes and prostitution originated, and that silent film enjoyed, particularly in the United States, a relative freedom from censorship compared with later decades.

There are no claims to exhaustiveness in my coverage of the field, and my sampling of films is entirely unscientific, determined by those that were available to view or synopsized in written sources in sufficient detail to be helpful. Nevertheless, without being encyclopedic, I have attempted to include a large number of examples, in order to demonstrate the widespread extent of the patterns discussed and the richness of variations upon them — it's my belief that genre and national cinema studies, for example, typically tend to work from too small a pool of examples.

The book is titled *Marked Women* in recognition of social structures and practices that single the prostitute out. At times in history, for example, a distinctive dress code for the prostitute has been compulsory; for the contemporary streetwalker, it's an economic necessity to signify her availability through her attire and posture, especially when the law forbids soliciting. The system compels the prostitute to mark herself off from respectable women, creating a coding of physical appearance, which is instantly recognizable and can be readily appropriated by the cinema.

There is a sense, also, in which sex workers are regarded like plague victims. There's a fear of contamination, an anxiety that respectable girls and women might become infected: hence the desire to contain prostitution within red-light quarantine zones. The stigma attached to the prostitute becomes a way of neutralizing the threat to the social order that she poses. For the pimp, on the other hand, the prostitute may be branded, tattooed, as a mark of possession; and if she tries to escape his control, she is in danger of being scarred by acid or razor. Frequently, in the cinema as in life, the prostitute is targeted for murder.

The Bette Davis film *Marked Woman* (USA, 1937) pays tribute to the New York prostitutes who helped put their gangland boss behind bars. Its rediscovery by feminist critics was part of a new wave of criticism and theory which revolutionized thinking about the portrayal of women in the cinema.[11] This book aims to contribute, as far as is possible from the necessarily skewed bias of a heterosexual male, to the discourse that developed from that point.

Cinema and prostitution struck up an early alliance. In 1896 French theater entrepreneur Charles Aumont toured Russia with the Lumière cinematograph/projector — and singer-prostitutes from his Paris *café chantant*. An observer wrote: "Aumont has added Lumière's cinematograph to the chansonettes, the can-can and the convenience of meeting his unfortunate creatures. . . . Without it many respectable visitors would be positively uneasy at going to Aumont's." Maxim Gorky encountered both the projector and the prostitutes at the Nizhnii Novgorod fair, and was to write a short story about their conjunction.[12] The potential for a reciprocal aphrodisiac effect was clearly grasped, and before long blue movies were being made and screened in brothels, or in private clubs to which prostitutes would often direct their clients.[13] Streetwalkers would loiter outside movie houses in red-light districts, and would at times conspicuously attend film screenings themselves, doubtless creating an air of sexual excitement for males in the audience.[14] In such a context, it would have been surprising if prostitute characters did not soon begin to crop up on screen.

It is likely that the first prostitute representations were in comic mode. The earliest film I have come across alluding to prostitution — *Scene in the*

Tenderloin, probably made in the United States in 1897 — is a comedy. The *International Photographic Films Catalog* (Winter 1897–98) describes it thus:

> Showing party of ladies strolling down the street. They are followed
> by young men, who in turn are followed by policemen. The ladies are
> arrested and taken to the stationhouse. The action of the ladies is most
> comical and laughable, and bound to please the most fastidious
> audience. Excellent film.[15]

The film itself is no doubt lost, and this description is teasingly ambiguous. The "ladies" might be either prostitutes — with the comedy derived from the physical vigor with which they resist arrest — or respectable women mistaken for streetwalkers because they're strolling in a
red-light district.

If the latter is the case, then *Scene in the Tenderloin* offers a prototype of
what was to become one of the favorite and enduring varieties of prostitute comedy, that of mistaken identity — the humor springing from the
application of an inappropriate category to the phenomenon in question:
virtue confused with vice, or the other way around. Other comic uses to
which the figure of the prostitute could be put may be illustrated by a few
further examples from early cinema.

Tenderloin at Night (USA, 1899) clearly identifies its three prostitute
characters, sitting gaudily dressed in a barroom, and locates them in a
criminal milieu. When a rube from the country comes in, one of the
women kisses and fondles him while her male associate slips knock-out
drops in his drink. With their victim unconscious, the prostitutes strip
him of his watch and wallet; a fight ensues when he comes to, which is
broken up by a cop. The prostitute here is a fake, a decoy, a thief in collusion with other criminals — a collusion that extends to the waiter and
perhaps to the policeman as well. Lending charm to this otherwise sordid little tale is the spontaneous jig the women perform, kicking up their
legs and holding their skirts, after the rube has been shunted out. The
lightness of touch is lacking in the otherwise similar *How They Do Things
on the Bowery* (1902), which shows a brazen streetwalker picking up a customer, clearly a naive fellow from out of town, taking him into a saloon,
drugging him and robbing him of his valuables, before he is run out of
the bar by the waiter and deposited by a cop in a paddy wagon.

In *What Demoralized the Barber Shop* (USA, 1901) it is the disturbance
that female sexuality (in the person of the prostitute) can engender, which
is given the comic treatment. In this short single-shot film a portion of

sidewalk can be seen at center above the interior of a basement barber shop, with the barber at work at left and a man receiving a shoeshine at right. The legs of two women appear. They are apparently streetwalkers, since they hitch up their skirts and sway back and forth, displaying their wares. The customer at right kicks over the shoeshine boy. The barber is so distracted he grapples crazily with his customer spread-eagled in the chair, lathering him blindly and taking to him with a blade while peering up and maneuvering to get a better view of the women. The maltreated customer waves his legs helplessly, while the shoeshine client topples off his high chair and gets up for another peek.

A reworking of this material, *The Barber's Dee-Light* (USA, 1905), is significant for the shift in emphasis away from comedy toward visual eroticism — until the end. The setup is the same, except now the sidewalk can be seen on the full width of the screen, and the action consists mostly of a series of women walking past, pausing, and displaying their stockinged legs, as the men in the barber shop gawk. Finally, however, after the prostitutes have been moved on by a policeman, another skirt appears, and the legs come down the steps into the shop. It's a man wearing a kilt. Here the erotic charge is intensified and then exploded in laughter.

Following hard on the heels of the comic treatment of the prostitute character was the melodramatic. Prostitution as a social phenomenon had a sensational profile in the era of silent film, particularly the years up to and including World War I, and melodrama was in fact to become the principal mode in which the subject was conceptualized in the cinema. Drawn from popular literature, the stage, and journalism, archetypal tales of the fallen woman and the white slave soon emerged on screen.[16]

An early appearance of the fallen woman story was in *The Downward Path* (USA, 1900), a five-part film with each scene listed separately in the Biograph catalogue.[17] This production (with a total running time of under fifteen minutes) was intended, according to the catalogue, "to convey a moral lesson in the career of a young country girl who succumbs to temptations, and becomes involved with the wickedness of a big city."[18] The protagonist is a chubby lass (whose size initially suggests comedy rather than melodrama) who rejects the advances of a rustic lad in overalls and instead runs away to the city with a roguish book agent. There she becomes a streetwalker, with the book agent acting as her pimp. When her parents appear she runs to embrace them, but the agent knocks her father down and drags her away, her mother faints, and a cop strolls past unconcerned. She is next seen as a "soubrette" singing and dancing in a cafe. After a dispute with her pimp, she takes poison and kills herself, her distraught parents rushing in too late to save her.

Here are many of the key elements in what was to become the recurrent tale, depicting the woman who descends into prostitution — to which a negative sign is almost invariably attached — as a figure of pathos. In the first major version of this story, as exemplified in *The Downward Path*, an innocent young woman is seduced or raped, and runs away or is cast out by her family. On her own, abandoned by her lover (or, as here, discovering that he is a procurer), perhaps with a baby to care for, and without a legitimate source of income, she sooner or later begins to charge for her sexual services. On the other hand, seduction may not be involved. The protagonist, in this case often a mature woman, strays from the path of virtue from force of circumstance or as an act of self-sacrifice. The outcome is, in any event, the same. As a prostitute the woman is degraded and trapped, condemned to a miserable fate unless fortune intervenes in granting her an opportunity to atone for her sins. She is likely to die at the end of the film, through suicide, illness, accident, murder or execution; the conventions of Victorian art and literature, Nina Auerbach notes, ordained that "a woman's fall ends in death."[19] Otherwise she may survive and save her soul through an act of redemption; frequently she is paired off with a good man whose upright character serves to cancel out the poor impression of the male sex given earlier in the film.

The version featuring a young woman protagonist is perhaps best exemplified by the many screen adaptations of Leo Tolstoy's novel *Resurrection*, first published in Russia in 1899 and adapted for the stage in Paris in 1902 and New York in 1903. The well-known story, set in Russia in the 1870s, tells of an orphaned peasant girl seduced by an aristocrat, Prince Dmitri Nekhludov, on his vacation. Becoming pregnant, Katusha is disgraced and leaves her godmother's service. After her child dies, she is reduced to prostitution. Following a trial in which she is convicted for a crime she did not commit, Katusha is sentenced to exile in Siberia. Dmitri, a juror in the case, feels remorse and offers to marry her. She, however, refuses him, accepts her lot as a prisoner, and is thus spiritually regenerated.

The novel and play were notably filmed by D. W. Griffith in his fragmented one-reel version titled *The Resurrection* (USA, 1909), which probably operated as a series of illustrated scenes from Tolstoy rather than as a narrative in its own right. Other silent adaptations included *Opstandelse* (Denmark, 1907), *Katusha* (Japan, 1914), *Vozrozhdennia* (Russia,

1915), *A Woman's Resurrection* (USA, 1915), *Resurrection* (USA, 1918), and *Resurrection* (USA, 1927).[20] Much of the enduring appeal of Tolstoy's tale, as in many fallen woman scenarios, must have resided in the essential moral ambiguity of the events of Katusha's life, inherent in the original novel,[21] and in the fascinating synthesis of virtue and vice in the one person. The story well exemplifies the "dual perspective" Auerbach writes of in analyzing Victorian fiction: "an explicit narrative that abases the woman, an iconographic pattern that exalts her."[22]

Where adaptations of *Resurrection* typify the version of the fallen woman narrative featuring a young, initially virginal protagonist,[23] the second version portraying a more mature heroine may be exemplified by another sob story warhorse. Alexandre Bisson's play *La Femme X . . .* (Paris, 1908) was filmed at least seven times, beginning with *Madame X* (USA, 1909).[24]

In the play, Jacqueline Floriot is driven from her home because of her rigid husband's suspicions regarding her relationships with other men. He keeps custody of their infant son Raymond and refuses Jacqueline permission to see the boy even when he becomes dangerously ill. After a suicide attempt, Jacqueline in despair leaves the country, becomes a woman of the streets, and over a period of years is destroyed by drink and drugs. When she eventually returns to Paris, Raymond has become a promising young attorney. To protect her husband and son from a blackmailer, she shoots the man and is put on trial for murder, with Raymond being assigned to defend her. Refusing to reveal her true identity, she confesses to the crime and dies happy in the knowledge that her son's life has not been tarnished.

Psychological demoralization, as here, often provides the impetus for the more mature protagonist of a fallen woman narrative to surrender her virtue.[25] Other motivating factors include abandonment by a husband, loss of custody of a child, and desperate poverty. Self-sacrifice for a loved one, particularly a son or daughter ignorant of the mother's true profession, is a persistent motif.

Although the trajectories are similar, the emotions generated by the two versions of the archetypal narrative can be very different. As the examples illustrate, the young woman is often far from blameless herself, whereas the mature woman is much more frequently obeying a higher morality in surrendering her chastity; the young woman can enjoy her life of sin whereas the mature woman seldom does. Nevertheless, the stories can have much in common; in daring to yoke together irreconcilable oppositions of guilt and innocence, of self-indulgence and self-sacrifice, the films attained much of their appeal.

For the male spectator, a major attraction of the fallen woman characterization would have been the admixture of virtue and vice in the one person, a woman who as fantasized object of desire could overcome (as explored further in chapter 2) the separating out of his affectionate and erotic feelings. It is the ambiguity with which the "fall" is frequently depicted, and the elusive, dynamic dialectic of purity and corruption, which preserve the woman's mystery and thus her allure. For the female audience, to whom the films were perhaps primarily directed, there was excitement in the transgressive nature of the story of the woman of good character (though sometimes with a rather too experimental approach to social mores) reduced to selling her body. As Auerbach writes of the motif in literature and painting, "the fallen woman, heartbreaking and glamorous, flourished in the popular iconography of America and the Continent as well as England. Her stance as galvanic outcast, her piquant blend of innocence and experience, came to embody everything in womanhood that was dangerously, tragically, and triumphantly beyond social boundaries."[26]

Of course, the heroine is typically punished for her transgression. Ideologically, the fallen woman film deals with the disturbance to the patriarchal order that occurs when a female is cast adrift from the family and is forced, bereft of protection from father or husband, to fend for herself. In its address to female spectators, the story will thus serve as a cautionary tale, illustrating what is in store for the woman who permits herself to stray from the path of virtue; for male audiences, the film may warn of the consequences of parental or marital failure. Ultimately the patriarchal pattern will be restored, whether through the straying lamb being brought back into the fold or through her elimination.

Nevertheless, there is always the chance of a narrative excess subverting the didactic purpose. It is in fact in interrogating the notion of "innocence" and what value it may have for women, regardless of the kudos that patriarchy attaches to it, that many fallen woman films begin to undermine the tenets of Victorian morality to which they pay lip service. Often it means in practice—as the films mischievously demonstrate—a cramped, narrow, subservient life, a submission to domestic chores or exploitative wage labor, a lack of fun or playfulness, an absence of intimate personal relationships outside the family, an inability to partake of entertainments such as dancing and drinking associated with urban night life, and of course a ban on sexual desire and its expression. For instance, the heroine's actions in *The Downward Path* in rejecting her rural suitor and eagerly eloping to the city with her rapscallion lover come across as the actions of a spirited young woman striking out for independence, while her supposedly degraded lifestyle in the city appears at times — when for example she dances a table-top jig and a female customer in the cafe joins in, slapping her knees — as just good fun. In *Der Mädchenhirt* (Germany, 1919), set in Prague, prostitution itself is never given a positive coloring but the frolicking hippielike life of the prostitutes and pimps on Kampainsel, a rustic island retreat, is contrasted favorably with the grim attachment to discipline and order represented (hypocritically) by the police inspector Duschnitz, who wants to sweep the island clean of its riffraff. *Das Tagebuch einer Verlorenen / Diary of a Lost Girl* (Germany, 1929) goes even farther in depicting life at a luxury brothel as decidedly more congenial than at the appalling regimented reformatory in which the heroine has formerly been confined for having given birth to an illegitimate child. Here, an indication that in this case ideological bounds had been broken is shown by the censorship problems the film encountered, as we will see in chapter 12.

The fallen woman narrative was predicated on (1) the belief that a single woman who is sexually active is morally corrupt, making her in the mind of many men ineligible for marriage, thus blocking off one avenue for her future, and (2) the barring of women from the vast majority of occupations in the workforce, including all well-paid jobs. In most industrial and post-industrial societies both these premises were well under way to obsolescence by mid-century. As a result, the concept of a loss of chastity leading inexorably to prostitution became no longer tenable, and most films with a fully developed fallen woman pattern were in fact produced in the silent era.

Related to the fallen woman narrative, but placing more emphasis on the element of coercion and hence on the potential of the imperiled protagonist's being rescued, was that of the white slave. Films structured on this story were sufficiently numerous and similar in nature to constitute a genre, which flourished particularly in the mid-teens but which continued, albeit hard hit by censorship, through the end of the silent era.[27]

The white slave traffic, "the widely accepted term for the procuring, selling or buying of women with the intention of holding or forcing them into a life of prostitution . . . the system by which vice markets are kept supplied,"[28] had been the subject of widespread public concern in Europe in the last years of the nineteenth century and the early years of the twentieth, resulting in a number of international conferences and a 1904 treaty, The Repression of the Trade in White Women. This treaty was agreed to the following year by the US Senate, and in the United States concern about the forcible entrapment of women in prostitution began to mount, reaching almost fever pitch by 1913. During this time, emphasis shifted away from the original preoccupation with international trafficking toward interstate trafficking, and indeed any form of coerced prostitution. Numerous investigations were held and accounts of the vice trade published, and popular fictional representations in the form of novels, plays, and films appeared. As a result of the public clamor, the White Slave Traffic Act (commonly known as the Mann Act), prohibiting the transportation of a woman across state lines for the purpose of prostitution, was passed in 1910, and many municipalities closed down their brothels and red-light districts.[29]

Ruth Rosen, in her well-researched study *The Lost Sisterhood: Prostitution in America, 1900–1918,* concludes that white slavery was probably experienced by fewer than 10 percent of the prostitutes working in the United States in the years prior to World War I.[30] There were nevertheless significant numbers of women being induced to work as prostitutes against their will, often in conditions of shocking brutality, as numerous case studies attested.[31] Films of the white slave genre appealed to, and helped fuel, public alarm over the situation by constructing highly emotional melodramatic narratives that placed their female characters in situations in which their virtue was imperiled.

Although short movies depicting women being strong-armed into streetwalking appeared in the United States as early as 1904—the short drama *Decoyed* contains in capsule form several of the elements that were later to become standard—it was in a series of increasingly elaborate films released in Denmark between 1907 and 1912 that a full-fledged genre emerged. The series, produced by Nordisk Films and its rival, Fotorama, included *Den hvide Slavinde / The White Slave* (Nordisk, 1907), *Den hvide Slavehandel / The White Slave Trade* (Fotorama, 1910), *Den hvide Slavehandel I / The White Slave / The White Slave Trade I* (Nordisk, 1910), *Slavehandlerens Flug / The Slave Trader's Escape* (Fotorama, 1910), *Den hvide Slavehandel II / In the Hands of Impostors* (Nordisk, 1911), and *Den hvide Slavehandel III / The White Slave Trade III* (Nordisk, 1912).[32]

These films typically tell the story of a young woman who, through deception, falls into the hands of white slavers in a foreign city such as London or St. Petersburg. Imprisoned in a brothel, she has to struggle to keep her virtue intact, before being rescued by her fiancé.

Exemplifying the argument that "white slavery represents the power of metaphor to reduce the complex problem of prostitution to a simple story of villain and victim,"[33] *Den hvide Slavinde* and its successors exalt the innocence of the heroine, who shows a fighting spirit worthy at times of a serial queen. In *Den hvide Slavehandel I,* for example, Anna repulses a client who has been brought into her by the procuress, knocking him senseless after a fierce struggle. Edith in *Den hvide Slavehandel II* has similar fighting qualities, but she is also subject to fainting spells; her resolution will preserve her just long enough for her male liberator to arrive.

The white slavers in this group of films are represented as unscrupulous confederates, working in a network to ensnare their prey, and prepared to use force to keep her in their clutches. Women are prominent among them, falsely masquerading as kindly maternal figures. Their bordellos service an upper-class clientele, who carouse in dinner jackets drinking champagne (in *Den hvide Slavehandel II,* a client who wishes to purchase Edith is identified as "Lord X"). The films thus appeal to class as well as chauvinist sentiments, depicting the heroine — who is typically from a humble background — in imminent danger of being debauched by the rich, shown by a repeated motif of her resisting the finery that is pressed upon her.

In showing the daughter's virtue being inadequately guarded, the Danish films record a failure of the patriarchy (the girl's father, in the first instance, and then the police, who invariably declare that they can do nothing about the situation). The younger male generation, however, comes to the rescue; the tale becomes one of the heroine moving from her father's care to that of her husband-to-be, and in thus reasserting patriarchal values the films repudiate prostitution as all that is evil, decadent, and foreign.[34]

Traffic in Souls and *The Inside of the White Slave Traffic,* released within a month of each other in November–December 1913, are the key works of the white slave genre in the United States, and have been subjected to extensive analysis.[35] For the purposes of this study, the crucial characteristic of these films is a shift in mode away from the melodramatic tale of a single female protagonist toward a quasi-sociological exposé of coerced prostitution.

In *Traffic in Souls,* there are several victims, representative of the three categories of vulnerable women reputedly targeted by the vice rings: two

1. *Traffic in Souls:* Lorna (Ethel Grandin) rescued by Officer Burke (Matt Moore). Courtesy of the Academy of Motion Picture Arts and Sciences.

Swedish girls from an immigrant ship, who are lured into a brothel on the pretence that it is an employment agency; a naive country girl who is spotted arriving at the railroad station and directed by a relay of pimps to the same establishment; and a candy-store employee, Lorna, who excitedly accompanies a procurer to a cafe and a dance-hall, is drugged, and ends up in a second brothel.[36] Once inside the houses, the young women are imprisoned by the beefy madams and their entourage of "cadets." Only smart work on the part of the heroine, Lorna's elder sister Mary, who cleverly procures evidence against the white slave syndicate, and Mary's fiancé, a policeman, secures their release.

Far from being the foreign villain of the Danish films and of earlier American films that had lain the blame on Chinese miscreants,[37] the kingpin (Trubus) of the vice racket in *Traffic in Souls* is a pillar of the local establishment and a respected reformer. *Variety* commented on the ironical physical resemblance of the actor who plays the part to John D. Rockefeller, whose report on white slavery in New York was supposedly the basis for the film.[38] *Traffic in Souls* makes a point of showing how Trubus personally supervises the extensive operation and collects its substantial profits; but in analyzing the control of brothel prostitution by organized crime and accusing apparently respectable citizens of being behind it, the film depicts the police as vigilant upholders of the law and makes no acknowledgment of the system of graft which the Rockefeller report had identified as a prime factor in enabling vice businesses to flourish.

There is no hierarchical syndicate in *The Inside of the White Slave Traffic*, merely a highly organized national network of procurers who trade their women from city to city, communicating by coded telegraph messages. As with *Traffic in Souls*, there is more than one victim: a machinist, Annie (Virginia Mann), who like Lorna falls for the blandishments of a pimp (George), is drugged at a restaurant and seduced; and an immigrant girl who is enticed into the life, it would seem (there is much footage missing from surviving prints), by the silk stockings and fancy dress that George's regular prostitute girlfriend holds out to her.

A striking feature — in line with the prefatory claim that the film is "a pictorial report of the life and habits of those engaged or associated with the White Slave Traffic . . . as they are in truth and fact, without any exaggeration or fictional indulgence" — is the absence of any melodramatic rescue mechanism. Annie is ordered out of her house by her father, "married" in a fake ceremony to George, and shortly afterward turned out as a prostitute. The film includes location shots, considered scandalous at the time, of her soliciting on New York streets. Abandoned by George, she is sold to a trafficker, Sam, and transported to New Orleans. Attempting to break away and work independently, Annie flees first to Denver, then Houston, "but the system is everywhere" and she is located and returned to Sam in New Orleans, where she "slaves for him again." Sinking into despair, she dies, "laid away, an outcast in Potter's Field." The immigrant girl, too, is delivered to New Orleans.

Seeking to ward off anticipated criticism, the distributors made much of the fact that *The Inside of the White Slave Traffic* was, as a title put it, "produced by Samuel H. London, the noted Sociologist, from facts gathered during his international investigation of the White Slave Traffic."[39] This, and the numerous endorsements from noted judges, doctors, writers and suffragists, failed to placate the outraged guardians of public morality. The graphic, factual depiction of prostitution — in addition to New York, scenes had been shot in the red-light districts of New Orleans and of El Paso, Texas — was not countered by the expected fictional punishment of the evildoers.[40] The film was banned in Chicago, and in New York Samuel London was convicted on a charge of holding an exhibition tending to corrupt morals. Further distribution of the film, which like *Traffic in Souls* had been highly profitable, was blocked.

As the campaign to close down the vice trade intensified, films that dramatized victories of the reform movement were in a stronger position than others to resist censorship pressures. Thus *The Fight* (1915) celebrates the successful campaign of a female candidate for mayor of a western city who has pledged to root out vice, outmaneuvering the machinations of her opponents who seek to entrap her in a bordello. *The Little Girl Next Door* (1916) was based on a report of the Illinois State Vice Commission and reportedly contained "actual testimonies of women who were forced into prostitution," their stories structured into a series of flashbacks.[41] *The Downfall of a Mayor* (1917) starred Los Angeles politician Charles E. Sebastian in a "picturized history of his public career as policeman, chief of police and mayor," with exploits that included saving "beautiful maidens from Chinese dens and white slave rings."[42] Finally, *The Finger of Justice* (1918) was produced by the Reverend Paul Smith, a leading figure in the campaign to close the Barbary Coast vice district in San Francisco, and dramatized his eventually successful battle against political corruption; the film was said to depict "in a straightforward and dramatic manner incidents in the lives of the women who inhabited this vice district . . . and the tragic scenes following the ousting of hundreds of women who knew no other homes than the home of vice and corruption."[43]

By and large, white slave plays and films received strong support from feminists in the suffragist movement, who applauded their exposure of crimes against women. One of the few females prominent in the motion picture industry, Alice Guy-Blaché, directed *The Lure* (1914), an adaptation of a controversial play about young women being entrapped in a brothel; she stated that she took on the project after several other directors had turned it down, and that she had some knowledge of the subject through her contact with a female lawyer who specialized in white slavery cases. Guy reports that when the film came before a censorship board, one of the women on the committee defended it by saying, "The subject was offensive — I believe that only a woman could have treated it with such delicacy." Having initially been banned, the film was passed.[44]

Little Lost Sister (1917) also had a strong feminist slant. Based on a popular novel by Virginia Brooks, the film denounces the exploitation of female workers in industry as a contributive factor to the growth of prostitution. The crusading heroine of the film upbraids a mill owner, warning him that "the day is coming when the employer who underpays his women workers, and thus subtly undermines their virtue, will be re-garded as a public enemy." One of his employees is in fact lured away to the city by a procurer, impressed into work at a cabaret-bordello, and at last rescued after the heroine induces the police to raid the shady estab-lishment.[45]

Production of white slave movies in the United States dropped off markedly following a December 1916 ruling of the National Board of Review that "No picture hereafter will be passed by the National Board which is concerned wholly with the commercialized theme of 'White Slavery,' or which is so advertised as to give the impression that it is a lurid 'White Slave' picture."[46] The interdiction against the subject of white slavery was reiterated in guidelines issued during the 1920s by the Mo-tion Picture Producers and Distributors of America (MPPDA), and later incorporated as an outright ban in the Production Code, adopted in 1930.[47] A few films, however, managed to sidestep censorship constraints, notably Mrs. Wallace Reid's 1925 production *The Red Kimona* (also known as *The Red Kimono*). Developing the feminist perspective of *The Lure* and *Little Lost Sister*, *The Red Kimona* offered a portrait of a white slave who is not rescued by external agency but instead herself shoots her procurer dead, becoming a prototype of the Avenger (see chapter 6).

Meanwhile, in Europe where, except for the United Kingdom, cen-sorship was less stringent than in the United States, the white slave theme was occasionally revived in films such as *Mädchenhandel / The White Slave Traffic* (Germany, 1926). Reverting to the original preoccupation with in-ternational trafficking, *Mädchenhandel* depicts a nefarious gang of white slavers plucking young women from Berlin, on the promise of legitimate employment abroad, and delivering them (via a relay point in Budapest) to brothels in Athens and Istanbul. Featuring Rudolf Klein-Rogge in the role of a foreign slave-trading kingpin who is a master of disguise, the film represents a late flourishing of the melodramatic impulse that marked the genre from its inception.

As a figure of comedy or pathos, erotic object or criminal, fallen woman or victim of a vice ring, early representations of the prostitute on screen give hints of the diverse and contradictory ways in which venal sex is conceptualized in patriarchal society. It is some of the root causes for this diversity that we explore in the next chapter.

2

Depicting Prostitution under Patriarchy

Men sense the contradiction in us. They observe our desire to be
prey. . . . In our fantasy life we submit even as in our real life we resist.
In their fantasy life they resist even as in their real life they submit.
—SHEILA ROWBOTHAM, *Woman's Consciousness, Man's World*[1]

I have suggested that the figure of the prostitute in film, and the depiction of female prostitution generally, is predominantly attributable to
the working of the male imagination, modified by the requirement for
a certain verisimilitude—the cinema being first and foremost a realist
medium—and by the conceptual framework of patriarchal ideology.

There is first the difficulty—some would say the impossibility, especially for a male critic—of thinking outside the dominant patriarchal
paradigm. This holds true, of course, for any critique of the ideological
formation of a society of which one is in some sense a part. In the case of
the representation of prostitution, the task is perhaps made easier by the
fact that patriarchal ideology is so demonstrably split on how to deal with
the social phenomenon in question, and by the vigorous debates within
the feminist movement—both about the representation of women and
about prostitution—that have occurred.[2]

The main problem with the argument, however, is that in placing so
much stress on the satisfaction of a narrowly conceived male agenda, it
underestimates the impact of other sociocultural forces. There are the
interests of an increasingly free-market capitalist system, which may no
longer mesh as well as they once did with those of patriarchy. There is
the impact of female spectatorship: for commercial reasons, prostitute
representations in the movies have from the outset deliberately appealed
to women as well as men, whether or not women have been involved in
a creative capacity as writers, directors, or producers. And finally, patriarchal ideology has been undermined or subverted in films that respond

21

to concerns of the women's movement, and it has met with outright challenge in the relatively few but highly significant productions that embody an overt feminist discourse.

If, then, prostitute depictions under patriarchy have tended to fall into recognizable patterns that survive for decades and crop up in the cinemas of very different countries, it is as a result of the interplay of a number of factors of which male fantasy, though undoubtedly the most important, is but one. The patterns are shaped within an intricate cultural force field of desires and prohibitions, dreams and dictates.

Male fantasy itself is not something fixed and monolithic. The nineteenth century masculine association of the prostitute with disease and decay, for example, prevalent in French writing of that era, did not survive long into the twentieth century: there are only a handful of films, mostly VD educational tracts, in which the prostitute is portrayed as a spreader of contagion.[3] And over the hundred-year-plus history of the cinema there are scenarios, such as the fallen woman story inherited from Victorian melodrama, whose popularity wanes, and new archetypes, like the Happy Hooker, which arise in response to changing social mores.

Moreover, to the extent that the psychological formation of male individuals is dependent upon their class affiliation, their imaginative creations are likely to take different forms: the aggressive "male fantasies" explored by Klaus Theweleit in his book of that title, for instance, belong not to all men, but to a particular stratum (upper-middle- and upper-class men who became officers in the Freikorps, and subsequently wrote about their experiences), at a particular period in German history. These were men whose psychological armoring was inculcated by a particularly rigid Prussian upbringing: as Theweleit acknowledges, "there was no basis among the workers for the types of fantasies we have come to associate with the men of the White Guard."[4]

Still, Theweleit does find ("a remarkable phenomenon") that "in their comments about prostitutes and women in general 'reactionary' and 'revolutionary' men are able to find some common ground. . . . The men are bonded together by their deep-seated fear of the vengeance of women."[5] This gender-based commonality holds good in the cinema. Despite variations attributable to class — and also ethnic, religious and national differences — and to historical change within society, representations of the prostitute in the work of male filmmakers do in fact exhibit a consistency that suggests that there is something common in their psychological makeup *as men*, which is finding expression in their fantasy creations.

American feminist theorists Nancy Chodorow and Dorothy Dinnerstein have argued that the roots of male attitudes toward women are to be traced to family structures, universal under patriarchy, which make childrearing an almost exclusively female responsibility.[6] In the nuclear family of advanced industrial societies especially, they suggest, the asymmetrical pattern of nurturing by the mother — the father being a comparatively distant figure — has a profound impact on the psychological development of people as gendered individuals in society. While children of both sexes must go through the difficult stage of separating from the mother, with whom they have formed a primary relationship charged with intense feelings of affection and dependence, the process is complicated for the boy by the fact that he must also acquire a masculine identity. In doing so he tends to repress his emotional and relational needs, denying his attachment to his mother and disparaging the feminine qualities he associates with her.

Two consequences of this growth pattern in particular would seem to be relevant to male fantasies about the prostitute. One is the development of feelings of anxiety about women, and in some cases intense hostility. The other is the phenomenon of the splitting off of lust from affection.

There is a strange moment in *Uncaged/Angel in Red* (USA, 1991) that illustrates in extreme form — perhaps deliberately (the director is female) — the kind of confused attitudes toward women that Chodorow is referring to. A pimp suddenly starts addressing as his mother the prostitute who has been holding out on him. He whimpers, sinking to his knees: "You don't love me any more, do you? You're going to leave me again, aren't you. You're going to come home again drunk, aren't you Mom. . . ." Then he batters her to death.[7]

In a male child, resentment of the power which his mother is capable of wielding over him by withholding affection or smothering him, may generate conflicted feelings of anger and aggression. In the normal course of development (or so the Freudian analyst would argue), these negative emotions will be dealt with and overcome. But in the fixated individual they may survive into adulthood, becoming displaced from the mother herself (since they are at odds with societal respect for motherhood) on to women in general or on to a particular substitute target. Chodorow declares, "I have yet to find a convincing explanation for the virulence of masculine anger, fear, and resentment of women, or of aggression toward them, that bypasses — even if it does not rest with — the psychoanalytic account, first suggested by [Karen] Horney, that men resent and fear women because they experience them as powerful mothers."[8] Anxiety about regressing to infantile dependence leads to a psychological hardening and the maintenance of rigid gender boundaries, in which the masculine is defined as all that the feminine is not. The male ego, on this scenario, is fragile, and threats to it may result in a lashing out in real or fantasized violence.

If he is successful in attaining the heterosexual orientation that patriarchal society expects of him, a man will look to a female partner for the satisfaction of his desires for erotic fulfillment and loving care. But in this relationship, as Dinnerstein writes, "he is in one very important respect more vulnerable than she is: she can more readily re-evoke in him the unqualified, boundless, helpless passion of infancy." If he does not guard against it, "she can shatter his adult sense of power and control." As a defense mechanism, a man may "renounce the opportunity for deep feeling inherent in heterosexual love" by keeping the relationship superficial; he may also "dissociate its physical from its emotional possibilities," adopting different behavior patterns either toward the same woman depending on the situation or mood, or toward different women.[9]

This separating out of erotic from affectionate feelings is significant in understanding the symbolic role of the prostitute in men's imaginative life. Freud found the phenomenon widespread at the time he was writing (1912): "In only very few people of culture are the two strains of tenderness and sensuality duly fused into one; the man almost always feels his sexual activity hampered by his respect for the woman and only develops full sexual potency when he finds himself in the presence of a lower type of sexual object."[10]

Freud attributes the condition — which he considers neurotic — to two factors: sexual frustration in adolescence as a result of societal prohibitions, and a strong incestuous fixation in childhood. The latter occurs (as part of what Freud would elsewhere describe as the Oedipus Complex) when the boy is required to repress any erotic impulse toward his mother in order to avoid transgressing the incest taboo. If the attraction to the incestuous object is sufficiently powerful, Freud contends, a form of impotence, either total or (in the much more common, less severe case) "psychical" may result:

> The sexual activity of such people shows unmistakable signs . . . that it
> has not behind it the whole mental energy belonging to the instinct. It is

capricious, easily upset, often clumsily carried out, and not very pleasurable. Above all, however, it avoids all association with feelings of tenderness. A restriction has thus been laid upon the object-choice. The sensual feeling that has remained active seeks only objects evoking no reminder of the incestuous persons forbidden to it; the impression made by someone who seems deserving of high estimation leads, not to a sensual excitation, but to feelings of tenderness which remain erotically ineffectual. The erotic life of such people remains dissociated, divided between two channels, the same two that are personified in art as heavenly and earthly (or animal) love. Where such men love they have no desire and where they desire they cannot love.[11]

For Freud, a crucial part of the theory was that the man suffering from psychical impotence could be sexually excited only by a woman whom society regarded as degraded: the woman of loose morals, and in particular the prostitute. In an earlier paper he investigated this "love for a harlot" and put it down to the circumstances in which a boy first obtains detailed knowledge of the sexual relations between adults: "The secret of sexual life is revealed to him then in coarse language, undisguisedly derogatory and hostile in intent." The boy is at first unable to attribute this activity to his parents, for whom he feels respect and tenderness, and his curiosity is aroused by learning of "the existence of certain women who practice sexual intercourse as a means of livelihood and are universally despised in consequence." Freud maintains that for the boy "this contempt is necessarily quite foreign; as soon as he realizes that he too can be initiated by these unfortunates into that sexual life which he has hitherto regarded as the exclusive prerogative of 'grown-ups,' his feeling for them is only a mixture of longing and shuddering."[12]

While much of the basis for this phenomenon may have disappeared with the waning of puritan morality, and in more recent years with a spreading of childcare responsibilities and hence a reduction in the emotional exclusivity of the mother-child relationship, there can be little doubt that it underpinned the workings of the male imagination throughout much of the twentieth century. In *The Dialectic of Sex*, Shulamith Firestone argues persuasively that under patriarchy the splitting process has had a widespread social effect: "One cultural development that proceeds directly from such an unnatural psychological dichotomy is the good/bad women syndrome, with which whole cultures are diseased. That is, the personality split is projected outward onto the class 'women': those who resemble the mother are 'good,' and consequently one must not have sexual feelings toward them; those unlike the mother, who don't call forth a total response, are sexual, and therefore 'bad.' Whole classes of people, e.g. prostitutes, pay with their lives for this dichotomy."[13]

A critical result of the psychological process is an alignment, and often a confusion, of erotic and violent impulses directed toward the "bad" woman, which may explain why the prostitute so often becomes the substitute target for the hostility of the frustrated male. Dinnerstein suggests that "lust then carries all the angry, predatory impulses from which the protective, trusting side of his love for woman must be kept insulated."[14] Repressed rage at a mother experienced as overwhelming or overdenying,[15] and disappointment at the discovery that she is in fact a carnal being ("he says to himself with cynical logic that the difference between his mother and a whore is after all not so very great, since at bottom they both do the same thing"[16]) may be condensed on to the figure of the prostitute as representative of all that is threatening as well as alluring in the female other.

Karen Horney was among the first psychoanalysts to recognize the link between male infantile experience and cultural representations of women in male-dominated society. In "The Dread of Women" she observes that "men have never tired of fashioning expressions for the violent force by which man feels himself drawn to the woman, and side by side with his longing, the dread that through her he might die and be undone." Horney cites the stories of Ulysses and the sirens, the riddle of the Sphinx, the goddess Kali (who dances on the corpses of slain men), Samson and Delilah, Judith and Holofernes, Salome, and Wedekind's "Earth Spirit" (the Lulu of *Pandora's Box*) as examples of depictions of women by means of which man strives to ward off his anxiety about female difference. "'It is not,' he says, 'that I dread her; it is that she herself is malignant, capable of any crime, a beast of prey, a vampire, a witch, insatiable in her desires. She is the very personification of what is sinister.'"[17] In the cinema this fictional tradition feeds into what I term the "Siren" and "Gold Digger" character types, but it is noteworthy that prostitute characters are very seldom depicted as purely monstrous or evil. Instead, they embody men's deep-rooted ambivalence to the sexual woman who is both intensely desirable and profoundly unsettling.

In projecting such feelings onto the already debased prostitute, man can keep the danger of woman at a distance and maintain his sense of superiority: as Horney writes, "from the prostitute or the woman of easy virtue one need fear no rejection, and no demands in the sexual, ethical, or intellectual sphere."[18] Examining French literature and art of the nineteenth century, Charles Bernheimer detects this process at work, arguing that "the prostitute is ubiquitous in the novels and paintings of this period not only because of her prominence as a social phenomenon but, more important, because of her function in stimulating artistic strategies to control and dispel her fantasmatic threat to male mastery."[19]

The discourse of prostitution in patriarchal film thus speaks of erotic yearning, of emotional deprivation, and of a hostility to women that constitutes a social pathology. The prostitute is in varying proportions an object of desire, representing those qualities in life for which the male experiences an aching want, and an object of hatred, symbolizing everything in the female other he wishes to deny or destroy. With her seductive power and her marginal, semicriminal status she typically poses a threat to male peace of mind, a threat that must be neutralized in the unfolding of the narrative. The two most common scenarios in which this is achieved are the love story, where she ceases to be promiscuous and is paired off with the protagonist, and the murder story, where she is killed off.

Male fantasy suffuses most but not all of the representations of the prostitute discussed in this book. The great majority of the character archetypes, for example, have a fantasy component satisfying psychological needs generated as a result of the processes discussed above. The Siren and Gold Diggers deal with men's fear of losing their power and their very identity to the seductive woman, while the Avenger, a nightmare of the male imagination, incarnates the threat of women taking retribution for all the oppression they have suffered at the hands of men. The other fantasies are more positive, in holding out an image of the fulfillment of desire, of pure indulgence of the pleasure principle. The Gigolette embodies sexual freedom in a context of puritanical repression; the Happy Hooker is the liberated woman whose only mission in life is to make sure that the erotic enjoyment you gain from your encounter with her is as great as hers; the Adventuress invites you to join her on her journey of sexual experimentation. For the masochist, the Business Woman dominatrix holds out the promise of an orgy of debasement amid chains, spikes, whips, and leather. Less sexual in emphasis, the Comrade is a fellow margin-dweller or companion in struggle, the Nursemaid a mother figure who enfolds but never engulfs. On the darker side, the Baby Doll caters to incestuous wishes generated in the father-daughter relationship, the Captive is an attractive woman trapped in men's power, while the Junkie offers up an image of the sexual woman in ultimate degradation.

There is a fantasy investment, too, in the narrative types. The fallen woman scenario explores male fascination with the metamorphosis of the good woman into the bad. The Love Story resolves the conflict many males—those who suffer from "psychical impotence"—experience in choice of love object: the prostitute as good-bad girl who is both nurturing and sexually alluring. A fantasy-rescue of the loved one — "the man is convinced that . . . without him she would lose all hold on respectability and rapidly sink to a deplorable level," writes Freud—may be entertained via the white slave paradigm.[20] The Prostitute and Pimp narrative deals with fears of dependency on the mother figure and difficulties of individuation and separation from her; it constructs a sadomasochistic fantasy of control over a woman who loves you unconditionally no matter how you treat her, who revels — or so you may like to believe — in the punishment you mete out to her. And what I have called the "Condemned to Death" story allows men to vent, in imagination, their hostility toward women and anxieties about female sexuality, by killing off the troubling specter in an act of cathartic violence. The fact that prostitute-killing is part of the real world and even regarded by patriarchal society as a professional risk for sex workers allows this aggressive fantasy to slip more easily past the superego.

A young man walks down a hospital corridor and enters a room in which a female patient is lying in bed, barely conscious. The nurse who showed the man in indicates she's popping out for a moment. The man speaks to the woman, who responds only by turning her head. She has facial injuries and looks as though she's been beaten up. His attention is caught by the drip, the long plastic tube feeding into her arm by means of a hypodermic needle. Slowly, deliberately, the man detaches the needle. We cut to a cemetery, where the woman is being buried.

This is the opening sequence of *Les Filles de Grenoble* (France, 1981). The man is a pimp, the woman a prostitute who had been working for him. The film, based on a real case, exposes the lethal brutality of a gang of pimps in controlling prostitution in the provincial city of Grenoble. Eventually, thanks to assiduous law enforcement and the courage of one of the prostitutes in testifying against her oppressors, the culprits are brought to justice.

Another opening sequence: A beautiful young woman is lying in bed, naked. She gets up, puts on stockings, panties, a bra, then glides over to the dressing table. There is an air of luxury. She applies lipstick, puts on some earrings, dons a white fur coat over her underclothes.

Then she leaves the house and gets in beside a man in the back seat of a limousine.

She is a prostitute, the man her client. The film is *Madame Claude 2 / Intimate Moments*, also released in France in 1981. It shows high-class call girls jetting to assignations with rich and powerful men around the globe and having a swinging good time doing it.

The glaring disparity of these diametrically opposed representations is indicative of the acute problems that venal sex poses for the ideologists of patriarchal society. So evident is the exploitation and oppression, generally, of prostitutes in real life, and so starkly does their trade clash with the ethic of home, family, and fidelity, that patriarchal ideology is severely stretched in seeking to contain it. Mostly, therefore, there is an attempt to disavow it, to deny the very existence of prostitution, or to displace all responsibility for it from the system as a whole, with its structured gender inequalities, and from men in general (and especially the clients) onto a certain criminal subculture (the pimps), or onto the prostitutes themselves. Alternatively, there is the totally opposite scenario — frequently handled in comic or quasi-pornographic mode — in which prostitution is depicted as not at all oppressive, and its function unobjectionable.

Denying its existence, erasing all trace of it, was the strategy adopted by British and American censorship authorities for several decades, until pressures for greater freedom of expression in the cinema became too great. I have elsewhere explored the justifications made in the United States for this policy of total exclusion and the difficulties it created for the authorities.[21] When total repression by means of censorship is unsustainable, what might be termed "official" patriarchal ideology deals with the irritant of prostitution by deeming it a bad thing, a necessary evil or an evil *tout court*, and the women involved victims, either of depraved men or of their own corrupt natures. The white slave films of the silent era and the Captive films (such as *Les Filles de Grenoble*) that began to appear in force in the 1950s, both of which depict prostitution as a criminal racket, clearly embody this ideology.

During the 1960s, however, this position was challenged as the sexual revolution got under way and a previously submerged, disreputable attitude toward promiscuity — that of celebrating rather than condemning it — gained prominence in popular culture and swept the depiction of prostitution up with it. Films such as *Pote Tin Kyriaki / Never on Sunday* (Greece, 1960) and *Tom Jones* (UK, 1963) captured the male imagination with their endorsement of prostitution as a force for the liberation of the libido, giving birth to the Happy Hooker archetype. This alternative, "unofficial" patriarchal ideology had the merit of acknowledging that prostitution was an institution created by male-dominated society to provide for men's carnal pleasures, but it resolutely closed its eyes to the human cost at which those pleasures were bought.

These two opposed positions have continued to find expression side by side in the cinema to the present day. When combined as they occasionally are in contemporary American films in which a traditional puritanism gets enmeshed with the Playboy philosophy, the "official" and "unofficial" lines form a composite ideological stance, which is shot through with contradiction. Despite their flagrant differences, the positions have one thing in common: the attempt to evade guilt for the oppression of women within prostitution. The unpleasant nature of the work itself and the psychological damage it can cause is seldom acknowledged. The profession is romanticized, glamorized. If the prostitute suffers, it may be because she herself is to blame: she is a sinner, a Gold Digger. The guilt that men experience for indulging their pleasures at women's expense may be dealt with in a tale of suffering and redemption: it is the Martyr's fate to live a life of sorrow and be rewarded by ultimate sanctification.

Never is the client to be held responsible for the prostitute's situation, all male guilt being deflected onto the pimp, who is regularly demonized, as in *Uncaged* and *Les Filles de Grenoble*. The nonviolent boyfriend pimp very seldom appears. The background of many prostitutes as victims of child abuse is alluded to only infrequently: the fact that such abuse usually numbs a woman's ability to enjoy sex is not admitted, and when rape or seduction at an early age is shown, it is usually portrayed as an act that sexualizes the victim and makes her promiscuous, not in a desperate effort to find love but because she's been "turned on."

The real-life prostitute is frequently defiant, contemptuous of the hypocrisy of a system that attaches the whore stigma to her. Patriarchal cinema does not care to show such a figure and works to neutralize the threat she might pose—particularly in combination with other like-minded sex workers. Prostitute characters in film, if they are fiercely independent, do not remain so for long and are seldom permitted to remain in their profession at the end: like other independent women in the movies, they are typically either married off or killed off.

There are fictional configurations in which the interests of male fantasy and patriarchal ideology converge. Nowhere is this more so than in the

love story. Here, the fantasy of the ideal love object fusing erotic and nurturing appeal works hand in glove with the ideological operation entailed
in attaching her to a husband. There are situations, however, in which
fantasy and ideology conflict.

Stories involving male violence against the prostitute, for example,
can pose problems. While such scenes can be satisfying psychologically
in a fantasy release of aggressive impulses, and in terms of narrative outcome it frequently serves ideological purposes to have the prostitute put
out of the way, it is not acceptable to the patriarchy for such violence
to be openly condoned — unless, of course, the perpetrator is provoked.
Hence the attacker is classically a bad guy — a pimp, for example — who
is not presented as an identification figure for male spectators and who
will typically be brought to (rough) justice for his crime. In *Magnum Force*
(USA, 1973), for example, a pimp kills a call girl by forcing her to drink
caustic drain cleaner. He is himself pumped full of bullets shortly after
he has committed the murder.[22] In the Jack the Ripper films, the protagonist is usually a detective and the killer unidentified until the end, thus
firmly positioning the audience on the side of law and order.

Serial-killer films, which tell the story from the murderer's perspective, revealingly provoke outraged reactions from censors and critics.
The protagonist of *Peeping Tom* (UK, 1959), for example, is a murderer of
women who films his victims at the moment of death; his first killing, that
of a prostitute, is shown from his subjective point of view through the
viewfinder of his home movie camera. Subjected to extensive cuts by the
British film censor,[23] *Peeping Tom* still provoked a now-notorious crop of
reviews, including: "It wallows in the diseased urges of a homicidal per-
vert. . . . From its lumbering, mildly salacious beginning to its appalling
masochistic and depraved climax, it is wholly evil" (Nina Hibbin, *The
Daily Worker*); "The only really satisfactory way to dispose of *Peeping Tom*
would be to shovel it up and flush it down the nearest sewer" (Derek Hill,
The Tribune).[24]

The film's invitation for pathological violence to be understood by
means of a psychological identification with the killer was one that British society was unwilling to take up — the film was a commercial failure.
Henry: Portrait of a Serial Killer (USA, 1986[25]), which likewise makes the
murderer the protagonist, prostitutes being particular targets of his
somewhat random violence, has similarly encountered censorship difficulties.[26]

Another area in which male fantasy may collide with patriarchal ideology is in the representation of promiscuity. *Bachelor Party* (USA, 1984),

for example, wishes to indulge the wet-dream vision of a stud party orgy while reassuring its audience that a real man (Tom Hanks) would never be unfaithful to his fiancée on the eve of his wedding. The embarrassed result has the groom's buddies avail themselves of the call girls' services while he himself virtuously abstains: prostitution is thus endorsed for the fulfillment of frustrated nerds who cannot score as the hero can, but negated in comparison with true love. The comic compromise here simply degrades the less socially adept males who have to resort to paying for their pleasure. The film fails to resolve the tensions implicit in the bachelor party tradition, which is a ceremonial way of marking the sacrifice of erotic choice a man makes in submitting to monogamy.

In the great expansionary phase of industrial capitalism — in the historical period, that is, in which the nuclear family became the basis of social organization — bourgeois and patriarchal ideology effectively buttressed each other. In the twentieth century and beyond, however, there has been an increasing divergence. Capitalism, now with a seemingly permanent surplus of labor to draw upon, has no longer a vested interest in the maintenance of the family as a social unit; indeed its breakup may facilitate the flow of workers to wherever they are needed. There is nothing to be gained by blocking the employment of women if they have skills that may be exploited. Hence patriarchal ideology, and patriarchy as a social system, is increasingly in competition with capitalism and its values, and is finding itself outpaced.

As far as prostitution goes, capitalism's interest lies in the orderly extraction of profit through the legitimation of the business. The marketplace is unpredictable enough as it is, without adding the problems of capricious law enforcement; and if money's to be made, why should it go to criminals? (In the Australian state of Victoria, brothels are listed on the stock exchange.) Bourgeois ideology easily accommodates the notion of prostitution as a legitimate business, by reference to liberal concepts of equality before the law, individual rights, and the minimization of government interference in the private sphere of human existence.[27]

The impact of bourgeois ideology on depictions of prostitution in the cinema is further discussed in chapter 11. The confusion of attitudes that results when free-market capitalism on the ascendant clashes with patriarchy on the decline is registered in such "Business Woman" films as *Money on the Side* (USA, 1982) and *Risky Business* (USA, 1983). Here, the initial endorsement of prostitution as a business practice like any other is radically undercut by the end of the movie.

For although its ideology, committed to fundamental inequality between men and women, is inherently less capable of rational justification than that of capitalism, patriarchy is nonetheless deeply entrenched and has vast resources at its disposal, the legacy of thousands of years of male-dominant culture. All the teachings of religion, for example, can be called upon; all the archetypal narratives and images depicting strong active men and submissive passive women can be revived in new forms. One of the stories of this book is how patriarchal ideology in the cinema, in the face of a variety of pressures, has maneuvered to sustain itself. The re-romanticization of the prostitute (despite the necessary explicitness) in the mega-hit *Pretty Woman* (USA, 1990) is a prime example of its success.

The phenomenon of *Pretty Woman* demonstrates that while prostitute representations in the cinema may primarily have been generated by male fantasy, they are also strongly influenced by the commercial advantages that accrue on appealing to a female as well as male audience. Female spectatorship has, in fact, been a major factor in the popularity and persistence of prostitute depictions in motion pictures ever since the fallen woman and white slave films of the silent era.[28]

Underlying the pleasures women derive from viewing prostitute stories may be a greater capacity for empathy than men typically experience, and a less judgmental attitude toward wrongdoers. In her psychoanalytic account of subject formation under patriarchy, Chodorow demonstrates that girls emerge from the oedipal period "with a basis for 'empathy' built into their primary definition of self in a way that boys do not," and that, in contrast to the "rigid and punitive superego" typically produced in masculine development, females are likely to develop a superego "more open to persuasion and the judgments of others, that is, not so independent of its emotional origins."[29] It would follow that identification of female viewers with stars portraying prostitute characters is potentially very strong.[30]

The prostitute figure may appeal to women in two contrasting guises: as a victim of patriarchy, and as a rebel against it. In the first category are those representations that show the character as degraded, trapped, and oppressed, in a white slave or Prostitute and Pimp story, for example, or as Captive, Martyr, or Junkie. In the second category are those that show her, at least for a time, as unbound by patriarchal constraints, achieving economic or sexual independence, as Siren or Gold Digger, for instance, Happy Hooker or Adventuress. In many cases there may be an admixture of both, and this is particularly so in fallen woman and Avenger stories.

2. *Pretty Woman:* Julia Roberts as Vivian.

The prostitute as victim may be typified by the character type termed the "Martyr." Here it is likely that the heroine as a locus of suffering, socially debased but spiritually transcendent, appeals to a woman's sense of powerlessness in patriarchal society. Patrice Petro writes of *Dirnentragödie/Tragedy of the Street* (Germany, 1927) that "the anticipated spectator is imagined to be female" and that "the very pathos surrounding Auguste's futile attempts at class rise would appear to address directly a female audience whose desire for mobility was not only similarly frustrated but also repressed in ordinary psychic and social circumstances."[31] A contemporary reviewer stated of Asta Nielsen's performance as the aging whore that "her acting presence is an event; her face is a concave mirror which can capture and reflect all the confusion of pain and bliss and dead void and radiant cosmos, intertwined, that we call human life."[32] Similarly, Molly Haskell refers to the culminating moment in *Street Angel* (USA, 1928) in which Janet Gaynor as the fallen woman is reconciled in church with the lover devastated by what she has become as "one of those scenes which to describe is to destroy, but to see is to succumb to completely"[33]; while a female fan said of Joan Crawford, who played prostitute or near-prostitute roles in *Rain, The Bride Wore Red, Strange Cargo,* and *Flamingo Road,* that she "could evoke such pathos, and suffer such martyrdom . . . making you live each part."[34]

As rebel, the attraction of the prostitute character is her defiance of patriarchal norms in striking out for, and often attaining, financial or sexual autonomy. Although such representations are usually finally contained within the dominant ideology, with the protagonist being reformed or punished, they undoubtedly offer opportunities for pleasurable spectatorship along the way.

Thus female audiences have reacted favorably—often to the alarm of moralists—to stories of women who barter their physical attractiveness for an improved standard of living. Commenting on the way that the archetypal fallen woman narrative was updated in the Hollywood of the 1920s and early 1930s, for example, Lea Jacobs notes a new emphasis on female aggressivity, and continues: "Moreover, the heroine appears in increasingly lavish and exotic settings, greatly attenuating the severity of the fall. It is as if Eve were admitted to the Garden of Eden *after* having tasted the apple."[35] In similar fashion, the prostitute protagonist (played by Hildegard Knef) of *Die Sünderin/The Sinful Woman* (West Germany, 1951) "gains economic independence, indeed wealth, by playing on the male desire," and would have appealed to German women of the postwar period, Heide Fehrenbach speculates, because at that time some of

3. *Dirnentragödie:* Asta Nielsen as Auguste. bfi Collections.

them "were reluctant to surrender their responsibility for their individual fates to men and reaffirm too quickly the principle of social patriarchy, especially when the projected patriarchs were not up to the challenge."[36]

Before being derailed by falling in love, Vivian (Julia Roberts) also has her eye on the main chance in *Pretty Woman* (USA, 1990), a film that strongly invokes a fantasy of social mobility. Kathleen Rowe remarks that it "conveys overwhelmingly reassuring messages about class," observing that "Vivian's transformation shows that the signs of class — upper or lower — are as easily taken up or discarded as a borrowed credit card" and that "after one week with Edward's card, Vivian seems born to wear the casual upper-class attire of designer blazer and jeans we see her in at the end of the film."[37]

Prostitute films can also, for some female spectators, mobilize fantasies of an illicit, promiscuous sexuality. The figure of the hooker takes on in this respect the qualities Nickie Roberts celebrates in *Whores in History:* "The whore *is* free in the sense that she does not bind her sexuality to any one man; on the contrary, she openly challenges the notion of female monogamy. Many women recognize this and identify their active sexuality as 'whorish' in their fantasies. . . ."[38] The American white slave films, as Shelley Stamp has demonstrated, attracted a large female audience by catering to "an openly voyeuristic, sexual gaze distinctly at odds with expectations about feminine decorum and reserve."[39] *Die Büchse der Pandora/Pandora's Box* (Germany, 1929) may have held a similar appeal for German audiences: Mary Ann Doane comments that "the androgyny attributed to Lulu is a fundamental aspect of her mutability, her free-spiritedness, the transgression of conventional boundaries—all of which constitute her eroticism, her desirability."[40]

Since the relaxation of censorship in the 1960s and '70s, the idea of sexual promiscuity has been more openly expressed in the cinema, particularly through the Happy Hooker archetype. Though such representations are clearly directed primarily at men, it is likely that they hold some appeal for female spectators as well. The female journalist investigating New York prostitution in *Hustling* (USA, 1975) remarks that "there isn't a woman alive who hasn't had the fantasy of going into a room with a stranger and selling herself for money." A feminist reflecting on her experience attending the Second World Whores' Congress (1986) commented: "When I see movies with whore characters—and of course harlot images come up all the time in films—I often identify with the whore. . . . I think that my promiscuous past with men and feeling that I often used men and wanted to have more power than them plus my knowing sexual stigma as a lesbian were a big part of my identification with prostitutes."[41] Linda Williams pertinently notes that there is strong evidence for the popularity of pornography—which often contains prostitute characters—among women.[42]

A woman's exploring her sexual desires in unconventional ways is highlighted in the character type of the "Adventuress." Exemplifying the pattern, Séverine (Catherine Deneuve) in Luis Buñuel's *Belle de Jour* (France, 1967) probes into her masochistic sexuality by taking an afternoon job at a brothel; and again, though it may be primarily a male fantasy that is finding expression on screen, there is certainly the possibility of a positive female response. Feminist critic Kathleen Murphy, for example, responds warmly to the characterization, asserting that "her fantasies may be kinky but they're certainly more fun, more richly devised and experienced, than anything that home, hearth and hubby can provide."[43]

The undercover vice cop (played by Theresa Russell) in the female-directed *Impulse* (USA, 1990) admits to having masochistic fantasies of taking her hooker masquerade all the way—"the guy's not handsome ... he's old and ugly and wants me to do all these degrading things— the worse it gets, the more excited I get"—and it is conceivable that certain prostitute characterizations, especially among the Captives and Junkies, mobilize equivalent desires, conscious or repressed, in female audience members. On the opposite side of the fence, sadistic and power-trip fantasies are catered to in the Business Woman films that feature a dominatrix.

Hooker as victim and hooker as rebel are fused in the potent image of the Avenger. Anger at abuse that she or other females have suffered at the hands of men drives her to a decisive act of revenge, not necessarily violent in nature, and guaranteed to afford satisfaction to women viewers. She is the bad girl *par excellence*. As Karyn Kay writes of *La Fiancée du pirate/A Very Curious Girl* (France, 1969), "Nelly Kaplan offers a villainous female heroine who gets away with her crimes, and for women such chances to be nasty, triumphant and terribly, terribly dirty come far too seldom."[44]

La Fiancée du pirate heralded a new wave of feminist challenges to the patriarchal representation of prostitution, which has continued intermittently to the present. With the explosion of communications technology and the globalization of media production enterprises, ideological shaping and control of cultural product has become less pervasive than it was through most of the twentieth century; moreover, women writers and directors are slowly making inroads into what has been an extremely male-chauvinist industry. The subversion of male modes of picturing prostitution began as early as the silent era—as we have seen with a film such as *The Red Kimona*—but really picked up strength only with the growth of the women's movement in the 1970s.

If in male fantasy the prostitute represents excitement, female sexuality, pleasure, and danger, the strategy of feminist-inflected films like Chantal Akerman's *Jeanne Dielman* (Belgium/France, 1975) and Lizzie Borden's *Working Girls* (USA, 1986) is to deny the element of erotic enjoyment for the woman, to delibidinize the sexual act and represent it as a burden, a dull and alienating routine (if at times leavened by the play-acting involved).[45] Deglamorized, the image of the prostitute in these films is stripped of the fetishistic eroticism it so often displays in films by male directors, and there is an outright refusal of heterosexual romance. The character type of "Working Girl," which has these features, is almost entirely feminist in inspiration. Films with a strongly female perspective will often too, as noted above, make of the prostitute an Avenger bent on repaying the patriarchy for the harm it has inflicted on women.

Beyond this, the orientation of the feminist film will depend upon which of the two main schools of thought about prostitution it adheres to. The prostitutes' rights movement, pioneered by COYOTE (Call Off Your Old Tired Ethics) in the United States in 1973 and in Europe by the Lyons prostitutes' collective in 1975, promotes a notion of sex work as a legitimate service occupation that should be decriminalized and accorded societal respect by the removal of the whore stigma. It contends that the great majority of prostitutes have chosen the work voluntarily. *Working Girls* is an example of a film that adopts this position, which clearly has much in common with the "unofficial" proprostitution patriarchal line and with the liberal/civil rights arguments of contemporary bourgeois ideology.[46]

In contrast, the radical feminist position, as advanced by theorists such as Kathleen Barry (author of *Female Sexual Slavery* and *The Prostitution of Sexuality*) and Sheila Jeffreys (*The Idea of Prostitution*) and by the American organization WHISPER (Women Hurt in Systems of Prostitution Engaged in Revolt), is that prostitution must be understood as an institution created by the patriarchy to exploit and abuse women. These antiprostitution activists deny that women choose sex work voluntarily, pointing to the loss of their sense of physical integrity, which children who are victims of sexual abuse suffer, as well as to male (pimp/brothel owner) control of the commercial sex business. They argue that the prostitute, far from being a rebel against the values of male-dominated society, is in fact conforming to one of the subordinate roles allocated to women under patriarchy, and they vigorously contest the view that making women's bodies available to men for money is socially desirable.[47] A film very much within this field of discourse, which paradoxically has affinities with the "prostitution is a bad thing" stance of "official" patriarchal ideology, is Marleen Gorris's *Gebroken Spiegels/ Broken Mirrors* (Netherlands, 1984).

The representation of female prostitution in the movies thus takes place in a complex, dynamic field in which the forces of male fantasy and patriarchal ideology (in two distinct guises) merge or collide, occasionally buffeted by free-market capitalist ideology, the interests of female spectatorship, and two opposed varieties of feminist discourse. The task of the remainder of this book will be to examine in detail the fascinating results of this cultural process.

3

Gigolette

On the grey days, when it was chilly everywhere except in the big cafés,
I looked forward with pleasure to spending an hour or two at the Café
Wepler before going to dinner. The rosy glow which suffused the place
emanated from the cluster of whores who usually congregated near the
entrance. As they gradually distributed themselves among the clientele,
the place became not only warm and rosy but fragrant.
—HENRY MILLER, *Quiet Days in Clichy*[1]

The "Gigolette" is a creature of habitat, whether a café in Clichy, a street
in Pigalle, a bordello in Rome, a waterfront bar, or a Wild West saloon.
Wherever prostitutes gather to ply their trade, she will be there, part of
the scenery. She is integrated into her environment, and although it may
be fairly limited, the milieu of pimps and criminals, she has a certain status within it.

With the Gigolette, in the cinema, prostitution is not problematized.
She accepts it as her occupation, performing a service for which there is
a public demand, as would a bus driver or a greengrocer.[2] Morally she
is no better or worse than other people in the milieu, or with whom she
comes in contact. Though she may get slapped around, she gives as good
as she takes, in one way or another. She is the easygoing tart. She is not
oppressed in her profession, afflicted by guilt like a fallen woman, nor is
she under the heel of gangsters; therefore there is no imperative to *save*
her. But if she does not suffer in her work, neither does she derive any special pleasure from it: the Gigolette is poised between Martyr and
Happy Hooker.

This position of delicate neutrality can often be sustained only at a
certain distance: the Gigolette is frequently a secondary character or
merely a background presence. A common ploy is to bring a female protagonist into close contact with prostitutes without her actually engaging
in the profession herself. In *The Bad One* (USA, 1930), for example, Lita

40

works in a French brothel but is "one of those maidens who passes out keys but never succumbs until her wedding day."[3] In *Babette s'en va-t-en guerre/Babette Goes to War* (France, 1959) Babette is evacuated from France to England along with a brothel madam and her colorful *cocottes*, but Babette herself is a hotel maid; the opportunity is taken to indulge in some risqué comedy of mistaken identity. Similarly, in *Lady L* (France/Italy/UK/USA, 1965), Louise is a laundress who regularly delivers to a house of prostitution in Paris. By means of this narrative device, the film can flirt with licentiousness while its heroine (Dolores Del Rio, Brigitte Bardot, Sophia Loren) retains her innocence.[4] In those movies in which she is the central character, the prostitute who outwardly displays the carefree characteristics of the Gigolette may not actually be very happy in her work: this is the case, for example, with Ballhaus-Else in *Razzia in St. Pauli* (Germany, 1932) and Dédée in *Dédée d'Anvers/Dédée* (France, 1948).

The Gigolette's function in the cinema is to provide the "rosy glow," to raise the erotic temperature. She is an insistent reminder of the claims and delights of the carnal. At her most idealized—in Jacques Becker's *Casque d'Or* (France, 1952), for instance—the Gigolette signifies the hope, the dream, the utopia of a liberated sexuality in a context of puritanical repression. As a love object she is attractive because of her simplicity: she bypasses all the business of courtship, of restraint before the wedding, of family arrangements and property settlements, which defer, complicate, and sometimes destroy the possibility of sexual fulfillment within the conventional marital tradition. The Gigolette's appeal thus belongs particularly to an age of strict sexual morality, in which the virgin/whore dichotomy had a much stronger sense than after the sexual revolution of the 1960s.

At the start, in movies, the Gigolette was far from idealized. She was, for example, just the slippery, seductive broad of Bowery saloons and sidewalks, pictured in films such as *Tenderloin at Night*, *What Demoralized the Barber Shop*, and *How They Do Things on the Bowery*, which have been described in chapter 1. Later, in Keystone comedy, she appeared on the vaudeville stage: in *The Ragtime Band* (USA, 1913), "two successive female dance duos hold up signs announcing their acts, then turn over the signs to show the audience their addresses written on the back of the sign." While feigning outrage, the bandleader "quickly writes the addresses on his sleeve." Douglas Riblet notes that "while the concurrent cycle of 'white slave' films adopted tones of moral outrage and/or sociological detachment in exploiting such racy subject matter, the Keystone film mocked such appropriate responses and reveled in the vulgarity of the subject matter."[5] Within the nascent gangster genre, the Gigolette features, for instance, as the woman in tweed jacket and turban drinking in a Bowery music-hall bar in *Regeneration* (USA, 1915): catching the eye of a young gang leader, she makes a head movement inviting him to leave with her and then, when he turns her down, simply shrugs.

But such untroubled representations could only flourish in a society that complacently accepted the validity of prostitution as a social practice. In the United States of the 1910s, this was far from the case. Motion pictures, in fallen woman and white slave stories, generally reflected the prevalent view of prostitution as a social evil that was to be rooted out. D. W. Griffith's *The Reformers, or the Lost Art of Minding One's Business* (1913) stood out against this trend in depicting the antivice crusaders as meddling busybodies who would snuff out, along with commercialized sex, all expressions of popular culture: these women in masculinized attire and their hypocritical mayoral candidate are shown closing saloons, dance halls, vaudeville theaters, and movie houses. Here, prostitution may be a problem for the League of Civic Purity, but for Griffith the problem is the reformers. The Gigolettes who strive to carry on their trade despite the crusade are just part of the urban scene, and so, it is implied, they should be. In the Modern Story of Griffith's *Intolerance* (1916) there is a more explicit handling of the theme, with images of the reformers looking on self-satisfied as a brothel is raided by police and prostitutes led away: the implication, by montage ("But these results they do not report") is that just as prohibition will lead to sly grogging and home distilling, closure of brothels will result in illegal streetwalking, with comparable undesirable consequences.

It is a short sequence; Griffith dwells much longer on his sensuous temple harlots in the Babylonian Story of *Intolerance*. It was to become an increasing tendency in American cinema to displace the site of prostitution, if it was not to be problematized, from the contemporary downtown urban environment to a waterfront enclave or farther afield: to a decadent, pre-World War I Europe — as in Erich von Stroheim's *The Wedding March* (1928) — to the Orient, or to the Wild West. Even in the case of the West, showing the saloon girls as prostitutes performing a valuable social service was often far from straightforward. In *Cimarron* (1931), for instance, Dixie Lee (Estelle Taylor) is kept from jail, to which the respectable citizens of Osage, Oklahoma, are about to consign her, by the intervention of the iconoclastic pioneer Yancey Cravat; but he has to convince the court of Dixie's merits by recounting the sad story of her tribulations as a fallen woman, and it is fully understood that she and her operation will pack up and leave town forthwith.

No such difficulties are likely to beset dockside working girls. Prostitution is typically presented as an accepted part of life in port city locales, on the unspoken assumption that for seafarers marriage is difficult, and it is appropriate that they be compensated for enforced sexual abstinence over long stretches of time while they are doing their job.

Louis Delluc's *Fièvre* (France, 1921), a short feature set in a waterfront bistro in Marseilles, offers a model for what was to become a familiar set of motifs. The prostitutes here are secondary characters who create a heightened, sensual ambiance for a tangled drama of desire and jealousy between bar staff and clientele, which is played out during the course of an evening. Gaudily dressed, diverse in age and appearance, they are pure Gigolettes: dancing, drinking, laughing, and singing as they eye up potential customers. They excitedly examine the exotic treasures a group of sailors have brought back from the Orient, and one tries on a slinky robe, exposing a breast as she does so. As the evening wears on, the dancing gets riotous and the *filles* drag men to their feet to join in the fun. Finally, as fighting breaks out, they launch themselves into the fray with abandon, although they do not participate in the serious violence that culminates in two murders. By intercutting, at the start, documentary footage of ships and the harbor with action in the bistro, *Fièvre* creates a convincing sense of authenticity in its representation of the characters and their milieu, and has been hailed as a forerunner of French poetic realism.[6]

In *The Docks of New York* (USA, 1928) and *Razzia in St. Pauli*, a prostitute moves to the center of the drama as the protagonist in a love story. Again, the rowdy bar full of sailors and women hopeful of picking up business from them provides the setting. Sadie (Betty Compson) of the silent *Docks of New York* is characterized in considerable depth: depressed, at the start—"You could have saved yourself the trouble, an' let me die" she tells the stoker who pulls her out of the water—she is, by turns, vivacious, cynical, affectionate, and angrily emotional. Sadie ("Nell" in some prints) displays a subdued, smoldering *joie de vivre*, in contrast to another floozy in the bar, Lou (Olga Baclanova), who is loud and extroverted. The rest of the band of Gigolettes are high-spirited and fun-loving, participating energetically in Sadie's impromptu marriage ceremony performed by

4. *The Docks of New York:* Sadie (Betty Compson) and Bill (George Bancroft).

Hymn-Book Harry ("If any of you eggs know why these heels shouldn't get hitched," one of them yells out, "speak now or forever after hold your trap!"). Like Sadie, Ballhaus-Else (Gina Falkenberg) of *Razzia in St. Pauli* is a creature of moods, afflicted by melancholy but at other times laughing happily and being tenderly loving, both toward her current partner Leo — who plays piano in the Kongo-Bar in Hamburg where she hangs out — and her new flame Karl. In this film the Gigolettes are a weary bunch half-asleep at the start of the evening, but they perk up and become animated as the night wears on, dancing gaily and joining in the folksinging, as potential clients filter into the bar. As is customary with Gigolette representations, the actual work is elided.

In *I Cover the Waterfront* (USA, 1933), set in a California seaport,[7] the locale for dockside entertainment is Mother Morgan's Boarding House, a brothel depicted as a watering hole for unattached males, somewhat clandestine but without much of a sense of either impropriety or illegality. Here, with the power of his purse, a grizzled, sozzled old deep-sea skipper can surround himself with attractive young women attentive to his comfort, appreciative of his modest efforts at the piano. The prostitutes themselves, scarcely characterized (except for a glimpse of thieving tendencies) are decorative objects in flimsy gowns whose function in the narrative is to tend to the male character's needs, without their own motivations or emotions being in question: Gigolettes, pure and simple.

The Docks of New York, *Razzia in St. Pauli*, and *I Cover the Waterfront* adhere to the realist conventions established by *Fièvre;* indeed, *Razzia in St. Pauli*, like *Fièvre*, has recourse to documentary footage, interspersing shots of the docks and city streets, and incorporating a final montage depicting the harbor, cranes, and machinery, together with the tramp of workers' legs, signifying the start of another working day. *La mujer del puerto* (Mexico, 1933), in contrast, shifts into highly stylized, melodramatic mode in its study of the fortunes of Rosário (Andrea Palma), who becomes the star of a cabaret in a tropical port and who, in one of the cruelest twists of fate ever inflicted on a fallen woman, enjoys the most passionate night of lovemaking in her life, only to discover the paragon of partners to be her brother. The other prostitutes in the film serve mainly as a supporting act in the cabaret, enhancing Rosário's preeminence; but there is one, outside, who is singled out for special treatment. Rosário's brother and his shipmates from an Argentinian vessel pass by a window covered in climbing plants, where a prostitute is smoking, cradling the head of an exhausted seaman, and singing languidly "I sell pleasure to the men who come from the sea and leave at dawn, why do I long to love?"[8] Here the poetic strain in Gigolette representation comes to the fore.

Later port-city films, reverting to the realist tradition, rework the familiar motifs. *L'Étrange M. Victor/Der Merkwürdige Monsieur Victor* (Germany, 1937), for example, shows sailors on the prowl for whores on the streets of Toulon[9]; *Die Grosse Freiheit Nr. 7/Port of Freedom* (Germany, 1944) is set in a Hamburg circus-club where seamen and prostitutes gather; while *Hamnstad/Port of Call* (Sweden, 1948), depicts a sailor, feeling depressed, getting drunk with a Gothenburg hooker. The action in *Dédée* centers on the nightclub near the Antwerp docks where crewmen from the ships in port come to relax with a band of battle-weary Gigolettes. For these women, it's a tough life, but one can't kick against one's fate; and there's fun to be had, too: the intimacy and solidarity and joking; the mothering of lost, lonely young men; the dancing with customers if they're attractive, or later, as dawn is breaking, with one another. It's a life that Dédée (Simone Signoret), less resigned to her fate than the others, tries to put behind her but, like Ballhaus-Else, cannot.

In the cinemas of Continental Europe, the representation of prostitution in the main urban centers was much less constrained than in the United States. The Gigolette characterization emerged strongly in societies such as Germany (prior to the advent of Nazism), France, and Italy, which openly acknowledged and to a great extent condoned the sex trade. In *Berlin — Alexanderplatz* (Germany, 1931), for example, the Gigolette type is embodied both by the three beauties from Pankow who have a fine time with protagonist Franz Biberkopf in the dance hall, drinking champagne, submitting laughingly to his one-armed embrace, and being entertained by his singing — performing the familiar function of warming up the erotic ambiance — and by Cilly (Maria Bard), a central figure in the lumpenproletariat milieu around the bar where Reinhold and his gang of burglars hang out. Cilly, a slightly built young prostitute inured to the life, submits to pressure from Reinhold to procure Franz for the gang, becomes attached to him, enjoys a taste of luxury with a client from West Berlin while Franz is in the hospital, and adapts resignedly to the situation when Franz drops her to take up with a street singer. The friendly attitude she adopts toward Mieze, the street singer, is reminiscent of the ties of solidarity between the women in the waterfront movies, while the vivid depiction, through location shooting, of the Alexanderplatz district of Berlin locates the film firmly within the realist tradition.[10]

In France, in the later 1930s, Arletty emerged as the Gigolette *par excellence*. With her thin, angular beauty, no longer youthful but tense with coiled-up energy, she incarnated in *Hôtel du Nord* (1938) and *Fric-Frac* (1939) the Parisian prostitute as a complex blend of forbearance and pugnacity, world-weariness and vivacity, carnality and small-girl innocence, shrillness and sensitivity. Observed at her makeup, in the privacy of her bedroom, she is contemplative, inwardly focused; yet among friends she is brightly extroverted. In both films, she has the cynicism of the person at the bottom of the social heap accustomed to finding herself and those she mixes with on the wrong side of the law: in *Hôtel du Nord*, she is locked up for four days because her papers aren't in order; in *Fric-Frac*, her boyfriend-pimp is doing a six-month stint in jail.

Raymonde in *Hôtel du Nord* is part of a small community at the hotel, which also includes her pimp, Edmond (Louis Jouvet). Edmond knocks her around (she sports a black eye for much of the film), excites her with the prospect of a trip to the Midi, and then dashes her hopes by going off instead with someone else. Their exchanges became famous for Raymonde's acerbic repartee. "I'm suffocating," Edmond says, "I need a change of atmosphere — and my atmosphere is you!" "This is the first

5. *Hôtel du Nord:* Edmond (Louis Jouvet) and Raymonde (Arletty). Stills Collection, New Zealand Film Archive.

time anyone's treated me like an atmosphere!" Raymonde retorts, and then, her fury rising, "Atmosphere! Atmosphere! Do I look like an atmosphere?" Raymonde starts up a liaison with a lock-keeper ("not because of attraction to him, not for personal revenge, but out of an instinct to console a man in need," Edward Baron Turk writes[11]), while Edmond returns from Marseilles to go to his death at the hands of an underworld rival settling a gang score.

In *Fric-Frac*, Loulou gets flirtatiously involved with a jeweler's assistant, Marcel, while simultaneously plotting a burglary of the shop where he works. At one point, after he has discovered to his disappointment that Loulou is a streetwalker, Marcel tells her animatedly of an idea he has had for a movie — about a *fille perdue* lifted up to honesty and morality. She slugs him. After further comic complications, Marcel and Loulou break off and he returns to the respectable daughter of his employer, who has been assiduously pursuing him all along.

In both films, the point of having a prostitute character, as is customary with Gigolette representations, is to infuse an otherwise banal tale with the thrill of illicit sexuality, not explicitly depicted but hinted at in generous glimpses of naked flesh (in *Hôtel du Nord*, Raymonde gets around easily in a state of undress) or risqué bits of business (in *Fric-Frac*, on a bicycle trip to the country, Loulou grinningly invites Marcel to feel down her back for an insect, and he does so, commenting delightedly that she is not wearing a bra). The working-class prostitute who is undamaged by her occupation, who is tough and retains her sense of humor and capacity for tenderness despite the rough treatment she at times receives, becomes an essential balancing factor in a social formation otherwise lacking the erotic dimension. In *Hôtel du Nord*, Arletty's Gigolette provides ballast for the ethereal lovers Pierre and Renée, whose listless *Weltschmerz* has brought them to the brink of death in a suicide pact; in *Fric-Frac*, she counteracts the bourgeois manners and values of the employer's daughter. Her very presence on screen is rich in connotation.

Simone Signoret took over the baton from Arletty in *Macadam/Backstreets of Paris* (France, 1946). As Gisèle, stylish and attractive prostitute operating out of the modest Hotel Bijou, she is quintessential Gigolette: an integral part of her milieu (there are others who also work from the hotel), associated with criminal elements (her pimp has been involved in robbery and murder), and a signifier of the joys of sexuality (contrasted with the hotel proprietress's daughter, who falls in love with the same man Gisèle does, but who is flat-chested, has very long hair pulled back severely in a bun, and is drably dressed).

Signoret went on to play a prostitute in *Dédée*, and then in Max Ophuls's *La Ronde* (France, 1950). Based on Arthur Schnitzler's play *Reigen* and set in a stylized turn-of-the-century Vienna, *La Ronde* positions the streetwalker as both the first and the last of sexual partners in a daisy chain of amorous encounters. But though Signoret's Léocadie is there at the start, she is not the initiator of events: she is on a merry-go-round propelled into motion by the master of ceremonies, obeying his instructions to station herself at the street corner and take the sixth soldier who appears. Initially reluctant, the soldier changes his mind when told it's for free: bizarrely, patriotic Léocadie informs him that "only civilians have to pay up." The couple do it under the arches; then the soldier rushes off, heedless of her pleas to give her his name, or at least a cigarette. Léocadie is left trying to dust off her feather boa, yelling abuse. In the final episode, an inebriated count picks her up and spends the night with her. We see him the morning after, getting up, hungover and confused as to what actually took place, as his companion lies in bed, sleepy and jaded.

The Gigolette here performs her usual function of foregrounding the sexual dimension to life, but the film adopts an unusually cynical tone. With the prostitute being placed at the start and finish, the commercial transaction becomes the paradigm for the other encounters: stripped of emotional warmth or commitment to a relationship, the sex between the other pairings tends to be as abrupt, meaningless, and casually brutal as it is between Léocadie and the soldier. As Raymond Durgnat writes in *Eros in the Cinema,* noting that most of the characters dash away to resume their social duties after their brief amorous bouts: "If Vienna was 'gay,' it was because of a patriarchal social structure almost as impervious to love, in the full erotic sense, as Victorian London. . . . The very poignancy of *La Ronde,* and its reputation as a 'romantic' film, is an affirmation that even mutilated love, even the mere illusion of love, is more satisfying than society's indifference to it."[12] It was to take another film, and another Signoret performance, for the Gigolette to be idealized into an image of erotic liberation in this era of repression, a signifier of the joys of passionate love nostalgically imagined as the utopian dream of the *belle époque.*

"*Casque d'Or* is a great, simple tribute of the glory of love and friendship," Signoret writes, in *Nostalgia Isn't What It Used to Be.* "While the film was being made we were all in a state of grace."[13] Gone is the ennui of the hard-bitten whores of *Macadam, Dédée d'Anvers,* and *La Ronde;* Signoret is radiant, transfigured by love. Set in Paris at the turn of the century, the film portrays the ardent, tragic affair of her character Marie — known as "Casque d'Or" for her head of golden hair — with a carpenter by the name of Georges Manda. Signoret recalls that she had just fallen in love with Yves Montand, "and Manda reaped the benefits."[14]

It is not that the Gigolette has lost her feisty qualities: Marie is disdainful of her pimp, Roland, when he slaps her, and later, after Georges has killed him in a duel, she gets in a fight with his successor, Félix. But

6. *Casque d'Or:* Marie (Simone Signoret) with Manda (Serge Reggiani). Stills Collection, New Zealand Film Archive.

as a lover, making the first moves in coming to seek out Georges at his workshop, she is a full-bodied figure of male fantasy, the luscious woman who falls into one's lap like a ripe fruit. There is a rival, as in *Macadam*— Georges's fiancée Leonie, who is everything that Marie is not, coiled inward, modestly covered at the neck, her shawl drawn tightly across her body by crossed arms — but it is no contest.

In the sensuous idyll that the lovers enjoy at a farm cottage on the banks of the Marne, it is the intimacy of the gestures that conveys the emotion: Marie tickling Georges's ears with straw, lying voluptuously asleep in bed alongside his naked body, or kissing and falling to the ground with him, in the woods. The only hint of disharmony comes when they look in at a wedding taking place in a church, and Marie, touched, is much more inclined than Georges to linger.

As usual, the prostitute's work is elided. We can see Georges practicing as a carpenter, but not Marie plying her trade. To do so, of course, would be to dispel the romantic aura that surrounds her. Put another way, Marie can exist as a love object for Georges (and by extension, the male audience) only if he can believe that her charms are for him alone, if he can suppress the knowledge that she sleeps with her pimp and sells her body to others. In the end, it is finding Marie's slippers by Félix's bed that fires Georges's jealous rage and brings about his ultimate downfall. The Gigolette's sexuality is thus intrinsically paradoxical: her promiscuity both excites her lover and makes a relationship with her impossible. In *Casque d'Or*, utopia is short-lived.

Federico Fellini's *La dolce vita* (Italy, 1960) heralded a new era in sexual mores and hence the representation of prostitution on screen. As sex outside marriage became much less the exclusive province of the prostitute, the Gigolette began to lose some of her power as a signifier of erotic liberation. Thus in *La dolce vita*, which is about the impossibility of the hero's finding in one woman a synthesis of the disparate feminine qualities that he desires, and his inability to choose between those who offer only partial fulfillment, the prostitute plays a surprisingly minor, supernumerary role. In the array from carnal to angelic, passing through the teasingly deceptive and the maternally clinging, the streetwalker proves of little interest to Marcello, her sole role being to provide a bed in her flooded basement apartment for him and his lover Maddalena to have sex on. Is it perhaps because she offers no complications, is straightforwardly attainable, and her availability kills desire? (It is noticeable that Marcello's libido peaks when the woman is elusive, out of reach, and plummets when she simply offers herself to him.) The prostitute here is not eroticized, in contrast to the unending parade of other women pirouetting around Marcello; she signals a necessary reworking of the Gigolette characterization within a more liberal social context.

Two new versions of Schnitzler's *Reigen* were indicative of the changed climate. *Das grosse Liebesspiel/And So to Bed* (Austria/West Germany, 1963), an updated adaptation, plays the series of sexual encounters as broad farce, while *La Ronde/Circle of Love* (France/Italy, 1964) retains the period setting, but without Ophuls's light sophistication of touch, and in an environment in which a challenge to repressive bourgeois morality can no longer provide piquancy, it is simply blasé.

Further evidence of declining faith in the erotic liberation associated with the Gigolette is offered by Marco Bellochio's *I pugni in tasca/Fists in the Pocket* (Italy, 1965). A little while after murdering his mother, the disturbed young protagonist Alessandro visits a prostitute. It is a woman whom elder brother Augusto—the only "normal" member of the family—has been seeing three or four times a month. There is a brief bed scene, then they dress. Alessandro asks about how well he did, compared with Augusto. She tells him he needs practice. The implication is that this is his first experience of sex, and that it may be liberating, his desires

previously being bottled up and channeled into intense romantic closeness with his sister — an aberration that has contributed to his murder-
ousness. The film ruthlessly shatters such expectations, however. Alessandro proceeds to drown his brother Leone in his bath, after giving him
a massive overdose of his medication. There seems little point to the
prostitute sequence if not to insist on the irrelevance of sex to a psycho-
pathological condition such as Alessandro's.

Swinging London of the 1960s is the ironic setting for *Mini Weekend/
The Tomcat* (UK, 1967). Sexually frustrated Tom "retreats into a world of
dreams where all women find him irresistible."[15] On his sortie to the
West End, the pub prostitute is just one of the range of females whom he
fantasizes about, in the context of a sexual revolution that he is missing
out on. The film is characteristic of a trend: the Gigolette representation
loses its distinctive quality when the prostitute is no longer sharply differentiated in sexual terms from other women.

The traditional Gigolette, however, held on strongly in period films. In
particular, she survived in the old-style brothel, which was outlawed by
the 1960s in most of Europe but was re-created in rosy-tinted hues in
films that celebrated, often in comic terms, the privileged sexual indulgence of males in a bygone age — most often the *fin de siècle*.

The bordello is represented as a site of sensual gratification, refuge,
nurture, conviviality. It is the place, for example, that a man can escape
to from his domineering, greedy wife, in *Dulscy* (Poland, 1976), set in
Cracow; it provides an idyllic existence for a poor Hungarian medical
student who takes a room there and becomes a favorite among the
women, in *Egy erkölcsös éjszaka/A Very Moral Night* (Hungary, 1977); it is
the gathering place for the patriarchal power elite in a small Spanish
rural community, in *La Belle Époque/The Age of Beauty* (Spain/Portugal/
France, 1992).

Typically, in a setting of opulent and often exotic decor, a bevy of
resident hostesses provide titillation and scopophilic pleasure for the
audience. In *Lady L* a dozen Paris prostitutes in Victorian underwear
scramble for money tossed up by a bank robber; in *The Assassination Bu-
reau* (UK, 1968), a raid on another Parisian brothel results in the scantily
clad inmates being dragged off, shrilly protesting, to the paddy wagon,
naked legs feverishly pumping the air; in *Zakat/Sunset* (USSR, 1991), a
bare-breasted bordello inmate in Odessa flings herself about, and others
lie around languidly in the nude.

The perspective being resolutely male, the prostitutes are generally subordinate figures and may scarcely be characterized at all. This is the case in *Lady L*, although this eccentric comedy does show one of the women attempting to radicalize her comrades ("We shall always be victimized, until we've organized ourselves into a union. . . . Long live socialized love!"), and, in a remarkably lengthy take, the faces of the Gigolettes as they listen entranced to a performance of classical music by a concert pianist. In the 1920s Berlin gangster comedy *Ganovenehre/ Thieves' Honour* (West Germany, 1966), the fiery temperament of the protagonist's girlfriend Nelly (Karin Baal), an employee at the Massage-Salon Venus von Milo, spices the characterization of the otherwise charming and loving dolly-bird prostitute, slim and blonde in flapper-era short skirts (and sometimes a perky sailor suit, for that fifteen-year-old look the clients like).

Male point of view is taken farther in *Ulysses* (UK, 1967), in which the prostitutes function purely to trigger off thoughts in the mind of protagonist Leopold Bloom and his companion Stephen Dedalus. The string of whores in and around Bella Cohen's "ten shilling house" in Dublin ("How's your middle leg, darlin'?") set off a chain of erotic/masochistic fantasy sequences, which establish a close association between the world of illicit sex and that of Bloom's imagination: the provocative trollops arouse his desires but also his fears, provoke reveries, sorcery, delirium, transformation. He is brought to trial for his past sexual offenses (mostly imaginary); he experiences transgressions of gender boundaries, indulges dreams of power and fame, submits to heinous degradation. Outside the whorehouse, it takes a fight brewing between Stephen and some soldiers over a streetwalker to bring him down to earth.

The durable appeal of the classic Gigolette characterization in period films is demonstrated in *Van Gogh* (France, 1991), in which the Gay Nineties Paris brothel is resurrected yet again. In a sequence that brings the erotic ambiance to a pitch of frenzy, the painter's prostitute friend Cathy (Elsa Zylberstein), all vibrant energy, cartwheels across the dance floor as *cocottes* and clients perform a wildly joyous cancan, while upstairs Vincent rips the bodice off his young lover and they allow their heightened sexual desires full rein.

It took a Taiwanese film, *Haishang hua/ Flowers of Shanghai* (1998) to begin to deconstruct the lingering fascination in male culture with the brothel of the *belle époque*. Here, in contrast to *Van Gogh*, the pace is languid, the sensuality refined. The beauty of the "flower girls" and their dedication to the gratification of their patrons accords with Gigolette convention, but they are given central parts in the small dramas that slowly unfold. The possibility that there may be a female subjectivity at odds with the assigned patriarchal role of pleasure-giver is, for once, acknowledged.

In the quasi-documentary *Roma/Fellini's Roma* (Italy/France, 1972), Fellini reflects upon the place of the brothel in the Italy of his youth. Prostitution is neither condemned nor celebrated, but represented as necessary in an age of strict sexual morality. (The taboo applied not to extramarital intercourse per se — as the film suggests, the Roman Catholic Church was quite willing to absolve peccadilloes with prostitutes — but to sexual relationships between boyfriend and girlfriend, particularly in the middle class.) Fellini explicitly contrasts the brothel-going of the 1930s with the freer sexual relationships of the 1970s, epitomized among the hippies — whom he films "huddled together like a basketful of kittens or a brood of chicks" on the Spanish Steps. "These disenchanted young people," the narration tells us,". . . remind us how different we were, how different our relationship to women. We had to hide to make love — in the kitchen, trying to finger the maid, in the darkness of movie houses, in the bathroom. It was so difficult to have a woman. So, one went to the whorehouse."

The film shows both working-class and luxury brothels. The decor varies, but the essential action remains the same: the prostitutes parading before the clients, enticing them upstairs with suggestive gestures and vulgar come-ons. There is no pretence that the women enjoy their work; they're just hustling as a job and slump down exhausted at the meal break. Still, the picture does not entirely escape an element of romanticizing. When one of the inmates (the most beautiful, in eighteen-year-old Fellini's eyes, at the high-class bordello) does get a chance to speak, she says nothing men don't want to hear ("I have no complaints, the old lady likes me, I have everything I need"). And when young Fellini invites her out on a date (lunch at the beach), *Roma* invokes the heightened erotic appeal of the girlfriend whose profession is sex and brings the representation of the Gigolette back toward that of the idealized love object.

In the Western genre, the relaxation of censorship in the 1960s allowed, for the first time since the early 1930s, the prostitute's profession to be explicitly identified, and she began to take a more prominent role in proceedings. In such films she is typically the consummate Gigolette, providing relief for the hero from the harshness of the terrain and the monotony of the all-male company he keeps. She awakens his long-buried libido, awards him for his feats of violence, consoles him for the fading of his dreams; she is both playmate of the sheriff and comrade-in-arms of the outlaw.

Little Big Man (USA, 1970), for example, features the highly sexed Mrs. Pendrake (Faye Dunaway), the reverend's wife turned "fallen flower," who on meeting up with her foster son Jack again ("Do you know I often had wicked thoughts about you?") sidles into the brothel bedroom through the swinging glass-bead curtain, strips off a black stocking and tosses it aside, unfastens her corset, and lies back on the bed with bare legs and midriff, invitingly. In *Pat Garrett and Billy the Kid* (USA, 1973), the cool sheriff finds himself in bed with four naked whores — not that he ordered any more than one. The others are a tribute by the hotelier to his prestige, the sexy women an item of exchange between powerful males. Ella (Isabelle Huppert) of *Heaven's Gate* (USA, 1980) greets the marshal delightedly, passionately, when he shows up at her log-cabin bordello and, after serving the hungry man coffee and pie, strips naked and races off into the bedroom, where she jerks his clothes off and climbs eagerly on top. Later, she bathes in the lake, her easygoing nudity an occasion for imagery of erotic lyricism.

In *Monte Walsh* (USA, 1970), Martine (Jeanne Moreau) is the fantasized ideal companion who's always there when you want a bit of female company, not there when you're in your man's world, and never makes demands, as a wife would. In Martine's case, she is so smitten with Monte (Lee Marvin) that she doesn't even make demands for money, so the sex is not a financial transaction. (Not that there is much emphasis on sex: they are both tired, don't have the energy for it. They spend most of their time in bed just cuddling and comforting.) If he is going to give her money ("This ain't money — it's capital"), then he decides when and how much, a matter of *noblesse oblige*. The film is about the pain of aging, the sadness of seeing one's life work diminished — with the skills of the cowhand no longer much in demand — and the way that the pain and loneliness can be assuaged by a nurturing prostitute.

The Ballad of Cable Hogue (USA, 1970) draws an insistent parallel between the waterhole for the parched man on the brink of death and the prostitute as lifesaver for the man starved of female company in the arid masculine world of the desert. In this lyrical tale of love springing up between prospector Cable Hogue (Jason Robards) and town whore Hildy (Stella Stevens), Hildy, like Martine, is quintessential Gigolette in incarnating the joys of sexual fulfillment without the hassles of possession. Cable stares at Hildy's breasts when he first catches sight of them

7. *The Ballad of Cable Hogue:* Hildy (Stella Stevens) with Hogue (Jason Robards). Stills Collection, New Zealand Film Archive.

with the same obsession that he previously exhibited in clawing at the moist sand to get at the water below. He just can't get those charms out of his mind; the editor cuts back to the close-up of cleavage time after time. She is his oasis, and the water imagery keeps stressing the metaphor: she scrubs him in her tub; he sponges her in his, out at Cable Springs; and water flows down the chute across the desert sands.

"You used to make me hotter than a June bride sitting bareback on a depot stove," Jane Greathouse (Jenny Wright) confides to Pat Garrett in *Young Guns II* (USA, 1990), "but I don't share my bed with the law." Now she's the defiant ally and lover of the outlaw Billy the Kid, sexy and young and slim, with curly red tresses hanging down to her breasts. When the sheriff, backed up by a lynch mob whose resemblance to the Ku Klux Klan is unmistakable, sets fire to her whorehouse to protect the "civic virtue" of the citizens of White Oaks, Jane strips naked but for boots and gloves, strides brazenly toward the assembled populace ("White Oaks, you can kiss my ass"), and then mounts a white horse and does a Lady Godiva act riding off out of town. Later, she smuggles a gun to Billy in jail, allowing him to make his escape. Confuter of straight-laced hypocritical puritanism and symbol of liberated sexuality, Jane upholds the Gigolette tradition even as the historical era to which she belongs recedes into the distant past.

In male action movies, the Gigolette's function is to redress the gender imbalance. In keeping with her tendency to mix in a criminal milieu, she is often found in detective and gangster films. Here, her role may be simply to constitute part of the scene, as for example in *Neige* (France, 1981), a study of Pigalle nightlife, where streetwalkers inevitably appear alongside addicts, cops, pushers, strippers, and transvestites. If she plays a larger part, it is often as desirable companion to the male protagonist on either side of the law, as in the Western. But it is in becoming involved in gangster violence herself that the crime-film Gigolette is most distinctive.

The desirable companion might be typified by Lily (Romy Schneider) in *Max et les ferrailleurs/Max and the Junkmen* (France/Italy, 1971), though paradoxically the lone-wolf police detective who becomes her sugar daddy has other things on his mind than sex. Lily is heart and beauty in an austere, rough milieu. Hanging out at a bar in Nanterre with other prostitutes, a couple of pimps, and a gang who sell stolen scrap metal and cut-up cars, she is different from the rest: a German, an independent operator who lives with her criminal boyfriend but doesn't support him. Max, the detective, targets her to get at the gang. In falling for his elaborate provocation, persuading the gang to carry out a bank robbery, she seals their fate as well as her own.

Despite Max's lack of sexual interest in her, Lily is, typically, eroticized, dressing in a variety of low-slung outfits and exposing a nipple when bathing in Max's apartment. Nudity for the crime-film Gigolette was to become increasingly obligatory, as exemplified by Elita (Isela Vega) in *Bring Me the Head of Alfredo Garcia* (USA, 1974) and Lydie (Sandrine Bonnaire) in *Police* (France, 1985), both of whom shower voluptuously in the presence of the male protagonist. Such characters decisively moderate the harshness of the violent underworld environment that they find themselves in: Elita, for example, by accompanying bar owner Bennie — who is in love with her — on his dangerous quest to retrieve a killer's body and claim the bounty; Lydie by rewarding police inspector Mangin with uncomplicated sexual pleasure for his part in helping her by planting drugs on her pimp and getting him arrested.

Other prostitute characters in the genre tilt the gender dynamics by taking part in violent crime themselves. Kansas City brothel inmate

Betty (Jocelyn Lane) in *A Bullet for Pretty Boy* (USA, 1970), for instance, becomes the gangster's lover and joins him on a crime spree that culminates
in a bank holdup in Pretty Boy's home town. Similarly, hooker Mona (Diane Varsi) joins the larcenous, murdering, incestuous Barker bunch in
the gangster parody *Bloody Mama* (USA, 1970). Although Mona provides
sexual divertissement—fornicating with the horny Arthur in the back
seat of an open touring car traveling through the South, to the accompaniment of country banjo and harmonica—she is no blonde bombshell, with her bony nakedness and cropped hair, and it is in her criminal
dimension that she comes into her own. In one exuberant car chase sequence, for example, the pregnant pistol-packing prostitute, a plume
trailing from her hair, fires two-fisted from her careering automobile at
the car behind, until finally it bursts into flames.

   Girls for Rent (USA, 1974) ups the ante, with prison escapee Sandra
Tate (Georgina Spelvin), who used to run a call-girl ring among other
criminal activities and is now enlisted as an enforcer for the mob, going
on a killing rampage. One of her victims is a hooker, Donna (Susan
McIver), who on gang instructions has slipped an awkward politician a
Mickey Finn without realizing it was lethal, and must now be eliminated
in case she talks. With an admixture of soft-core copulation (Spelvin had
starred the previous year in the breakthrough pornographic feature *The
Devil in Miss Jones*), *Girls for Rent* becomes a hotly spiced cocktail of sex and
violence, illustrating the evolution of the Gigolette archetype in response
to the loosening of social constraints.

The 1980s saw the Gigolette being used increasingly in comic scenarios.
In *Porky's* (Canada, 1981), for example, "exotic dancer" Cherry Forever
(Susan Clark) burlesques the suffusion of lust among sex-starved young
males at a 1950s Florida high school; in *¿Qué he hecho yo para merecer esto?/
What Have I Done to Deserve This?* (Spain, 1984), call girl Cristal (Veronica
Forque) plays a crucial part in a savage spoof of Spanish machismo. But
there was a darker side, too, as the hopes of erotic liberation that had
been pinned to the figure of the carefree prostitute began to fade. With
sexual morality changing so that the good girl/bad girl dichotomy hardly
applied any more, and fierce debate beginning to rage in feminist circles
over the nature and desirability of prostitution, Gigolette characterizations took on a new aura of disenchantment.

   Thus in *The Men's Club* (USA, 1986), a bunch of misogynists get together to lament the inadequacies of their current women, and then
truck on down to the brothel where their money can buy sex objects more

adequate to their fantasies. What results is the wet dream of the uptight, patriarchal middle class, exposed in a series of ugly, violent vignettes in which the men take out on the hookers their accumulated resentments without fear of reprisal, and the women take it as par for the course. "Do I remind you of your wife?" Allison (Marilyn Jones) asks her client, Solly. "Not yet," he replies, "Complain about something." When she invites him to her room, he pulls her up the stairs, slams her against the wall and, it seems, almost rapes her on the spot. Allison responds, "I'll give you what you want," allows him to pick her up in his arms, and then giggles: hence the violence is validated. There is dancing, and there is sex, but *The Men's Club* can offer only a bitter parody of the exuberant *fin de siècle* brothel scenes featured in more characteristic Gigolette films.

Letzte Ausfahrt Brooklyn/Last Exit to Brooklyn (West Germany/USA, 1989) is also dark. There is an aspect of the Gigolette to Tralala (Jennifer Jason Leigh), the voluptuous blonde with "the best tits in the Western world," the woman who can offer a soldier off to Korea a glimpse of heaven before he ships out to hell. But Brooklyn 1952 is not bathed in any golden hue of nostalgia, and Tralala shocks because of her total lack of romantic inclinations and because of the harsh explicitness with which the film depicts her at work. Prostitution is not problematized in this film; it is just another ugly, alienated routine in a world permeated by corruption and brutality.

Claude Chabrol's very loose adaptation of Henry Miller's *Quiet Days in Clichy, Jours tranquilles à Clichy* (France/Germany/Italy, 1990), registers the changing mood, turning a warmly nostalgic memoir, whose charm is in its closeness to lived experience, into a chilly fantasy linking libertine/commercial sex with death. Despite the explicit depiction of clients dallying with naked prostitutes both at the luxurious brothel that the American writer's friend has (conveniently) inherited, and at an art deco nightclub, there is nothing of the joyous celebration of the libido that marks classic Gigolette representations as well as Miller's book. Instead, a morbidity pervades the film, induced in the first place by the framing situation, which depicts the aged, decrepit writer approaching death, choleric, trying unsuccessfully to persuade a naked young woman sixty years his junior to fuck him, and reinforced, as we enter the main story, by the sight of a well-preserved but dead old whore lying in a coffin in her baroque bordello.

But perhaps the most deadly blow to the Gigolette as twentieth-century cinema knew her is delivered by David Cronenberg's *Crash* (Canada, 1996), a film that asks what function the prostitute figure can

8. Jennifer Jason Leigh as Tralala in *Last Exit to Brooklyn*.

perform in a field of rampant polymorphous promiscuity. She does not even point the way to freer sex: the movie's swinging married couple are way ahead of her there. She's just in it for the money; the forbidden excitement she used to provide is now supplied by car crashes. Here, in this realm of postmodernity in which the distinction between respectable and disreputable has been blurred, the moral imperative against infidelity rendered null and void, the prostitute can no longer symbolize either a necessary sexual liberation or a temptation to be spurned. She is simply another piece of flesh: splayed legs, bared nipples, thrusting pelvis, jerking knees, exposed rounded buttocks—the anonymous airport hooker, earning her sixty bucks in the back seat of a battered '63 Lincoln convertible, manhandled by an awkward john, getting her "scenic ride," splashed with cold light on the urban night freeway.

4

Siren

Beware of whores, for they be the sirens that draw men on to
destruction; their sweet words are enchantments, their eyes allure,
and their beauties bewitch. Oh, take heed of their persuasions, for
they be crocodiles, that when they weep, destroy.
—ROBERT GREENE, *The Black Book's Messenger* (1592)[1]

The siren is the woman of myth whose sensual allure is such that men fall
under her spell and are drawn on toward their destruction. This *femme fatale* obviously need not be a prostitute, and in many versions of the story
(the typical vamp narrative of silent movies, for example) she is not. Yet
as the above quote suggests, there is an inveterate association between
the siren's bewitching beauty and the practice of prostitution, which a
significant body of work in the cinema draws upon.

This is likely because making the heroine a professional sex practi-
tioner sharpens the contradiction between what she is and what her lover
dreams of her becoming, intensifying his anguish when the impossibility
of possessing her for himself alone becomes apparent. From the woman's
point of view, having a freelance source of income buttresses her independence and enables her, when she is so inclined, to resist the blandishments of her importunate admirers.

The Siren's story in film is characterized by a number of recurring
features, among which the troublesome consequences of her fickle, flirtatious nature are often to the fore. The barfly from Buenos Aires in
Stormy Waters (USA, 1928) seduces David, a seaman, away from his fiancée, after which "the fiery Lola destructively flirts with several of the
crew" on the boat on which they are sailing, even attempting to ensnare
his brother Angus, the captain.[2] Similarly the "unscrupulous German
tart" in *The Rough and the Smooth/Portrait of a Sinner* (UK, 1959) seduces "an
upper middle-class archaeologist on the verge of marriage to a newspaper heiress" and "drags him into a network of unsavory relationships

which very nearly destroy him."[3] Ultimately she may drive her lover to suicide, as in *The Woman in the Case* (USA, 1916), in which an American marries a French prostitute and subsequently kills himself because of her, or *The Amazing Woman* (USA, 1920), in which a dissolute playboy commits suicide because the woman he is in love with, a prostitute who plies her trade in order to raise money for a hospital for crippled children, refuses to marry him.

The Siren is often responsible for wreaking havoc with a man's family. After being led astray by a woman of the streets, the respectable judge in *Sensualidad* (Mexico, 1951) asks his wife for a divorce, precipitating her early death. In *Nihombashi* (Japan, 1956) Denkichi, the owner of a seafood store, falls obsessively in love with Otaka, a geisha who does not reciprocate his feelings, whereupon his wife dies and he leaves his children. When the happily married Sigismond in *La Marge / The Margin / The Streetwalker / Emmanuelle '77* (France, 1976) becomes infatuated with a Parisian whore, his son drowns, and his wife in despair jumps to her death from a tower.

Intoxication with a Siren is also likely to prove hazardous to a man's financial and business affairs, and may well lead to a life of crime and its consequences. The formerly upright judge in *Sensualidad* embezzles money from the police commissariat, kills his lover's accomplice, and finally strangles the object of his passion. He is arrested. Denkichi in *Nihombashi* goes bankrupt, threatens Otaka with a knife, and eventually kills her aunt and an apprentice geisha, only to be killed himself by Otaka. In *Secrets of a Married Man* (USA, 1984), aeronautical engineer Christopher Jordan becomes passionately attached to a high-class hooker and as a result is embroiled in a blackmail plot concocted by her pimp, comes close to losing his job, and is almost murdered. Chan Chen-Pang in *Inji kau / Rouge* (Hong Kong, 1987), smitten by the singer-courtesan Fleur, is seduced away from a successful business career, brought to the verge of death in a suicide pact, and then condemned to a life of minor theatrical parts followed by pitiful obscurity and penury. In *Hong fen / Blush* (China / Hong Kong, 1994), a young man from a prerevolutionary landowning family falls in love with two former prostitutes and, driven to distraction by their expectations, embezzles a large sum of money from his employers. He is arrested, sentenced to death, and executed by firing squad.[4]

What is fascinating about the Siren (as opposed to the Gold Digger — see chapter 8) is that despite her destructive impact on the lives of her admirers, little moral opprobrium is directed at her. The men enamored of her, frequently of high station in life, are instead gently or occasionally savagely satirized for their folly in becoming obsessed with a woman of the streets, while the Siren herself, from a humble background, may become an object of admiration for her skill at parlaying beauty and vivacity into a luxurious lifestyle, subsequently to become an object of pathos if things fall apart and she in turn is marked for punishment or destruction.

The first appearance of the Siren in film was probably in early adaptations of several popular literary and dramatic works, which were to become standard source texts. The Abbé Prévost's *Histoire du chevalier des Grieux et de Manon Lescaut* (1731) was filmed as *Manon* (France, 1910), *Manon Lescaut* (Italy, 1911), *Manon Lescaut* (USA, 1914), *Manon Lescaut* (Germany, 1926), and *When a Man Loves* (USA, 1927), with a probable updated variant in *Manon de Montmartre* (France, 1914). Émile Zola's novel *Nana* (1880) appeared on screen as *A Man and the Woman* (USA, 1917)—though the synopsis of the film bears little resemblance to the original.[5] Finally, Frank Wedekind's plays *Der Erdgeist* (1895) and *Die Büchse der Pandora* (1904) were brought to the screen as *Lulu* (Hungary, 1917) and *Erdgeist* (Germany, 1923). The available evidence suggests that these first versions, while placing the erotic woman and her danger to the man in love with her at the center of their narratives, tended to downplay the element of prostitution. This was more conspicuous, as we shall see, in two key works of the 1920s, Jean Renoir's Nana (France, 1926) and G.W. Pabst's *Die Büchse der Pandora / Pandora's Box / Lulu* (Germany, 1929).[6]

The fully fledged Siren prostitute emerged before then, however, in Karl Grune's *Die Strasse / The Street* (Germany, 1923). Identified only as "Die Dirne" (as the protagonist is simply "Der Mann"), the woman (played by Aud Egede Nissen) whom the bourgeois citizen encounters during his night on the town is the conduit by which he is drawn into a nightmare world of sensuality and crime. (Commentators have made comparisons with the feverish post–World War I visions of big-city streets as the locus of a dance of death in the paintings of George Grosz and the expressionist drama of Georg Kaiser, whose *Von Morgens bis Mitternacht* was filmed in 1920.)[7]

Lured into the street by a hallucinatory vision of the excitement to be found there (a rapid superimpositional montage in which the close-up of a smiling woman is sandwiched among images from busy traffic, a circus, a roller coaster, and a fireworks display), the man hesitantly ventures into the red-light district. Here the hallucinations, filmed in expressionist style, continue but begin to take on a disturbing tinge: the face of a streetwalker metamorphoses into that of a skull. Following the prostitute played by Nissen into a dancehall, he is enticed by her into a gambling den, where he comes close to being totally fleeced. Later in the night he goes back to the prostitute's apartment, and here, before his fumbling groping at her can come to anything, he finds himself framed for a murder, which takes place in the next room. At the police station, the woman directly accuses him of the killing. In despair, he is making a noose out of his belt when he is reprieved: the real killer has confessed. Shaken, the man returns home where his middle-aged wife, as she had done at the start of the film, serves him up a bowl of soup. He goes to her, his head slumped on her shoulder in a gesture of submission to a routine respectability.

The execution of the film is mediocre, but it has attained its place in film history no doubt on account of its highly charged narrative of the middle-class male lured into a nighttime lumpenproletarian milieu who, almost engulfed, retreats to his foyer and his wife a wiser man, a story reprised, for example, in *Dirnentragödie* (1927). Grasping the role of the prostitute is inhibited by confusion in the narrative and mise-en-scene (this is a case where the determination to tell the story without benefit of titles has mixed results), but she nonetheless plays her part symbolically as a composite figure condensing sex and criminality, the eroticism absent in the bourgeois household and the male protagonist's projected fear of the illicit. She is temptress (under her spell he gambles away even his wedding ring), betrayer, and harbinger of death. At the end, with the protagonist safely back at home, patriarchal normality is restored, but the Siren is still out there, in the wild zone of the city, waiting to snare her next prey.

What is striking here is the draining away of the man's willpower after his coming in contact with the prostitute, and this becomes the central motif of Renoir's *Nana*. Selecting from the Zola original those episodes detailing Nana's relationship with three of her admirers — Count Muffat, Count Vandeuvres, and Georges Hugon — the film details how each in turn is destroyed, until the courtesan herself comes to a bitter end.

Captivated by Nana at a theatrical revue in which she is appearing as "La Blonde Vénus," Muffat (Werner Krauss) comes to her rooms, declares his love, and volunteers to make any form of sacrifice for her. When she tells him she can't accept, he buries his head in her lap, pleads, and debases himself. For a moment she smiles and strokes his hair, but then she thrusts him away ("l'argent, je crache dessus!"), and the Count, robbed of vitality, can get to his feet only to slump into a chair. On a later occasion (Nana this time consenting to receive him only after receiving a lavish box of chocolates in which a wad of money has been conspicuously stashed), Muffat is reduced to a puppy dog who crawls after Nana on his hands and knees, making little leaps for the chocolate, which she dangles above him; his unmanning is completed when finally he collapses on the rug, and she steps on him with her heel.

Nana here plays the Siren as the opposite of the Nursemaid, a role that she parodies. She is the bad mother as against the good mother; she denies the breast. With the power to infantilize her admirer, she rejects his cry for nourishment, abasing him further, scorning him, trampling on him. She is the destroyer, as the Nursemaid is the healer, a figure of nightmares rather than dreams.

Muffat survives (though at the end his life is imperiled); Vandeuvres and Hugon do not. Vandeuvres is driven to act dishonorably (by cheating at the races) out of desire for Nana; subsequently, ruined, he asks for her hand in marriage, is disdainfully rejected, and commits suicide by taking poison. Hugon, a younger lover, commands more of Nana's affection but has the misfortune to witness her intimate games of humiliation with Muffat; at this, "intoxicated with shame and jealousy" (as a title informs us) he too is reduced to quivering jelly, and he stabs himself to death with a pair of scissors.

Nana's end comes after she is infected with smallpox. Lying delirious in bed, she is assailed by accusatory visions of Hugon and Vandeuvres; but she is granted release when Muffat, who has broken off with her, relents and comes to her bedside. Even in her dying moments, Nana exerts such a pull over the Count that in taking her in his arms to comfort her, he will put his own life at stake.

In terms of its story line, the film is clearly a pivotal work in the fleshing out of the Siren archetype. This is less the case, however, in relation to performance. As Nana, Catherine Hessling gives a curiously stylized interpretation with broad semaphoric gestures, which at times become so jerky that she flings her arms about and tosses her head like an automaton whose mechanism is failing. Renoir comments that she carried stylization "to the uttermost extreme. She was not a woman at all, but a marionette." Her seductiveness, at the level of performance, failed to carry conviction, and her stylized acting was, Renoir says, a "transfiguration" that "the public could not accept."[8] The honor of being the screen's first full-blooded Siren should perhaps therefore go to Louise Brooks as Lulu in *Pandora's Box*.

As in *Nana,* the courtesan protagonist in *Pandora's Box* is also, and

9. The showgirl: Louise Brooks as Lulu in *Pandora's Box*. David Lascelles Stills Collection.

perhaps primarily, a showgirl. What the showgirl and the prostitute have in common is a sexualization of the body and its display for the titillation of spectators, principally male. But with the showgirl the pleasure stops at voyeurism.[9] Her naked legs are a tease, a come-hither but a don't-touch. For the man in the audience the excitement is safe and legitimate; he can go home with his wife, or to her, with a clear conscience. The prostitute, however, is not teasing; what she offers she will supply, at a price of course, but one that is fixed in advance.

The Siren as incarnated by Nana and Lulu is closer to the showgirl than to the prostitute proper. It is her tantalizing behavior, her failure to deliver in full measure the pleasure she promises with the beauty of her body and the enticement of her smile, that drives her victims to self-destruction. Unlike the common prostitute, she makes no straightforward cash transaction; but like her, she is no man's sole possession. To believe, as Dr. Schön (Fritz Kortner) in *Pandora's Box* does, that he can have Lulu all to himself, either as mistress or as wife, is to make a fatal blunder.

Here a useful comparison may be made with Josef von Sternberg's *Der Blaue Engel/The Blue Angel* (Germany, 1930), in which prostitution is not a factor but where many of the same dynamics are at play. Like that of Lulu, the eroticism of Lola Lola (Marlene Dietrich) is public and hence inevitably shared, promiscuous. She makes a spectacle of her body simultaneously for Rath (Emil Jannings) and for the crowd at the Blue Angel. This eroticism cannot be privately appropriated, since it exists only through and for a paying audience — it is both pleasure and work. Rath's mistake (equivalent to that of Schön, who promotes Lulu's appearance in a musical revue) is to believe that Lola Lola's sexuality, when she is off stage, can be for himself alone, a mistake that the episode with the postcards (titillating images of herself, which Lola Lola sells) quickly demonstrates. The way is always open for Rath to find other work and support her, but he recognizes instinctively that it is with Lola Lola the performer that he is in love. He must live out his destiny in the showbiz world, joining it himself to become pathetic clown to her ever more brazen chanteuse.

Like Lola Lola, Lulu cannot be possessed. Though she may take him in her arms, flirtatiously, affectionately, there are no scenes of her in bed with a lover. On his wedding night, before he can have his wife to himself, Schön is killed. Even at the end, when in desperate poverty Lulu solicits in the street, her client (Jack the Ripper) is clearly impotent. Likewise she cannot be bought: she angrily repudiates a scheme to sell her to an Egyptian brothel. A teasingly chaste aura accompanies Lulu's depiction as erotic spectacle, a paradox that reinforces the way in which she eludes categorization.

For, like other Siren characters at the ambiguous margins of prostitution, Lulu cannot be pinned down. Although Louise Brooks herself refers to the character as a prostitute, there is little to identify her definitely as such until the final sequence, in which before she can take on a paying customer she is murdered.[10] The quality of scandal that Lulu provokes arises from the game of alternation she plays between private and public woman, blurring the distinction between respectable and disreputable. It is typical of the film's strategy of confounding expectations that in the introductory sequence Lulu is seen giving, rather than accepting money. And it is her ambiguity that is troubling to the male characters, especially Dr. Schön. From what we can tell on the evidence presented she is not *in fact* unfaithful, and her affection for Schön is genuine, but she refuses to play the role of the good, virtuous, submissive wife, the woman who acknowledges only one master, allows intimate acquaintance with no man but her husband. It is her *apparent* promiscuity, and the uncertainty he experiences as to whether her feelings are feigned or real, that inflames his jealousy and drives him to violence.

The climax of this drama occurs in the wedding party sequence, which brings together the key figures up this point: Lulu; the newspaper magnate Schön, who has forsaken his high-society fiancée for her; the old tramp Schigolch who was, it seems, Lulu's first sugar daddy; her would-be trapeze partner Rodrigo; and Alwa, Schön's son, who has fallen in love with her. Lulu's carefree reveling, in the marital bedroom, with Schigolch and Rodrigo, followed by her maternal nurturing of the troubled Alwa, both of which are witnessed by Schön, are enough to unhinge his mind. In the action that follows, Schön forces a gun into Lulu's hands telling her to kill herself; when the gun goes off, however, it is Schön who is shot.[11]

And yet despite the ambiguity surrounding her mode of life, Lulu is not constituted as the typically enigmatic *femme fatale*. Only hints of her background are given — just what role Schigolch has played in her life is unclear, and the lesbian Countess Geschwitz exclaims at Lulu's trial, "Mr. Prosecutor, do you know what would have become of your wife if she had to spend all the nights of her childhood in cafes and cabarets?" — but the past is not presented as a mystery to be unraveled as an explanation for her current conduct. Her desires, by and large, are clearly enough expressed: she does not want to perform in front of her lover's fiancée, she does not want to go to work in a bordello in Cairo; she does not want to starve to death in a freezing, leaking attic. She does want to freely give and receive affection. She also no doubt enjoys the comforts that Schön's money can buy, but there is nothing mysterious in that.

This transparency is reinforced, for the male spectator, in the fact that there is no male character with whom he is invited to identify, no character who is *more* transparent than Lulu, and whose perception of her as enigmatic he might therefore be called on to share (as, for example, with Rath in *The Blue Angel*). On the contrary, Lulu is the pivot of the narrative; the male characters circle around her, substantially more opaque than she is. We have to guess at the reasons for Schön going berserk with a gun, for his son prostrating himself before her and subsequently fleeing with her from the law, fetching up on a ship where he loses all his money gambling. The nature of their fixation on this woman is obviously erotic — and here the much-praised magnetic performance of Louise Brooks, with her seductive vivaciousness and highly energized but graceful physical movement, is crucial in creating plausibility — but what the lovers want of her beyond a momentary satisfaction remains as obscure to us as it probably does to them.

Lulu is perhaps only a mystery to the man, like Schön, who cannot understand why a woman might not wish to belong to himself alone—and a man in his social position![12]—forsaking all other intimacy; might not want to conform 100 percent to the submissive role patriarchy has allotted to her. This is a strength of the film, that it endorses Lulu's desire for autonomy so flagrantly. Yet, of course, she cannot triumph. She is a provocation and a threat, uncorraled because of the corrupt ineffectuality of father-figure Schigolch and the pathetic inadequacy of husband Schön. To neutralize her, finally, male society's enforcer, Jack the Ripper in his first fictional outing is wheeled onstage, a killer ex machina. Lulu is written out, erased, stabbed to death and left off-screen, while her male companions in misfortune, Schigolch and Alwa, damaged but intact, go on with their lives.

A different fate awaits the protagonist of *Sadie Thompson* (USA, 1928), distinctive for the earthiness of its Siren characterization and for the adoption of a point of view, which is firmly on her side. Produced by its star Gloria Swanson in defiance of the industry's censors,[13] the film was based on a W. Somerset Maugham short story and its theatrical adaptation, *Rain*, which had been a hit on Broadway. *Sadie Thompson* is the drama of a battle of wills between a young woman with a shady past—implicitly prostitution—and a puritanical reformer intent on changing her ways. Taking place among a group of American travelers, servicemen, and expatriates in Samoa, it uses the exotic setting and the pressure-cooker confinement of its characters, several of whom are detained unwillingly on the island because of a quarantine emergency, to mount a damning critique of holier-than-thou arrogance.

It is the infectious vulgarity of the gum-chewing Sadie that marks her at the start. After sashaying down the gangplank she is tapped familiarly on the rump by a ship's officer as she is introduced to a squadron of marines, with whom she is shortly drinking and dancing to jazz records. Her flashy outfit, replete with feathers, fox-fur stole, pearls, gaudy bangles, dangling handbag, and parasol, overdetermines her as prostitute, suggesting excess, parody, and even perhaps denial—the hint that appearances may be deceptive. In the 1932 sound remake *Rain*, featuring Joan Crawford, the suggestive attire is fetishized into a visual trope, a rapid montage of close-up details of bejeweled wrists and ankles clad in fishnet stockings, which serves to introduce Sadie for the first time. *Variety* called the costuming "bizarre," commenting: "Pavement pounders don't quite trick themselves up as fantastically as all that."[14]

Sadie's adversary is Davidson[15] (Lionel Barrymore), whose belief that "the knife of reform is the only hope of a sin-sick world" makes him

10. *Sadie Thompson:* Gloria Swanson as Sadie, with marines.

11. *Rain:* Joan Crawford as Sadie.

determined to put her on the path to salvation. For days he denounces her as an "evil woman" and endures her contemptuous ripostes ("mealy-mouthed hypocrite," "psalm-singing louse") before, by playing on her guilt, he induces her to pray for redemption. But having achieved his goal, he comes under the Siren's spell: a demonic, possessed look takes over his countenance and he goes to Sadie, raving about "flaming — hot eyes — Aphrodite — Judas!" and declaring "You are radiant — You are beautiful!" The next morning it is clear that Sadie has been sexually violated ("You men are all alike — pigs — PIGS!"), while Davidson's body is hauled up from the sea in a fishing net . . . he has cut his throat.

In this sober reassessment of erotic obsession and its fatal consequences, no blame is attached to the woman. The cause of the man's mental instability and violent actions cannot be attributed to anything that she does; instead it is blamed firmly on his warped, repressive attitude toward sexuality. The Siren's vivacious carnality, on the other hand, is endorsed, associated with naturalness, openness, and gregarious good times.

But in the dynamic interplay between the two, it is not only Davidson who is changed. Moved to repentance, Sadie is transformed, appearing desexualized, devitalized, in a modest dressing gown. It is true that following the physical encounter with her reformer she reverts to the prostitute's attire, but only as a gesture of bitter disillusionment. She will not be taking up again her happy-go-lucky promiscuous ways; instead, she will sail for Sydney and the prospect of marriage to the marine sergeant who has fallen in love with her. Patriarchal ideology here spares the independent woman her life and takes the other route to neutralization. Sadie learns that her sexuality, rather than being flaunted to all comers, must be reserved for the one individual: the wild woman is tamed.

After the silent period, the popularity of the Siren archetype declined. The power of the temptress whose sensuality enticed her victims away from the straight and narrow path waned as sexual morality became less rigid. In a more cynical age, she tended to metamorphose — as with Manon Lescaut — into the Gold Digger, the one prostitute type generally portrayed negatively: the woman whose lust for the things that money can buy induces her to betray her lover in unforgivable ways.

Yet the Siren, the sympathetic seductress, continued to crop up, intermittently, in sound film. There were productions such as those mentioned at the beginning of this chapter, and new versions of the classic tales of Nana and Lulu. But perhaps the most significant films were those that attempted a modernist, self-conscious reworking of the archetypal material, including Joseph Losey's *Eve/Eva* (France/Italy, 1962), Masahiro Shinoda's *Shinju ten no amijima/Double Suicide* (Japan, 1969), and Rainer Werner Fassbinder's *Lola* (West Germany, 1981). Meanwhile, a baroque twist saw the Siren emerging as the vampire hooker in comic horror films.

In *Eve*, a project to which he had a high personal commitment, Losey aimed to present "that which most people do not wish to see, and which is unpleasant to examine: what it is that destroys a man and a woman."[16] It is a tale of the cruelty of unrequited passion set in contemporary Italy on the fringes of a milieu that was very much Losey's own — the European film industry.

A Welsh writer, Tyvian (Stanley Baker), attending the Venice Film Festival for the premiere of the film that has been made from his best-selling book, makes the acquaintance in unusual circumstances of a high-class French call girl, Eve (Jeanne Moreau). A turbulent relationship ensues, despite her warning him not to fall in love with her. Tyvian is physically attacked by her and humiliated; he loses his newly acquired fortune gambling and catering to Eve's expensive tastes. He marries his beautiful young fiancée, Francesca, but when she discovers that he is continuing to see Eve, she commits suicide. Tyvian goes to Eve intending to kill her, but he cannot go through with his strangling attempt. He implores her, instead, to reciprocate his love, but she contemptuously drives him off with a riding whip. Two years later, he remains obsessed with her, attempting to make a date for when she returns from the Greek islands with her latest client.

It was vital, in Losey's view, to mitigate the harshness of the subject matter with a treatment both lyrical and compassionate.[17] In many respects this is achieved, despite damage inflicted (in Losey's view) by re-cutting of the picture and sound track by the producers.[18] Moreau is svelte and lissome in the role of Eve; something of the playfulness as well as the dark moodiness of her Catherine in Truffaut's *Jules et Jim* (1961) lingers. In one scene she slaps, kisses, and decorates a series of Roman marble busts. There is a striking baroque elegance to the photography and mise-en-scène: one critic describes the film as "a ravishing *tour de force*."[19] And the jazz soundtrack of Michel Legrand, highlighted in particular by the Billie Holiday songs "Willow Weep for Me" and "Loveless Love," has a dulcet but heart-wrenching resonance, going far toward creating what Losey had hoped for (although Miles Davis had been his

12. Jeanne Moreau in *Eve*. Stills Collection, New Zealand Film Archive.

first choice for composer), "a dialogue of different kinds of anguish and loneliness between a man and a woman."[20]

Tyvian has an arrogant bravado but also a vulnerability. He is a phony: his riches have been fraudulently acquired, since the book he is famous for was in fact written by his brother, now dead. His downfall, then, is more complex than that of many of his predecessors as victims of the Siren. He has a guilty conscience, which no doubt pricks him when Eve brands him a "loser." In the scene in which he confesses to her, breaking out into sobs, she lies with him on the floor, and he draws his head down to her breast, while stroking her hair. There is a pan to her face, impassive: here, like Nana, Eve infantilizes her lover, but the interpersonal dynamics run much deeper than the caricatured infatuation of Renoir's silent film.

Eve is, possibly, from a troubled background; she tells Tyvian a tale of being orphaned, of poverty, of sexual abuse at the age of eleven — but then laughs and says, "You'd believe anything." Whatever the etiology, her attitude toward Tyvian as toward her other clients is clearly that of a refusal to become emotionally involved and an unwillingness to be dependent on anyone else. Losey speaks of her as having more lucidity and honesty than Tyvian; she does not prostitute herself, he argues, but she knows that she gives pleasure and for that she should be paid. No question of sin or guilt is involved.[21]

Losey also refers to Eve's "determination to maintain some kind of independence in a world that's not a woman's world, and where women are the extremes of various things — such as Eve's particular extreme — because of what's demanded of them by men."[22] We may be in the presence, then, of a protofeminist text, a reading, which could be sustained by noting that Eve is spared the Siren's customary comeuppance and left to carry on with her scandalous (in the eyes of the patriarchy) lifestyle, trailing victims (not only Tyvian but also his wife) in her wake.

Such a reading, however, would need to be qualified by consideration of the opening and closing sequences, which invite an essentialist interpretation (Eve as Woman) likely to be anathema to feminists. Both sequences feature statues of Adam and Eve in a Venetian piazza, accompanied by biblical quotations in voice-over, "And the man and the woman were naked together, and were unashamed." The theme is reinforced by a Michel Legrand song, "Adam and Eve," reprised at various times during the film. Losey is evidently angling for the Tyvian-Eve relationship to be taken as paradigmatic of heterosexual relationships in general — in an interview he claims to have been aiming for "some sort of statement about marriage, about middle-class marriage and about middle-class male-female relationships in a particular society."[23] If the story could be taken in this way, the director would have succeeded in confounding the very distinction between wife and prostitute upon which the Siren archetype is founded. But the evidence of his film is against him: Francesca is the typically bland and safe wife, just as Eve is the familiar alluring and dangerous courtesan.

What Losey *has* succeeded in doing is infusing the Siren story with his own bleak vision of love as unreciprocated erotic obsession. "With *Eve* I wanted to make a picture . . . about the particular destruction and anguish and waste of most sexual relationships,"[24] he has said. His biographer David Caute notes that "there is not a single depiction of mutual sexual passion or love in his films."[25]

With *Double Suicide,* in contrast, the passion is reciprocated. In relating the love story between a paper merchant and the courtesan to whom he is irresistibly drawn, Shinoda reworks Monzaemon Chikamatsu's classic puppet play of 1720 into a highly formal and yet intensely emotional study of the clash between duty and desire.[26]

In this film version, the puppets are replaced by actors, but in overt acknowledgment of the *bunraku* theater tradition, the doll figures are shown, in a precredits sequence, being prepared to enact the drama, and the black-clad puppet handlers or *kurago* reappear throughout. Self-referentiality is attained via a telephone conversation during the titles sequence in which the director advises the screenwriter that the script is acceptable apart from the suicide scene, which must be made more realistic. Other formal elements, which work to distance the spectator from the action, include a restrained expressionist acting style, visuals emphasizing geometrical patterning and high-contrast chiaroscuro effects, and a spare use of music, composed by Toru Takemitsu, in which percussion is dominant.

In *Double Suicide's* familiar tale of man so enamored of a prostitute that he is prepared to put both his business career and his family life at jeopardy for her, two features stand out. One, perhaps associated with the Buddhist tradition from which the film springs, is the mutual respect between wife and mistress. The other is the intensity of the lovers' erotic passion, handled with an unusual (for the time) sexual explicitness.

Because of Jihei's social obligations and because he cannot afford to redeem Koharu from the teahouse where she is in bondage, the lovers find themselves in an intolerable situation and have considered committing suicide. When Jihei overhears Koharu denying that this is her intention, he is devastated at this apparent infidelity and breaks off with her. But the truth is that Koharu is feigning indifference out of concern for his wife, Osan, who had written to her asking her to save Jihei's life. Learning this, Jihei's passion is revived, whereupon Osan, in a reciprocal self-sacrificial gesture, offers to give up her private savings and clothes in order that he may have enough to redeem his mistress. The complementarity of the two women in Jihei's life is reinforced by the fact that they are played by the same actress, Shima Iwashita.

The lovers' acute desire for each other is expressed in restrained but anguished dialogue ("I wanted nothing but to be with you. I shouldn't fall in love. A courtesan must sleep with hundreds of men. . . . Why can't I fall in love like any other?") but more particularly in the sex scenes, which, in contrast to *Eve*, are not elided but depicted with a frankness all the more startling for the context of classical formalism in which they appear. It's interesting to note that the British Board of Film Censors refused to grant *Double Suicide* a certificate unless the shots of cunnilingual love-making were cut. The scenes, especially a climactic graveyard sequence in which the lovers have orgasmic sex amid a dense cluster of tombstones, are the revelation of the erotic impulse that draws Jihei irresistibly to Koharu despite all conventional good sense, and impart an extraordinary power to the film. Extending this emphasis, the Siren archetype was later to develop in the direction of soft-core pornography with *La Marge* and the 1982 Italian version of *Nana*.

Osan's willingness to sacrifice her personal property to further her husband's dalliance with a prostitute is not permissible in the patriarchal society to which she belongs. Osan's father intervenes, demanding a divorce. Jihei abducts Koharu, and the doomed lovers commit a ritual murder/suicide under the watchful eye of the masked *kurago*. Executed with a rare grace and elegance, the scene is the culmination of a remarkable work that elevates the Siren movie to the level of tragedy.

Fassbinder's *Lola*, in the satiric mode, has a very different feel. Originating in a plan to do a new adaptation of Heinrich Mann's novel *Professor Unrat* (which had provided the basis for *The Blue Angel*), it took on new dimensions when the director and his screenwriters recognized that Mann's story was too much of its pre–World War I-era to be plausibly set in the 1950s, the decade in which Fassbinder was particularly interested.[27] *Lola* ended up as *BRD 3*, the third film in narrative chronology (after *The Marriage of Maria Braun* and *Veronika Voss*) in Fassbinder's trilogy of features dissecting the history of the German Federal Republic.

An old-fashioned, middle-aged civil servant, von Bohm (Armin Mueller-Stahl), takes up a position as building commissioner in the Bavarian town of Coburg and falls for Lola (Barbara Sukowa), a singer-prostitute at the local brothel. This is the skeleton of a recognizably Siren-type narrative, but Fassbinder's film, in self-consciously elaborat-

ing upon the familiar elements, works a significant twist: under Lola's influence, von Bohm loses not his money or his business or his family, but
simply his integrity.

An honest man ("You're simply not corrupt," Lola will later tell
him), von Bohm begins his job determined to wield a new broom, but he
is a realist. Though willing to grant some truth to the claims of his left-
wing assistant Esslin that building in the town is dominated by a corrupt
clique led by property developer Schuckert, he is inclined to the view
that profiteering is an inevitable concomitant of the reconstruction of
Germany under the free-market system. His outlook changes, however,
when he discovers that the demure young woman he has been courting
is actually the prime attraction at the town's brothel, the Villa Fink, and
the "private whore" of its owner, Schuckert. Enraged, von Bohm tells
Schuckert that he is going to destroy him, "Destroy and annihilate, all
of you and your whores along with you." He puts a stop to work on the
Lindenhof development — the largest building project in the town's history — and commences an anticorruption crusade targeted at Schuckert
in particular. Radicalized overnight, he frenziedly denounces "the whole
lying system" that "deforms and distorts people and makes them sick."

In response, Schuckert plays on the building commissioner's weakness for Lola. "Take her," he lewdly urges von Bohm, "Take off her
clothes. Throw her on the bed. Do with her what you want. She's a
whore." Taking up the suggestion, von Bohm goes to the Villa Fink and
makes a public announcement to Schuckert: "I want to buy your whore!"
Lola is accordingly made available. Von Bohm gets her to undress and
put on sexy underwear, but then he sobs and breaks down, collapsing on
the bed. Lola comforts him, declaring in wonder, "You love me!"

It is a degrading encounter for Lola, but not unlike what she regularly
endures from the vulgar Schuckert, who is fond of declaring that she has
"the sweetest ass in NATO." The star attraction at the Villa Fink is
acutely and bitterly aware of her stigmatized status; she even tells her
young daughter Marie that she is "a whore with leprosy." Having initially
held hopes that von Bohm could be the man to rescue her from her situation, she renounces them when she realizes the inevitability of his discovering her true identity. With the turn that events have taken, however,
Lola sees an opportunity.

A deal is done. Von Bohm withdraws his objections to the Lindenhof
development (at the ground-breaking ceremony, he vigorously applauds
the speech extolling "our free enterprise system, which points beyond
the past toward the progress that the future will bring"). Lola and he are

married: having previously complained that the town's power brokers "won't let me play along," she is able to tell Frau Schuckert triumphantly, "I'm now one of you—so to speak." The couple receive as a wedding present from Schuckert the Villa Fink, in trust until Marie's twenty-first birthday. A grateful Lola prepares to have sex with her "sweet pig" Schuckert—he would like her to leave her bridal veil on, but that, she tells him, costs extra—von Bohm contentedly declares to Esslin, who has left his building commission job to work for Schuckert "I'm happy."

Conflict between the antithetical roles of wife and prostitute has been resolved. In a heavily ironic ending, the protagonist both secures the woman he desires and solidifies his position in the community by coming to an accommodation with the corrupt power elite. The Siren, incorporated under the wing of the patriarchy by being married off, simultaneously enters the ranks of the bourgeoisie as the co-owner of a profitable entertainment enterprise.

While *Eve, Double Suicide,* and *Lola* are representative of the evolution of the Siren archetype within art-house cinema, a contrasting trend was evident in genre-based commercial film. In the horror movie, the threat of female sexuality as embodied in the prostitute took on nightmarish, hallucinatory dimensions. "Don't let them bite or they'll suck you dry," warns the video cover of *Vampire Hookers* (USA, 1979), describing the spectral creatures of an unidentified foreign port who lure red-blooded American sailors to their crypt for orgies of sex and death. "These girls are illusions," goes the theme song. "They slit throats from ear to ear. They want you for transfusions . . . and blood is not all they suck." The mesmerizing power of seductive women, mingled with the fear of sexually transmitted diseases, is here intensified in a camp fantasy leavened by bad jokes. The theme is reprised in *I, Desire* (USA, 1982), featuring a blood-sucking Los Angeles streetwalker. Just as lethal as these vampires are the gory, hustling cultists in *Hollywood Chainsaw Hookers* (USA, 1988) who dismember their clients out of reverence for Elvis Presley (in what is described as a "love-and-cleave-them racket"), and the patchwork organic automaton of *Frankenhooker* (USA, 1990), welded together from the choicest body parts of exploded prostitutes, who herself takes to streetwalking and blows up her unappealing clients in the throes of intercourse. The vampire motif returns in *Gore Whore* (USA, 1994), featuring a dead streetwalker who is reanimated and stays alive through the consumption of human blood, and *Bordello of Blood* (USA, 1996), in which the undead inmates of a brothel in a funeral home fulfill men's erotic fantasies while draining them of their life blood. In the twenty-first century

13. Bernadette Lafont as Marie in *La Fiancée du pirate*.

it is perhaps only in such campy comedic form that the myth of the Siren will live on.

Nelly Kaplan's *La Fiancée du pirate/A Very Curious Girl* (France, 1969) deploys the Siren's tale to work a feminist satire of the patriarchal regime in sexual relations. Marie (Bernadette LaFont), downtrodden outsider in a French village denuded of all charm and sentiment, gets her own back on the exploitative locals by becoming a prostitute and using her considerable sensual charms to ensnare them. The raging lust of the menfolk, which will brook no denial even after she has hiked her rate higher than that of Parisian professionals, is subjected to Buñuelian parody:[28] bedridden old Papa, practically gaga, grunts and slurps his food at the very sight of her; Duvalier, the postman/game warden, sniffs and pockets Marie's panties, snoops around her house, and spies on her from a treetop roost; Leduc, the mayor, comes to caution her but instead succumbs in bestial fury to her seductive wiles. Bedazzled by Marie ("that bitch has cast a spell on them," declares Duvalier), the men relinquish their heirlooms, neglect their work, endanger their businesses, denounce their wives. Julien, the farmhand, steals from his female employer to pay for sex with Marie, and in consequence is flogged with a riding whip and fired; subsequently, denouncing her as "a poison weed," he pathetically begins to strangle her before she knees him in the testicles and kicks him, reduced to a quivering wreck, out of her hut. By the end of the film he has become a beggar.

La Fiancée du pirate celebrates the Siren as a woman who revels in her sexuality — or to be more precise, the display of herself as erotic object, for there is no evidence that Marie has sexual desires or pleasures of her own — and the power that it brings her. At the end of the film she wreaks her final sweet revenge on those who have oppressed her, and her gypsy mother before her. Having tape-recorded her sessions with the menfolk, she sets the machine going, out of reach on a high altar, during a well-attended church service. Leduc is heard speaking of his wife: "She's old, she's ugly, and cold as ice." Félix, the cafe owner, calls his spouse "a bore — she drinks like a fish, she snores." Paul, the pharmacist, is exposed in his attempt to squeeze a percentage out of Marie's earnings; the priest himself is compromised. There is fury, tumult, but Marie has slipped away. Having skewered the hypocrisy of the male power brokers, she skips out of town, Siren turned Avenger, a jaunty independent vagabond.

5

Comrade

On October 7, after mutinying and trying to escape along the platforms of the Gare du Nord, the women got off the train, bodices open. Then, *L'éclair* reports, they lifted up their skirts, exposed their bellies, and attracted passers-by with their shouts. On January 14, 1909, after a new mutiny a group of the detainees had to be transferred to the prison of Bonne-Nouvelle; throughout the journey they continually sang the "Internationale."[1]

Admirable! La révolution, et . . . la prostitution! Quel beau programme!
—*Boule de Suif* (France, 1945)

By the turn of the twentieth century something of a consensus in the socialist attitude to prostitution had emerged. As Alain Corbin remarks in his study of venal sex in France after 1850: "Prostitution was regarded by the socialists as a scourge that was spreading." It accompanied the expansion of capitalism, to which it was necessary because, as Ferdinand August Bebel had argued, the capitalist regime creates "a state of contradiction between man, qua natural sexual being, and man considered as a social being." The nature of the bourgeois family induced a demand for pre- and extramarital sex which could only be met by debauching working-class girls, a process facilitated by poor working conditions and low wages. In the socialist discourse the traditional values of chastity and fidelity were assumed, and the boss came to symbolize the vice that threatened proletarian virtue.[2]

The anarchist discourse, on the other hand, was much less wedded to conventional sexual morality. While denouncing capitalist society for generating prostitution, anarchists did not regard the prostitute as any more degraded than a female wage worker exploited by her employer. As one militant declared: "In present-day society, there is not only the prostitution of sexual organs; there is a prostitution of arms, bodies, brains. . . . The working woman who works for the profit of her employer is just as much a prostitute as the woman who sells her flesh. What I deplore and what will be abolished only when the rotten society we are living in is crushed is prostitution in general."[3] Indeed, the prostitute could be valorized for her defiance of bourgeois mores, anticipating the sexual liberation that would be a necessary part of any genuine social revolution.[4]

With such divergent viewpoints in the broad left field of politics, it is unsurprising that in films of a left-wing tendency there is a wide diversity in the symbolic uses to which the figure of the prostitute may be put. There is a split, for a start, based on the subjectivity of the prostitute character herself. If she accepts the values of capitalist society with its commercial ethos (typically in works of satire or social analysis), she is likely to epitomize the very characteristics that are under attack, becoming archetypally a Business Woman (see chapter 11). But if, subjectively, she is in revolt against a society that has consigned her to the bottom of the heap, she becomes a positive figure in the fight for justice and liberty, a Comrade.

As one might expect, the Comrade comes in many stripes. At a basic level one can distinguish traditional socialist representations from those indebted more to the anarchist tradition. *The Jungle* (USA, 1914), based on Upton Sinclair's famous muckraking novel, exemplifies for example the "socialist" strand. Here the prostitute is a victim of capitalist rapacity: during a strike of stockyard workers, Ona's family is evicted and, destitute, she has sex with her husband's foreman "in exchange for money to feed her starving child" (who dies nonetheless); another worker, Marija, becomes a prostitute after having been drugged and raped by the stockyard owner's son.[5] In contrast, *Die 3-Groschen-Oper / The Threepenny Opera* (Germany/USA/France, 1931),[6] Pabst's film version of the Brecht/Weill play, is in the "anarchist" vein. In this satirical portrait of a corrupt and inequitable society, the whores of Turnbridge Alley are cheerful and resilient margin dwellers, good mates of the criminal Mack the Knife. Just as Mack is an outlaw hero for refusing to lead the downtrodden life that respectable society consigns the poor to, so the prostitutes will not be "good" girls, and while dreaming of ultimate revenge (the song "Pirate Jenny" is sung by Jenny the prostitute rather than Polly Peachum, as in the stage version) they make of their brothel an amenable women's space.

Looked at more closely, the figure of the defiant prostitute in the imagination of the left-wing artist can be seen to occupy a position on a passive-active continuum ranging from victim/outcast at one end, through outlaw/rebel, to militant/partisan/revolutionary. I have chosen the one term, "Comrade," to denote a single archetypal representation to acknowledge that beneath the very real differences, there is a bedrock of commonality. Always, the Comrade is a locus of virtue in a vicious world: either innocent, or if compromised not as corrupt as those around her, meaning the men with power (in these films, the conventional reputable-disreputable opposition is turned on its head). Then, too, she is steeled through hardship and will often have a political consciousness, an awareness of exploitation, oppression, and social injustice. And almost invariably, whether passive in her suffering or active in her fightback, the Comrade highlights the mercenary nature of capitalist society, exposes the hypocrisies of the bourgeoisie, and incarnates the virtues of solidarity and comradeship in a proletarian or lumpenproletarian milieu.

At the victim end of the continuum the Comrade shades off into the Martyr, who also suffers and endures. But the Martyr films are apolitical, or to put it another way, entrenched in the status quo: the prostitute's suffering is necessary, the way of the world. Comrade films are calls to change the world, or at least to recognize its absurdity. At the opposite, revolutionary, end of the spectrum, the Comrade approaches the Avenger, who likewise takes up arms to right the wrongs she has been subjected to and fight for a better world. But whereas the Avenger is out for personal revenge and directs her anger at men and the patriarchy, the Comrade (typically a product of the male imagination) is less individually motivated and usually just takes a place alongside her companions, both men and women, in the anticapitalist or antifascist struggle.

In *The Jungle*, the ruthless drive for profit by the capitalist class (represented by stockyard owner John Durham) reduces workers to penury and forces women to turn to prostitution to survive. The immediate cause for the workers' strike is a large wage cut, a motif that had earlier been adopted in *By Man's Law* (USA, 1913), in which "an oil magnate ruthlessly buys up independent rivals until he controls the industry, then cuts wages and closes factories, causing much suffering among the working classes."[7] Among those affected is a young working woman who becomes unemployed, is forced into seeking work as a prostitute to feed herself and her family, almost falls into the hands of white slavers, and eventually dies.[8] Like Ona in *The Jungle*, she is a prototypical representative of the Comrade as victim of an exploitative system.

By Man's Law exposes (as D. W. Griffith's *Intolerance* was to do several

years later) the hypocrisy of the wealthy magnate who contributes to societies for moral uplift while reducing his employees' wages; *The Quality
of Faith* (USA, 1916) takes the ethical challenge a step farther by making
the protagonist a minister of the church who leads a campaign of protest
against the oppressive working conditions in a mill, and encourages the
workers to go on strike. The minister meets and falls in love with a prostitute who had previously been a worker at the mill, and though his former fiancée, the mill owner's daughter, attempts with some success to
woo him back, "he finally realizes how far superior Marna is to Louise,
and rejects his old sweetheart in order to marry his new one."[9]

Despite the unemployment depicted, these films were made at a time
when the American economy was in an expansionary phase. A group of
left-wing German films from the 1920s, on the other hand, reflect a much
less stable and buoyant capitalism, responding to both the postwar infla-
tionary chaos and the impending Great Depression.

G. W. Pabst's *Die freudlose Gasse/The Joyless Street* (1925), set in Vienna,
is structured around three parallel fallen woman narratives.[10] Grete
(Greta Garbo), the daughter of a newly retired white-collar worker who
loses his pension money owing to manipulation of share prices by speculators on the stock exchange, is driven finally by the family's dire financial straits to consent to appear as a prime attraction in Frau Greifer's
bordello-cabaret. Maria (Asta Nielsen) also has a starving family, but
her prime motivation in becoming one of Frau Greifer's stable would
appear to be to escape from her situation at home and further her love
affair with a young businessman. In contrast, there is no doubt that a
third young woman, Else (Hertha von Walther) prostitutes herself to a ra-
pacious butcher solely because she is poverty-stricken, living in a stable
with an unemployed husband and an underfed baby. Else later gains her
revenge, hacking the butcher to death with his own hatchet when he
refuses to give her meat.

The socially critical stance of the film is encapsulated in a celebrated
montage sequence intercutting the Viennese bourgeoisie reveling at Frau
Greifer's establishment with poverty-stricken citizens, mostly women,
lining up for meat. Grete, who is among those in the line, faints from cold
and hunger. The political thrust of the film, in which the three female
characters are driven to the brink of prostitution or beyond as a result
of societal economic collapse, was not lost on the German censorship
authorities, who wrote: "The essential content of the film consists of
showing how Viennese girls are forced to sell their moral honor and to
earn their bread in brothels as a result of need and the misery of infla-

tion. . . . Through this forced situation, in which the girls are brought without exception into depravity, the impression must emerge that the girls' action is the necessary consequence of misery and need."[11] The heavy cutting the film was subjected to attempted to rectify this unfortunate impression.[12]

There is nevertheless some equivocation in Pabst's representation of prostitution (in Maria's story, for example, and in the elegance and luxury associated with Frau Greifer's business operation), a tendency that was reinforced in his 1929 film *Das Tagebuch einer Verlorenen/Diary of a Lost Girl*, which came under censorship pressure for depicting brothel life as pleasurable for the inmates (see chapter 12). There is no such ambivalence in two films released the same year by Prometheus, the small production and distribution company linked to the German Communist Party (KPD). Both *Jenseits der Strasse/Beyond the Street* and *Mutter Krausens Fahrt ins Glück/Mother Krause's Journey to Happiness* adopt the traditional socialist stance toward prostitution as symbolic of the degradation and corruption of capitalist society.[13]

Jenseits der Strasse shows hopes for a nascent love, joyful and delicate, between a prostitute (Lissi Arna) and a young unemployed worker (Fritz Genschow) being dashed by their poverty. At the end of the film he is wanted for murder while she is back at work, picking up a lecherous bourgeois client with prominent potbelly, her face a mixture of assumed gaiety, world-weariness, and disgust. *Jenseits der Strasse* takes it as an outrage that attractive working-class women should belong to the rich, not the poor, and mercilessly exposes the distortion of values — especially those to do with relations between the sexes — which occurs as a result of the class inequities of capitalism.

Mutter Krausens Fahrt ins Glück is a proletarian family melodrama centering on the consequences of unemployment and the housing shortage. Set in the working-class district of Wedding, Berlin, and adapted from stories by the artist Heinrich Zille, it shows a young woman, Erna, almost taking up prostitution out of desperation when her mother undergoes a financial crisis brought on by the misdemeanors of her son Paul. Erna is following in the steps of a streetwalker, Friede, who boards with the family, and is urged on by Friede's boyfriend, a pimp, who also lives there and has been subjecting Erna to sexual harassment. In the critical scene, Erna strives to surrender herself to a fat, middle-aged man for the twenty Marks that her mother needs. In a subtly modulated performance illustrative of silent film acting at its best, Ilse Trautschold vividly registers Erna's nervous flirtatiousness followed by visceral revulsion when her

14. Lissi Arna as the prostitute in *Jenseits der Strasse*. Stiftung Deutsche Kinemathek — Filmmuseum Berlin.

would-be client lays a hand on her knee. Erna's refusal to succumb to the prostitute's fate — after a struggle, she succeeds in repelling the man's advances and making a run for it — is emblematic not of maidenly virtue (for we know that she has already slept with the pimp) but of working-class rebellion, a point reinforced when she then joins her militant boyfriend Max marching in a workers' demonstration.

With Erna's story, *Mutter Krausens Fahrt ins Glück* delivers a decisive riposte to *Jenseits der Strasse*. Refusing victim status, Erna gives herself to a proletarian socialist comrade rather than a bourgeois oppressor, showing the way for other women similarly pressured by economic circumstances. (In his room Max — who has a picture of Marx on his wall — shows Erna a copy of Bebel's *Die Frau im Socialen Kampf*.) This radical optimism is not matched in the other narrative threads of the film, however. Friede (Vera Sacharowa) remains trapped in her profession, as her boyfriend, along with Paul, is arrested for burglary, while Mutter Krausen, utterly despondent, commits suicide, taking Friede's young daughter along with her on her "journey to happiness." This is a society that, except for those who struggle to change it, can deliver only misery.

15. *Mutter Krausens Fahrt ins Glück:* Erna (Ilse Trautschold) resisting prostitution. Stiftung Deutsche Kinemathek — Filmmuseum Berlin.

As Prometheus was linked with the KPD, so the Indian People's Theatre Association (IPTA), launched in Bombay in 1943, was informally affiliated to the Communist Party of India (CPI). Several Indian films made within its ambit or under its influence significantly reproduce the traditional socialist attitude toward prostitution, adapting the critique to serve as an attack on imperialism and neocolonialism.

The first of these, *Dharti ke Lal/Children of the Earth* (1946), was collectively produced by IPTA members under the direction of Khwaja Ahmad Abbas, a founder member of the association. It depicts with documentary realism a rural Bengal family forced to leave their farm and go to Calcutta in the wake of the 1943 famine — caused, the film reveals, by grain reserves being drawn on by the British for the war effort. Joining a throng of starving, homeless people in the city, the family is reduced to destitution, and the younger son Ramu's desperate search for work is intercut with his wife Radhika's selling her body as the only way of keeping their child alive. Ramu and Radhika are too alienated by their experience to join in the positive action with which the film ends: "Before dying, the patriarch enjoins his family to return to their native soil where the farmers get together and, in a stridently celebratory socialist-realist ending, opt for Soviet-style collective farming."[14]

Nagarik/The Citizen was produced in 1952 but not released until 1977. Written and directed by Ritwik Ghatak, who had been active as a playwright, director, and actor in IPTA, the film also deals with a family of migrants to Calcutta, driven to the city this time by the Partition of Bengal. Forced to give up their individual aspirations and observing an acquaintance turning to prostitution, they eventually move into a working-class slum and become politicized . . . at one point the "Internationale" plays on the soundtrack.[15]

Satyajit Ray's *Ashani Sanket/Distant Thunder* (1973), less directly political than its predecessors, returns to the 1943 Bengal famine. Here, however, the action is set wholly within a remote village where the food shortage has a devastating effect. War profiteers attempt to turn the situation to their sexual advantage, and one woman, Chutki (Sandhya Roy), is driven to prostitution in return for rice. She later becomes an Avenger in beating to death a man who had made a sexual assault on another female character.

The last in this small group of leftist Indian films depicting prostitution as the deplorable outcome of an exploitative system is *Tarang/Wages and Profit[s]/The Wave* (1984). Directed by Kumar Shahani, a former student of Ritwik Ghatak at the Film and Television Institute of India, *Tarang* is an ambitious attempt to adapt the classical epic tradition represented by the *Mahabharata* to the cinema. A scathing dissection of contemporary Indian class relationships and the ruthless exercise of power in industry, the film has as its pivotal female character a woman whose husband, a union activist, is killed on the job. Reduced to prostitution, Janaki (Smita Patil) furthers her husband's commitment to the working-class cause and donates her earnings as the mistress of a member of his former employer's family to the movement. In a subsequent development, Janaki is manipulated into the position of scapegoat in a murder plot, and she is forced back to the streets. At the end, *Tarang* shifts into mythical mode and Janaki becomes an accusatory voice of history.

In *Una novia para Davíd* (Cuba, 1985) a teenage student trying to create a sex life for himself comments to a schoolmate on the disappearance of the brothels: your father would take you there, he says, when you were thirteen — they were a social disgrace, but they should have kept one open for students, for educational purposes. In Communist societies, the conceptualizing of prostitution as symptomatic of a capitalist decadence now transcended becomes an orthodoxy, and any suggestion of the sex trade continuing under the new regime becomes quickly taboo. Interestingly, Dziga Vertov's documentary *Kino-Glaz / Cine-Eye* (USSR, 1924) does include shots of prostitutes in contemporary Soviet society, linking them with speculators as undesirable manifestations of the New Economic Policy, the partial restoration of the free market which the film is implicitly critical of.[16] The survival of prostitution is also acknowledged—as a scourge to be eradicated—in Vertov's later documentary *Shagai, Sovet! / Forward, Soviet! / Stride, Soviet!* (USSR, 1926), in which "a series of titles, presented as a series of slogans, informs the audience of the activity of the [Moscow City] Soviet to:

DECLARE WAR ON RUIN . . .
DECLARE WAR ON UNEMPLOYMENT . . .
DECLARE WAR ON PROSTITUTION . . .
DECLARE WAR ON ILLNESS . . .
DECLARE WAR ON DIRT . . .
DECLARE WAR ON BANDITS . . ."[17]

Vertov's fellow documentarian, Esfir Shub, was later to plan (but not realize) a film about the status of women in the Soviet Union, in which "an ex-prostitute is rehabilitated and becomes a 'shock-worker.'"[18]

In the few Soviet fictional features to incorporate prostitute characters, the treatment would typically picture them as outcasts in pre-revolutionary society, victims of an oppressive class structure, kind-hearted women with an affinity for the alienated and rebellious. In *Foma Gordeyev / The Gordeyev Family* (1959), based on the Maxim Gorky novel, for example, the prostitute Sasha (Marina Strizhenova) becomes the companion of the disillusioned son of a wealthy grain merchant who is in revolt against his father's values. Similarly in *Voskreseniye / Resurrection* (two parts, 1960/1962), one of the numerous adaptations of the Tolstoy story, Katyusha (Tamara Syomina), the peasant girl who is seduced and abandoned by Prince Nekhlyudov, subsequently to become a prostitute and convict, refuses the prince's marriage proposal (after he has had a change of heart) and chooses to remain in exile in Siberia at the side of political prisoners.

East German films inherit this approach. A four-part television miniseries from 1965, *Wolf unter Wölfen*, for instance, is set in Berlin in the turbulent years of 1923–24 and depicts several female characters engaging in prostitution because of the lack of alternative employment opportunities. One in particular, Petra (Annekathrin Bürger), is driven into the streets for lack of money to pay the rent and is subsequently imprisoned on a solicitation charge. Petra is the tender, sensuous, and devoted lover of a feckless youth; the facial transformation she undergoes as she walks downstairs steeling herself to approach clients, accompanied by a subjective voice-over: "What is hell? That's the end . . . quiet, quiet . . . step, step . . . right, left, always going further down . . ." and captured in a slightly jerky long take, powerfully registers the damaging human impact of a disintegrating capitalism.

The working-class milieu of Berlin at the turn of the century is the setting for *Zille und Ick* (East Germany, 1983), a musical about the life of Heinrich Zille (whose stories had inspired *Mutter Krausens Fahrt ins Glück*). Here, too, prostitution has a negative sign attached to it: a young singer, Jette (Daniela Hoffmann), is almost forced into it out of poverty, while the aging streetwalker Olga (Angela Brunner) is afflicted by a *Weltschmerz* alleviated only by the sight of Jette being reunited with her heart-throb, a socialist (SPD) militant currently engaged in a campaign against child labor. Unlike *Wolf unter Wölfen*, however, *Zille und Ick* is very much a male-perspective film; it never comes close to communicating Olga's subjective experience, and it is content to derive a bit of rowdy fun from the spectacle of her ample buttocks being bared to serve as a card table for the guys in the bar she hangs out in.

Der Lude/The Pimp (East Germany, 1984), though set in a similar East Berlin milieu, is no light-hearted musical. The time is the early 1930s, and the film, based partly on factual incident, demonstrates how Communist activity was suppressed and the Nazis consolidated their power base with the collusion of the police and the judicial system. The prostitutes and their pimps are pawns in this sinister political game. One pimp, an SA Sturmführer, is killed by a rival over a woman.[19] The authorities seek to portray it as a political murder, and another pimp, Bello, is blackmailed by police into implicating Communists in the alleged plot. The apolitical Bello is compelled to collaborate, since his streetwalker girlfriend, Frieda (Michele Marian), is underage. Bello recants his testimony in court and escapes retribution, but later, after the Nazis have come to power, he is murdered by the SA. Here prostitution is portrayed as a symptom of a decaying capitalist system rapidly sinking into fascism (a Jewish activist significantly tells Bello that "pimps and Communists don't mix"), but the women involved remain largely uncorrupted by their profession: Frieda, like Petra in *Wolf unter Wölfen*, is a warm and loving companion to her unemployed boyfriend.

The moral integrity of the prostitute in contradistinction to the stigma attached to her by polite society is most vividly represented in those films that take their cue from Maupassant's story "Boule de Suif." The heroine, an outcast flung together in a coach with respectable citizens who would normally shun her company, exposes by her self-sacrificial action the craven natures and self-interested hypocrisy of her social "betters." The tale becomes — particularly in the hands of left-leaning filmmakers — a means of attacking bourgeois society and vindicating the prostitute as representative of an unjustly despised proletariat.

In John Ford's *Stagecoach* (USA, 1939), loosely derived from the Maupassant story, for example, prostitute Dallas (Claire Trevor) is marched out of town by a posse of prim, grim-faced dowagers calling themselves the Law and Order League, and en route is given the cold shoulder by Army officer's wife Lucy Mallory (who softens after Dallas assists her in childbirth), embezzling banker Gatewood, and notorious gambler and Southern gentleman Hatfield. The disreputable/respectable divide is again undercut in the two remakes (1966 and 1986), though it carries less weight in the more permissive climate of the times in which the later films were made. A somewhat similar story is told in *La spiaggia/La Pensionnaire/ The Beach* (Italy/France, 1954), in which a former prostitute is cruelly spurned when vacationing at a fashionable hotel on the Italian Riviera, and receives sympathy only from the young left-wing mayor.

In the direct adaptations of "Boule de Suif," the prostitute is a pivotal figure in a study of social stratification and patriotism. The story is set at the time of the Franco-Prussian War, and Élisabeth Rousset, nicknamed Boule de Suif, joins a group of Rouen dignitaries fleeing the occupied city by coach. Along the way the party is held up by Prussian troops, and the commanding officer lets it be known that they will not be allowed to resume their journey until Boule de Suif consents to sleep with him. She refuses for some time but eventually yields to the patriotic pleading of her fellow passengers. The following day, on the road again, Boule de Suif is once more ostracized by the respectable citizens traveling with her.

The original setting is retained in *Pyshka/Boule de Suif* (USSR, 1934) and its musical remake *Ruanskaya deva po prozvishchu Pyshka/Boule de Suif* (USSR, 1989), a TV film also known under the title *A Girl from Rouen Nicknamed Doughnut*, and in the French adaptation, *Boule de Suif/Angel and Sinner* (1945). Other versions give the story a different historical context: *The Woman Disputed* (USA, 1928) is set in Lemberg, Austria, during the World War I; *Maria no Oyuki/Oyuki, the Madonna/Oyuki, the Virgin* (Japan, 1935) transposes the action to Meiji Japan during the Seinan War (a samurai uprising of 1877); the story of *Hua guniang/Flower Girl* (Hong Kong, 1951) takes place in China during the Sino-Japanese War. Although interpretations vary, the core concept of the moral superiority of the despised prostitute to those who look down on her remains constant; while in the French *Boule de Suif,* the combination of the original story with another Maupassant tale, "Mademoiselle Fifi," transforms the prostitute protagonist from stigmatized victim to heroine of the partisan cause.

The prostitute character who figures as outlaw or rebel in a left-wing narrative does not internalize the shame that polite society heaps upon her. Having likely come from a background of poverty and abuse, she is hardened to a life on the margins and scornful of conventional mores. Sometimes the brothel where she lives and works is a site of solidarity with other stigmatized women and a place where the weaknesses and hypocrisies of the male power-brokers in society are exposed. Colored with an anarchist brush, she is self-assertive and defiant but has a strong empathy with other outsiders.

Pabst's *Threepenny Opera* paints a caustic portrait of a class-divided capitalist society. In its satirical mode, the film likens business methods to gang crime and lays bare the fundamental drives of self-interest that underlie all social relationships whatever the moralizing veneer: the police chief is corrupt, the beggars are impostors, and the like. If this cynicism were thoroughgoing, the whores would be Gold Diggers pure and simple — but they're not. Jenny (Lotte Lenya in the German version, Margo Lion in the French) betrays Mack out of jealousy and for a wad of cash, but then assists him in eluding the police at the brothel and subsequently engineers his escape from prison. One could argue that having gotten her money she's simply looking after her best interests by keeping in well with Mack, but the impression from the performance — a playful tussle, a grin, and a hug in their moment of reconciliation — is that there's real sentiment involved. Jenny certainly comes across as a good person at heart who suffers a momentary weakness, rather than a bad person whose mercenary motives result in despicable betrayal of others.

The prostitute as companion to the man on the wrong side of the law has a long pedigree in the cinema, in Westerns, adventure films, and crime thrillers in particular. Dallas, for example, teams up with the Ringo Kid in *Stagecoach*. In films with a left-wing slant, this relationship is given a political inflexion, becoming an act of solidarity in defiance of bigotry and injustice. *Easy Rider* (USA, 1969) exemplifies this tendency, which intensified in the era of the Vietnam War and generated romantic outlaw stories infused with the values of the counterculture.

In *Easy Rider*, hippie bikers Wyatt (Peter Fonda) and Billy (Dennis Hopper) become targets of redneck America's intolerance toward the nonconformist, the connection with the war being made in particularly pointed dialogue delivered by a hip ACLU lawyer (Jack Nicholson): "Don't ever tell anybody that they ain't free because they're gonna get real busy killin' and maimin' to prove to you that they are." After the lawyer is bludgeoned to death by local thugs, Wyatt and Billy, severely beaten up themselves, continue on to New Orleans for Mardi Gras. Here they drop acid with two prostitutes (Toni Basil and Karen Black) who share the bikers' grief and pain, performing their duty of solidarity and solace in a strangely unexplained context of abundant Christian imagery (and with the Apostles' Creed being spoken in voice-over).[20] The psychedelic experience and the sexual activity that Billy and his partner engage in are conveyed in an avant-garde flurry of whirling images, with the hint of a bad trip for the hookers at least, and then the women are left behind as our male heroes hit the road again in search of America . . . bein' *free* man, ain't that what it's all about?

Hippie disenchantment with mainstream America surfaces again in *Steelyard Blues* (USA, 1973), in which Jane Fonda and Donald Sutherland team up as a countercultural couple (she's a hooker, he's a thief) in a curious whimsical narrative laced with stoned humor. Political content in the film itself is minimal, but audiences would have understood a strong antiestablishment message, given that Fonda and Sutherland were well known as left-wing activists who had had a touring antiwar stage show.[21] The tradition of portraying prostitute-criminal camaraderie in a morally bankrupt society is continued in a later offbeat comedy, *Love and the Midnight Auto Supply* (USA, 1978), in which a hooker (Colleen Camp) joins forces with a car-parts thief who is assisting agricultural workers combat corrupt politicians.

Although in most of the outlaw/rebel films the prostitute serves as adjunct to the male activist, there are a handful in which she begins to emerge as a politically conscious individual in her own right. A significant early example is provided by *The Money Master* (USA, 1915), in which a prostitute (Fania Marinoff) whose father was ruined by an industrialist who has risen to the top through "ruthless and illegal machinations" is "influenced by anarchists" and attempts her revenge by shooting at him; he survives and becomes a philanthropist.[22] *Keetje Tippel/Cathy Tippel*

(Netherlands, 1975) is more thoroughgoing. Based on the autobiographical memoirs of Neel Doff, the film depicts the extreme poverty suffered
by Keetje's working-class family in 1880s Amsterdam, which drives first
Keetje's sister and then Keetje herself—after having been raped by her
boss at a hat-maker's establishment—into prostitution. Refusing to accept this fate, Keetje (Monique van de Ven) extricates herself as an artist's
model and as the mistress of a bank clerk, while becoming increasingly
politically aware. During a workers' hunger march she sings the "Mar-
seillaise," flings cobblestones at the attacking riot police—and helps a
wounded demonstrator, who turns out to be a wealthy socialist whom she
is destined to marry.

Keetje Tippel is firmly within the mainstream socialist tradition in its
negative depiction of prostitution; attitudes in Lina Wertmüller's *Film
d'amore e d'anarchia/Love and Anarchy* (Italy, 1973), on the other hand, are
complicated by its falling under the anarchist influence that its title suggests. As in *The Threepenny Opera*, the brothel is presented as an agreeable
milieu—despite the draconian madam—where female camaraderie
flourishes, while the presentation of the work itself is shot through with
ambiguity, especially as the clients are the agents and beneficiaries of
Mussolini's hated regime.

This is particularly apparent in the displaying-the-wares montage.
To the accompaniment of a chirpy French song sung by a female vocal-
ist, the prostitutes trip down the stairs and offer themselves to the morning clientele. Posing, gesturing, beckoning, the women in detail shots expose their flesh, a nipple here, full-bodied breasts there, now an upper
thigh, all proffered with seductive winks, grins, and pouts. Intercut, the
customers appraise the stock. It's a charade, but one the women seem to
enjoy playing. The Bacchanalian revelry promised by this constructed
ritual appears only slightly parodied, undercut here and there by an expression of boredom or an overplayed gesture. Why this carnivalesque?
Only occasionally in conversation elsewhere in the film is the unpleas-
antness of being flattened underneath the fascist pigs mentioned. One
might claim it as a feminist celebration of women's control over the activity: this is a wild zone where they serve men, to be sure, but they do it
their way. Or is the sequence evidence, rather, of a brainwashed female
director, serving up a familiar male fantasy replete with scopophilic delights, fragmenting and objectifying the women's bodies to do so?

There is a parallel ambiguity in the political thematics. A young peasant, Tunin (Giancarlo Giannini), has come to Rome on a mission to as-
sassinate Mussolini, not so much out of thought-through anarchist con-

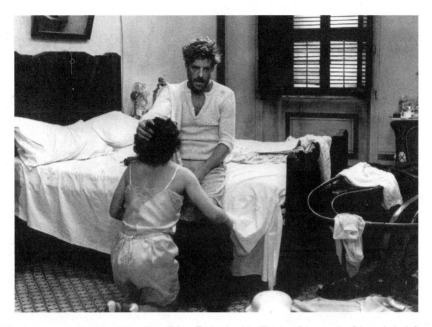

16. *Love and Anarchy:* Tripolina (Lina Polito) with Tunin (Giancarlo Giannini). bfi Collections.

viction as out of a desire to avenge a childhood hero of his, killed before he could carry out the deed. He is assisted by Salome (Mariangela Melato), a prostitute who likewise has personal reasons to throw in her lot with the anarchist cause. Inconveniently, Tunin falls in love with another of the brothel inmates, Tripolina (Lina Polito), in the days leading up to the scheduled assassination attempt. He is not about to let this deflect him from his mission, but Tripolina, convinced that the attempt will be suicidal, deliberately fails to wake him on the date set. Salome tries to intervene and fights with fury over the key to Tunin's room; but then, changing her mind, allows Tripolina to have her way.

The antifascist prostitute despises herself for giving in to the pleas of her companion who puts love above politics; but Wertmüller also sets up another reading, which would make Salome's falling in with Tripolina's desires an act of political principle. Earlier, Salome, in chiding Tunin for his naive zeal declares, "In my opinion, all idealists make a mess of the world in the end"; and at the end of the film, a title quotes the eminent anarchist Errico Malatesta: "I would like to stress again the horror I feel towards assassinations. Aside from being evil acts in themselves, they are foolish acts, for they harm the very cause they were to serve. . . ."

Wertmüller herself makes a claim for Salome's political sagacity, arguing: "If you look more closely, you must see that although these women are prostitutes who sell their bodies to men for their livelihood, that even in this most subjugated condition, they still manage to actively engage in political struggles against the bourgeoisie. Mariangela Melato is the political mind of this picture. It is she who is torn between pragmatically using the politically naive Giannini to commit this political act, and wondering whether he is prepared for this action and its consequences."[23]

It is doubtful if cinema audiences, seeing only a woman desperate to save Tunin's life, whether out of regard for Tripolina's feelings or out of love for him herself, were alert to such subtleties. Staunch and belligerent, but soft and gooey, Wertmüller's anarchist prostitute is a very picture of contradiction.

There is much less equivocation in *La Putain respectueuse/The Respectful Prostitute* (France, 1952). An adaptation of Jean-Paul Sartre's play set in the American South, the film (somewhat labored in its English-dubbed form) features a white nightclub singer/prostitute who is pressured into giving false evidence against a black man being framed for murder, but who then saves him from a lynch mob.

Defying the corrupt, racist senator whom she is earlier respectful toward, the prostitute heroine (played by Barbara Laage) declares at the end of the film that she will testify against him and his family. The senator's nephew is in fact guilty of the crime, and in a pose, which is held and frozen, the heroine places her hand in solidarity on that of the accused black man. A superimposed quote from Lincoln (". . . all men are created equal") drives home the message and confirms the prostitute in her role as a rebel fighter against injustice and racism.[24]

Another European take on American racism, again featuring a singer/prostitute, is Rainer Werner Fassbinder's *Whity* (West Germany, 1971). In this camp melodrama set in a white supremacist Southwest in 1878, the self-abasing black servant to a decadent seignorial family is made conscious of his servile condition and urged on to kill his oppressors by the flamboyant but world-weary saloon entertainer Hanna (Hanna Schygulla). The deed executed, the two outcasts-turned-rebels dance a melancholy waltz together in the desert.[25]

Political consciousness is the hallmark of the cinematic prostitute who becomes an active participant in the socialist or antifascist cause, often moving from a supporting to a principal role. Having experienced poverty and exploitation herself, she has no difficulty identifying with the

17. *Whity:* Whity (Günther Kaufmann) and Hanna (Hanna Schygulla). Stiftung Deutsche Kinemathek — Filmmuseum Berlin.

struggles of the proletariat and in throwing in her lot with those fighting for a better society or resisting aggression. If the need arises she has no compunction about resorting to violence, no doubt as a result of having been on the receiving end herself.

I compagni / The Organizer / Les Camarades (Italy / France / Yugoslavia, 1963) deals in tragicomic style with a strike among Turin textile workers at the turn of the twentieth century. Protesting against a fourteen-hour working day and unsafe working conditions, the strikers are led by a political refugee, Professor Sinigaglia (Marcello Mastroianni), who is harbored by a prostitute (Annie Girardot) when the order is given for his arrest. *The Jungle* similarly exposes appalling working and living conditions with consequent human tragedies, but it ends on an optimistic note when Marija (Alice Marc), now a prostitute, is saved from drowning herself by the former stockyard worker Jurgis: he has been inspired by a Socialist Party rally, and Marija, who has always been attracted to him, joins him to "work for the establishment of a 'cooperative commonwealth.'"[26]

In much more prosperous times, sex workers themselves become

18. *Never on Sunday:* Illia (Melina Mercouri) and rebel prostitutes in jail. David Lascelles Stills Collection.

organized in *Pote Tin Kyriaki/Never On Sunday* (Greece, 1960), under the charismatic leadership of the prototypical Happy Hooker Illia (Melina Mercouri). Protesting the exorbitant rents charged by local vice czar No Face for their waterfront apartments, the prostitutes rebel when a fleet of sailors is in town, tossing their beds into the street. They end up in jail where their solidarity enables Illia to negotiate a massive reduction in their rents. It is, of course, a comedy, written and directed by the American leftist Jules Dassin, in European exile to escape the blacklist.

In the French *Boule de Suif,* filmed in 1945 with the recent German Occupation very much in mind, the prostitute, ostracized by collaborating members of the bourgeoisie and aristocracy, becomes — thanks to the incorporation in the script of material from "Mademoiselle Fifi," — a patriotic heroine.[27] Élisabeth (Micheline Presle), kidnapped along with other women in the coach to cater to the pleasures of Prussian officers at a drunken party, acts defiantly, eventually stabbing to death the arrogant Lt. Fifi and making her escape. As a fugitive, Élisabeth is hidden by a partisan priest and remains at large, an inspiration to the "maquis" of 1871, as the film ends.

If *Boule de Suif* is metaphorically about World War II, a number of later films featuring prostitute characters deal directly with combating the Nazis. In *Nous sommes tous des assassins/Siamo tutti assassini/Are We All Murderers?* (France/Italy, 1952), a French prostitute murders a German soldier. *La guerra continua/La Dernière Attaque/Warriors Five* (Italy/France, 1961), set in Italy in 1943, features a sabotage unit comprising principally an American paratrooper and an Italian soldier with his prostitute girl-friend. The unit blows up a bridge and wipes out a German camp. In *Castle Keep* (USA, 1969), Nazi troops attacking a Belgian castle containing priceless art treasures are resisted, unsuccessfully, by American GIs and women from the local brothel hurling Molotov cocktails at the advancing tanks.

A famous Parisian bordello kept open under the German Occupation is the initial setting for *Soft Beds, Hard Battles* (UK, 1973), a comedy vehicle for the protean talents of Peter Sellers. The madam, enlisted as an undercover agent by the Resistance, oversees the poisoning of a whole company of German officers. Forced to flee, the prostitutes disguise themselves as nuns but later return, dressed in SS uniforms, to foil Hitler's plans to destroy Paris. Tampering with the Nazi explosives, they make sure that the Gestapo chief blows himself up instead. In a more melodramatic vein, *Salon Kitty/Madam Kitty* (Italy/West Germany/France, 1975) is set in a Berlin brothel to which girls from National Socialist families are assigned to become spies on the clientele. One of them, Margherita (Teresa Ann Savoy), falls in love with a disaffected German officer who is planning to defect ("I'm going to fight against Hitler. Against his madness. Against the violence which is corrupting us all."). Margherita does not betray him, but his intentions are discovered and he is hanged. When a fellow officer gloats at the brothel that he "got a kick out of seeing that bastard hanging up there like a stuffed pig," Margherita shoots and kills him.

The revolutionary prostitute in film is relatively uncommon. Xiao Feng-xian (Li Lihua) in *Xiao Fengxian/The Little Phoenix* (Hong Kong, 1953) is "a classic sing-song girl: well-versed in poetry, an able performer of opera skits, and so beautiful that generals and statesmen vie to risk their reputations and careers over her."[28] The story is based on historical events and centers on the conspiracy of Xiao Fengxian and her lover, the revolutionary general Cai Songbo, to undermine the rule of the first president of the Chinese Republic (founded in 1911), who is aiming to proclaim himself emperor. In much less exalted circumstances, a young woman (Joan Anderson) in *Lonnie* (USA, 1963) prostitutes herself for the cause of a Spanish revolutionary living in the United States. The Mexican revolutionary movement against the French is the setting for *Two Mules for Sister Sara* (USA/Mexico, 1970), in which the brothel whore, disguised initially as a nun (Shirley MacLaine), reveals that her hatred of the imperialists is derived from her experiences with them as clients. Benefiting from the toughness she has acquired from her profession, Sister Sara is able to rival men in the physical feats the struggle calls for. She teams up with a mercenary (Clint Eastwood) contracted to the cause, and shows herself to be eminently capable of slugging him when he gets drunk and of climbing a high trestle bridge to plant dynamite. She is, however, consigned to the sidelines when the climactic battle to capture a French fort rages. In contrast, *Co Gai Tren Song/The Young Woman on the Perfumed River* (Vietnam, 1987) chronicles contemporary events. Based on a true story, it depicts a prostitute who assists a Vietnamese revolutionary cadre and is disowned by him after reunification and his appointment to a government position.

The key study of the prostitute in a revolutionary context is however Vicente Aranda's *Libertarias/Freedomfighters* (Spain, 1996). The film, based on fact, dramatizes the struggles of the anarchist women's organization, Mujeres Libres, as it strives to sustain revolutionary momentum and especially the liberation of women during the bitter Spanish Civil War. Although part of the anarchist movement, Mujeres Libres had a traditional socialist attitude toward prostitution, regarding it as degrading to women: a Mujeres Libres poster shows a miserable naked woman with the caption "Every person is born with the capacity for dignified work and a human existence,"[29] and this is reflected in an early scene in *Libertarias* in which the revolutionaries confront the inmates in a brothel. Attempting to persuade them of their oppressed condition, one of the militiawomen argues: "Our country is now in revolt. The symbols of oppression are burning. The workers have organized the factories and barracks. . . . We cannot aspire to any kind of justice while the greatest slavery still exists. It forces you to renounce love, tenderness, friendship and waste your lives on the sexual voracity of strangers. . . . Comrades, sisters, in the name of all Spanish women, we open our arms to help you regain your dignity as workers, sisters, or mothers. Join the liberation of prostitutes! Long Live Free Women and the libertarian revolution!" Exasperated with the blank-faced response of the prostitutes, the leader of

19. *Libertarias:* Charo (Loles León), center, with the militia. bfi Collections.

the Mujeres Libres squad takes up the challenge: "For Chrissake! What is it you want? To be whores all your life? To have cocks stuck up you ten or fifteen times a day and all for a bowl of stew?"

Finally the women are won over and enthusiastically pledge to support the revolutionary cause. As the militiawomen close down the brothel, they are guaranteed a "decent job," and one of them, Charo (Loles León) proceeds to join the militia group herself, fighting at the front against the fascists . . . and on one occasion reluctantly providing sexual solace to a desperate militiaman.

After the war has continued for some time, Charo receives a letter that indicates that the closure of the brothels in Republican areas has not proceeded: "One day Olga asked me to come and see a girl from the old days. We were amazed to see that the pussy game is more popular than ever. Anyway, the union guys gave us a house and we've set ourselves up. There is a constant line of militiamen. It's better than before for there's no one bossing us. We've become a collective and formed a committee like that militiawoman said. I'm the treasurer and Julia's the secretary. . . ."

Signifying a defeat for Mujeres Libres, for whom the "liberation of prostitutes" means closing down the brothels and finding the women alternative employment, this development paradoxically conforms more closely to predominant strands in anarchist thinking on prostitution: the women have seized power themselves and collectively taken control of their own working life.[30] The Comrade, a valorized figure in all of left-wing cinema, here becomes quintessentially the prostitute as activist heroine: antifascist militiawoman at the front; provider of guilt-free, because egalitarian, sexual pleasures behind the lines. It is pertinent that this state of affairs is short-lived: at the end Charo, along with others in the Mujeres Libres squad, has her throat cut by Franco forces.

There are several films that refuse the dominant tendency to romanticize the prostitute as a heroine of resistance or rebellion. Thus Matilde Landeta's *La negra Angustias* (Mexico, 1949) endorses the revolutionary cause, but its female protagonist, who becomes a colonel in the Zapatista army, is a goatherd. The film's other women characters, who include prostitutes in the cantinas, are by contrast "depictions of vulnerability, powerlessness and the renunciation of desire."[31] With similar patterning, *Bread and Roses* (UK/France/Germany/Spain/Italy/Switzerland, 2000) celebrates the struggle being waged by underpaid, mostly Latino, janitors in a Los Angeles office building for union rates and conditions, but the militant activist in the campaign is the naïve young Maya, not her elder sister Rosa (Elpidia Carrillo) who sells out her fellow workers in the hope of gaining promotion to supervisor and who, it is revealed, is weary from a lifetime of prostituting herself to support her impoverished family. When Maya confronts her, Rosa bitterly tells her the truth: "For five fucking years in Tijuana, every single night. . . . Let her suck everybody's fucking dick—black, white, sleazeballs, slimebags. Let her fuck everybody, right?" The film thus reverts to a traditional socialist representation of the prostitute as victim of economic inequality and social injustice.

Dusan Makavejev's *Sweet Movie* (France/Canada/West Germany, 1974), on the other hand, is profoundly skeptical about the revolutionary movement itself. More circumspect and disenchanted than his *WR: Mysteries of the Organism*, *Sweet Movie* seems to set up a familiar Reichian opposition between authoritarianism-virginity and revolution-promiscuity, with sexual liberation affording the antidote to the murderous puritanism of Stalin, only to radically undermine it.

The libertine Anna Planeta (Anna Prucnal) is skipper of the ship *Survival*, which cruises the canals of Amsterdam with a gigantic bleached head of Marx at the prow and a crew that sing upbeat socialist anthems. The "radical prostitute"[32] whose eager seduction of men and youth aboard her vessel does not seem to be undertaken for money, even though she does accept gifts for her services, is a Comrade only in the sense of subverting the political romanticism of earlier portrayals. She is not the rock solid ally of the radical fighting man but the executioner of the revolutionary party as it turns in on itself. Liberated sexually she may be, but her seductiveness seems directed only at recruiting new victims for slaughter. The ship of revolution carries, it turns out, a cargo of corpses (associated with the victims of the Katyn massacre — attributed to Stalin — by direct montage), and Anna herself plunges the knife into her proletarian lover, the sailor from the Potemkin, as they copulate in a vat of sugar. The revolutionary prostitute has turned butcher of her comrades.[33]

6

Avenger

> But as to the men, those two-legged animals, I'll infect every one of
> them! I've been getting back at them every night. Ten, fifteen of them
> every night! Let them rot! Let them give syphilis to their wives and
> sweethearts! Yes, yes, to their mothers and fathers too! Let them all
> croak, the bastards!
> —ALEXANDER KUPRIN, *Yama: The Pit* (1914)[1]

The "Avenger," as I have termed her, is the prostitute who fights back
against the conditions of her oppression, or the oppression suffered more
generally by girls and women in a sexist society. In a common scenario,
she gets even with the seducer/procurer who is responsible for her downfall. Often she will act on behalf of, or in combination with, others who
are being exploited in the prostitution business. She may inflict retribution on men guilty of rape or sexual abuse. Perhaps most provocatively,
from a male point of view, she may exact vengeance on men in general
for the violence they have inflicted on female victims, with her targets—
selected from among her clients, for example—not necessarily personally guilty but standing in for the actual culprits, since like all men they
profit from a system of gender inequity.

Because she has been criminalized as a prostitute, the Avenger has no
investment in the established regime of law and order, which she often regards with scorn as being male-imposed and hypocritical. Bearing the
whore stigma, she is unlikely to be moved by the suggestion that using violence is unfeminine. She is tough and angry, intent on making sure that
the oppressor gets as good as he dishes out—and if there's any woman,
like a brothel madam, profiting from colluding with the enemy . . . she'll
be in the line of fire too.

Nevertheless, violence is not her only weapon. The Avenger can use
the tactics of scandal, blackmail, and public humiliation to wreak her revenge. And it is in drawing attention to the seriousness of crimes against

females in society and in raising questions about the legitimacy of retaliatory violence that the Avenger film is inevitably caught up in debates about sexist oppression and techniques of combating it.

The Avenger narrative made its appearance in the cinema at a time of widespread concern, particularly in the United States, at coerced prostitution and in the context of a vigorous feminist movement. It re-emerged in strength with the development of second-wave feminism, accruing strong affinities with the conventions of the rape-revenge cycle in American cinema analyzed by Carol J. Clover.[2] For obvious reasons, it has appealed to women producers and directors. The patriarchal power structure, on the other hand, has been concerned to contain the radical and subversive implications of the Avenger characterization, seeking to ensure that the target of the prostitute's vengeance is limited to the demonized bad guy, usually a pimp, and not widened to implicate men in general.

No doubt because of its potential to generate strong emotions in an audience through identification with the female protagonist — anger when she is mistreated and rejoicing when she inflicts her revenge — the Avenger formula has proved enduringly popular and occasionally controversial. This chapter studies the evolution of the archetype by concentrating on a select few films that are representative of particular tendencies.

In *The Wages of Sin* (USA, 1914), former mill hand Barbara, seduced and abandoned by Stephen, throws a drink in his face when he ventures into the saloon where she is now evidently plying a different trade, and later she goes for his throat and attacks him with a chair. In *The Conspiracy*, of the same year, Margaret kills the boss of the white-slave syndicate responsible for her abduction and captivity in a brothel. Such pictures paved the way for perhaps the most significant Avenger film of the silent era, *The Red Kimona* (USA, 1925).

In a scene near the start of the film, a man in a jeweler's store is seen selecting a wedding ring, trying it out on his little finger. A woman comes up behind him and says "Howard." He turns, disdainfully looks her up and down, then without a word resumes his transaction. The woman backs away, trembling. Then, in trepidation, she steels herself and, with a pistol concealed in the pocket of her fur coat, fires. The man topples over, dead.

The Red Kimona develops the popular thematics of the white slave and fallen woman narratives in a scandalously feminist direction by having the wronged heroine wreak personal retribution on the man who has betrayed her — and get away with it. Gabrielle Darley (Priscilla Bonner) has learned that her fiancé, having abandoned her in New Orleans, has come to Los Angeles to marry another woman; Gabrielle has followed and tracked him down. In flashbacks she goes on trial for murder, and we discover how the situation came about. A girl from a country town, she falls in love with a stranger, Howard, and is lured to New Orleans on the promise of marriage. There he puts her to work in a crib in the red-light district, where she endures "years of bondage — sorrowful — sordid," represented elliptically by an eloquent scene in which the bruised, world-weary woman bolts her door against two prospective clients and then, resignedly, powders her face and reaches for the latch. As she explains to the jury, it was the sight of him buying a ring with money she had earned through prostitution that induced her to pull the trigger.

Gabrielle is acquitted by the all-male jury. Taken up briefly as a notoriety by a society woman and becoming friendly with her chauffeur, she is subsequently unable to find work because of her past and, forlorn, returns to New Orleans to resume life on the streets. The money for her train fare comes from a prostitute friend, Clara, answering the call in the "tradition that help comes wholeheartedly from the Sisterhood of Sorrow." Run over in the act of escaping from a rapist, she is hospitalized and then becomes a volunteer nursing aide; meanwhile, the chauffeur who has followed her to New Orleans declares his love. Gabrielle in joy and sorrow vows to wait for him as he ships off to war.

The Red Kimona was produced by Mrs. Wallace Reid (Dorothy Davenport), and effectively codirected by her.[3] It was based on real events and scripted by Dorothy Arzner from a story by Adela Rogers St. Johns, who had covered the case as a reporter in 1917.[4] Mrs. Reid appears on screen in opening and closing scenes consulting a newspaper file and speaking to the camera, cautioning viewers — in titles — about the nature of the story ("If it contains bitter truths, remember that I only turn the pages of the past") and finally averring: "You have seen the temptations and struggles of this modern Magdalen, and though she won her redemption and found love and happiness — there are others — countless others — and it is toward these, that we women must face our responsibility, if we would fulfill the duty of true womanhood."

It was only because Mrs. Reid's company was not a member of the MPPDA that the film was able to be made, since the Hays Office had a policy of eliminating pictures that were "based on white slavery."[5] It suffered, however, at the hands of state censor boards. Kevin Brownlow reports that "it was subjected to no less than twenty-five cuts in Pennsylvania, where the censors changed the entire plot, for good measure, by ordering all the titles to be reshot."[6] Some measure of the consternation *The Red Kimona* caused in the American establishment may be gauged by the vituperative reviews it received at the hands of male critics, who were perhaps less disturbed by the mere fact that it dealt with white slavery — their ostensible cause for concern — than by the feminist perspective that it brought to the topic.[7]

While the suffering of the fallen woman is imprinted into Gabrielle's face in virtually every scene of the film, and her redemption conforms to the familiar pattern, what is distinctive about *The Red Kimona* is that its authors allow the protagonist to kill her male oppressor, escape punishment, and end happily in the arms of her lover. This signals a very significant twist to the old tale, opening up cracks in the patriarchal facade. Is the film implying that all hard-done-by women, especially those trapped in prostitution, should take a lead from the example it offers? In a telling moment, Clara cuddles and comforts Gabrielle, saying of Howard that "they're all alike." Gabrielle Darley is one of the earliest incarnations of the Avenger triumphant, and the film illustrates the troubling challenge this figure can pose to the patriarchy.

Violence is not the only instrument in the hands of the Avenger, as *Das Tagebuch einer Verlorenen/Diary of a Lost Girl* (Germany, 1929) demonstrates. Directed by G. W. Pabst, the film was based on a 1905 novel by Margarethe Böhme, previously adapted for the screen in 1918. The book has been praised for allowing a prostitute to speak for herself, and there is some suggestion that the diary entries were not fictional but those of a real woman.[8]

In Pabst's version, Thymian Henning (Louise Brooks) is the daughter of a well-to-do pharmacist, celebrating at the start of the film, at the age of perhaps seventeen, her confirmation. On this eventful day the household governess is expelled from the house for being pregnant by Thymian's widowed father, and she commits suicide; Thymian, upset, is seduced by Henning's sleazy assistant Meinert. Thymian gives birth to a baby daughter, and when Meinert refuses to marry her (she would in any case have turned him down), she is packed off to a reformatory while her baby is put out to care with a midwife. The reformatory is an oppressive, punitive institution, mercilessly satirized by Pabst, and Thymian manages to escape, with the help of the young ne'er-do-well Count Osdorff, a family acquaintance. She goes to the midwife, only to find that her

20. Louise Brooks as Thymian in *Diary of a Lost Girl*. Stiftung Deutsche Kinemathek — Filmmuseum Berlin.

baby is dead. Thymian then joins her friend Erika (Edith Meinhard), who escaped with her, at a glamorous nightclub/brothel. Her first night is so enjoyable that the next morning, when the madam hands her her client's payment, she is bemused and refuses to take it. She nevertheless becomes installed at the bordello and is enjoying raffling herself off as a prize one night when she catches sight of one of the clientele — her father, who, devastated, simply looks on with an impotent gaze. Several years later Thymian learns of his death. Osdorff, a frequenter of the brothel, agrees to marry her but kills himself on discovering that she has given her inheritance to her two young half-sisters, so they will not have to lead the life she has. Osdorff's uncle, the elderly count, marries Thymian instead. Thymian enters polite society and is courted by a reform association. Attending a meeting at her old correctional facility, at which Erika is being disciplined for repeated escapes, Thymian scandalizes the good citizens by declaring that she knows exactly what sort of place this is as she was an inmate once herself, she walks off arm in arm with Erika.[9]

Thymian's revenge consists only in this small gesture of defiance and solidarity with the rebellious prostitute, but it is nevertheless a powerful repudiation of the institution whose project is to teach wayward young women to accept the male power structure. Throughout the film, despite her vicissitudes, Thymian never evokes pathos or bears the mark of the trapped victim. In Louise Brooks's beautifully judged performance, Thymian emerges as a fallen woman whose will to life will not be crushed and whose morality lacks for nothing in comparison with the corrupt men who would judge her and bend all young women to their will. The exquisite disdain with which she eyes the repugnant director of the reform school in the final scene is characteristic of an Avenger who triumphs without a blow being struck or a shot fired.

Later nonviolent Avengers would take a cue from her, using a variety of tactics to get back at the person who wronged her. In *Elmer Gantry* (USA, 1960), for instance, the prostitute gets her vengeance on the opportunist evangelist who seduced her by taking compromising photographs and issuing them to the press. Maddalena in *Accattone* (Italy, 1961) denounces her pimp to the police, while Rosemary in *Greed: Pay to Play*, Bette Gordon's contribution to *Seven Women — Seven Sins* (West Germany/France/USA/Austria/Belgium, 1986), pins a murder on her pimp in an act of solidarity with the humiliated lavatory attendant who actually did the killing. Karla in *Der Besuch/The Visit* (West Germany/France/Italy, 1964) returns to her home town a multimillionaire and publicly shames the prominent citizen who abandoned her when she was pregnant and forced her to become a prostitute. The high-class call girl in *Iki kadin/Two Women* (Turkey, 1992) takes out legal proceedings against the politician who rapes her. And as we have previously seen, Marie in *La Fiancée du pirate* (France, 1969) achieves her revenge by public exposure of her oppressors, while Diane in *Broken Mirrors* (Netherlands, 1984) deliberately renounces the opportunity of using the pistol in her hand to kill, opting instead simply to walk out of the brothel in a radical act of repudiation of all that it stands for.

While many Avengers are concerned only with personal redress, Kelly (Constance Towers) in Sam Fuller's *The Naked Kiss* (USA, 1964) is a prime specimen of the prostitute heroine who battles also on behalf of others. Kelly's fascination is as the violent woman who attacks any man abusing his position of power to exploit women or girls. And she will mete out the same treatment to offenders of her own sex if necessary.

The precredits sequence boldly introduces her. To the accompaniment of hot jazz, Kelly grapples with a man in an apartment, and in the course of the struggle her wig slips off to reveal that her head is shaved.

21. *The Naked Kiss:* Kelly (Constance Towers) grapples with former pimp Far-lunde (Monte Mansfield) as Griff (Anthony Eisley) looks on.

Swinging her handbag she then knocks the man out cold. She rifles through his wallet ("Eight hundred dollars! You parasite!") and takes "only what's coming to me." In a later scene, Kelly explains what provoked the attack. The man, Farlunde, was her pimp. "That parasite held out on me — held out on all of us," she recounts. "So I got six of his best girls to walk out on him. To get even, he spiked my drink with a knock-out pill, and he cut off my hair. I was bald! I waited, I waited until he was drunk, and then I took exactly what was coming to me — seventy-five dollars and not a penny more." Kelly goes on to relate that following this incident word was out in the underworld to throw acid in her face, so she ran and worked small towns for two years before arriving at Grantville, where the action of the movie takes place.

As an independent prostitute, Kelly has a front as a traveler in sparkling wine ("Angel Foam goes down like liquid gold, and it comes up like slow dynamite"). But shortly after peddling some of her product to police captain Griff, she has a good look at herself in the mirror ("I saw a broken-down piece of machinery — nothing but the buck, the bed and the bottle for the rest of my life") and decides to pursue other avenues of employment. She gets a job as nurse's aide at an orthopedic hospital and thrives. The female superintendent enthuses that "she was born to handle children with crutches and babies in braces."

An unhappy young workmate of Kelly's is tempted by the prospect of becoming a "bonbon" at Candy's club across the river. Disturbed, Kelly tells Buff just what to expect: "After a steady grind of making every john feel at home, you'll become a block of ice. . . . Your world with Candy will become so warped that you'll hate all men. And you'll hate yourself, because you'll become a social problem, a medical problem, a mental problem. And a despicable failure as a woman." Furious at the madam's approaches to Buff, Kelly belts her repeatedly about the face with her bag and then stuffs the twenty-five dollar advance into Candy's mouth.

Kelly's final task as Avenger is to deal with her fiancé. She has become engaged to J. L. Grant, "society's most eligible bachelor," who is not put off by her former profession. He is also, however, a child molester. Coming upon him one morning with a young girl, Kelly is not impressed by his appeal for understanding ("My darling, our marriage will be a paradise because we're both abnormal") and kills him with a well-aimed blow of the telephone. Kelly has some difficulty convincing Griff of her story, but eventually the girl corroborates her claims, and the charges against her are dropped. The ex-prostitute walks from Grantville a free woman, saluted by the townsfolk.

Like Gabrielle in *The Red Kimona*, Kelly breaks the taboo against female violence and gets away with it. Taking on masculine fighting attributes and stripped of female markers (the shaven head, the ambiguous name), she is also, at other times, feminized as the mother *manquée*—being infertile herself, she is a lover of babies and a nurturer of children. This compensatory eulogization of surrogate motherhood—together, no doubt, with the negative portrayal of prostitution—satisfied the U.S. Production Code Administration but not the British Board of Film Censors. *The Naked Kiss* was banned in the United Kingdom.[10]

The enraged prostitute who directs her anger at her clients has attained potent symbolic force in the cinema, as in literature. An early equivalent in film of Kuprin's ferociously disillusioned brothel inmate (see the quote at the head of this chapter) is the unnamed girl of the streets in *Damaged Goods* (USA, 1915), based on the notorious stage play *Les Avariés* by Eugène Brieux. The prostitute explains to the protagonist, who has caught syphilis from her, that she herself "contracted syphilis from a wealthy man, who remained respected, while she was refused treatment at hospitals. Angered, she decided to infect men from the upper classes. . . ."[11]

Likewise, Kumiko (Tomie Tsunoda) in *Yoru no onnatachi / Women of the Night* (Japan, 1948) contracts syphilis and avenges herself on men by infecting her clients.[12] The "myth of the woman who takes revenge on all men for mistreatment by a few" is explored further in *Irezumi / The Spider Tattoo* (Japan, 1966), in which Otsuya (Ayako Wakao), having been sold to a geisha-house owner, becomes a "tough, man-eating prostitute" who "delights only in duping men and taking their money"; she eventually turns the knife on the jealous lover with whom she first eloped and kills him.[13] Another variant on the theme is proffered in *The Girls That Do* (USA, 1967). Gigi, whose boyfriend "tricked her into selling her body to pay his debts," enlists the help of her roommates Sylvia, whose husband turned into a sadist, and Ruth, a model who was nearly raped by a photographer, when she brings home a man who has been pestering her: "The three decide that they will take revenge on the male sex by torturing him."[14]

Kidnapped, delivered to a brothel and forced to become a prostitute, Ai Nu (Lily Ho) in *Ai Nu / Intimate Confessions of a Chinese Courtesan* (Hong Kong, 1972) exacts her revenge by acquiring martial arts skills and murdering her clients one by one. *Thriller — en grym film / Thriller / They Call Her One Eye* (Sweden, 1974) develops this theme further, in expanding upon the melodramatic potential of the material. Frigga (Christina Lindberg) is raped at the age of seven, and is thereafter unable to talk. At nineteen, en route to a doctor's appointment, she is picked up by a young man, Tony, who treats her to a meal. He then drugs her wine, pays an evil doctor to inject her with heroin, gets her hooked, locks her up and recaptures her when she attempts to escape, and compels her to take up prostitution. When she scratches the face of her first customer, Tony pokes a knife into her eye. Operating from his apartment, Frigga services under duress a series of clients, including a lesbian, who treat her roughly; her fellow victim Sally (Solveig Andersson), who confides in Frigga that she is saving money for expensive treatment at a narcotics clinic in Switzerland, disappears, leaving behind a bed soaked in blood and a slashed pillow. Meanwhile Frigga's caring parents commit suicide, shattered by her apparently heartless abandonment of them.

Frigga plots her revenge. Still mainlining heroin, she takes lessons and becomes expert in rally driving, marksmanship, and kung fu. She then shoots and kills three of her clients, among whom is the lesbian. Tony takes a contract out on her life, but Frigga has no trouble disposing of the gunmen. With her martial arts and driving skills she is able to elude the police. Finally she challenges Tony to a duel, outwits him when he accepts, buries him up to his neck, and has his head yanked off by a draft horse.

Stretching plausibility beyond the breaking point, *Thriller* collapses into a series of sadistic set pieces, lent a veneer of legitimacy by the oppressed-woman-seeks-justice motif. The dramatic effectiveness is not enhanced by the one-note performance of Christina Lindberg, who seldom relinquishes her customary expression of sullen hostility. *Thriller* has its limitations, yet in its oddly serious, humorless absurdity it highlights the profile of the Avenger who has been hurt so egregiously by male-dominated society that she will strike back with lethal violence against anyone responsible, to whatever degree, for her suffering.

Thriller is male-directed;[15] no greater contrast in style can be imagined than with Chantal Akerman's contemporaneous *Jeanne Dielman, 23 Quai du Commerce, 1080 Bruxelles* (Belgium/France, 1975), a work of feminist structural-minimalism. "No man could have made this film," asserts its star, Delphine Seyrig; "It is a totally feminine film."[16]

In three hours and twenty minutes, *Jeanne Dielman* depicts three days in the life of a petit-bourgeois single mother who each afternoon receives a client as a prostitute. Jeanne's daily routines of childcare, housekeeping, shopping, and cooking are shown at length, while the prostitution, on the first two days, is elided. On the third day, Jeanne is shown having sex, and reaching orgasm, with her customer. She then dresses, takes a pair of scissors, and stabs the man, who is lying back on the bed, in the throat. Having killed him, Jeanne sits motionless and expressionless at the dining room table, as the shot is held for a considerable length of time.

Jeanne Dielman is filmed at medium distance, with a camera that never moves, in long takes that preserve real time. Access to Jeanne's subjectivity is hindered by the absence of close-ups and reaction shots; there is no voice-over, thought-revealing dialogue, or subjective imagery. We do not learn of anything in her past that would seem to motivate her recourse to violence. The film is a conundrum: if the murder is the act of an Avenger, on whom or for what is Jeanne taking revenge?

In a movie such as *Thriller*—indeed, as a general rule—the Avenger, no matter the traumas to which she has been subjected, is lucid, focused. The killing in *Jeanne Dielman*, on the other hand, gives the appearance of a spontaneous deed by a woman whose mental processes are confused: "a desperate, insane act," one critic describes it.[17] The lack of explanation is the film's provocation, and it is left to the viewer to conclude, first,

22. Delphine Seyrig in *Jeanne Dielman*. bfi Collections.

that Jeanne's act is a protest against the soulless routine of her life ("It's the logical end to what was going on before," argues Akerman),[18] and second, that Jeanne has struck out against her client because he symbolizes a patriarchal regime that purchases men's pleasures at the expense of women's independence and freedom. Whether positing such random violence as an act of liberation is a good thing has been a matter for some debate within the feminist movement.[19]

Chinamoon (USA, 1975) is a fifteen-minute, 16mm film by Barbara Linkevitch. Set entirely in one room of a stylized brothel, it shows the interaction of four inmates with their clients. The prostitutes "are depicted with tenderness and sensitivity; not as sex objects, but tragically, as tired, sexually depleted women." The focus is on the boredom of their existence, the camaraderie between them, and their contempt for the men. As in *Jeanne Dielman*, things move to a violent climax: "The finale of the film is a pagan chorus, in song and rite. Having shown the use of women's bodies which destroys their souls, a ritual murder of the men who have come in contact with them takes place."[20]

Utopie/Utopia (West Germany, 1983) is also set in a brothel, but it rivals *Jeanne Dielman* in length, and though similar in some respects to *China-*

23. Renate (Imke Barmstedt), Helga (Johanna Sophia), Susi (Gabriele Fischer) and Rosi (Gundula Petrovska) in *Utopie*. Stills Collection, New Zealand Film Archive.

moon, it bears the marks of male authorship.[21] In particular, it displaces all guilt for the imposition of the suffering experienced by the women onto one man, the pimp/brothel owner.

Heinz works the streets of Berlin with Renate (Imke Barmstedt), who is approaching middle age. He expands his operations by opening the Club Arena and attracting four other workers to service the clientele: Susi (Gabriele Fischer), a bored linguistics student; Helga (Johanna Sophia), a divorced woman hoping to open a cosmetics boutique; Rosi (Gundula Petrovska), an experienced, cynical prostitute dissatisfied with her previous place of work; and Monika (Birgit Anders), a novice getting away from an unsatisfactory affair with a married man in a small town. Heinz, who has gang connections, is dictatorial and brutal, inclined to bang the women's heads against the wall or punch them in the face at any sign of dissent. Monika, who is a failure as a whore, slits her wrists, and Rosi has to be rescued from throwing herself out the window. Susi leaves after being beaten up, but then returns. The representation of a white-slave style institution can be made plausible only by exaggerating the psychological spell that Heinz casts over his women: a sadomasochistic hold (especially with Renate, Helga, and Susi) is postulated, which makes the prostitutes complicit in their slavery.

The clients — unlike those in *Broken Mirrors*, for instance — are not portrayed as aggressive. Typically they are merely lumps of flesh to be endured, grinding away as the woman stares to the side, expressionless. But one in particular is depicted with some sympathy, in his protest against Monika's cold behavior ("You lie there like a stone — how can I like that?"). Another sign of difference from the female-authored works is that the interaction between the women is more often than not negative — icy, bitchy, quarrelsome.

There are, however, moments of closeness and affection, and solidarity in the classic Avenger finale. After having considered defenestration and cyanide, Renate eventually, like Jeanne Dielman, selects scissors as her weapon of preference, wounding Heinz in the stomach. The groaning man is then stabbed and battered to death, with Renate now using a knife, Rosi a stool, and Susi an iron. Judicial consequences do not enter into it; in an ironic, nonfeminist coda, the Heinz regime is replaced not by a women's cooperative but by a renewed authoritarian structure with Renate at the head.

Though the writers and director of *Nuts* (USA, 1987) are male, the driving force behind the production seems definitely that of producer/star Barbra Streisand, and the film has a feminist agenda comparable in some respects to that of *The Red Kimona*.[22] In both films the prostitute protagonist is able to demonstrate to the satisfaction of the justice system that her act of homicide, while deliberate, was justified; and the proceedings in each case, in bringing to light the appalling history of maltreatment she has suffered, expose the oppressive, sexist nature of the society that has permitted it to occur.

In *The Red Kimona*, Gabrielle is a victim of coerced prostitution; in *Nuts*, Claudia Draper (Streisand) has been subjected to childhood sexual abuse. The facts come out during a court hearing to determine if the feisty, unruly call girl is psychologically fit to stand trial for the manslaughter of a client in her apartment. Fighting what she perceives as a conspiracy to have her locked away in a psychiatric institution, Claudia publicly slugs the lawyer hired by her upper-class parents, and in conjunction with his replacement, a legal aid attorney, goes on to win the right to stand trial for the offense. An end title informs us that she was acquitted.

The circumstances of the killing are shown in flashback. An importunate client refuses to leave when time is up, suggesting that he and Claudia take a bath together. When she demurs ("I don't do baths"), he slaps her, chases and seizes her when she gets away, slams her head against the wall, throws her down, and eventually, after she has once more escaped, forces her to the bathroom floor and begins to strangle her. Claudia stabs him with a shard of glass from a mirror that has shattered in the fray.

The situation may well have triggered childhood memories, as becomes clear later in the hearing. Claudia's attorney elicits from her stepfather that he used to bathe her as a child, and fragmented flashbacks that follow Claudia's anguished interjections reveal a pattern of sexual abuse (her favors purchased with $20 bills) that continued until she was sixteen. A brief shot of her client pinning Claudia to the bathroom floor is incorporated in a flurry of images that culminates with uproar in the court and Claudia breaking down in frantic despair. "I didn't know," Claudia's mother will later say. "You didn't want to know," Claudia retorts.

Like the fallen woman narrative, the Avenger story often deals with the girl who turns bad after being sexually exploited. But whereas the fallen woman is depicted as guilty for becoming a prostitute, the Avenger film lays the blame for the victim's situation squarely at the feet of her violator, and beyond him, at men in general who allow such abuses to occur. When she has power, the Avenger will retaliate.

In doing so, she may, as Claudia does, refuse patriarchal definition by scandalizing and turning the labels against her accusers ("Don't judge my blow jobs — they're sane!"). Claudia continually refuses to be good, quiet, polite, to obey the rules of the court, even when to do so, it seems, would be in her own best interest. *She* will define what her own best interest is. Given the crimes committed against her in her childhood, and the attack against which she has recently had to defend herself, the patriarchy has no moral credibility. The anger that suffuses *Nuts* is that of the bad girl Avenger who is impelled to strike back. In protecting herself against her client she does what she wasn't able to as a child; by insisting on her day in court she takes a stand on behalf all girls and women who have suffered abuse. A male critic calls it "an intolerably smug film": is he perhaps disturbed, like the detractors of *The Red Kimona*, by the uncompromising feminist perspective?[23]

Unforgiven (USA, 1992), directed by its star Clint Eastwood, raises issues relating to retribution for the wronged whore in a different context. A

24. Anna Thomson as Delilah in *Unforgiven*.

Western set in Wyoming in 1880, it commences with the slashing of a saloon prostitute's face by a cowboy client ("I'll brand you like a damn
steer, bitch," he yells). Her transgression, it appears, is to have giggled at
the sight of his "teensy little pecker." In the fracas, the assailant is assisted
by his partner in holding the woman down. The rest of the film is concerned with the prostitutes' determination that the men involved pay for
their crime, and the chain of violence that is set off as a consequence.

Though Delilah (Anna Thomson) will be scarred for life, it is not her
personally (she "doesn't care one way or the other") but the leading figure among the hookers, Strawberry Alice (Frances Fisher), who insists
on taking action. The initial impulse of Sheriff Little Bill Daggett is to
bullwhip the cowboys for the assault, a punishment Alice considers gro-
tesquely inadequate. However the saloon-keeper, Skinny, brandishes a
"lawful contract" between himself and Delilah, representing his "investment of capital" and demands recompense for the damage to his "property"—"like if I was to hamstring one of their cow ponies." Little Bill
comments: "Are you figurin' nobody will want to fuck her now, right?"
Accepting Skinny's claim, he orders the attacker, Quick Mike, and his
partner, Davey Bunting, to deliver a total of seven ponies to Skinny in the
fall, and foregoes the whipping.

Outraged ("That ain't fair, Little Bill!"), Alice stirs the prostitutes into pooling their savings as a bounty for the killing of Mike and Davey. "Just because we let them smelly fools ride us like horses don't mean we gotta let 'em brand us like horses. Maybe we ain't nothin' but whores, but by God, we ain't horses." The plan is agreed to, the hookers let it be known that a reward is offered — infuriating the dictatorial Daggett — and bounty hunters swing into action.

The ethical and emotional conflicts entailed in the decision to pursue an Avenger scenario are beautifully encapsulated in the scene in which Mike and Davey bring their ponies to town. They are pelted with mud by the women. As a gesture of recompense, the young Davey has brought an extra horse, "the best of the lot," for Delilah. Clearly repentant, he cuts a sympathetic figure. But Alice angrily rejects the offer: "A pony? She ain't got no face left. You're gonna give her a goddamned mangy pony?" We are abruptly swung around to her point of view and the rightness of scorning a horse in return for permanent disfigurement. The prostitutes resume their pelting, but Delilah, standing sorrowfully apart from the others, does not join in.

Mike and Davey will both be killed, as will a number of others in acts of retribution. Alice and her colleagues will be denounced as "murdering whores" by the townsfolk, but perhaps their clients will think twice before coming at them with a knife in future. A powerful meditation on the very notion of justice, *Unforgiven* depicts an Avenger whose taking of the law into her own hands is seen as a logical inevitability in the context of a system that treats prostitutes as chattel.

Two years later, the gender-bending *Bad Girls* (USA, 1994) reprises some of the same themes, in lighter vein. Here, however, retribution is exacted instantly. A client hassling Anita (Mary Stuart Masterson), one of the hookers in a Colorado parlor house ("I paid for a goddamned birthday kiss, I'm gonna get one") is shot and killed by a fellow prostitute, Cody (Madeleine Stowe). The injudicious Colonel Clayborne topples from the balcony to the floor of the saloon, and a hue and cry arises for Cody's execution. She is about to be strung up by a group of evangelical antivice crusaders when she is rescued by Anita and the two other saloon girls, Eileen (Andie MacDowell) and Lilly (Drew Barrymore). The four race out of town, leaving their old profession behind them and making a seamless transition to outlaws.

Their anger against male society mounts when Anita learns that her claim to land in Oregon, held jointly with her late husband, is now worthless under the law. The gang of Avengers now find themselves in the vanguard of the armed struggle for women's rights — at least to the extent that this fundamentally conventional Western permits. The appeal here—as in the urban prostitute-vigilante pictures such as *Streetwalkin'* and its remake, *Uncaged*—lies in giving the Avengers access to high-powered weaponry, including a Gatling gun, and allowing them to shoot to kill with impunity. In a lawless territory (the marshal sleeps as the lynching is prepared)—but one where the law can still be invoked to deprive women of their rights, as in Anita's case—the fantasy of decisive direct action against the oppressor can be indulged. That in the popular imagination it is the prostitutes who become the gunfighters in the feminist cause is significant: it is they who have had the most direct and varied experience of the enemy.

Similarly, in the notorious *Baise-moi/Rape Me* (France, 2000), it is a prostitute and a porn actress who embark on a killing rampage—this time without the distancing of a period genre, and in a work by women. (The film was codirected by Virginie Despentes, who wrote the novel on which it is based, and Coralie Trinh Thi). Hooker Nadine (Karen Bach) witnesses the murder of a close drug-scene friend and flips, strangling her nagging female roommate to death. Porn performer Manu (Raffaëla Anderson) is viciously raped in a scene that shows hard-core penetration and then kills her brother when it appears that he is less concerned with her feelings than with getting revenge. Nadine and Manu join up and skip town together, heading off on an orgiastic spree of sex and violence. If the sheer randomness with which the pair select their victims—women as well as men—means that Nadine is not strictly an Avenger within the terms set out in this chapter,[24] *Baise-moi* remains as chilling testament to the devastating psychological impact of male oppression in society in general and in the sex trade in particular, and a blunt warning that there are those who will not take it any more. It is a production, of course, which has met with severe censorship problems.

Baise-moi, as a highly colored fantasy, pays no heed to the encounter with the law likely to be in store for any real-life hooker who starts killing. But the legal consequences and the concomitant ethical issues raised when a woman takes lethal revenge for the ill-treatment she has endured, while often sidestepped—as in *Utopie*, for instance—are at times, in the cinema, crucially emphasized. Thus in *The Wages of Sin* (USA, ca. 1938), an independent exploitation movie unrelated to the 1914 film, Marjorie goes on trial for killing the man who promised to marry her and forced her into prostitution instead; she also shoots the new girlfriend with whom he is making love. "During deliberations," the synopsis states, "the jury becomes hopelessly deadlocked, unable to decide whether Marjorie committed murder, whether it was justifiable homicide, or whether she is not guilty by reason of insanity."[25]

The jury in the Aileen (Lee) Wuornos case had no doubts. A prostitute charged with killing her client, Richard Mallory, in Florida in 1989, Wuornos was found guilty of first-degree murder and subsequently sentenced to death. Although she made a plea of self-defense, evidence regarding other killings to which she had confessed was introduced at the trial, and may have affected the outcome. Wuornos ultimately admitted to killing six other clients picked up on Florida highways during 1990, stating that one had raped her and five had attempted to; after having pled guilty to further charges, she received additional death sentences.

The British documentary *Aileen Wuornos: The Selling of a Serial Killer* (1992) includes footage of Lee testifying at her trial. She describes in graphic detail the rape and torture Mallory subjected her to, along with his death threats: "He said, 'You're going to do everything I tell you to do, and if you don't I'll kill you right now, and I'll fuck you after, just like the other sluts I've done.'" Finally, Wuornos says, she spat in his face; he said, "You're dead, bitch, you're dead," and she grabbed her pistol and shot him as he was coming for her. Some time after her trial, it was revealed that Mallory had a history of violent sexual assaults and had been imprisoned for a number of years in Maryland for attempted rape.[26]

The television movie *Overkill: The Aileen Wuornos Story* (USA, 1992) significantly omits the Mallory killing and the trial. It covers the period from the discovery of Lee's fourth victim up to her arrest following a police investigation, with flashbacks to her childhood. The effect is to downplay male violence as an immediate causative factor in the killings and to stress Wuornos's culpability. Details reinforce the impression of a woman who commits premeditated murders: thus we are shown her packing in a bag, when she prepares to go out to work, both a pistol and a bottle of window cleaner, the better to remove fingerprints; and when driving with her final victim, she says: "Think you're going somewhere special? Well guess again, honey. You ain't goin' nowhere." A point is also made of Wuornos's prior criminal record — auto theft, drunk and disorderly, concealed weapon, forged identification, and the like.

The representation of the killings themselves again positions Wuornos (Jean Smart) as the guilty party, overreacting to a tense situation — and perhaps deliberately provoking it. The title, a reference to the number of bullets Wuornos fires — "Nine times? Talk about overkill!" — identifies her violence as, precisely, excessive. Two homicides are depicted only by means of sound track flashback, in both of which Lee is heard to respond to cries of "whore" or "slut" by taunting her victim: "You want to rape me? Come on, come on, over here baby, come on!" "What were you gonna do with this, cowboy?" Then the shots ring out.

The third killing is depicted visually. It is nighttime, and Lee and her client have parked in the woods to have sex. She asks for money. He responds by showing her a police badge, saying "If you treat me real good, I won't arrest you for prostitution."[27] Angered, she denounces him as a phoney and pulls out her gun. There is a struggle, and he wrestles her to the ground, knocking the gun away and pinning her down. Lee gets away, recovers the pistol, and shoots him point blank.

It is evident that *Overkill* is not prepared to show Wuornos's victims as the violent rapists that she claimed them to be. To portray a string of her customers as brutally aggressive would be, of course, to give a very negative image of men — and to let the dangerous notion creep in that she might have been right to do away with them. Still, the film does attempt an explanation for her murderous rage.

During the encounter with her last victim, when Lee is pinned to the ground, there is a cut to flashback images of her as a young girl being held down by a youth or young man who looms over her. She struggles but cannot move. And interspersed elsewhere there are other flashbacks: Lee as a girl of about five, twirling to the sound of a music box, being advanced on and struck by a stern older male; Lee as a girl of thirteen having her baby ripped away from her; Lee as a young girl pointing a gun at herself, perhaps contemplating suicide. The detective investigating the case confirms our suspicions, telling his wife that "there's a pretty strong indication that she was raped by both her grandfather and her brother." The men Lee kills are thus substitutes for those who abused her as a child: the parallels with *Thriller* and with *Nuts*, for example, are clear.

But if Lee's violence is understandable, it is not excusable. "How do you make a life from that?" the detective's wife asks him, after he has explained her family background. "I dunno," he replies. "Maybe you don't. But how do you decide to take people out in the woods and kill them?" What the film is not ready to grant is that any of Lee's crimes may be justifiable. She is not afforded the opportunity to articulate a rationale for her actions, and at one point says herself that she is crazy.

Most strikingly, *Overkill* neutralizes the threat that Wuornos as Avenger poses by making her repentant at the end. Her final confession speech contains no defiance, anger, or reasoned defense; simply remorse and confusion. "I just wish I'd never got that gun," she says. "Wish to

God I'd never been a hooker. I just wish I'd never met those guys and done what I did. I realize I don't have a family and I don't understand, but I know that I have hurt these families very badly." Lee Wuornos's actual confession, as shown in original police footage incorporated in the documentary, commences virtually identically.[28] But the statement carries on rather differently (it is one continuous take): "I still have to say to myself, I still say that it was in self-defense. Because most of 'em were either gonna start to beat me up or were gonna screw me in the ass . . . [unintelligible] and they'd get rough with me, so I'd fight 'em and I'd get away from 'em. . . ." As for the families of her victims, Wuornos had this to say in a television interview in August 1992: "Here's a message for the families. You owe me. Your husband raped me violently, Mallory and Carskaddon. And the other five tried, and I went through a heck of a fight to win. You owe me, not me owe you."[29]

Overkill thus takes the sting out of the Avenger, making her, in the end, more to be pitied than feared. The patriarchal nightmare of "overkill," of the abused woman taking violent and somewhat indiscriminate revenge on her sexual partners because "all men are rapists," has been skirted but held in check. From death row, Lee Wuornos condemned this version of her life: "the movie *Overkill*, that is a total fictional lie."[30]

Wuornos had no opportunity to comment on *Monster* (USA/Germany, 2003). Patty Jenkins's biopic went into production after Lee's execution in October 2002. But the film differs from *Overkill* in representing Wuornos's violence as she herself saw it, as self-defense—at least at the start.[31]

The first victim of Aileen (Charlize Theron) in *Monster* is clearly a slightly fictionalized depiction of Mallory.[32] The whiskey-slugging client viciously belts her when she refuses to suck his penis because it is not part of the deal. Later, as she lies tied up, barely conscious and bleeding profusely from the head, he shoves a metal rod up her, kicks her, and grabs her hair, yelling "Do you want to die?" He then pours caustic liquid over her raw flesh: "I'm gonna clean you up," he explains, "because we've got some fucking to do." Screaming in agony, frenzied, she works her hands loose, grabs her gun, and shoots him eight times. Then she ferociously batters the twitching body.

The killing in self-defense reinstates precisely that which is elided in *Overkill*. Aileen's subsequent homicides shift the ground toward other dimensions of the Avenger archetype. Having renounced prostitution, she tries unsuccessfully to get an office job and reluctantly goes back on the highway ("I've been hooking since I was thirteen, man," she tells her lesbian lover, "Who the hell am I kidding? I'm a hooker."). But when a client entreats her to call him "daddy" while she has sex with him, she can take it no longer. Overload is signaled by the music shifting into a crescendo of noise, and she guns him down, the act here a more generalized retaliation for the relentless abuse of sex workers by customers with perverted lusts.

Aileen's third victim, on the other hand, stands in for the man who raped her as a child, and the father whose friend it was and who didn't believe her story. "There was this old guy," she tells the client, "who used to rape me when I was eight. Real good friend of my dad's, you know. So I go to my dad, tell him what's going on. My dad don't fucking believe me so his friend keeps raping me for years. And the fucking kicker to the story is that my dad fucking beats me up for it." Sensing trouble, the client reaches in his pocket for a gun, but Aileen is too quick, and shoots him dead. Finally, *Monster* depicts Wuornos simply lashing out from the depths of despair, killing without evident provocation or motivation a man who has done nothing but offer to help her in response to her hard-luck story. Here the film, in refusing explanation, approaches the abstraction of the violence perpetrated by Jeanne Dielman on her client; it is a cry of rage and a defiant act of vengeance, perhaps, directed against all males and the power they wield.

Blotchy-faced and stringy-haired, with a gangling walk and towering with her massive frame over her diminutive lover (Christina Ricci), Aileen in Theron's richly detailed and chillingly persuasive performance offers up an image of the Avenger whose authenticity is based upon, but not limited by, the fidelity of the production to the details of Wuornos's life.[33] Stripped of the transcendent romance of *The Red Kimona*, the saccharine sentimentality of *The Naked Kiss*, the melodramatic excess of *Thriller*, the sadistic fantasy of *Baise-moi*, *Monster* is the least embellished portrait to date of the prostitute who claims personal redress for the hurt inflicted on women under patriarchy.

7

Martyr

It is the body of the young harlot
Somewhere, I forget just where I saw it—
Above a doorway of the cathedral at Chartres
Or it might have been at Rheims—
Naked and beautiful, a very human beauty
And therefore a beauty whose meaning is pity,
Carried shoulder-high
By the hawk-headed demons.
—JAMES K. BAXTER, *The Harlot*[1]

From that time—the winter of 1916–17—I became eager to pierce
the mystery of Mary Magdalene, the lover of Jesus Christ, the only
woman who made Our Saviour weep. . . . I believe today I have
penetrated into the very soul of the Penitent of the Holy Ointment and
am capable of writing the story of her mystic wedding rites and of her
contemplative life . . . from which I will draw a film that I will produce
in the very heavens once the war is finished. . . . Sanctus! Sanctus! My
squadron will sing like giant organs and will disappear into the host of
angels transporting Mary Magdalene to heaven, naked under her
adorable locks. . . .
—BLAISE CENDRARS, from *The Detonated Man* (1945)[2]

Alberto Cavalcanti's *La P'tite Lilie* (France, 1927) is a short, stylized,
silent-film illustration of a song, whose lyrics are interspersed in the action as titles. Lilie (Catherine Hessling, giving a more restrained comedic performance than in *Nana*) is a pert, orphaned teenager bored with
operating a sewing machine in a Paris dressmaking workshop. Her lively
beauty is admired by people on the street who watch her go by. The
milkman declares she is an angel passing, and lo and behold, she is suddenly transformed into an angel in white tutu as she trips past a cop and
a lamplighter. One day, however, she falls victim to the enticements of a

procurer whom she meets at a dance. He compels her to leave her job, promising she will find a better one. She forthwith becomes a saucy streetwalker, giving one potential client a boot in the rear when he doesn't respond to her solicitation. The passers-by sadly observe that she is not made for this life, and Lilie finds she doesn't have her heart in it. On one occasion when her pimp angrily demands more money than she is able to give him, she runs off but is pursued by him to the edge of the Seine. In a comic, melodramatic gesture, she presents her back to him, and he thrusts his knife in. She falls, lifeless; he calmly sits down beside her to wipe the blade clean. A fisherman sees the corpse and calls a cop, as the pimp, blasé, knife still in hand, walks off. Lilie's soul now rises from her body as an angel and floats heavenward, kicking her feet one last time as the innocent girl we saw at the start of the film. "She has returned home," the final verse tells us, as the policeman and fisherman gesture skyward, witnessing this playful miracle.

The motif of the prostitute as martyr, suffering and degraded in life but spiritually transcendent, did not originate in the cinema. Eric Trudgill, in *Madonnas and Magdalens: The Origins and Development of Victorian Sexual Attitudes*, draws attention to a 1795 poem by a clergyman, George Richards, titled "Matilda; or the Dying Penitent," which comprises "a loving description in lachrymose couplets of a magdalen's terrible sufferings and contrition, ending with her final ascent on angel's wings to heaven."[3] The idea initially centered on spiritual reward for the "magdalen," or reformed prostitute, but it gradually came to embrace, as in the "fallen angel" characterization embodied in *La P'tite Lilie*, the notion of the woman who sells her flesh being sanctified — if she is pure at heart — *in her very identity as prostitute.*

"Christianity, while condemning the procurer, introduced a charitable attitude toward the prostitute," the *New Catholic Encyclopedia* tells us, regretting that "the compassion manifested by Jesus toward Mary Magdalen is not more clearly reflected in attitudes toward the prostitute in contemporary society."[4] There is no doubt that the Martyr archetype in Western cinema is heavily Christian, and specifically Catholic, in origin, although there may well be analogs in films drawing upon other religious traditions — Sumita S. Chakravarty points out, for example, that in *Pakeezah/Pure Heart* (India, 1971), a film that explores the Muslim culture of northern India, the courtesan's body is the site where "the trade of the flesh is sublimated into a metaphor of the purity of the soul."[5]

Whether in its development in the cinema the Martyr characterization is overtly religious or not, it is consistent in suggesting that the prostitute's suffering is not in vain. In this regard it performs the ideologically valuable function of assuaging the guilt that accrues when men's sexual pleasures are purchased at the expense of a class of women who are degraded and oppressed in the process.

The prostitute suffers, in the films considered in this chapter, since that is her metaphysical destiny. Patriarchy displaces the agony of Christ onto his female surrogate, and holds her ordeal to be necessary. In the Martyr's journey through life she will seldom escape the vale of tears; on her face will be registered all the physical pain and emotional heartbreak that a human being can undergo. No matter how brutal, no matter how unjust the blows of her pimp or the violence of her client, she will not fight back — or if she does she will quickly pay for it; her virtue is endurance. Through all her tribulations will often ripple a joyful innocence, as with Marie in *La Dérobade* (see chapter 18): she is not corrupted by the sordid world she inhabits. And there is generally an optimism that will sustain her unless it, too, finally succumbs to despair.

The Martyr's background, if we are privy to it, is familiar from the fallen woman paradigm. She has very likely been abused as a child or adolescent, like Angela in *Everybody Wins* (USA, 1990), who tells of being repeatedly raped by her father.[6] As an adult she may be seduced and betrayed, sexually violated, shamed. Her adoptive father acts as her pimp, in *Malu tianshi / Street Angel* (China, 1937); her mother makes her a prostitute, in *La mujer del puerto / Woman of the Port* (Mexico, 1992).[7] If married, she may have the misfortune to have a husband who dies, deserts her, or is a hopeless drunk; in *Jeg — en Kvinde, II/I, a Woman, Part II* (Denmark/ Sweden, 1968), he is an unregenerate Nazi who forces her to take up prostitution. Most commonly, however, it is sheer poverty that drives the Martyr out onto the street.

The work itself is misery. Most Martyr films, especially those toward the sentimental end of the spectrum, tend to bracket out the daily grind of servicing clients, though telling references to it are not uncommon. The grim experience of the heroine (Greta Garbo) in *Anna Christie* (USA, 1930) is etched on her face, when she tells her father and lover that she was "no nurse girl these last two years. . . . I was in a house, that's what! Yes! That kind of a house. The kind that sailors like Matt and you go to in port. . . . And all men, I hate them!" Equally worn down by the job is Liz (Theresa Russell) in *Whore* (UK/USA, 1991): "Me, I don't want to see another dick as long as I live," she says. "I used to love sex."

Liz, on one occasion, is seized by men in a van who pull her over into

25. Theresa Russell as Liz in *Whore*.

the back and rape her many times over, tossing her out in the end dazed and bleeding. Barbie of *Barbie's Hospital Affair* (USA, ca. 1970) is a former top call girl suffering from amnesia "caused by a severe beating she received from three men who forced her to have sex with them all simultaneously."[8] At the mercy of clients, the Martyr is also of course vulnerable to violence from her pimp. Cigarette burns are a preferred form of torture, employed for example in *Dédée d'Anvers* (France, 1948), *Hustling* (USA, 1975), *Shirins Hochzeit* (West Germany, 1976), and *Les Filles de Grenoble* (France, 1981). Many Martyrs, like prostitutes of other stripes, are heavily battered by their pimp, as discussed in chapter 18—Marie of *La Dérobade* being a prime example—while Liz of *Whore* is almost strangled to death, when she naively pursues the idea of going independent.

The prostitute victim is likely to find herself further penalized by the attachment of the whore stigma to her. She may be ostracized, driven out of town by morally concerned citizens, like Glory in *The Tower of Lies* (USA, 1925) or Dallas in *Stagecoach* (USA, 1939, 1966, 1986). Prejudice against her occupation may cause her, nobly, to sacrifice her love for a man from respectable society, as Camille does, and Irene in *The Painted Soul* (USA, 1915) who, on "realizing that marriage with her would make Barnard a social outcast . . . continues her life in solitude."[9] The motif continues in *Waterloo Bridge* (USA, 1940) in which Myra, rather than ruin the life of the man with aristocratic family connections who loves her devotedly despite her past, throws herself in the path of a truck.[10] On the other hand, the groom's father may call the wedding off, as in *Dharmapatni* (India, 1940), or the man himself may find her past life too hard to stomach, which is the case for Marcelle in *Marchandes d'illusions/Women Without Hope/Nights of Shame* (France, 1954) and Charity Hope Valentine in *Sweet Charity* (USA, 1969). The prostitute's own brother spurns her in *Umrao Jan* (India, 1981); in *Bidaya wa nihaya/The Beginning and the End* (Egypt, 1960), Nafisah helps to put her brother through the military academy with her earnings as a prostitute, but when he discovers her profession he forces her to commit suicide. The whore stigma is affixed to the seduced and abandoned peasant girl Mari in *Tavaszi zápor/Marie, légende hongroise/Spring Shower* (Hungary/France, 1932), even though she is employed at a brothel as a maid rather than prostitute: "when she returns to the brothel, Mari's daughter is taken from her at the request of a group of stony-faced bourgeoises who think that the child may be in moral danger."[11]

Akasen no hi wa kiezu/Tainted Flowers (Japan, 1958), taking a sociological stance rare among Martyr films, is an exposé of the way in which the whore stigma operates as systematic discrimination against prostitutes who are attempting to leave the life. When the 1958 antiprostitution law closes the red-light district where they have been working, Nobuko (Machiko Kyo) and Hideko (Hitomi Nozoe) determine to find other employment. Nobuko is denounced and fired from her first job after the boss has attempted to rape her, and is sacked from another job when, because of her past, she is suspected of stealing. She cannot acquire a permit for a food stand without sleeping with the man who can get it for her, which she is unwilling to do. Hideko is fired from work at a restaurant because of her previous occupation, and subsequently has a troubled relationship with a man who marries her but has difficulty accepting her past. Both women end up at an illegal brothel, along with many other former residents of the red-light district who have found it impossible to make the change-over to legitimate work. The story ends on an optimistic note, however: the women talk to the police, Nobuko is given hope by a counselor from a rehabilitation center, and Hideko is reconciled with her husband.

Imprisonment may heighten the Martyr's suffering, barred doors clanging shut on her hopes for life. In *The Painted Lady* (USA, 1924), *The Sin of Madelon Claudet* (USA, 1931) and *Orizuru Osen/The Downfall of Osen* (Japan, 1935) she is imprisoned for a crime she did not commit. She is

sent to jail in *Chhaya/Holy Crime* (India, 1936) after having been forced to
kill her child; in *Salón México* (Mexico, 1948) after having become entangled in a robbery with her pimp; in *Víctimas del pecado* (Mexico, 1951) for
killing a pimp when he tries to hit her adoptive son; in *Appassionate/Pas-
sionate Women* (Italy, 1999) for killing a client. Lina (Giulietta Masina) goes
to prison in *Nella città l'inferno/ . . . And the Wild, Wild Women* (Italy/France,
1958) an innocent, deceived young housemaid, but after doing her stint
and being released, she soon returns, transformed into a prancing, heavily made-up woman of the streets. Meanwhile, Egle (Anna Magnani), the
older prostitute experienced in the ways of the world, continues to serve
her sentence, slowly breaking down under the impact of the relentless,
soul-destroying prison regime.

Illness—frequently terminal (see chapter 19)—is also liable to strike
the Martyr down, intensifying the pathos generated by the misfortunes
of her life. Venereal disease, as in *The Downfall of Osen, Mukti* (India, 1970)
or *Yingzhao nülang/The Call Girls* (Hong Kong, 1973), for example, is especially poignant in that it is contracted from her work as a prostitute. *The
Footstep Man* (New Zealand, 1992), in its film-within-a-film depiction of
the painter Toulouse-Lautrec and his female friends, offers a powerful
account of a prostitute devastated on discovering that she has syphilis:
earlier, at one of the brothel women's regular medical inspections,
Mireille (Jennifer Ward-Lealand) has seen a colleague diagnosed with
the disease and has subsequently found her in hospital covered with ugly
red sores on her hands and face, staring lifelessly, a portent of Mireille's
own future.

Just the prospect of growing old as a whore may be gut-wrenching
enough. In the 1930 *Anna Christie*, Anna dejectedly observes the alcoholic
wreck (Marie Dressler) sitting across from her at a saloon table and says,
"You're me, forty years from now." In *Dédée*, the young nightclub prostitute (Simone Signoret) hurries uneasily past older women lining the
Antwerp streets and says to her lover, "It makes me think of later." In the
comparable performances of Garbo and Signoret there is a poignant lucidity about their characters' bleak prospects for the future, a fate from
which Anna is rescued by the sentimental optimism of Hollywood but
to which Dédée, victim of European pathos, is condemned.

"Asta Nielsen: aging prostitute" is the statement that *Dirnentragödie*
(Germany, 1927) makes and repeats, ad infinitum. Since the livelihood
of prostitutes depends on their ability to attract men, and the older a
woman is the less attractive (in conventional terms) she becomes, the
aging prostitute is ipso facto a figure of pathos. But Auguste's tragedy is

26. Greta Garbo in *Anna Christie*.

played out on a higher plane than this. She can still attract clients; and what is more, she no longer has to, having saved enough to buy herself a cake shop. It is her delusion that she can be found genuinely appealing by a young client, and that she can keep him if the competition is eliminated, which leads to her downfall. Felix, the wayward bourgeois youth who is the object of her passion, is only temporarily in need of a maternal substitute; once his anger at his family subsides, he can go back home to his mother. Auguste's desperation expresses itself in violence directed not against men, but against her perceived rival — her friend, roommate, and fellow prostitute, Clarissa, whom she induces her pimp to kill — and then, in consequence, against herself. She commits suicide.

In contrast, it is not pathos but horror that the figure of the aging hooker evokes in *L'ultimo tango a Parigi / Le Dernier Tango à Paris / Last Tango in Paris* (Italy / France, 1972). At 4 AM, a streetwalker (Giovanna Galetti) knocks on the hotel door, demanding her usual room for half an hour. Through the glass door, in the half light, she looks rather glamorous. But when the door opens and she turns to camera in close-up, her appearance is shocking: sagging face, heavily made-up, plastered in white, with black around the eyes and scarlet lips, like a death mask.[12] (Paul, the inheritor of the hotel, has just been wiping the cosmetics off his wife's laid-out corpse, saying, "You look ridiculous in that makeup. Like the caricature of a whore.") *Last Tango in Paris* here pivots on the unsettling effect of the trade in aging flesh (Paul earlier describes one of the hotel's residents: "Right here is the beautiful Miss Blowjob of 1933. She's still making a few points when she takes her teeth out.") The prostitute's appearance contrasts with the young ripe body of Maria Schneider's Jeanne, who engages in sex not for money but for the love of it, and who offers the film's only hope for this character Paul (Marlon Brando) obsessed with death. In this negative, atheistic strand of the Martyr archetype the dimension of sacrifice is downplayed, toward the ultimate pessimism of suffering without purpose, a mortality of the flesh with no hope of transcendence.

In the Bible, Mary Magdalene is the possessed woman whose devils are driven out by Christ, and who is later made holy by proximity to the divine being, the risen Lord. By conflation, in Catholic theology, with the woman taken in adultery, Magdalene becomes a prostitute, creating a neat dichotomy: she is the Mary of the flesh, as the Virgin is the Mary of the spirit. Through her, as through the Madonna, humanity can find the path to God.

As an object of compassion for the suffering she has undergone, Magdalene becomes herself the symbol of the charitable attitude. In *The Eternal Magdalene* (USA, 1919), leading citizen Elijah Bradshaw is about to start a crusade to drive out the town's prostitutes: "Only one person stands against Bradshaw and cites Christ's charity to Mary Magdalene as the example that they should follow." Bradshaw discovers that his daughter Elizabeth is involved with his secretary, and orders her out of his house. But then he dreams of Magdalene "who shows him men in bread lines given hymn books instead of food; a church where the poor cannot reach the door latch; Elizabeth driven from a brothel and depositing her child in an asylum" and other calamitous consequences of a rigid moralism. Horrified, Bradshaw stops his daughter from leaving, cancels his crusade, and "begins to implement compassionate reforms."[13]

Taking her cue from this Magdalene image, the Martyr in film is, very often, the very incarnation of self-sacrifice and altruistic devotion to others. The polar opposite of the Gold Digger, she engages in prostitution not to benefit herself but as the only way she knows of helping someone close to her who is in dire need. Most characteristically, she becomes a prostitute to support a sick or injured relative: mother, in *Street Angel* (USA, 1928) and *Bokuto kidan / The Twilight Story* (Japan, 1960); brother, in

Holy Crime; husband, in *Faithless* (USA, 1932) and *Another Day, Another Man* (USA, 1966). In *The Enemy* (USA, 1927) and *Subarnarekha* (India, 1962) she is forced to resort to prostitution to feed her child. The heroine puts her son through medical school in *The Sin of Madelon Claudet;* assists a poverty-stricken rickshaw driver she has befriended to receive medical training, in *The Downfall of Osen;* enables her sister to receive expensive private education, in *Salón México;* becomes a part-time call girl to make sure that her son can receive the special schooling he needs, in *Money on the Side* (USA, 1982). And the pattern of self-sacrifice continues: in *Tian ruo you qing er/A Moment of Romance II* (Hong Kong, 1992), the immigrant from mainland China raises money through prostitution to bribe officials who have imprisoned her brother.

The Martyr has a particular affinity for persons suffering from a physical disability. In *Für zwei Groschen Zärtlichkeit/Call Girls* (West Germany/Denmark, 1957) Madeleine's husband is crippled; in *Bonitinha, mas ordinária/Pretty But Wicked* (Brazil, 1963) Rita's mother is an invalid; in *Warm Nights on a Slow Moving Train* (Australia, 1988) Jenny's brother is a paraplegic. The religious connotations become apparent in *Le notti di Cabiria/The Nights of Cabiria* (Italy/France, 1957), in which Cabiria, making a pilgrimage to pray to the Madonna, finds herself in a church lined with what we presume are the abandoned crutches of the handicapped who, through the miracle of faith, now walk again.

A revealing indicator of the Martyr's compassionate nature is her sympathy for the man on death row. In *Tonka Sibenice/Tonka of the Gallows* (Czechoslovakia/Germany, 1930) and what appears to be a later variant, *Hold Back Tomorrow* (USA, 1956), she is induced to spend a night with a condemned criminal and is strongly affected by the experience;[14] in *The Front Page* (USA, 1931) and its 1974 remake, she gives unwavering support to the unhinged radical awaiting execution for the shooting of a cop, much to the amusement of the cynical, wisecracking press corps. Christian allusions are never far from the surface. In the 1974 *Front Page*, Molly berates the journalists for the stuff they have been writing about her: "Calling me an 'angel of the pavement,' 'the midnight Madonna'! Who are you kidding? I'm a two-dollar hooker from Division Street and you know it!" A religious thematic is overt in *Tonka of the Gallows*, in which Tonka's face is superimposed on that of the condemned man at the hanging, and a black cross becomes the dominant feature of the image. "This strange romance profoundly affects Tonka," writes Peter Hames, "giving her a quasi-religious insight into the meaning of life that goes beyond the values of the society in which she lives."[15]

"The cinema of prostitutes, as the title of its first representative makes explicit," writes Jorge Ayala Blanco, discussing a genre of Mexican film for which he takes *Santa* (1931) to be the model, "is in its origins a veiled form of Christian martyrology."[16] The extent to which overt religious allusions are made in the development of the Martyr characterization varies, but they are often quite insistent.

Such allusions sometimes take the form of a paradoxical association of the prostitute with the Virgin Mary. Thus in *The Informer* (USA, 1935), Katie (Margot Grahame) appears almost as an image of the Madonna, but then slips back her head scarf to reveal the bleached blonde hair and painted face of a streetwalker. The identification is made systematic in *My Madonna* (USA, 1915), directed by Alice Guy-Blaché: a visionary artist finds in Lucille (Olga Petrova), a high-society prostitute, the ideal model for his portrait of the Madonna. She poses for him and falls in love, but his painting propels him to fame and he turns away from her. After many vicissitudes in their separate lives, "Robert finds his way to a church where his Madonna painting hangs. By chance his flesh and blood Madonna also appears, and the two happily reunite."[17] In a very similar scenario, Angela (Janet Gaynor) in *Street Angel* poses for a Madonna portrait, and she and the artist, Gino, fall in love, without his knowing that she has been streetwalking to obtain medicine for her mother. Circumstances tear them apart, and on learning of her past Gino becomes so embittered toward Angela that he tries to strangle her. She rushes into a church, however, and he follows. There he sees his Madonna painting, and on it, superimposed, an image of the woman he loves. He collapses before the altar, and the couple are reconciled.

The title of Kenji Mizoguchi's *Maria na Oyuki/Oyuki, the Madonna* (Japan, 1935) makes the intended analogy explicit. In this tale of two prostitutes with contrasting responses to their oppressive condition, Okin (Komako Hara) is "for resistance, for meeting hostility with all the small hostility someone in her position can display," while Oyuki (Isuzu Yamada) "stands for acceptance, for submission to circumstance. Though a social outcast herself, she is still capable of compassion."[18] A comparison with the Virgin Mary is again drawn in Mizoguchi's later *Yoru no onnatachi/Women of the Night* (Japan, 1948). After desperately appealing to her sister-in-law not to join her in the profession and almost being lynched by a band of prostitutes as a result, Fusako (Kinuyo Tanaka) escapes behind a bombed-out chapel, where the camera pans along a fresco of the Madonna and child, "providing a parallel"—Keiko McDonald comments—"that is all too obvious."[19]

A whimsical variation on the theme is offered in *Appassionate*. While the imprisoned prostitute Maria Maddalena (Anna Bonnaiuto) is assailed by memories of unhappy loves, a bucolic Madonna leaves the countryside and enters the streets of the city, accompanied by a bevy of chickens.

In Jean-Luc Godard's *Vivre sa vie/My Life to Live* (France, 1962), the identification made is with Joan of Arc. Nana (Anna Karina), about to enter a life of prostitution, goes to the cinema to see Dreyer's *La Passion de Jeanne d'Arc*. The sequence of Joan being told that she is to die at the stake—her eyes slowly turning heavenward, as she declares "It will be my martyrdom!"—is silently intercut with close-ups of Nana totally absorbed in the drama, tears rolling down her face. Nana herself is to die, gunned down in a battle between pimps. On the other hand, a parallel with Christ's own martyrdom is drawn in *Maynila: sa mga kuko ng liwanag/Manila* (Philippines, 1975). The protagonist's lover Ligaya Paraiso (Hilda Koronel) is held captive on Misericordia Street. "Arranging to meet her in church, he elects instead to take her to a moviehouse where they can speak more freely: the film being screened is Nicholas Ray's *King of Kings* and the scene being shown is that of Christ carrying the cross on his ascent to Golgotha."[20] Ligaya's fate is to remain unknown: she vanishes in the labyrinth of the city.

As in the climactic scenes of *My Madonna* and *Street Angel*, the prostitute being seen in church strengthens the sense of the sinner being sanctified. In *Senza pietà/Without Pity* (Italy, 1948), Angela prays in church and is joined there by Jerry. She urges him to return the money he has taken in a robbery, but he persuades her instead that they should go through with their plan of escape. Shortly afterward, Angela is shot dead. The prostitute protagonist (Anna Magnani) of *Mamma Roma* (Italy, 1962) also attends church, and though it is perhaps with the pragmatic purpose of currying favor with the priest whom she hopes will help in finding employment for her son, her action adds to the Christian allusions that become attached to the character. The elusive Manuela (Liv Ullman) in Ingmar Bergman's *Das Schlangenei/The Serpent's Egg* (West Germany/USA, 1977) tells her brother-in-law that she works in a whorehouse in the mornings, but when he follows her she enters a church, and after the service discusses with the priest the guilt she feels for her husband's suicide. Another prostitute to attend a church service is the psychologically unstable Angela (Debra Winger) in *Everybody Wins*: she takes communion and lights some candles, and the priest tells her boyfriend Tom that he is her lifeline now—"You're all that connects her to reality."

The roof of the Milan cathedral is the setting for the pivotal meeting, in *Rocco e i suoi fratelli / Rocco and His Brothers* (Italy/France, 1960), between Nadia (Annie Girardot) and Rocco. She is framed against gothic arches as she declares her love for him, and Rocco tells her that they mustn't meet again, that she must return to Simone. Nadia runs off in despair along the elevated balustrade, a lone, distant figure between the finials. Nadia is to become Simone's murder victim (see chapter 19)—a sacrifice for the (male) future represented by the two youngest Parondi brothers: "Some say the world will never be any better, but I think it will," Ciro tells Luca. "And you'll have a better and more honest life."

"Religioso overtones throughout the film add piquancy through contrast," opined *Variety* in reviewing *The Pyx* (Canada, 1973), a thriller about the murder of a hooker, Elizabeth (Karen Black).[21] Among the songs composed and sung by Black is one with lyrics drawn from the *Song of Solomon*. In a corrupted Montreal, devil worship is afoot; Elizabeth is killed at a Black Mass, when she refuses to commit sacrilege against the Host. Religious associations of a different sort accompany Jenny (Wendy Hughes) in *Warm Nights on a Slow Moving Train*, who is an art teacher in a Catholic girls' school when she is not entertaining passengers for cash in the train's Judy Garland suite. In this film, though there is a good deal of explicit sex, the viewer's attention is riveted not on Hughes's body but on her face, where suffering is welded with an indomitable willpower, the self-alienation of whoring buttressed by a sense of self-righteousness at pain undergone for a higher good.

In the performance of Anna Magnani in Pasolini's *Mamma Roma* there is a vivaciousness, a gaiety, but we must guess at how forced it is; for much of the film her character, like Jenny in *Warm Nights*, must bear the weight of the world on her shoulders. Having discussed metaphysical issues with the priest, Mamma Roma at one point asks, "Who's responsible?" and looking skyward, calls out: "Explain to me, because I'm nobody and you are the King of Kings."[22] Naomi Greene reports that Pasolini, "deeply religious as an adolescent . . . had experienced mystical longings so intense that—as he confessed in his diary—at times he seemed to see 'images of the Madonna move and smile.'"[23] Christian iconography in *Mamma Roma* begins with the banquet table (for the wedding of Mamma Roma's pimp) in the opening scene, which suggests the Last Supper; while "Mamma Roma, pushing her fruit and vegetable cart before her," argues Greene, "seems to be mounting the hill of Calvary."[24] The death of her teenage son Ettore, on the other hand, through similarity in composition to Mantegna's painting *Cristo morto*, positions the

27. Nadia (Annie Girardot) with Rocco (Alain Delon) in *Rocco and His Brothers*.
Stills Collection, New Zealand Film Archive.

youth as Christ and hence his mother as the Virgin — but in this rereading of myth, Chris Chang argues, Ettore is no savior, and he "must die for
the sins of the Mother."[25] For all the religiosity, the prostitute here cannot
shake the guilt that clings to her.

Yet in the tradition of the Victorian Magdalen, there is always the potential for redemption. In *The Painted Soul*, for example, Irene is selected
by an artist to model for a portrait of "The Fallen Woman," but when she
catches sight in the studio of an inspired image of *The Resurrection*, she is
profoundly affected and no longer able to pose as a fallen woman nor,
presumably, to practice as a prostitute. Anna in *Anna Lans / The Sin of Anna
Lans* (Sweden, 1943) makes up for the mistakes of her past by joining the
Salvation Army.

For the character who does not survive, the film is likely to offer up
the religious gestures associated with dying: Gertie, in *The Angel of Broadway* (USA, 1927), as she is about to pass away, seeks someone to pray for
her; Madame Hortense, in *Zormba / Zorba the Greek* (Greece/USA, 1964),
clutches a cross on her deathbed. But it is Mari, the brothel maid from
Spring Shower, who gets the most spectacular send-off after La P'tite Lilie:
"The bells of the church seem to call her, she stalks madly up the aisle,
reaches for the statue of Mary, and dies. But she is seen to ascend to
heaven. . . ."[26]

If many suffering prostitutes are released from earthly travail and end
up literally or metaphorically heavenward-bound, Giulietta Masina's
Cabiria is the paradigm of the Martyr as survivor. Just as *Nana* is Renoir's
portrait-of-the-wife-as-prostitute and *Vivre sa vie* is Godard's, *The Nights of
Cabiria* is Fellini's, the realization of a character study he had been developing in his mind since at least 1947.[27]

The film has a simple, episodic narrative. At the start, Cabiria is
cruelly mistreated by a lover who pushes her in the Tiber and steals her
purse; at the end, she is callously deceived by a fiancé who makes off with
her life savings ("You couldn't believe," she tells him, "what I had to do
to scrape even that much money together.") In between, we see something of her house (a hut of concrete blocks) and place of work (the rough
Passegiata Archeologica quarter of Rome), meet other prostitutes and
some pimps, and accompany Cabiria on three small adventures: spending a night with a famous actor (rather than sleep with him, Cabiria is
shut in the bathroom, since the actor makes up with the elegant girlfriend
he has quarreled with); going on a pilgrimage to the Madonna of Divine
Love; and appearing onstage in a hypnotist's show.

28. Giulietta Masina in *The Nights of Cabiria*. Stills Collection, New Zealand Film Archive.

We do not see Cabiria have sex with a client or with anyone for that matter: her character is in fact systematically stripped of sexuality. In appearance, even with a tight wet dress clinging to her, Cabiria is not eroticized; in contrast, the large, opulent body of her friend Wanda is emphasized by a low-cut frock, which puts her breasts on display. The opposition assists the paradoxical characterization of Cabiria as the whore of spirit rather than flesh, whose innocence and virtue are intact. Her slight build, in addition, appeals to an audience's compassionate empathy, her seeming fragility belied by strength and endurance.

Cabiria's character yokes feistiness with gullibility; she is emotionally volatile, moving readily from tears to smiles, intensely felt hurt to a joyful exuberance expressed in spontaneous breaking out into dance. With her ability to live life to the full emotionally for the moment, and her propensity to change moods like quicksilver, there is something childlike about her.

On her pilgrimage, a crucial sequence in terms of the film's religious connotations, Cabiria is accompanied by friends from the milieu, including the crippled uncle of a pimp. There is a procession, with crucifixes held aloft; and in the church, with its illuminated "MARIA" sign, there is a crush of people chanting "Praise Madonna!" Cabiria joins in, then kneels and prays: "Madonna, oh Madonna, make me change my life. Please help me, Madonna." She breaks down, sobbing.

Outside, Cabiria laments the fact that "nobody changed"—like the cripple, who is still lame. "What do you expect to change, Cabiria, you fool?" asks Wanda. "I'm through with this life," Cabiria replies; but she is not. It is her destiny, like Wanda's, to be a prostitute and to suffer; but Wanda has the lucidity to recognize it. Cabiria will not be getting married and setting up as a storekeeper, as she later, like Auguste in *Dirnentragödie*, fondly hopes. In the final sequence, after a night of lonely despair in the woods, Cabiria is serenaded by a group of itinerant young partygoers, and there is a close-up of her smiling amid her tears. She glances briefly at camera: she has accepted her lot in life.

"A lyrical, musical outburst, a serenade sung in the woods ends this last film of mine (which is full of tragedy)," wrote Fellini to a Jesuit priest, "because in spite of everything Cabiria still carries in her heart a touch of grace. We must not try to discover just what is the nature of this grace; it is kinder to leave Cabiria the joy of telling us, at last, whether this grace is her discovery of God."[28]

The Martyr's death, when it occurs, whether from illness, accident, murder, or as is very frequently the case, suicide, is by definition not in vain. Sacrificial overtones tend to be particularly stressed in films with a setting of religious or sociopolitical crisis, as four examples will show.

The pretext for Ingmar Bergman's *Fängelse/The Devil's Wanton/Prison* (Sweden, 1949), discussed in a prologue by a film director and his former mathematics teacher, is existential angst at a world of atomic bombs, a world seemingly abandoned by its creator. The subject is rejected as unsuitable for filmic treatment. Instead, we become involved in the story of a writer, Tomas, and his brief relationship with a seventeen-year-old prostitute, Birgitta-Carolina (Doris Svedlund). The young woman is tormented with guilt for having abandoned the baby she was too young to keep, and which was subsequently drowned. Trapped in her profession and tortured with cigarette burns by a former pimp, Birgitta-Carolina stabs herself to death. Her death frees Tomas, who has been on the verge of suicide himself, to return to his wife, revived by his encounter with the prostitute. "Meeting her has had a liberating influence on him," writes Birgitta Steene. "She has acted out his frustration and suffered in his place."[29] And though in the framing story the director remains unconvinced of the value of the idea that has been put to him, for Bergman the suicide of a prostitute has provided a subject by means of which he can explore in concrete dramatic terms the abstract theme of the absence of God.

WUSA (USA, 1970), an exposé of American death culture at the height of the Vietnam War, is too mired down in the pessimism it generates to succeed on any dramatic level, yet its use of the figure of the prostitute is revealing. The lucidity of downtrodden hooker Geraldine (Joanne Woodward) about her own situation and by extension that of the racist, warmongering nation — one guesses this: she never actually expresses any political views — only sinks her deeper into depression, and accordingly limits the nurturance she can offer to the alcoholic drifter Rheinhardt whose values are always truer than those of the degenerate radio station he works for. Crushed by life, Geraldine hangs herself in a police cell with the steel chain of her bunk. Visiting her grave, her lover is cleaned up, smartly dressed, moving on out of town. A hippie calls out, "Don't worry about it, Rheinhardt. Everything's dying." "Not me," Rheinhardt replies. "I'm a survivor."

The crisis in István Szabo's *Édes Emma, drága Böbe/Sweet Emma, Dear Böbe* (Hungary, 1992) is that of the East European nation on the collapse of communism. Reasonably paid work for young women is desperately hard to find; some audition as nude extras for a film company, while Böbe (Enikö Börcsök) supplements her meager income as a language tutor by picking up foreigners. Her despair is such that after a run-in with the police for drug-dealing and prostitution, she commits suicide by jumping from a high window. She is survived not by a man but by her friend Emma, who may have a better future to look forward to.

Finally, we may consider *Bawang bie ji/Farewell My Concubine* (China/ Hong Kong, 1993), directed by Chen Kaige. The moment of crisis in this historical epic of China in the twentieth century is reached with the outbreak, in 1966, of the Cultural Revolution. In a frenzy of public denunciations, leniency is extended only to those who condemn their own pasts. Opera star Duan renounces the woman who has been his partner for nearly thirty years, the beauty he plucked from the House of Blossoms. It is true she was a prostitute, he declares. "I don't love her. I'll never have anything to do with her again." Soon after, the body of Juxian (Gong Li) is found: she has hung herself. The tainted woman — "once a whore, always a whore" the madam warned her, when she left the brothel — dies, but the great opera singer and the tradition he stands for lives on.

In these four films, the prostitute takes upon herself the suffering of humanity, concentrating it in her own body. She kills herself, perhaps, because she perceives with greater clarity than those around her the corruption of the world they live in, and has endured more that she can bear. Her sacrificial suicide is a sad but necessary ritual for the renewal of male-dominated society.

Fourteen minutes in the latter half of *The Sun Shines Bright* (USA, 1953) is devoted to the funeral of an unnamed prostitute whom we have scarcely seen. As a piece of propaganda — fully consistent with John Ford's other work, such as *The Informer* and *Stagecoach* — for the charitable, Catholic, attitude toward the woman who has led a life of sin, it usefully encapsulates many of the assumptions underpinning the Martyr characterization.

Several decades after the end of the Civil War, a mortally ill prostitute who was involved in a scandal some years before returns to her home town of Fairfield, Kentucky, to die. Judge Priest risks his reelection chances in arranging — at the request of Mallie Cramp, proprietor of the town's brothel — the dignified funeral that she does not dare approach the preachers about: "It would ruin any man," the judge concurs.

In the funeral procession, to begin with, there is just the hearse, the judge, and a handful of women from Mallie's establishment. But one by one the more compassionate townsfolk drop what they are doing and join the parade, braving the scorn of their respectable fellow citizens, who turn up their noses or jeer at the prostitutes in mourning. By the time the procession reaches the church — outside which an African-American choir is singing spirituals — there is quite a crowd.

At the service, the judge preaches the sermon. Although he declares that "upon me who has never attempted such an undertaking devolves the privilege of speaking a few words about her," he says nothing about the dead woman as an individual, other than to imply that she was a sinner. He tells the congregation that he thought of using for his text the words of Saint Mark: "The Lord and Master took a child in his arms, and he said, whosoever receives a child in my name receiveth me." Instead, he reads the story from the Gospel of Saint John about the woman taken in sin, and the accusers who slink away when Jesus challenges them with the words, "He that is without sin among you, let him first cast a stone at her." "Bye and bye," says the judge, "every last one of them common scoundrels were gone." The story ends, of course, with the Lord saying to her, "neither do I condemn thee." At the judge's request, one of the mourners then says a prayer: "Gentle Jesus meek and mild, look upon a little child. Pity her simplicity. Suffer her to come to thee. Amen."

The conjunction of ideas is revealing. The woman who is being buried is *guilty*—that is her defining characteristic. And yet this person who died in middle age had the innocence of a child, stripped therefore of any responsibility for her actions, of any adult individuality, of any freedom. She should not be shunned. Her life was one of *necessary* suffering, the film implies: she should be honored for serving her purpose in God's plan, and the patriarchy's.

In contrast, the Protestant version of the Martyr story, as exemplified by Lars von Trier's *Breaking the Waves* (Denmark/Netherlands/Sweden/France, 1996), is crueler, and bleaker. Even a human sacrifice cannot warm the hearts of the frigid pious fraternity of this island off the coast of Scotland, religiously condemning Bess (Emily Watson) to hell for her sins of the flesh.

The sexually innocent young woman ("What do I do?" she asks, when offering herself to her husband for the first time), desperately in love, paradoxically becomes a prostitute after Jan has been paralyzed in an oil rig accident. "I want you to find a man to make love to, and then come back and tell me about it," he asks of her. "Now that will keep me alive." Hating it (her face screwed up in anguish as she fucks), ostracized by the community, locked out of her own home by her mother, almost committed, once again to a mental institution, Bess seeks out, clad in red vinyl hot pants and patterned tights, ever more dangerous sexual encounters, convinced that in relating to Jan what happens—or later, so she believes, communicating the experience by spiritual telepathy—she will save him from dying and enable him to walk again.

Bess has her own, personal style of religious observance. In the austere church—from which the bells have been removed—she engages in dialogue with God, playing both roles herself. At the start, she promises simply to be a good girl; later, as things become confused, she is distraught by a lack of response to her prayer for guidance. Still, she is unwavering in her belief that she is on the right path: "Forgive me Father, for I have sinned. Mary Magdalene sinned, and she's among thy dearly beloved."

On one occasion, visiting a trawler that none of the other ship girls will service, Bess has the back of her blouse sliced with a knife after one of the crewmen gets rough. Undeterred, she goes back. This time, when she returns, it's as an ambulance case, with deep cuts and severe internal injuries. Face striated, she bears the stigmata of her sacrifice. Shortly after, she dies.

Jan, though, lives — and walks. Outwitting the censorious elders who have denied Bess a funeral service, he substitutes sand for her body in the coffin, and takes her out for burial at sea. He and his mates tip the body overboard. Suddenly, they are transfixed and stare at the sky. Up in the clouds, high above the oil rig below, church bells ring.

The pain and suffering has been transcended, to the greater glory of God. If there is a feminist response to this matrix of ideas, it is that there is no transcendence, only the endless agony. Take *Purge* (New Zealand, 1994), for example, a concentrated, ten-minute character study of a prostitute by the name of Belladonna (Carol Smith). The film, by Rachel Anderson and Bridget Lyon, is heavily stylized; it depicts Bella as a hooker in long diaphanous blue dress, her eye sockets darkly mascaraed, her face pale, her lips rouged. She's young but has the look of the Martyr already imprinted on her. Oblique, fragmentary flashbacks hint strongly at a history of childhood sexual abuse by her father ("Why did he do it? He never goes away. He never leaves me. Always his face and his hands. Over and over again.")[30]

Bella's wish for an angel is granted in the person of a heavy, camp transvestite in red-checked gingham tunic, miniskirted, sporting outsize wings. But this Gabriel is no help; eventually she says, "Fly away angel, you're frightening the trade." Bella takes on a customer: they copulate in a bar full of posturing young people, she bending down over a pinball machine, he entering from the rear, his trousers round his ankles. We view from above, and then front on, as he thrusts and grunts, in a scene heavily reminiscent of *Broken Mirrors*. He comes, with an agonized expression. She reaches back, swabbing between her legs.

Now Bella is descending steps in the night, dangling her handbag. "Buy my body in black fucky lace," she says. "Exploit me! Exploit me! Exploit me! I want to be exploited. Stick your finger up my five-year-old cunt. Burn me with your cigarette. Piss on me." She bumps against a wall, and staggers on. "Fuck me with your fist. Jam your dick down my throat. Tear me to pieces and freeze me. Slap me around. Shove a beer bottle up me. Slice my breasts with your big man knife. I want to be exploited!"

She invites martyrdom: "Nail me to a cross and I'll die for your sins";

29. Belladonna (Carol Smith) in *Purge*. Rachel Douglas.

later, driving with Gabriel, she tells him, "I think Mary Magdalene suffered more than Christ." The last we see of Bella, she is hanging on a pole, naked but for a G-string, nipple rings, and a crown of red roses, suspended in the blue-lit alley at night. "Fuck off, angel!" she tells Gabriel, as he goes flying past, and she stays there, female flesh hung out for the butcher.

The patriarchal Martyr suffers on behalf of mankind; Belladonna just suffers. "Well what did you expect?" as her voice-over asks. "There are worlds without poetry."

8

Gold Digger

Men always praise an honest whore, keen
for the price of what she proposes to do,
but to promise & break promise
frequently taking & never giving
proves the woman, Aufilena, inimical to men.
—CATULLUS (ca. 60 BC)[1]

Keep cool and collect.
—MAE WEST[2]

In *Today* (USA, 1930), Eve Warner (Catherine Dale Owen) is unwilling to adjust to a more modest lifestyle when her husband Fred goes bankrupt. Without Fred's knowledge, she becomes a high-class prostitute. When he finds out, Fred kills her. In one version of the film, the story stops there, with Fred calling the police; but in the more generally released version, Eve then wakes to find that it has been a nightmare.

It is an embarrassingly poor, poverty row production, with very stilted dialogue, excruciating acting, and a primitive sound track. But the narrative is nonetheless fascinating in its unequivocal representation of the prostitute as Gold Digger, morally reprehensible because she puts greed ahead of love and decency. "You forced me to give up my very life!" Eve accuses Fred, when he confronts her at her bordello. "Stifled me in that rotten, crowded place. I wanted furs, clothes, jewels. Well, I've got them!" The point of view is decidedly male, offering Eve no grace at all. Fred's behavior is impeccable throughout—if one excuses, as one is expected to, the act of violence at the end; Eve is unfeeling, uncaring, dominated by her desire for luxury. If the tacked-on ending is to be taken seriously—*Variety* reported that "customers giggled scornfully" at it[3]—then this judgment is qualified by the consideration that it is all Eve's

147

"nightmare"—but why should she have internalized such an exceptionally negative evaluation of herself, if it's not true?

Eve is not the only woman in *Today* to stray from the path of devotion to her husband. At the beginning of the film, Fred's colleague Greg tells him: "Women are all the same nowadays. They're raised with the one idea of annexing a bank roll. When they get it, they won't give it up." He has no illusions about his own wife, who later runs off to Paris and gets divorced; Eve's close friend Marian, who introduces her to prostitution, is also married.

Although it is based on a 1913 play, first filmed in 1917, *Today* in its updated version registers an acute anxiety over the collapse of male prerogative and authority following the 1929 stock market crash—a headline announcing the event is the first shot of the film. Marian's husband George, for example, is a weak character who connives at what she is up to—Fred refers to him as a "worm." The institution of marriage, structured at that time on inequality of male and female earning capacity, is revealed to be vulnerable when the income stops flowing: romantic love, the ideological tie, is stretched to breaking point. *Today* is unusual in the baldness with which it presents the extinction of love within a marital relationship: Eve's scathing "It would bore me to tears," for example, to Fred's suggestion of a romantic moonlight boat ride is never (except in the tacked-on finale) rescinded or moderated—indeed her attitude when confronted by Fred at the climax reinforces the statement. She just doesn't love her husband any more, does not even care enough about him to spare his feelings, for old times' sake. (In the version in which Eve awakes from her nightmare, she declares her love for Fred, urges him to take her jewels if they'll help him, and says she will stand by him.)

Here the low-budget programmer is able to say things that the A-movie can not: that a woman could quite well fall out of love with her husband and prostitute herself to buy fineries, and that such a person might not be an extraordinary, evil creature, but indeed fairly typical of women of 1930 whose husband's income has been affected by the onset of the Depression.

While the economic crisis brought such anxieties to the fore, fear of women slipping out of male control has been an ongoing condition of patriarchy and is undoubtedly a major factor in the generation of what I have termed the Gold Digger archetype, to which Eve Warner so closely conforms. The one prostitute type in the cinema that is predominantly portrayed negatively, the Gold Digger is the figure on whom male insecurities about the female—about her sexual independence, in particu-

lar — are condensed. She is a provocation of the highest order, the woman who exploits men's natural sexual desires to effect a redistribution
of wealth in her favor. Painted, therefore, as morally corrupt, very frequently beyond all redemption, she is an object of misogynist contempt — sometimes mixed with sneaking admiration for her chutzpah.
Though related to the Siren in her destructive impact on men, she seldom has the charisma to swing audience sympathy in her favor. Thinking only of herself, she is a polar opposite of the Martyr, and her death, if
it comes, will serve no higher purpose.[4]

Because she is unsympathetic, the Gold Digger is often not the chief
protagonist of a film. Sometimes, as in *Today,* the story will be told from
the perspective of the man who is duped or hurt or corrupted by her.
Another device is a pairing: the Gold Digger as the less ethical of two
women friends who are trying to get on in the world. This is the case, for
example, in *Scandal* (UK/USA, 1988), a dramatization of the 1962 John
Profumo affair. Christine Keeler (Joanne Whalley-Kilmer) is warm,
sincere, a little bewildered; she has never been a prostitute, she insists at
Dr. Stephen Ward's trial, and though she has received gifts, in one case
money, from her lovers, she remains, in the eyes of the filmmakers, guilt-
less. Mandy Rice-Davies (Bridget Fonda), on the other hand, is brassy,
uppity, unlikable: she does not love Stephen as Christine does, of course,
and in brazenly specifying the sums of money she received for sex is
shameless, shameful.

The background of the Gold Digger is not often gone into. The assumption in many cases is that she is a fallen woman, with the narrative of the
film concentrating not on the descent from virtue to vice, but on the latter phase, when she is already corrupted. It's significant that in the film
Christine is given a modest home in the country and a mother, whereas
Mandy has only someone on the phone whom she tells lies to. By omitting information that might induce us to empathize with her, this rhetorical strategy makes a negative judgment against the Gold Digger that
much easier to elicit, the explanation for her behavior tending toward
the essentialist: she is bad because she is a (sexual) female.

It is precisely because the film provides such background information
that the young prostitute in *La Petite Lise* (France, 1930) escapes the Gold
Digger categorization. It is true that Lise (Nadia Sibirskaia) kills a pawnbroker in the course of robbing him with her pimp, but we learn about
her difficult past: she has had to fend for herself from the age of ten, when
her father murdered her mother in a fit of jealousy and was sentenced to

a penal colony. Lise's lack of moral restraint can be attributed to parental failure, and she is, we are led to believe, good at heart; her father's action, now, in taking the blame for her crime is portrayed as a noble gesture.

The Gold Digger, on the other hand, is simply venal. Mary Magdalene (Jacqueline Logan) in *The King of Kings* (USA, 1927) provides something of a model: she is a whore, it would seem, for the sensual pleasures the profession offers (silks and perfumes) and for what it can buy her in terms of material goods and power (personal slave, charioteer, and the like). That this is a form of corruption in the film's terms is amply evident in the scene of the casting out of the seven deadly sins, among which Greed is prominent, and from Mary's subsequent adoption of modest dress and renunciation of finery in adornment, hair styling, and makeup. Her life is, of course, turned around by personal contact with Jesus; later Gold Diggers, without such fortune, are much less likely to reform.

Myra Madden (Loretta Sayers) in *Fifty Fathoms Deep* (USA, 1931), for example, is a choice specimen. She marries a deep-sea diver, Pinky, without letting him know that she is a waterfront prostitute, and secures control of his bank account. Then, when he is away on a job, she "absconds with the money and returns to her old life." She gets involved with Pinky's friend Tim, who spends all his back pay on her, and then leaves him for Brewster, a millionaire. When Pinky returns, Myra causes trouble between the friends by telling her husband that Tim assaulted her, but she is prevented from further mischief-making by being drowned when Brewster's yacht is wrecked.[5]

A love of money above all else is the most common defining characteristic of the Gold Digger. Mae in *Gambling with Souls/Vice Racket* (USA, 1936) is living "frugally, but happily" with her husband until she "becomes addicted to gambling and expensive living." She abandons him and becomes one of the women on offer in a vice ring.[6] The escort girl/cabaret singer who is the protagonist of *Yuye gesheng/Song on a Rainy Night* (Hong Kong, 1950) is "a woman who cannot resist the materialistic life."[7] The rejected mistress of a member of parliament, in *Ratai/The Body* (Japan, 1962), "aspiring to a life of luxury, and well aware of her physical attractiveness to both men and women," becomes a prostitute.[8] In *The Hot Pearl Snatch* (USA, 1966), an old sailor acquires a map "marking the most valuable pearl oyster bed in the Caribbean," and "all those who hear the sailor's tale become dominated by greed . . . women offer their bodies in return for a share of the treasure."[9]

Often it is a young woman contemplating her options for whom the temptations of the luxurious life prove irresistible. Myrsini in *Ta kokkina phanaria/Red Lanterns* (Greece, 1963), the newest inmate of a brothel in Piraeus, "loves the lustful life of prostitution and its financial rewards" and determines to carry on clandestinely after the government closes down the red-light district.[10] Teenager Amy in *Marked for Love* (USA, 1967) "enjoys the money and the favors older men bestow upon her."[11] In *Trackdown* (USA, 1976), teen runaway Betsy, told by the organizer of a Los Angeles call-girl operation "I need girls with your kind of looks, if they've got the brains and ambition to cash in on their assets," is sufficiently excited by the sight of a luxury penthouse and the prospect of earning $500 for a night of sex to put the rape she's already been subjected to out of her mind. Similarly, Julie in *Beverly Hills Madam* (USA, 1986) hitchhikes into town, is picked up and accommodated in grand style by the madam of a Beverly Hills high-class call-girl operation, and is easily seduced into the life by the visible evidence of its rewards: jewels, fur coats, limousines. . . .

Imagery frequently associates the Gold Digger with money. In *Ikiru/To Live* (Japan, 1952), the charge by the writer who is showing his friend a night on the town that "these girls are the most avaricious among existing mammals" is later supported by a shot of a prostitute in their car counting out a wad of cash, while her colleague applies lipstick and tears off her false eyelashes. Similarly, *Akasen chitai/Street of Shame* (Japan, 1956) contains a shot of the gold-digging prostitute Yasumi counting out the large sum of money she has received under false pretenses from a suitor. In more comic vein, one of the sketches ("Roman Nights") in *Le Plus Vieux Métier du monde/L'amore attraverso i secoli/Das älteste Gewerbe/The Oldest Profession* (France/Italy/West Germany, 1967) shows Flavius Caesar's wife Domitilla claiming that her appearance, disguised, at a brothel was purely to revive the emperor's flagging interest in her; however when he pulls off her toga, a number of gold coins fall to the floor. Annie in *Money on the Side* (USA, 1982) is, pathetically, a clandestine Gold Digger: after she has hung herself, husband Jack discovers a white fur coat hidden away in the closet, along with rolls of paper money that he spills out over the bed. "Why didn't she spend it?" he wonders, desolate. "How many guys is all this money?"

An exception to the essentialist characterization of the Gold Digger occurs when her mercenary motives are attributed to corruption by foreign influences. Thus in *Ch'il-su wa Man-su/Chilsu and Mansu* (South Korea, 1988), Chilsu's sister becomes a prostitute for American soldiers and then goes off to the United States, "contaminated by American cultural imperialism."[12] *Interdevochka/Intergirl* (USSR/Sweden, 1989) shows a Leningrad hard-currency hooker "attracted to life in the fast lane, which includes pop fashion and material goods,"[13] who succeeds in pulling off an advantageous marriage with a well-off Swedish business-man, enabling her to escape the USSR. In the female-directed *Saikati* (Kenya, 1992), Monica (Susan Wanjiku) is a young Nairobi woman whose values have been distorted by the experience of becoming a pros-titute catering to an expatriate European clientele: she leaves the up-bringing of her infant daughter to others; she has been less than frank in enticing her cousin Saikati to come to the city from her village; and she is clearly after a good time at the expense of care and concern for Saikati. The alienation entailed in forgoing African dress, customs and relation-ships for European style and European men — something that Saikati is in the end unwilling to do — is an obvious, but unspoken subtext.

The acquisition of money may also mean a shift in the established balance of power in gender relationships and the opportunity to achieve upward social mobility. In *Mandalay* (USA, 1934), Tanya, a Russian refu-gee in Rangoon, "uses sex to gain power."[14] In *La mujer sin alma / The Woman Without a Soul* (Mexico, 1944), "The beautiful Teresa . . . seduces her way up the social ladder. . . ."[15] *The Oldest Profession* offers another ex-ample, in comic mode: in "The Gay Nineties" Nini, discovering that the elderly man she has picked up is a banker, refuses his money and succeeds in convincing him that she is a respectable woman, finally going to the altar with him. If the Gold Digger is able to lever her desirability in this way to her personal advantage, she represents a disturbing threat to male prerogative, frequently inviting narrative punishment, as we discover in chapter 19. Moreover, as Lea Jacobs has demonstrated in relation to American films of the Depression era, the figure of a woman "calculat-ing and exploitative in her relations with men, [who] is also sexually knowing, aggressive, and unashamed" is highly likely to provoke sup-pression by means of whatever censorship mechanisms are available.[16]

The Gold Digger's greed is usually associated with other moral fail-ings, and often with criminality. Like Monica in *Saikati*, for example, she is likely to be a poor mother. A classic exposition of this motif is contained in *La Maternelle* (France, 1933), in which the girl Marie, neglected and pe-riodically abandoned by her streetwalker mother (Sylvette Fillacier), at-tempts suicide. In the 1949 remake, the woman is given an opportunity to tell her life story, which includes abusive treatment in correctional in-stitutions: thus her neglect of her daughter, while no less morally repre-hensible, is given a sociological and biographical context. The blowzy prostitute Rose-Ann (Shelley Winters) in *A Patch of Blue* (USA, 1965) keeps her eighteen-year-old daughter — whom she accidentally blinded when throwing a bottle at her husband some years before — cooped up in their apartment as an uneducated menial drudge, raped on one occasion by one of her customers. Another exemplar of maternal failing is Ginger (Sharon Stone), queen of the Las Vegas hustlers in *Casino* (USA, 1995), who in refusing to have her wings clipped by motherhood ties her daughter up in bed and locks her in her room.

Criminalized, generally, by the very act of exercising her profession, the Gold Digger shows little compunction about engaging in other forms of criminal conduct. As early as 1899 in *Tenderloin at Night,* she is shown stealing from a barroom customer (see chapter 1). Sade in *Lady in a Cage* (USA, 1964) plans to loot the mansion of the wealthy woman trapped in her elevator, although things go awry. Melanie in *The Banker* (USA, 1989) finds a thousand-dollar bill serving as a book mark at her client's apartment and tucks it down her front. The call girls in *Dutch / Driving Me Crazy* (USA, 1991) extricate the wallet of the hitchhiker they pick up while he's asleep and later drive off with his bag. Double-crossing their gangland confederates and making off with the loot is the name of the game for the lesbian hooker and her lover in *Lisa's Folly* (USA, 1970) and *Bound* (USA, 1996) — though in these cases, since the action is all contained within the criminal milieu, their larcenous behavior does not attract the moral opprobrium that might otherwise accrue.

The Gold Digger goes in for swindling in *Sailor's Holiday* (USA, 1929) — telling gullible sailors that she is looking for her long-lost brother — and fleecing men on a Mississippi steamboat in *Bed of Roses* (USA, 1933).[17] She develops a line in blackmail in *Madeleine Tel. 13 62 11 / Naked in the Night* (West Germany, 1958) — the enterprising young prostitute sets up a hidden camera to photograph herself with her clients — and also, for example, in *Chair de poule / Highway Pickup* (France / Italy, 1963), *Sensation / The Seducers* (Italy, 1968), *Sale destin* (France, 1987), and *Liste noire / Black List* (Canada, 1995). Vicky in *High / In* (Canada, 1968) dabbles in credit card fraud, while the racket of the hookers in *Sweet Trash* (USA, 1970) is loan-sharking. Tralala in *Letzte Ausfahrt Brooklyn / Last Exit to Brooklyn* (West Germany / USA, 1989) is in league with a male gang to beat up and rob her customers.

The Gold Digger's unscrupulous criminality escalates to murder in, for example, *Highway Pickup* and *O Dragão da Maldade contra o Santo Guerreiro / António das Mortes* (Brazil / France, 1969), discussed later in chapter 19. In *Mandalay*, Tanya (Kay Francis) poisons her former lover — who has been causing her trouble — on board ship, and he falls over the side to his

death; similarly Violet (Jennifer Tilly) in *Bound* pumps her gangster boyfriend full of bullets. In the melodramatic narrative of *Setenta veces siete/
The Female: Seventy Times Seven* (Argentina, 1962), the woman (Isabel Sarli)
who is now a prostitute in a decrepit brothel recalls the traumatic moment in her past when, unable to choose between a sheepherder and a
horse thief, she leaves them both in a well to die; Sarli also stars in *Intimidades de una prostituta/Sex is the Name of the Game* (Argentina, ca. 1973) as a
hooker who, caught in the act of robbing a client, shoots him dead. In
Shanty Tramp (USA, 1966), the promiscuous sharecropper's daughter (Lee
Holland) carves out a trail of destruction in her southern town, including
stabbing her alcoholic father to death. Perhaps most representative of
such homicidal tendencies is Vicky (Astri Thorvik) in *High* who, annoyed
by the attitude adopted by a client ("You lousy bastard! Just because you
drive a big car and have a fat wallet you think you can push people
around") bludgeons him to death with a metal bar — and then, laughing
hysterically, props his body against a tree, dances through the grass with
her boyfriend, strips naked, and makes love.

Vicky ditches her boyfriend before the film is through, and it is in her
interaction with a male partner — especially when he is an empathetic
figure for the audience — that the Gold Digger's corrupt nature is painted
in blackest colors. She is portrayed, variously, as untrustworthy, dishonest, heartless, treacherous, incapable of fidelity. Inverting the terms of the
Love Story, the prostitute in this incarnation is seen as immutably hardened by her profession and hence an unsuitable person on whom to lavish one's affection.

   Much of the male anxiety that underlies this representation may well
derive from the prostitute's status in real life as an actor, a performer. It
is a feature of her profession to simulate, to counterfeit, whether the
cruder pleasures of intercourse (fake orgasm) or the subtler attention,
concern, tenderness she may seem to offer her client. So long as the lines
are clearly drawn, this causes no problem; it is, implicitly, a mutually
agreed form of playacting. But should a relationship with a prostitute
evolve into something more, or on the other hand, should the woman
whom the man thinks respectable turn out to be, or have been, a prostitute, there is ambiguity and the potential for emotional confusion. With
the hooker, whose show of excitement or affection he is well aware is
feigned, the man knows where he is; but with a lover, whose gestures pur-
port to be genuine but may not be so, he can never be sure.
   En cas de malheur/Love is My Profession (France/Italy, 1958) is a case in

point. Well-to-do lawyer Gobillot falls in love with the pert young hooker
Yvette (Brigitte Bardot) whom he has defended on a robbery charge. She
apparently reciprocates the affection — her face is all softness and gentleness when they embrace, and she tells him how much she enjoys their
lovemaking — and he sets her up in an apartment. Meanwhile, however,
she continues to see her boyfriend Mazetti, a medical student, and she
may also still be practicing her profession. Neither man, aware of the
other's existence, knows quite where he stands. Yvette is the deceptive
female, the woman who, because she cannot be trusted and resists as-
signment to one or other of the categories allotted to her by patriarchy —
one man's woman (wife, mistress), every man's woman (whore) — must
be destroyed. It turns out to be Mazetti who slits her throat.

In registering disillusionment with the prostitute as love object, the
Gold Digger archetype in the cinema indicts the alluring female for failure to conform to the ideal her male partner has formed of her. It is no
coincidence, given the nature of prostitution as a trade in appearances,
that much of what in the male mind is unacceptable behavior relates to
a perceived lack of genuineness, of truthfulness.

Who's Your Neighbor? (USA, 1917) takes up an aspect of this concern.
With the closure of red-light districts across the United States, prostitutes
are setting up shop in formerly respectable neighborhoods. Hattie Fen-
shaw (Christine Mayo), compelled to seek her livelihood "in the better
residential section of the city," meets Dudley Carlton and "through her
feminine wiles, convinces him to abandon his sweetheart." Her dissimu-
lation creates havoc in Dudley's life, while she is also successful in gaining the confidence of a "pillar of the church" who later, "rudely awak-
ened . . . learns the value of segregating houses of prostitution from the
rest of the community."[18]

Deception of a different stripe is dissected in Kenji Mizoguchi's *Street
of Shame*, which contrasts five prostitutes belonging to a brothel in Yoshi-
wara, the pleasure district of Tokyo. One of them, Yasumi (Ayako
Wakao), is motivated solely by the desire to make money in order to be
able to set herself up in business and is willing to be ruthlessly manipulative to achieve this end. She lies to an admirer, letting him understand
that if he finds 150,000 yen to clear her debts — and later another 100,000
yen, to pay hospital bills — she will marry him. The man embezzles the
money from his place of work and is plunged into desperation when Yasumi informs him that the marriage is off: "I may sell my body, but my
life's not for sale." He attacks her, but she is not badly injured; before long
she is the proud proprietor of a linen shop.

30. Yvette (Brigitte Bardot) with Gobillot (Jean Gabin) in *En cas de malheur.*

In *Tumult/Relations* (Denmark, 1969), affluent middle-aged business-man J. P., "frustrated by his wife's frigidity," succumbs to the sexual prop-osition of a promiscuous sixteen-year-old, Sonja (Gertie Jung). A rela-tionship commences, "but J. P. gradually realizes that he is being lied to and degraded," discovering that Sonja is under the sway of her pimp who has engineered the affair to extract money from him. "For a brief mo-ment it seems that Sonja's feelings for J. P. are strong enough for her to break with the pimp," but she does not do so.[19]

In a similar tale, *Sale destin* depicts a luscious young hooker, Rache (Pauline Lafont) swearing to the married, middle-aged butcher, François Narboni, who is crazy about her, that "there's no one apart from us two," while meanwhile involved in a plot with her pimp to blackmail him. An integral part of a sleazy milieu, she is not to be trusted one centimeter, and she certainly has no genuine emotion for François: we see her finally at a Martinique resort hotel with another client, while the double-crossed butcher, unable to disentangle himself from the underworld characters he has hired to deal to the blackmailers, is blown up in his car.

Angela (Debra Winger) in *Everybody Wins* (USA, 1990) is a highly un-usual combination of the archetypal opposites Martyr and Gold Digger, which makes her a double-whammy enigma. She exhibits the classic Martyr's attitude of endurance toward the violence inflicted on her body and has self-sacrificial traits, but all she's really after, her lover Tom finally discovers, is money and status. A private investigator in an indus-trial town in Connecticut, Tom is hired by Angela to get to the bottom of a case she has an interest in. As he becomes romantically involved, he finds her changeable, erratic, mysterious, untrustworthy, but with a mag-netic charge that draws every man within her ambit into her power. Tricky and manipulative, she uses Tom to maneuver her out of an awk-ward situation, plays on his attraction for her without developing any real affection for him, and forms a liaison at the end with the judge, as she had previously with the doctor and the state's attorney. Tom is left out in the cold.

The discovery that his affection is not returned, that it has all been a con game and that he is merely a client after all, is a devastating moment for the Gold Digger's lover. In Jean Renoir's *La Chienne* (France, 1931), middle-aged cashier — and Sunday painter — Maurice (Michel Simon) is abruptly brought to the realization that Lulu (Janie Marèze), the beauti-ful young streetwalker he is in love with, has stayed with him not on his own account but for his artwork, which she is able to sell at a tidy profit. "What'd you expect?" she asks, inviting her unprepossessing admirer to take a look in the mirror. "What a fool I was," he says, "You make me sick." Lulu is caustic. "You think it didn't make me sick? If it wasn't for your money, I'd have dropped you like a hot potato. You wanted to be loved for your own sweet self. What a laugh!"

A comparable reckoning awaits the handicapped artist Henri de Toulouse-Lautrec (José Ferrer) in *Moulin Rouge* (UK, 1952). Having fallen in love and become obsessed with a woman of the streets, Marie Charlet (Colette Marchand), he seeks her out in a dingy tavern in a slum area of Paris. No matter that she once assured him that she didn't care about his legs and that she reciprocated his love — "I'm all yours, for as long as you want me" — now she introduces him to her pimp as "my rich cripple from Montmartre" and scornfully asks, "Why do you think I stayed with you one night even? For love of your ugly face?" There is not the slightest trace of affection in her expression as she continues: "You made me sick when you touched me. I'd never have come back, except for Babare, to keep him in silk shirts and pomade."

Much the same is in store for Philip Carey, the protagonist of *Of Human Bondage* (USA, 1934, 1946; UK, 1964), based on the novel by W. Somerset Maugham. This is particularly so in the 1964 version, in which the development of the character of Cockney waitress Mildred Rogers (Kim Novak) as a prostitute is the strongest. "You ought to take a look at yourself," she tells the clubfooted Carey (Laurence Harvey), who has become besotted with her. "I used to feel sick when I let you kiss me. . . . We laughed at you, Miller and me, and Griffiths and me, especially. . . . I used to say, wouldn't the cripple like to be here kissing me now! That's all you are. Just a cripple!" In her gaze, there is a hint of supplication, a plea perhaps for him not to believe her, but it is of no avail . . . she will shortly die of syphilis.

The emotional dynamics of *Moulin Rouge* and *Of Human Bondage* are very similar. Carey, too, is a painter — though not of Lautrec's stature! — and both men are highly self-conscious about their physical disability. It is perhaps his lowered self-esteem, and the associated masochism, that prevents the tortured protagonist from loving the woman of his own class — the cultured model Myriamme in *Moulin Rouge*, the novelist Norah in *Of Human Bondage* — who genuinely desires him.

Rache of *Sale destin* betrays her lover for her pimp, as does Lulu of *La Chienne* and Marie of *Moulin Rouge*. The Gold Digger's other treacherous specialty is to work as a prostitute without her husband's knowledge. This is what Eve in *Today* does, and Myra in *Fifty Fathoms Deep*, Domitilla in *The Oldest Profession*, and Annie in *Money on the Side*. In *Women of Desire*

31. Cécile Aubry in *Manon*. Stills Collection, New Zealand Film Archive.

(USA, 1968), Pat has racetrack gambling losses and succumbs to the enticement of the easy money to be made working as a hooker out of a motel; her husband, meanwhile, believes she has a job as a nurse. But perhaps the most biting exploration of the theme is in *Manon* (France, 1949), an updated adaptation of *Manon Lescaut*.

Robert and Manon (a sixteen-year-old Cécile Aubry) meet at the end of the war: he is an activist in the Resistance, she a suspected collaborator whom he rescues from an angry crowd. They fall in love and go to Paris, where Manon's brother Léon is active in black-market profiteering. Work is hard to come by, and prices high; Robert suggests they go to the provinces to live, but Manon is much too taken by the gay life of the capital to countenance the idea. They stay, and Robert becomes a courier for one of Léon's dubious schemes while Manon gets work as a fashion model. Intrigued by the dresses and jewelry Manon seems able to afford on her salary, Robert gets one of her rings valued and finds that it is worth a considerable sum. Checking at her fashion house, he discovers that she left two months ago; he then follows her to the upscale brothel where she is working and confronts her.

Unlike Eve in *Today,* Manon is apologetic rather than defiant. She sobs, speaks of her unhappiness. Robert, declaring he's leaving her, spits out his contempt. When she taunts him ("always the hero!") he throttles her, and then, releasing his grip, rests his head on her breast and pleads for forgiveness. Manon grants it, stroking his hair. Asked for her reasons ("You weren't happy at home?") she responds simply, "I detest poverty — it was too strong for me." There is no mistaking where Manon's priorities lie, and whatever her love for Robert — and it is certainly more genuine than that of many another Gold Digger — it will always take second place.

The couple are reconciled; but, typically, Manon is not capable of fidelity for long. A compulsive promiscuity is a feature of many Gold Digger characterizations, even when she is nominally attached to one man. Thus Mildred in *Of Human Bondage* defies Philip with a series of affairs and becomes a prostitute, and Marie in *Moulin Rouge* reverts to her life on the streets. Mob kingpin Sam Rothstein in *Casino* is confident he can convert Ginger from her fast lifestyle when he marries her, but he's wrong. With Manon, it's a case of falling for the American officer who has been instrumental in helping them set up a penicillin racket. He asked me to marry him, she tells Robert, who laughs. I've accepted, she continues — he's got dollars.

By this stage Robert, former man of integrity, fighter against the Nazis in the Maquis ("I was pure," he recalls) has become significantly corrupted by his contact with the unprincipled Manon. This, too, is a theme that recurs in Gold Digger stories, the negative influence that the degraded woman may exert on the man who falls in love with her.

The effect may be confined to a self-destructive demoralization, as in *Moulin Rouge,* in which Toulouse-Lautrec, embittered by his experience with Marie ("she opened doors for me that might better have remained closed"), becomes a hopeless alcoholic. Frequently, however, the Gold Digger's lover is drawn into criminality and its consequences.

In *La Chienne,* for example, Maurice embezzles from his employer in order to set Lulu up in an apartment. Angered by her admission that she was only after his money, he then stabs her to death — and allows her pimp to be convicted and executed for the crime. At the end, this formerly upright member of society has been reduced to a down-and-out tramp. In *Mr. Broadway* (USA, 1933), waterfront worker Bob is urged by the hooker Daisey (Dita Parlo), with whom he has started a relationship, to get his hands on the valuable necklace that his old pal Sam has found—"they could get away and start over in a new place."[20] Bob confronts Sam and kills him—only to return to Daisey to find her pleasurably entertaining another man. When she lies about it and then says "What of it?", he commits suicide.

As has been mentioned, Yasumi's lover in *Street of Shame*, like Maurice in *La Chienne*, steals money from his employer. In *Carmen, Baby* (Netherlands/USA, 1967), a version of the Prosper Mérimée story and Bizet opera, the young policeman seduced by waitress/prostitute Carmen (Uta Levka) kills his superior when he finds him with her. He then gets involved with her in smuggling and blackmailing tourists, commits another murder out of jealousy, and finally stabs Carmen to death. Tom in *High* is already a petty criminal at the time he meets Vicky, but the scale of his offending escalates as he teams up with her on a search for kicks, culminating in his being accessory to murder. *Sweet Trash* encapsulates the theme: "Honest dockworker Michael Donovan is drawn into the loan shark racket by a group of Manhattan prostitutes and 'businessmen' who easily corrupt the susceptible man. Donovan proves unable to adjust to his new role as a loan shark out to cheat his friends and co-workers, and he becomes a helpless alcoholic."[21]

In *Manon*, Robert gets into a fight with his tricky sweetheart over the American officer she wishes to marry. Her brother intervenes, locking Robert up in order to allow Manon to get away and goading him about his inadequacies in providing for her expensive tastes. Robert strangles him.

Both *Manon* and *Carmen, Baby* engage in cynical rewriting of a classic melodrama in order to strip it of its romantic trappings. This deromanticization becomes a systematic project in *La dama delle camelie/The True Story of Camille* (Italy/France/West Germany, 1981), whose object is to retell, one more time, the story of *La Dame aux camélias* by offering an allegedly authentic biographical account[22] of the woman, Alphonsine Plessis, who was the inspiration for Dumas's heroine.

The idea was not new. In *Figures of Ill Repute*, Charles Bernheimer points out that even in the 1850s, "rival dramatists made a point of critically updating Dumas's portrayals by offering what they claimed to be more realistic depictions of the vicious world of *galanterie.*" He cites *Les Filles de marbre* by Barrière and Thiboust, produced a year after *La Dame aux camélias*, which "features a venal heroine, calculating and avaricious, who drives her lover to suicide" and Emile Augier's *Le Mariage d'Olympe*, produced a year after Dumas's *Le Demi-monde* of 1854, which "desentimentalizes Dumas's portrait of the *cocotte* by showing her to be motivated by heartless, mercenary ambition."[23]

The True Story of Camille takes a similar line. Although, in scenes showing Alphonsine's early life in the country, her father is presented as a pill-addicted panderer who sells her to a neighbor for the pleasures he derives, apparently, from making her undress, she is depicted less as a victim than as the author of her own fall from virtue. Thus when reporting her situation to a priest, she seduces him by persuading him to read from the *Song of Songs* and then stretching out on the sofa, exposing her thighs. In Paris, where she flees after the priest's suicide, she quickly makes the transition from seamstress to theater-based prostitute, known for her salacious ways. On one occasion she descends her lover's staircase, naked, observed by many of his friends — "Since I'll end up in their beds," she declares, "it's only right." Greedy and unscrupulous, she makes her way up the social scale, being married at one point to Count Perregaux, and causing Count Stackelberg to sell land and forests in order to accommodate her demands. While in Dumas's play, which we see being rehearsed at the start of the film, Marguerite Gautier remains pure at heart, Alphonsine easily adapts to the decadence of her wealthy circle. As the heroine, Isabelle Huppert is a skinny young thing, attractive but without voluptuousness or magnetism: no Garbo she, which is no doubt connected to the film's deromanticizing project.

The part of the young lover, Armand Duval in the play, is here taken by the writer Dumas fils himself. But far from the reciprocated passion of his imagination, Alphonsine's devotion to him is strictly circumscribed by monetary concerns. When he confesses his love, she tells him bluntly that she is a whore who spends 100,000 francs a year — Dumas père explains to him that the top Paris courtesans require three or four patrons to keep them in style — and that she wants a lover "without rights — I like the hellish life I lead."

The True Story of Camille succeeds in convincing us that the idea that there was something noble about the woman known to posterity as Camille is merely a romantic fiction. Like the other idealized love objects discussed in this chapter, she turns out on closer inspection to be merely a Gold Digger.

The Gold Digger narrative has three possible outcomes. The woman may emerge from her dubious dealings triumphant and scot free; she may see the error of her ways and reform; or she may be punished, very often by death.

The triumphant Gold Digger is epitomized here by Yasumi in *Street of Shame*, Vicky in *High*, Rache in *Sale destin*, and Angela in *Everybody Wins*. In *Intimidades de una prostituta*, Maria "is found not guilty of the murder of her client because he actually died of a heart attack." She goes on to marry a handsome, wealthy man with an idyllic country estate. Her former pimp and criminal accomplice returns from time to time to cause trouble, but he fortunately falls to an accidental death.[24] In *Scandal*, Mandy's victory is reserved for the end titles: while Christine Keeler, we are told, was accused of perjury and sent to prison, "Mandy Rice-Davies became a cabaret singer, left the country, and opened a string of successful nightspots in Israel. They were called Mandy's." The message for men in the audience is clear: there are unprincipled, mercenary women out there, on the loose — watch out!

The model for the repentant Gold Digger is of course provided by Mary Magdalene in *The King of Kings;* she is also represented by the Eve of *Today* who wakes from her nightmare to a horrified realization of her sinful desires. *Beverly Hills Madam* offers a more modern, secular variant of seeing the light. Julie (Terry Farrell), the naive debutante in the call-girl business, gets flown by Lear jet to Acapulco and then taken out to a yacht to initiate the eighteen-year-old scion of a wealthy family into sex. She is successful — so successful that she believes Justin has fallen in love and wants to marry her, a delusion of which she is quickly disabused ("Look, I don't know what kind of game you're trying to pull, but my son doesn't date whores"). Informing Lil, the madam, of her decision to quit, Julie asks "How can I make love to a man for four days and come away with nothing?" Lil points to the $25,000 she has earned — "I don't call that nothing." "I mean nothing inside," Julie replies, "I feel like I don't exist." Lil says she'll toughen up, but Julie is unmoved. "No, it's too big a price. For what? So I can wear fancy clothes and ride around in a limousine? Go on fancy yachts? . . . I'd rather be a waitress, or a farmer, or even a street hooker. At least they don't pretend to fall in love with you."

Julie gets out while the going's good. Many another of her kind is not so lucky. Gold Diggers to incur severe retribution for their crimes include, preeminently, Eve in *Today* (if it's not a nightmare), Lulu in *La Chienne*, Yvette in *Love is My Profession*, and Carmen in *Carmen, Baby*, all killed by a husband or lover; Betsy in *Trackdown* and Melanie in *The Banker*, killed by a client; and Maria in *Highway Pickup* and Ginger in *Casino*, killed by an associate in her criminal milieu. The guilty woman may also succumb to accidental death (*Fifty Fathoms Deep*, *Women of Desire*, *Antônio das Mortes*,

Intergirl), illness (*Of Human Bondage, The True Story of Camille*), or suicide (*Money on the Side*). Spared death, Tralala in *Last Exit to Brooklyn* receives a different form of punishment. The woman who is a cheat and a thief, whose one ambition seems to be to obtain money by any means open to her, who provocatively flaunts her sexuality, is in the end gang-raped by a platoon of drunken servicemen and workers until she is bleeding and senseless.

In *Manon*, after murdering Léon, Robert escapes on a train to Marseilles — and Manon, with a change of heart, joins him. The couple stow away on a ship carrying illegal Jewish immigrants to Palestine, and though they are discovered on board, the captain, having heard their story, allows them to go ashore with the other passengers. As they are trekking through the desert, the refugees are attacked by Arabs, and Manon is shot. Dying, she clutches Robert in an agonizing embrace, declaring "Nothing can ruin our love now," and then falls back with blood seeping from her mouth. There follows what must be the most excruciatingly drawn-out ending in the history of cinema. Deciding that she should be buried by the water's edge, Robert hauls the body over rocks and sand dunes and through cactus until he finally collapses, exhausted. Then, covering her with sand but for her face, he hears her voice: "I am your wife." He lays his head alongside hers and, sobbing, assures Manon he will not leave her. The audience is given ample time to contemplate the gruesome fate of the Gold Digger who pledges true allegiance but is always ready to prostitute herself for a little more of the good life, and of the man who is fool enough to believe her, and forgive her.

Mizoguchi paved the way for a possible feminist reexamination of the Gold Digger archetype with *Gion no shimai/Sisters of the Gion* (Japan, 1936). Omocha (Isuzu Yamada), rejecting the notion of *giri* or social obligation to which her elder sister Umekichi adheres ("Has that society ever treated us like human beings?"), contends that men who come to the geisha district "use their money to make playthings out of us." Since the clients are "hateful enemies," she is quite prepared to lie and manipulate, to "make them pay and pay." Using her wiles to procure a luxury kimono from Kimura, the clerk at a dry goods store, she immediately drops him in favor of his boss. Kimura, who is fired and bitterly resentful, attacks and injures her, and Umekichi suggests that this should be a lesson to her: "Don't trample on people's feelings." Omocha repudiates the idea: "Doing like you say simply means being defeated by men." In a final, passionate outburst emphasized by a track in to medium close-up, Omocha implies that acquisitive behavior is only a logical response to the gendered injustice of prostitution: "If we're sharp in business, we're criticized. What are we going to do? What do they want us to do? Why must we suffer so? Why are there such things as geishas in this world? Must they exist? It's wrong. Entirely wrong."

In the Communist China of *Hong fen/Blush* (China/Hong Kong, 1994), Omocha's plaint has been heeded: prostitution has been abolished. But in the early years of the new regime, old habits die hard. Li Shaohong offers a portrait of two women from the Red Happiness Inn whose lives are thrown into turmoil by the closure of the brothels and who do not adapt easily to the demands of the revolution. Her film indicts Qiu Yi (Wang Ji) and Xiao E (He Saifei) for indolence and greed — something of the idea of their being symbols of the old society sticks to them indelibly — but exposes what lies behind the negative Gold Digger archetype: insecurity, intensified now that the women are deprived of the only way they know to make a living.

In the case of Qiu Yi, who escapes compulsory rehabilitation and goes to live with a former client, Lao Pu, the precariousness of her situation is given prominence. Although he is passionately attached to her, Lao Pu is forced to accede to his mother's wishes and ask her to leave when family members, having had their land taken, arrive from the countryside. At his suggestion of installing her in a "love nest," Qiu Yi throws a tantrum, demanding money from him. "Just pay up! I've slept with you every night. You didn't think it was free, did you?" He hands over a wad of bills, but she tears them up, saying, "Have I ever asked you for money?" The contradiction is graphic evidence of the bind she is in: genuinely in love with him, later confirmed by a voice-over narration, but totally lacking financial independence.

For Xiao E, put to work in a factory and hating it, marriage is an escape route. With Qiu Yi gone to live in a Buddhist convent, Lao Pu is available, and before long Xiao E is pregnant and the two are married. They quarrel: Xiao E is disappointed that he can't provide the comfortable lifestyle she had expected — never mind that Lao Pu has given her plenty of advance warning. After the birth, she expects to be waited on hand and foot. While little sympathy is extended toward her, her background is not forgotten: she was born at the Red Happiness Inn, "born to be a whore." But one line of dialogue, again pointing to insecurity and lack of economic independence, is particularly telling. "You're a man," she tells Lao Pu. "It's your duty to support me. In the past, I could have supported you. I wouldn't have had to care what you thought."

Sisters of the Gion and *Blush* displace the locus of guilt for the Gold Digger's money hunger from the prostitute herself to the inequitable, male-dominated society that has created her profession. In doing so they issue a disturbing challenge to the man who would condemn her: the root of evil may not lie, as he would have it, in the brazen sexual female, but somewhat closer to home.

9

Nursemaid

I'm like a mother to 'em. Only they can't fuck their mother, so they
come here.
—prostitute in *The Missionary* (UK, 1982)

By the poolside at a desert motel, an attractive hooker spills Scotch down
her front, tugging at her bathing suit so her breasts are exposed, allowing
the liquid to flow onto her nipples, inviting her alcoholic lover to lick it
off. Liquor as milk, the prostitute as bounteous mother, dependency as
the oceanic bliss of infancy, *Leaving Las Vegas* (USA, 1995) offers a particular vision of the archetypal figure that I have termed the "Nursemaid."

For Ben Sanderson, ex-successful Hollywood script agent, divorced,
deliberately drinking himself to death in Las Vegas, Sera (Elisabeth
Shue) accompanying him on his final existential journey is a dream
come true. "What are you, some sort of angel visiting me from one of my
drunk fantasies?" he asks, at one stage. He has even imagined, earlier, a
scene in which he pours out his fantasized fusion of liquor and sex in addressing a female bank teller: "If you spread your legs and you had bour-
bon dripping from your breasts and your pussy, and said 'Drink here,'
then I could fall in love with you. . . ."

Sera has it rough, cut up and beaten by her pimp, battered and raped
by her clients, but she is not in the least psychologically damaged, just
lonely ("The only thing I have to come home to is a bottle of mouthwash,
to take the taste of cum out of my mouth"). She has a fund of affection
waiting to flood out onto the first trick she has ever felt anything for; she
snuggles up to him, hugs him. Despite his misgivings ("I'm not much
good in the sack, Sera," "I knock things over, I throw up all the time"),
she will invite him to come and live with her. Her blonde beauty enhanced by soft golden light, the mood intensified by the romantic lyrics
of the soundtrack ("The touch of your hand is like heaven"), she will declare her love for him. When he is flaked out at her gate, when he goes

167

berserk in the casino, when he smashes a glass table at the motel, she will come to his aid; when he gets his nose bashed, she will sponge off the blood. Marginalized herself, she is the fitting partner for the man who is on the downward slide. At the end, she tells her unseen interlocutor, "I accepted him for whoever he was, and I didn't expect him to change."

There are a handful of films that position the prostitute as nurturer to another female character. In *This Woman* (USA, 1924), for example, a poverty-stricken woman is prevented from committing suicide by Rose, a streetwalker, who then buys her a meal in a "cafe of questionable reputation."[1] Maria, the protagonist of *La peccatrice* (Italy, 1940), tends her sick friend Anna in the brothel where they are both working; likewise Corrie in *The Reivers* (USA, 1969) looks after Hannah in their whorehouse in Memphis ("She nursed me through double pneumonia and she spoon-fed me tapioca for two solid weeks"). In *The Killing of Sister George* (USA, 1968), prostitute Betty Thaxter lends a sympathetic ear to George's tales of troubles, while in *Trois couleurs bleu / Three Colours Blue* (France/Switzerland/Poland, 1993), it is the friendship of a sex worker, Lucille, that brings the classical composer Julie back from the abyss when she is suicidal after the death of her husband and daughter.

But the small number of such films in comparison to the many that depict the nurtured character as a boy or man suggests that the Nurse-maid archetype is deeply entrenched in male fantasy fulfillment. The filmic representations may in fact compensate for what is lacking in real life.

If quick sexual relief is what most clients get from a prostitute, it's not necessarily what they want. Consider the complaints that come in: prostitutes are too cold, too mercenary. And the testimony of sex workers, who say that many of their customers are after companionship.[2] It would probably be true to say that clients, often, want to assuage a loneliness, want a contact that is both physical and nonphysical, want, in fact, a kind of love—love that is missing in their lives. The idealized prostitute of many of the films considered in this chapter is a figure who can offer this love—an understanding and nurturance miraculously combined with an erotic allure. Such a woman is without children, so that there is no competition for her mothering. She has no other commitments: for the time that he has paid for her, she is all his. And she is a mother with no authority over the person at her breast, unlike the real mother: she nurses him to just the extent that he wants and permits it, no more. He has no obligations to her; all his liabilities can be discharged by a cash payment. And there are no psychological bonds: no deep-rooted antagonisms complicate the affection that can flow between them, in this momentary utopia of a sexual transaction. In creating the Nursemaid, the impossible Oedipal dream fusion of lover and mother, male filmmakers are indulging a fantasy and raising a protest against the dehumanization of life.

Why a prostitute for this figure — why not any fantasized lover? Of course, many love stories posit just such an ideal combination of qualities in the object of desire. But the prostitute has particular characteristics that can be appealing. First of all, her generosity. She *gives* to men, many men; she is not a taker. The money, in this vision, is irrelevant; after all, one has to live. As a giver, she is not one to *possess*, as another woman might wish to possess her man. She is after neither a man's property nor his soul. And then, the time limit on the interaction with the prostitute has its appeal, too, to those who are daunted by the prospect of living happily ever after; even in those stories that move toward marriage, the relationship is still surrounded by an aura of bliss-for-the-moment that can henceforth be renewed indefinitely at will, but is free of the usual connotations of heterosexual pairing.

In the film narratives we are concerned with, it is not necessarily the prostitute-client relationship that is emphasized, since for male audiences there may be a certain discomfort in positing as a hero the man who has to resort to paying for his sexual gratification. There is, at times, an element of displacement, with an adult male character being absent, or the man encountering his prostitute lover in some capacity other than customer. Yet the nurturing qualities this mother-surrogate embodies remain constant, no matter on whom she lavishes them.

The Nursemaid can suckle infants and succor children. She can take care of a young man's sexual initiation and passage to maturity, and be on call thereafter as sexual counselor and therapist. She can supply shelter for the homeless or the man on the run, and nursing for the sick and wounded. She can help resolve a man's mental anguish or emotional problems, giving him courage. For the man who experiences a lack of love in his marriage, she can offer solace. She is often an agent of regeneration, helping the hero out of the depths of despair; and she can provide comfort to him in old age. Most important of all, perhaps, the Nursemaid can be the nurturer and muse of the creative artist, in whose dramatized figure, no doubt, the male filmmaker sees an image of himself.

"When Captain Lief Erickson finds a baby abandoned in a lifeboat on his ship," a plot synopsis of *Sal of Singapore* (USA, 1929) tells us, "he abducts a waterfront prostitute, Singapore Sal, to care for the child; despite her outrage, Sal takes pity on the little tyke and manufactures a bottle for him out of an empty whisky bottle and the finger of a rubber glove." Sal (Phyllis Haver) subsequently has to fight for the baby's life when he becomes ill. The experience makes her "suddenly ashamed of her old calling"; as for Erickson, he has no doubt seen in Sal an ideal fusion of desirable qualities, for he battles a rival captain and crew in order to win her as his bride.[3] In contrast, Maria (Paola Barbara) in *La peccatrice* becomes, literally, a nursemaid prior to taking up prostitution — her own illegitimate baby having died, she cares for sick and abandoned infants at a children's hospital and later takes fulltime charge of one on a farm — but because the film is structured on flashbacks from the brothel, the two images of the "sinful woman" tend to merge into one. A similar conjunction of images occurs in *Casa de mujeres* (Mexico, 1966), set at a brothel where the prostitutes are able to "fulfill their frustrated maternal longings" with a baby boy who miraculously appears on Christmas Eve.[4]

For the older boy, the Nursemaid will often function as substitute mother in the absence of his own. The teenagers in *Wild Boys of the Road* (USA, 1933) who leave home and take to living off their wits because their unemployed parents cannot support them receive, briefly, nurturance from a brothel madam. A gangster's young son in *Five Came Back* (USA, 1939), included among an odd assortment of characters who are forced to fend for themselves when their plane crashes in a Central American jungle, comes under the care of a streetwalker, Peggy — whose ministrations win her the respect of the pilot. The farm boy in *Terror in the City* (USA, 1966) runs away to New York, where after being beaten up by a gang "he is rescued by a prostitute, Suzy, who takes him home, washes his wounds, buys him clothes, and shows him the sights of Manhattan."[5]

Corrie (Sharon Farrell) of *The Reivers*, as well as caring for her fellow inmate at the brothel, takes eleven-year-old Lucius in hand. The boy, who is on an illicit trip to the city with the family's hired hand Boon, has gotten into a brawl with her nephew, who had called her a whore, and Corrie wipes away his tears, tends his injury, and gets him a glass of milk; at the end, Corrie and Boon will decide to marry ("You'll make a good nurse," says Lucius). *The Reivers* is set in 1905; a world and the best part of a century away, in the confusion of the Lebanese civil war, another boy is served with a glass of milk in a brothel. Here, in *West Beyrouth / West Beirut* (Lebanon/France, 1998), Tarek has strayed into the bordello by accident, and it is the amply figured madam (Leïla Karam) who looks after him and becomes an incipient maternal substitute: his own mother is too preoccupied with her professional life as a lawyer and too freaked out by the fighting to give him the mothering he craves. Significantly, the brothel is sited on neutral territory between the warring factions, an oasis of peace. An actual adoptive motherhood is the subject of *La Vie devant soi/Madame Rosa* (France, 1977), which dramatizes the relationship between Rosa (Simone Signoret), an aging former prostitute who cares for the children of streetwalkers, and Moma, one of her charges, whom she brings up as Muslim although she herself is Jewish.

The motif is persistent. In *Dutch/Driving Me Crazy* (USA, 1991) a call girl comforts twelve-year-old Doyle — whose mother has angered him by divorcing his father — and he finds temporary respite sleeping with his head resting on her breast; in *Milk Money* (USA, 1994) a beautiful hooker (Melanie Griffith) befriends the adolescent Frank, whose mother died in childbirth, and ends up fulfilling his yearning for a nurturing female in his life by falling in love with his father. But it is perhaps *Pixote: a Lei do mais Fraco/Pixote* (Brazil, 1981) that most vividly invokes the narrative configuration, only to cruelly dash the fond fantasy invested in it. Ten-year-old Pixote escapes from an oppressive reform school and with some older companions takes to the streets, getting mixed up in theft and drug dealing. The youths team up with a disenchanted prostitute, Sueli (Marília Pêra), who has just gone through a painful self-inflicted abortion. They scheme to rob her clients at gunpoint. On one occasion Pixote accidentally shoots his accomplice dead and then the customer; he is left in a state of shock alone with Sueli. When he abruptly vomits, she places her hand on his forehead, wipes his chin with her fingers, and embraces him. Then, in one remarkable three-minute take, she comforts him on the bed, hugging him to her breast, rocking and patting him like an infant, and offering him her nipple. "Baby suck it," she says, "Mummy's with you." He does so, gratefully; and then, as he shows no sign of letting up, she gets impatient. "Let go," she demands. "Let go, Pixote! I don't like it! Take your dirty mouth off me!" She shoves him away. "I'm not your mother!" she shouts. "Do you hear? I don't want a child! I hate children!" Sueli orders him out: for those on the margins in Brazil, *Pixote* suggests, there is precious little solace.

Asked by a psychologist at his reformatory if he has ever been to bed with a girl, young Antoine Doinel in François Truffaut's *Les 400 Coups/ The 400 Blows* (France, 1959) smiles playfully, says no, and then sheepishly recounts how he went one time to the Rue Saint-Denis, got bawled out by some of the women, and then waited in vain for a young prostitute who, he was told, would go with "young kids and all that." In the cinema this is one of the Nursemaid's important functions, to assist the youth emerging from adolescence to shed his virginity, and scenes in which this occurs may be both comic and touching.

Thus, in *The Dirty Girls* (USA, 1965), Parisian streetwalker Garance's first customer for the evening is "a shy young student whom she gently initiates into a world of sexual pleasure"[6]; in *The Learning Tree* (USA, 1969), sensitive teenager Newt Winger, injured in a tornado in his small Kansas town, is "rescued and initiated into sex by Big Mabel, the local whore."[7] Similarly, in *Le Souffle au coeur/Murmur of the Heart* (France/Italy/West Germany, 1971) fourteen-year-old Laurent has his first sexual experience when his elder brothers take him along to a brothel in Dijon. His allocated partner, Fréda (Gila von Weitershausen), is gentle and comforting, stroking him but refusing to allow him to kiss her, telling him he's cute and advanced for his age, remarking on his soft skin, drawing him down on top of her — and then, laughingly protesting that he's going too fast and hurting her, commending him on "doing well for the first time." His brothers, against Fréda's furious protests, then come and drag him off, but Laurent has learned enough. Later in the film, he will be seduced by his own mother.

A young soldier or sailor is often the subject. In *The Virgin Soldiers* (UK, 1969), which focuses on the sexual tensions of British conscripts in Malaya in the early 1950s, Private Brigg is initiated by the voluptuous Juicy Lucy (Tsai Chin), his first vigorous but unconsummated attempt at intercourse being intercut with the commandant's daughter eagerly losing her virginity to an experienced sergeant, the men unwittingly emulating each other thrust by thrust as in a shearing contest. When Brigg stops, a pained expression on his face, Lucy taunts him about his being — still — a virgin, but generously gives him his money back and then kindly offers to show him how it's done. *The Last Detail* (USA, 1973) depicts diffident eighteen-year-old sailor Larry Meadows, while en route to military prison, being treated by his escorts at a Boston brothel. The anonymous young whore (Carol Kane) whom he chooses for his sexual debut has the archetypal tenderness of the Nursemaid — overcoming his embarrassment at coming while she's giving his penis a precautionary wipe-down, and then praising his efforts second time around ("Well, you got off to a shaky start — after that you took to it like a duck to water") — and is uncommonly attractive: in the brothel parlor, with her auburn hair pulled back in a bun, she seems plucked from an old Dutch Master, but in the bedroom, her hair tumbling down over the slender nude body to her waist, she's like a Pre-Raphaelite Madonna, out of scale with the hunky young sailor awkwardly feeling his way through his first sexual exchange. *Biloxi Blues* (USA, 1988) portrays the maturation rite in a similar gently comic vein. The erotic is downplayed: prostitute Rowena (Park Overall) is not unappealing, her underwear is standard sexy, and she poses, one leg bent, in a clichéd seductive manner, but there's no sexual excitement here. It's broad daylight, and the apartment is down-home domestic, with clothes suspended on a folding rack and snapshots pinned to the wall. Scared, embarrassed young soldier Eugene just wants to get it over with, regressing almost to a helpless child: "Come to momma," Rowena says, helping him to arrange his limbs as if he were a toddler trying to climb a staircase for the first time. Put off by the nurturing manner ("Would it be OK if we didn't use the word 'momma'? It makes me think of my mother and that sort of kills it, you know"), Eugene eventually clambers gawkily on top, omitting to remove his shorts and sticking his knee in her stomach. He starts thrusting, stops breathing ("My nose is running"), then grunts and collapses, exclaiming "I did it!" after fully ten seconds' exertion.

The West German comedy *Auch Fummeln will gelernt sein* (1972) works a variation on the theme. A young soldier who is about to be married confesses to one of the women in a brothel that he is a virgin ("*Er hat noch nie gebumst!*" a title exuberantly declares). There follow a series of flashbacks to his childhood and youth, in which the comedy resides in his sexual inexperience in contrast to the licentious goings-on around him, such as copulating Punch-and-Judy show puppeteers. Here the brothel provides an erotically stimulating environment in which questions of sexual performance can be addressed, and the prostitute a comforting breast on which to pour out one's anxieties. At the end, the soldier has sex not with her, but with his bride.

The Nursemaid thus eases the transition from youth to manhood, her sympathy and understanding like a soothing ointment on the raw wounds of inexperience. The nurturing may well occur beyond the point of first sexual experience. In the "Rue Saint Denis" episode of *Paris vu par . . . / Six in Paris* (France, 1965), for example, the maternal prostitute (Micheline Dax) indulges her comically immature, perhaps impotent client (though he says it's not the first time) to the point at which he may possibly find himself capable of fornication, the substitute-mother through whom he will perhaps resolve the Oedipal struggle with his father — presumably the stern patriarch whose portrait on the wall is laboriously intercut with the couple to make a point about emasculation. Similarly *Jamón Jamón / Salami Salami* (Spain, 1992) positions the mature prostitute Carmen (Anna Galiena) as maternal surrogate for the infantilized José Luis, assisting him to negotiate the incest taboo in being a legitimate object of erotic desire — her breasts on display particularly excite him — while simultaneously providing the mothering he craves.

The Nursemaid can function, too, as counselor and therapist to any man experiencing lack of sexual fulfillment. In *The American Success Company* (USA, 1979), for instance, the American businessman in Germany who feels that he is a failure in life hires a hooker to mentor him in enhancing his sexual potency.[8] In the hardcore *Throat — Twelve Years After* (USA, 1984), a repressed married man "has recourse to a prostitute, who pities his constrained sex life and instructs him on how to please her," and that night he and his wife "enthusiastically seduce each other in a number that emphasizes cunnilingus and fellatio equally."[9] Or to take another example, the experienced streetwalker Odette in *Un héros très discret / A Self-Made Hero* (France, 1996) gives the young man recently arrived in Paris lessons in elementary sexual technique: "Make it last! You're like greased lightning. . . . Imagine you're in a restaurant. . . . When the grub arrives, don't gobble it. Savor it, eat it slowly."

Former stud Jonathan in *Carnal Knowledge* (USA, 1971) needs no technical instruction, but when his potency in middle age sadly withers, he resorts to a call girl, Louise (Rita Moreno) for reinvigoration. She duly agrees with his belief that all women are "ball-busters," and rehearses for him a litany of praise for his manhood. He is, she proclaims, "a man who inspires worship because he has no need for any woman, because he has himself," and the words have their desired effect: "You're getting hard — more strong, more masculine, more extraordinary. . . . It's rising, virile, domineering, more irresistible. It's up! It's in the air!"

The prostitute recites the script that the client has written. By insisting on her being word perfect and throwing a tantrum if she isn't, Jonathan (Jack Nicholson) can retain a sense of his masculine authority, can persuade himself that the ball-busters haven't got him, no way. The money he pays, as a prosperous attorney, for this service is of no consequence. One of the Nursemaid's functions therefore is to be that woman over whom the male can feel superior; he uses the gendered disparity in earning capacity that patriarchy delivers to reassure himself of his potency (where the sexual symbolizes the sociopolitical). The role takes on greater importance in a context of women's liberation and challenges to traditional male prerogatives in personal relationships and elsewhere; the period of *Carnal Knowledge*'s production is of course important here.

Louise is not a woman of striking beauty or of extraordinary figure, like Jonathan's former wife, played by Ann-Margret. What is it then that he finds arousing in her? Precisely her submissiveness, the guise she adopts of adoring slave to the macho master. The film in satirizing Jonathan — the all-powerful stud reduced to this — cuts sharply into the male-chauvinist culture of life achievement measured by sexual prowess, but the patriarchal assumption that the prostitute is available for whatever tasks men set her, including parroting a pathetic paean to virility, remains untroubled.

But it is not only in providing sexual services that the Nursemaid excels. She can offer shelter to the man in need, for instance. In *Tadbir* (India, 1945), Kanhaiyalal and his mother "find shelter in the house of Saguna . . . a prostitute who eventually sacrifices her life to save the hero's."[10] In a very different context, the World War II veteran in *Act of Violence* (USA, 1948), on the run from a relentless pursuer bent on vengeance, is harbored temporarily by a middle-aged streetwalker. When philandering André Ripois in *Knave of Hearts/Monsieur Ripois* (UK/France, 1954) finds himself at a low ebb in London, penniless and homeless, he is taken in hand by a matronly prostitute who provides him with food and beer and offers him a place to stay indefinitely. Similarly, a blonde prostitute in *Rue des Prairies/Rue de Paris* (France/Italy, 1959) picks up a youth who has run away from home and lets him stay with her — sharing her bed — when he explains he has no money; in the morning, however, shocked at finding how young he is, she turns him in to the police.

Looking after the sick and injured is also a distinctive characteristic of the Nursemaid. Drawing on her caring disposition, former prostitute Grace in *The Waiting Soul* (USA, 1917) in fact becomes a nurse, while Gabrielle of *The Red Kimona* (USA, 1925), as we have seen, redeems herself by offering her services as a nursing volunteer during the World War I flu epidemic. The Russian Baroness Natalie Ivanoff, a high-class prostitute, takes to nursing wounded soldiers during the emergency of the Boxer Rebellion, in *55 Days at Peking* (USA, 1963). In *The Front Page* (USA, 1974), hooker Molly recounts how when Earl Williams was beaten up by a pimp for distributing leaflets saying prostitutes were exploited by capitalism, she took care of him, nursing him for three days; and later, when he is hiding out after making his jail escape, she bandages his wounded arm. Likewise, prostitute Kate in *Stormy Monday* (UK/USA, 1988) looks after Brendan when he is battered and bruised following an encounter with his gangster employers: she sponges him in the bath, tends to his wounds, and makes love to him for the first time. A variant on the theme is provided by *Sansar Simantey* (India, 1975), in which the streetwalker Rajani "shelters the thief Aghor but he steals her money." She nurses him back to health after having had him beaten up by a mob.[11]

If the Nursemaid caters to a man's physical needs, she also, and perhaps more importantly, helps calm his emotional turmoil. It may be Gypo Nolan in John Ford's *The Informer* (USA, 1935), tormented with guilt for having turned in a wanted IRA man to the British, confessing to his girl-friend Katie (Margot Grahame)—in a composition reminiscent of the Pietà, he lies by the fireplace while Katie gently strokes his hair and kisses him, saying "I'd lay down my life for you."[12] Or it may be the troubled boarding-school student in *Der junge Törless/Young Torless* (West Germany/France, 1966), passively complicit in the increasingly sadistic torture of a boy who has been caught stealing, who turns to the sympathetic village prostitute Bozena (Barbara Steele) for comfort when the stress becomes too much for him to bear. The inveterate nature of the compassionate role assigned to the Nursemaid is suggested by *El jardín de tía Isabel/Aunt Isabel's Garden* (Mexico, 1972), in which prostitutes calm the fears of the soldiers, friars, and liberated prisoners in a sixteenth-century Spanish expeditionary party shipwrecked on the American coast and decimated by an earthquake as they trek through the forest.

At times the Nursemaid provides the only light in the darkness. In Ingmar Bergman's *Das Schlangenei/The Serpent's Egg* (West Germany/USA, 1977) circus performer turned prostitute Manuela (Liv Ullman) soothes the angst of her former partner Abel, who is mired in depression over his brother Max's suicide. Having been Max's wife, she shares Abel's grief, taking his head in her hands, kissing him, assuring him that "everything is all right"—although in the context of the nightmarish tension of Munich in 1922 with its incipient fascism, this is far from the case. A similar oppressive mood pervades Fassbinder's *In einem Jahr mit 13 Monden/In a Year of 13 Moons* (West Germany, 1978), set in Frankfurt in 1978. The film positions caring prostitute Zora (Ingrid Caven) as the main support of the lonely, desperate transsexual Elvira, who has been beaten up by street youths, abandoned by a lover, and stricken by unresolved issues of gender identity. Zora plays the traditional comforting role, at one point telling a bedtime story to a child-like Elvira tucked up under the covers, explaining, "You're supposed to sleep, Baby." Her help is unavailing; Elvira commits suicide.

The sympathetic prostitute is the woman a man turns to when his marriage isn't working out. In *Gone With the Wind* (USA, 1939), Belle Watling (Ona Munson) gives Rhett Butler the loving he's desperate for, and which Scarlett refuses him; goodness flows from her ample bosom like mother's milk. Similarly, in *Faces* (USA, 1968), call girl Jeannie (Gena Rowlands) is a gentle substitute for the wife whose love, after fourteen years of marriage, has ebbed away; jaded Los Angeles businessman Richard spends a night with her and bathes in the warmth of her company, receiving a foot massage, pouring out his "demented dialogue," dancing to romantic music with her in the dark, going to bed, and then, in the morning, being served breakfast by a vision of loveliness in a soft diaphanous robe, her immaculate blonde hair falling lightly to her shoulders. For neurotic Lenny Weinrib in *Mighty Aphrodite* (USA, 1995), whose wife has become cold and businesslike, the kooky prostitute Linda (Mira Sorvino), comically towering over the diminutive sportswriter, stroking his hair, kissing his hand, nibbling his ear, telling him "It looks like it's been a long time since you had a great blow job," holds out an alternative female role model, subordinate and submissive — one that his wife will return to by the end of the film.

For these men, the prostitute offers temporary solace, but for businessman Kresten in *Mifune* (Denmark/Sweden, 1999) the substitution is definitive. His married existence has scarcely begun before he discovers that the boss's daughter was the wrong choice, and that gorgeous blonde Copenhagen call girl Liva (Iben Hjejle), who strays into his life by chance and tenderly ministers to him after he's been beaten up, has something to offer that is worth much more than advancement in the company.

When he reaches old age, a man's loneliness can be assuaged by a sympathetic prostitute. In *Death of a Gunfighter* (USA, 1969), for example, Marshal Frank Patch is progressively deserted by all his former friends and allies, but Claire Quintana (Lena Horne), owner of the local bar and brothel, remains staunch and, finally, marries him. In *The Great Smokey Roadblock* (USA, 1978), terminally ill trucker Elegant John embarks on a final cross-country run, hauling hookers out of town; his "one-time romance" Penelope (Eileen Brennan) gives him the job, and "as they ride to the finish, John dies in Penelope's arms."[13]

It is not necessarily by means of the physical caress that the Nursemaid performs her narrative function, as Jean-Luc Godard's *Une femme est une femme/A Woman is a Woman* (France/Italy, 1961) illustrates. Protagonist

32. Jeannie (Gena Rowlands) with Richard (John Marley) in *Faces*.

Émile, disturbed that his girlfriend Angela may be seeing a friend, Alfred, because he has refused to entertain her desire to have a baby, allows himself to be picked up by a streetwalker (Marion Sarraut). With her he seems more interested in philosophy than sex: there is a shot of him sitting on a chair saying "And so it is, unconsciously, that we are guilty of injustice, are intolerant and evil." There is a cut to the prostitute, slim, brunette, lying naked in bed, on her stomach, bared to the waist, her image doubled in a mirror alongside. "Unconsciously, at least, so it seems to me," she replies, smiling tolerantly.

The prostitute appears in only two shots, but her structural function in the drama is crucial. She is the fulcrum on which Émile turns. She is the public woman, just as Angela is, when working as a stripper; it is Angela's wish to become the private woman, the mother, to differentiate herself from the others, which he realizes he must now indulge. This woman does not take Émile in her arms, rest his head on her breast, at least not on screen, but she is a Nursemaid nonetheless, offering a sounding board for his ideas and in so doing soothing his emotional unrest. She is the nurturer par excellence, and all she does is expose her body and repeat his words, not unkindly; we imagine the rest. And having unburdened himself to this understanding, anonymous woman, he can return to his girlfriend, fall in with her desires, laughing, loving.

In *Anticipation,* his contribution to the omnibus film *Le Plus Vieux Métier du monde/The Oldest Profession* (France/Italy/West Germany, 1967), Godard further develops the theme by positing a future in which specialization has resulted in one category of prostitute who caters to the body (she doesn't talk), another to the mind (she doesn't strip). This creates a problem for the intergalactic traveler who is having his needs met at a space station on earth. He is unmoved by the silent nudity of "'Miss Physical" (Marilu Tolo), and agrees with her replacement "Miss Conversation" (Anna Karina), who explains that she knows all the words of love, that it is sad and illogical that she is not permitted to "speak" with her legs, breasts and eyes. But suddenly the traveler has an idea: he touches her lips. She understands: the mouth is one part of the body that she is able to use. As they kiss, the image flashes for the first time from a solarized single tone into full color, there is a burst of music, and the voice-over announces that "Traveler 14 and Prostitute 703 have discovered something. . . . They feel at the same time spiritually and physically." The split has been overcome, a synthesis has been achieved— Prostitute 703 has become the fully fledged Nursemaid of the year 2000.[14]

Celui qui doit mourir/He Who Must Die (France/Italy, 1957) is significant in another way for its reexamination of the role of the nurturing prostitute within the Christian tradition. Adapted from the novel *Christ Recrucified* by Nikos Kazantzakis and directed by Jules Dassin, it is set in 1921 in a Greek village under Turkish domination and structured around a performance of the Passion Play. An illiterate shepherd, Manolios, is assigned to the role of Jesus, while the village whore, Katerina (Melina Mercouri) plays Mary Magdalene. When a party of starving refugees arrives, villagers are ordered by the local administration, fearing trouble with the Turkish authorities, not to feed and shelter them; but Manolios, emboldened by Katerina, with whom he has begun a love affair, defiantly disregards the edict and, with others, guarantees that the refugees receive the assistance they need.

In this rereading of the gospels to accord with a radical political agenda, critical reversals occur. Becoming the spirit of rebellion, Katerina/Magdalene feels no shame as a prostitute, but pride in her female strength. "I've known men, so many," she tells Manolios. "It's always interesting when they come to make love. They make big chest, they show their muscles. But in truth they're fragile, defenseless." The nurturing which she provides—here, particularly, to Manolios, in a serene and maternal way—is calculated to calm a man's passions but not to make him pliable and submissive: on the contrary, she aims to ease his fears so that he will have the courage to revolt. Later, when Manolios is captured for his insurrectional activities and then fatally stabbed in the church, it is Katerina who cradles him like the Virgin Mary with the body of Christ in her arms.

But if the class politics of *He Who Must Die* are provocatively left wing, the gender politics are somewhat more ambiguous. Katerina is valued for the services that she provides for the men; as in Dassin's later *Never on Sunday*, the prostitute has no relationships, virtually no contact (except for a fight with a jealous wife) with nonprostitute women in the community, who are by and large excluded from the action. As Katerina, shedding tears, holds the dying Manolios, fourteen men surround them, a reminder that it is the Nursemaid's dedication to serving male needs that defines her.

In an adaptation of another Kazantzakis novel, Martin Scorsese takes the remodeling of the character of Mary Magdalene a stage farther. In *The Last Temptation of Christ* (USA, 1988), while retaining her nurturing qualities, she scandalously incites Christ's tormented lust and eventually, in an extended vision of the life that might be his should he escape crucifixion, becomes his sexual partner. Jesus and Magdalene (Barbara Hershey) are presented as former childhood sweethearts, now estranged; to see her he must wait as she services a series of clients behind a filmy gauze curtain. When they are together, Magdalene rejects his plea for forgiveness, challenging Jesus to recognize the life of the body. Baring her breasts, she tells him: "If you want to save my soul, this is where you'll find it." Like Katerina with Manolios, she taunts him with his timidity ("You never had the courage to be a man"), but then comforts him, running a tender hand down his cheek and across his knee, assuring him that "all I ever wanted was you." Magdalene later appears to Jesus as a serpent in the desert, tempting him; and then, in his dream of being rescued by an angel from the cross, as the woman who caressingly sponges the blood from his wounds prior to making passionate love. The prostitute has become the Nursemaid of God, forcing Jesus to acknowledge that only as a sinner with sexual desires like anyone else can he be fully human.

It is often the Nursemaid's function to be an agent of regeneration, assisting a man to emerge from a low point of demoralization. Her care and concern is crucial in enabling him to climb back up out of the depths.

He may be just released from jail, as for example in *Die Verrufenen / The Slums of Berlin* (Germany, 1925), *Camille of the Barbary Coast* (USA, 1925), *Burai yori daikanbu / The Gangster VIP* (Japan, 1968), and *Trading Places* (USA, 1983). In *The Slums of Berlin*, Kramer is unable to find work, is reduced to taking refuge in a night shelter, and goes farther and farther under. He is about to take his own life when he is rescued by a streetwalker, Emma (Aud Egede Nissen), under whose nurturance he recovers, finding employment with a photographer and subsequently becoming an engineer.[15] In *Camille of the Barbary Coast*, drifter Robert Morton meets Camille (Mae Busch) in a San Francisco dive, and she is instrumental in his rehabilitation. "Robert gets a job, but he is fired when his prison record becomes known. Camille sticks by him, and they are married. Robert obtains another position and gradually works his way back to self-respect."[16] Goro Fujikawa of *The Gangster VIP* shows less gratitude toward his benefactress: "Out of prison, he joins a small gang and is nearly killed by a rival group, only to be nursed back to health by his girlfriend, who becomes a prostitute to pay for his medical expenses. Once healthy, he joins a larger gang, marries another woman, and has a son." He finally decides to go straight.[17] In the twisted plot of *Trading Places*, businesslike prostitute Ophelia (Jamie Lee Curtis) takes commodities broker Louis under her wing when he is down-and-out, looking after him when he contracts a cold (the treatment includes slipping into bed nude with him, when their relationship has been strictly nonsexual up to this point), and assisting him to regain his severely dented self-esteem.

The weak-willed stowaway in *The Singapore Mutiny* (USA, 1928) is in ill health and at a loose end; the kind treatment he receives from "Broadway jade" Daisy (Estelle Taylor) gives him the strength to act heroically in a crisis.[18] Similarly, the help and encouragement that prostitute Perla (Stella Stevens) affords the drunken, misanthropic doctor in *El mal / Rage* (Mexico/USA, 1966) enables him to stop drinking and to reach a medical center in time to treat the rabies he has contracted; while in *Cuori al verde / Love Money and Philosophy* (Italy, 1996), the love of call girl Lucia (Margherita Buy) brings the suicidally depressed intellectual Stefano back from the abyss, allowing him to flourish.

Finally, the Mexican whore Maria Elena (Cordelia González) in *Born on the Fourth of July* (USA, 1989) is the agent of Ron Kovic's recovery. It is her sexual attention to the embittered, paraplegic Vietnam War vet that will, after a little more degenerate behavior, pull him out of the hell of guilt and self-loathing and give him the courage to face the family of the man he killed, eventually to become a prominent antiwar activist and author. Maria Elena is a substitute for the mother who won't hear the word "penis" spoken in her house, who drives Ron from his home; it is she who insists on seeing his paralyzed member, on forcing the cripple to face the truth — which doesn't exclude sexual pleasure. It's a liberation.

It is as nurturer and muse to the creative artist that the Nursemaid attains her full dignity, transcending her degraded status in society. Reinforcing the Romantic notion of artist as outsider, she offers her solidarity to the troubled and misunderstood protagonist, instilling in him the strength of purpose that will enable his creative talents to flourish.

In *Perdida* (Mexico, 1950), the prostitute becomes muse to a composer; in *l'Esclave / The Slave* (France / Italy, 1953), she befriends a musician who is addicted to morphine, helping to effect a reconciliation with his wife. The voluptuous, easygoing Clarisse (Michèle Mercier)[19] in François Truffaut's *Tirez sur le pianiste / Shoot the Piano Player* (France, 1960) offers her body freely to the morose pianist as an act of neighborly companionship (and, no doubt, because she enjoys the sex, shrieks of laughter coming from beneath the sheets); she also cooks meals for his young son. *Antony Firingee* (India, 1967) recounts the legend of an early nineteenth-century Portuguese-Indian who becomes a Bengali poet-musician and falls in love with the renowned courtesan Shakila (Tanuja): "She then agrees to marry Antony and they try to overcome social ostracization when, under her tutelage, he defeats a series of famous poets in the tradition of the Kabir Larai (contest between poets emphasizing improvisation)."[20] In *Van Gogh* (France, 1991), the prostitute Cathy (Elsa Zylberstein), whom the painter has known in Arles, meets up again with in Auvers and subsequently becomes reunited with in Paris, is the only person among those close to him who believes in his work; with her he can freely discuss his psychological problems, dance fast and furiously in a nightclub brothel, and have playful, uncomplicated sex — the sensual, intellectual, and maternal rolled into one. For the opera singer Cheng Dieyi in *Bawang bie ji / Farewell My Concubine* (China / Hong Kong, 1993), the former House of Blossoms prostitute Juxian (Gong Li) is a bitter rival, since she has married the partner he is in love with; but when he is suffering the agonies of opium withdrawal, it is she who calms his frenzy, covers him to ease his shivering, cradles him, takes him to her breast. He gets through the crisis, to reemerge as a star of the Beijing Opera.

Two films are especially representative of the Nursemaid's relationship with the artist. They are *Die Sünderin/The Sinful Woman* (West Germany, 1951) and *Pyaasa/The Thirsty One* (India, 1957).

Die Sünderin, which unleashed a storm of controversy on its release because of its representation of an unrepentant prostitute as its heroine, depicts a passionate and tragically doomed love affair between Marina (Hildegard Knef), who has drifted into prostitution after an upbringing disrupted by the war, and the painter Alexander Kless, a former military officer demoralized by the German defeat.[21] Marina literally picks Alexander up from the gutter, after he has been ejected as a drunk from a Munich bar. She takes him home, and a relationship commences, which will see Alexander, basking in Marina's adoration, overcoming his self-doubt to eventually become a critically acclaimed artist. Their happy times together, on a trip to Italy and after they have moved to Vienna, are sensuous idylls in which he paints her nude. Alexander, however, suffers from a brain tumor, which is inclined to make him moody and violent toward his lover, and the prognosis for which is blindness and death. The operation he undergoes — which Marina finances by returning, with difficulty, to prostitution — is successful, but only temporarily; at the end, his eyesight gone, he induces her to give him a fatal dose of Veronal and she also takes the pills, dying in his arms.

The film's complicated flashback structure enables episodes from Marina's troubled adolescence — parental disharmony, initiation into sex for money by her stepbrother, being ejected from the house — to be interwoven with her relationship with Alexander, enriching the portrait of the "sinful" woman whose early love of luxury and finery is displaced by self-sacrificing devotion, whose rebellious independence as a young woman gives way to total immersion in the life of the man she loves. As Marina, Hildegard Knef — with her long blonde hair, sculptural features, and body that can appear both teenaged and motherly — is the very incarnation of the Nursemaid as model and muse to the talented male artist.

While Alexander gratefully reciprocates Marina's love, the tormented poet Vijay in *Pyaasa* does not recognize where his true feelings lie until the end of the film. Rejected by publishers, thrown out of the house by his brothers for not earning a living, abandoned by his sweetheart from college days, Vijay is drunk and in a near-suicidal depression when he is taken in and comforted by the prostitute Gulab (Waheeda Rehman), who unlike the professionals can discern the beauty of his poems and songs. His equilibrium restored, Vijay resumes writing. Later,

33. Marina (Hildegard Knef) with Alexander (Gustav Fröhlich) in *Die Sünderin*.
Stiftung Deutsche Kinemathek — Filmmuseum Berlin.

when he is thought dead, she gives up all she has in the world to have
his work published. Ironically, the book is a huge popular success, but
Vijay chooses not to make his existence known and reap the rewards;
instead he heads away as a vagrant with Gulab.

Giving the lie to initial appearances — on the first occasion on which they meet, Gulab scornfully dismisses Vijay as a pauper — the prostitute is paradoxically presented as a figure of sensitivity and integrity in a world corrupted by commercialism. She sings Vijay's songs and acts as a surrogate mother in his time of dire need (significantly, his real mother has just died), inviting him to come and rest in her house, assuring him that "the world needs you and your poetry." Then, in the extraordinary melodramatic projection of paranoia in which the latter part of the film is steeped, with all of the writer's family and erstwhile friends out to deny and/or exploit him, virtually the only character who remains true to him is Gulab, deeply in love and untouched by the mercenary fever in which everyone else is gripped. For the troubled poet — undoubtedly a figure with whom *Pyaasa*'s writer-director Guru Dutt, who plays the part, closely identified[22] — the Nursemaid is both lifeline in the present and promise of sexual and emotional fulfillment to come.

Michelangelo Antonioni's *Il grido/The Outcry* (Italy/USA, 1957) portrays the despondency of the rejected male, so thrown that he cannot readjust to life without the love object, paralyzed, indecisive. In following the wanderings of a sugar-refinery worker whose common-law wife has left him, Antonioni draws a portrait of the prostitute that strikingly undercuts the male-fantasy components of the Nursemaid characterization. Precisely at the point of the story at which she would appear, normally, to mother him tenderly out of his miseries, Andreina (Lyn Shaw) crops up — ill, requiring Aldo to care for *her*. Then, quickly recovering, she joins forces with him but shows little interest in providing the emotional sustenance that might help him emerge from his depression and inertia. They're in a leaking shack in a rainstorm, without money, without food; faced with Aldo's inability or unwillingness to do anything about their plight, she takes the initiative and heads off to find a client. Though this finally spurs him into action, it's simply to attempt a prohibition, which is too late and spurned. Refusing the role allocated to her by the patriarchal imagination — but not characterized negatively as a result — Andreina throws the embedded assumptions of the Nursemaid archetype into sharp relief.

10

Captive

Now the film you are about to see deals with a seamy, almost frightening subject: prostitution. Now the crooks who run this highly organized racket are utterly ruthless.
—FABIAN OF THE YARD in *Passport to Shame* (UK, 1958)

I lived with Champa and her husband, Yongyuth, who beat me and forced me to work as a prostitute. My virginity was sold for 20,000 baht, but I never saw the money. Throughout the three years I worked in that massage parlour, I never received any money for my body.[1]

In *The Pawnbroker* (USA, 1965), a black prostitute (Thelma Oliver), desperate to make extra money for her boyfriend, offers herself to the Jewish protagonist. She warns him that she is risking a beating: "Because if my boss finds out I've been messing around in private. . . . You see he don't hold still for nothin' like that, so if it was to get out to him, he'd make me old before my time." As she strips in the back room of the shop, baring her breasts, the aging pawnbroker suddenly begins to get flash memories of a concentration camp, of being compelled to watch his wife, half-naked on a bed, becoming sexual prey to Nazi officers. The montage intercutting makes a powerful equation between the slavery of the camps and pimp-controlled Harlem prostitution. The distraught pawnbroker covers the woman up; later, he will tell her "boss," for whom he has been laundering money without being aware that it is the profits of prostitution, that he will no longer do so, "because it's money that comes from filth and horror."

Terrified of being found out for acting on her own, the anonymous hooker of *The Pawnbroker* exemplifies the character type I have termed the "Captive." The modern successor in the movies to the white slave, she is the woman who is trapped in her situation as a prostitute, at the mercy of the pimp, brothel owner, or criminal organization she works for. In the narratives in which she features, the imperiling of female virtue is no longer the focal point that it was in the silent era, when stories were typically infused with a Victorian melodramatic aesthetic and puritan moral values. The Captive is not discredited for being sexually experienced: what is deplorable about her condition is not a loss of chastity, but the brute fact that she is forced to sell her body and exploited in doing so.

Two powerful motivating forces behind this archetypal representation, quite different in nature but readily coalescing, have led to its frequent recurrence in the cinema. On the one hand, there is outrage at the enslavement and exploitation of women in coerced prostitution, a stubborn social reality whose locus may shift, in global terms, but whose incidence remains high. On the other hand, there is the potent male fantasy of the sex slave, the attractive female who may be stripped, shackled, and raped at will.[2]

It is this dual aspect that has resulted in the representation of forced prostitution in the cinema often being highly controversial, and inclined to trigger, as I mentioned in chapter 1, stringent censorship. Thus it was only the abolition of censorship in Germany for a brief interlude following World War I that enabled a film such as *Das Frauenhaus von Brescia/The Women House of Brescia* (1920) to be made. A romance of the Lombardy wars of the early fourteenth century, it depicts female captives being placed in the house of pillory, "a building where the local prostitutes are incarcerated as punishment under the authority of the city hangman Luigi and where every free citizen has the right to use and abuse them as he sees fit." The film was, unsurprisingly, rejected by the British Board of Film Censors.[3]

In the United States, the industry's self-imposed ban on the depiction of white slavery, which came into effect around 1917, was reinforced in the Production Code adopted in 1930, with an explicit interdiction of the topic. The small independent companies not affiliated to the Motion Picture Producers and Distributors of America were however not bound by the Code, and it was in their hands that the white slave characterization evolved in the early years of the sound era into that of the Captive.

The low-budget independent "quickies" produced by these firms had an exploitation agenda that may be illustrated, for example, by *The Cocaine Fiends/The Pace That Kills* (USA, 1935). In this film, "Nick, second-in-command of a powerful mob that peddles drugs to teenagers, lures small town girl Jane Bradford to the city and gets her addicted to cocaine. Jane, who calls herself Lil, marries Nick and he abuses her. Soon the racketeering boss, Farley, orders Jane to work at the Dead Rat Cafe, a dive infamous for its sleazy clientele."[4] *Slaves in Bondage/Crusade Against Rackets* (USA, 1937) similarly depicts a sex industry gang that recruits women for its nightclub brothels by attracting women from small towns to the city, in this case using a barbershop manicure business as a front: "Soon the girls are adrift and alone in the city, and become easy prey."[5] In *The Wages of Sin* (USA, ca. 1938), a poor laundry worker becomes the target of a pimp who entraps her on false promises of marriage: "Using threats, Tony now turns Marjorie into a hotel call girl."[6] The theme continues in *Mad Youth* (USA, 1939), in which Marian, who has been leading a wild partygoing life, discovers that her friend Helen "is living in a brothel, where she has been forced to work after being lured to the house by the prospect of marriage. Marian is taken prisoner and a similar fate awaits her."[7]

The well-publicized prosecution and conviction of Mafia boss Charles "Lucky" Luciano for compulsory prostitution in New York City in 1936 inspired several films dedicated to exposing the control of the vice trade by organized crime. *Gambling with Souls/Vice Racket* (USA, 1936) is structured as a courtroom drama with Mae Miller (Martha Chapin) accused of the murder of "Lucky" Wilder, the owner of a gambling and prostitution house. In flashbacks, Mae reveals how she went from being a happily married woman to a gambling addict, $10,000 in debt to Wilder. Her friend Molly, who introduced her to Wilder's club, "has been running a sex exchange . . . luring thrill-seeking girls into gambling, then forcing them to entertain Wilder's male clientele when they can no longer pay their debts." Under pressure, Mae leaves her husband and "becomes one of Wilder's girls"; later, her younger sister is also trapped in the same way, and dies after an abortion. In court, Mae admits that she killed Lucky in revenge.[8] Another quickie, *Smashing the Vice Trust/Confessions of a Vice Baron* (USA, 1937), identifies abduction as the chief method by which females are recruited for the gang-controlled brothels, and stresses the ruthlessness of the racketeers. Vice syndicate boss James "Lucky" Lombardo, complaining to his associates that profits are down, "demands that his henchmen get new, younger, and prettier girls for his bordellos. When one of his henchmen, Eddie, refuses to kidnap any more high-school girls, Lucky has him killed." Other gang members are more pliable, restocking the houses with girls abducted from "local high schools and dance halls"—one of whom eventually commits suicide "rather than have her sorry fate discovered." Lucky is put on trial, the prostitutes testify against him, and he is sentenced to twenty years to life.[9]

The motif of the victims having the courage to testify against their oppressor was the highlight, too, of the Warner Bros. version of the Luciano case, *Marked Woman* (USA, 1937), but because it was a major studio production the protagonists had to be identified as "nightclub hostesses" rather than prostitutes.[10] This censorship-evading stratagem reduced the narrative to implausibility and incoherence, with the women, allegedly employed to soften up high-rolling gamblers so they could be gypped, told by mobster Johnny Vanning to "kick back part of what you make to me" (from their wages?), freely leaving the club with male patrons during the course of the evening (though only to be taken, in the example we are given, "from one chop suey joint to another"), and routinely being given $100 "cabfare" simply to attend parties. The story in fact only makes sense if the women are prostitutes, though where and how they exercise the profession is difficult to determine from the details revealed.

Given these constraints, *Marked Woman*'s exposé of the vice racket is necessarily blunted, and indeed Vanning is indicted on a charge of murder rather than compulsory prostitution. Still, the film attains some power as a portrait of the Captive and the pressures under which she works through its unsentimental and unsensational script, and particularly through the restrained and moving performance of Bette Davis as one of the women, Mary Dwight. Mary is no innocent lamb to the slaughter; she knows just what she's getting into when she decides to accept Vanning's offer of employment — making "about fifty times what you're getting now" — at the club he has taken over and is turning into a clip joint. "This isn't the only way to make a living," one of her fellow hostesses points out. "Do you know a better one?" Mary retorts. "We've all tried this twelve-and-a-half-a-week stuff. It's no good! Living in furnished rooms, walking to work, going hungry a couple of days a week so you can have some clothes to put on your back."

She's aware of the risks. She knows of Audrey Fleming, who wound up in the river when she got to know too much about Vanning. Mary "is not getting into his trap." She tells her friends that "some will wind up with the short end, but not me, baby. I know all the angles, and I think I'm smart enough to keep one step ahead of them, till I get enough to pack it all in, and live on easy street for the rest of my life. I know how to beat this racket." But if *Marked Woman* initially offers a less deliberately shocking and more plausible account than *Gambling with Souls* and *Smashing the Vice Trust* of how recruitment to gang-controlled prostitution takes place, allowing for an element of free choice and self-interest for the women involved, an underlying coercive aspect is revealed as events

34. Mary (Bette Davis) with the investigating attorney (Humphrey Bogart) in *Marked Woman*.

unfold. When Mary's kid sister Betty, on her first night as a party girl, won't be friendly enough to one of the punters, she is knocked down the stairs and killed by Vanning. Then, when Mary defiantly refuses to keep away from the investigating attorney, she is beaten nearly to death and winds up in hospital, her cheek slashed with Vanning's doublecross trademark.

Mary will testify against Vanning—allowing the grandstanding prosecutor to flay the "vice czar, who at this very moment is exacting his staggering tribute from a supine and cowardly city," using the tactics of "insidious bribery to corrupt, brutal violence to intimidate, and cold-blooded murder to silence any who dared protest"—and he will be found guilty. But Mary's future is uncertain. "I'll get along," she says, in an ending admired for its toughness, as she and the other women who had the nerve to take the stand "walk off, arm-in-arm into the fog."[11] It's odds on Mary Dwight won't be working again as a "hostess" anywhere Vanning's syndicate holds sway.

Rounding off the cinematic fallout from Luciano's demise, Columbia Pictures also released a version of the case, *Missing Daughters* (USA,

1939). Censorship is again averted by depicting the victimized women as "nightclub hostesses," although as one unfortunate recruit discovers, the truth is that "the hostess racket is just a cover for the white slave traffic."[12] She is killed on the orders of gang boss Lucky Rogers; her sister then infiltrates the operation in order to expose it. Once again, the Captive is portrayed as trapped in her position through physical force and intimidation.

In the 1950s and 1960s there appeared an international cycle of social-problem dramas devoted to coerced prostitution. Reviving many of the motifs of the white slave genre and its 1930s successors, particularly in detailing the methods by which young women were procured for the sex trade, the films of this cycle typically adopted the conventions of the crime thriller and reserved a privileged role for the police in combating the social evil. No doubt with an eye to warding off accusations of exploitative intent and, in Britain and the United States, to breaking through the censorship barrier, the pictures insisted on their seriousness of purpose, often by means of direct address to the spectator.

Thus *Les Compagnes de la nuit/Companions of the Night* (France, 1953), which ushered in the cycle, opens with a title that asserts, in part: "If the characters and the action of this film are imaginary, the problem with which it deals is sufficiently real, indeed alarming, that we have felt it desirable to present it to the public in an authentic light. . . . It has seemed to us that in order to contend with one of the most menacing scourges of our century, there is no better remedy than showing the true face of the evil."

In keeping with this declaration, *Les Compagnes de la nuit* follows *Marked Woman*'s lead in having a self-assured protagonist with no illusions, it seems, about what she is letting herself in for — and the French film benefits from not having to beat about the bush. For Olga (Françoise Arnoul), who has been in and out of correctional institutions since her early teens, prostitution is her *métier* and she's proud of it. She has only scorn for the truck driver, Paul, who has fallen for her and wants her to quit the life: "You've got a lighthouse keeper complex," she tells him.

When, after being released from jail, she signs up with Monsieur Jo as her pimp in Paris, it's like a business deal, with him generously advancing the capital. As Olga herself tells us in voice-over: "I wasn't one of his victims . . . I'd freely chosen. Dressed, accommodated, fed, my son examined by the best medical specialists and now at the Pension Geneviève. Monsieur Jo respected the terms of the marketplace." All she had to do, she tells us, was to pay her dues each week at the "headquarters of the enterprise" — a legitimate car dealership that serves as Jo's front.

Of course, as for Mary Dwight, things are not quite like that. Slapped around when she spends money on a leg brace for her boy Jackie without Jo's permission, Olga still believes she is an independent agent and, since she does not sleep with Jo, she can leave when she wants. An older member of Jo's stable, Pierrette, chillingly disabuses her. "Leave?" she says. "Look at me, Olga. I've done Chicago to Panama. What's the name of your kid?" Pierrette had a boy, it turns out. "They killed him."

Things come to a head when Olga finds herself in love with Paul after all. She decides to take him up on his offer and go and live with him, together with Jackie. She is clear, now, that it will be difficult ("I'm not free, you don't know how I can't escape"), though Paul is naively confident ("We're not in the Middle Ages. These days a woman has the right to do what she likes."). Getting wind of the plan, Jo serves warning on Paul and tells Olga not to think about going to pick up Jackie — "he's changed address." Meanwhile another of Jo's prostitutes, Ginette (Marthe Mercadier), trying to sneak away after Jo has told her she can't keep her newborn baby, is caught and severely beaten up; while Yvonne (Nicole Maurey), the woman he has just seduced into the business in classic pimp style, protests, is belted by him, and dies when her head strikes a chest of drawers as she falls. In the action that ensues, Ginette, a witness to the assault, is run over and killed by Jo's confederates, and Paul, too, is run over. It is made very clear that if the prostitute steps out of line, the pimp will have no qualms about using violence, either in momentary fury or as a calculated elimination of risks.

As a crime thriller, *Les Compagnes de la nuit* takes the form of a mystery, with a complicated flashback structure. Early on, we are shown Jo being gunned down by an unseen assailant. As the film draws to its conclusion, the identity of the killer is revealed. Olga, who thought herself a Business Woman and discovered instead she was a Captive, has turned Avenger. The police are on hand to mete out justice and restore the prestige of the patriarchy.

When Yvonne's body is pulled out of the canal it is found to have been *vitriolé*, presumably as an attempt to obliterate her identity and perhaps, also, as a generic warning to prostitutes who hear the news. *The Flesh is Weak* (1957), a British entry in the cycle, picks up the motif, with the difference that acid is thrown on the woman's face while she is still alive. The film takes what is a subordinate plotline in *Les Compagnes de la nuit* — the pimp's recruitment of a woman into the trade by means of

35. Olga (Françoise Arnoul) in *Les Compagnes de la nuit*. Stills Collection, New Zealand Film Archive.

charm, seduction, and false promises — and elevates it into the main story. Marissa (Milly Vitale), age twenty-one, newly arrived in London, falls for pimp Tony of the notorious Giani brothers vice ring. She is gradually eased into prostitution, but rebels when she discovers how fraudulent his professions of love have been. Misguidedly taking to the streets as an independent ("You'll never get away with it," the motherly Trixie warns her, "No girl walks out on them"), she is framed for assault on one of Tony's other women, convicted, and imprisoned. The story then follows the *Marked Woman* pattern: on release, Marissa becomes a witness against Tony in court. The final image is of a newspaper billboard with the words TONY GIANI SENTENCED — THE END OF VICE GANG.

The sight that persuades Marissa to take the stand is the acid-burned face of Doris, the woman who served as Tony's accomplice in recruiting her into the business: she has been punished for having allowed Marissa to stay at her flat after breaking with Tony. Aside from this vicious act, the British gangsters are markedly less violent than their French counterparts, part of a deliberate strategy to avoid the police coming down hard on them. Much of the emphasis of the film is, in fact, on the police,

36. Tony (John Derek) and Marissa (Milly Vitale) in *The Flesh is Weak*. bfi Collections.

and their successful tactics in preventing the outbreak of warfare between the Gianis and a rival gang seeking to muscle in on their territory. The social-issue approach is also advanced through the character of an investigative journalist who promotes the idea of a law change to legalize streetwalking, but on the whole, as the *Monthly Film Bulletin* observed at the time, *The Flesh is Weak* is a film "dealing with, but not one feels very gravely concerned about, the real life problem of organized prostitution."[13]

Passport to Shame / Room 43 (UK, 1958) proclaims its serious intent by means of an introductory address to camera by Fabian of Scotland Yard. "This city probably has the worst prostitution problem in the world," he tells us. In terms very reminiscent of the opening title in *Les Compagnes de la nuit,* he continues: "You'll see for yourselves the terrible methods used to turn innocent girls into prostitutes. And the film deals with the problem frankly, dramatically, and accurately. And by exposing this racket as it does, I think it will make us all realize what is going on, and maybe it will do something towards wiping out this awful social evil."

The recruitment technique, in this case, is entrapment rather than seductive charm. Parisienne Malou Beaucaire (Odile Versois) is tricked into traveling to London on the understanding she will be given work as a lady's companion, and then manipulated into a marriage (British citizenship, it is explained, will prevent her being deported if she's picked up as a streetwalker by police). It is at this point that she is put under heavy pressure to join Nick Biaggi's stable, subjected to violence by his toughs when she tries to make a getaway, and intimidated by the threat of disfigurement.[14] The voluptuous Vicki (Diana Dors) is at present Nick's favorite; he draws Malou's attention to Vicki's sister, a young woman with an acid-scarred face: "Maria too was a girl who couldn't look at a man," he tells her, "Now no man will look at her." Given a drugged cigarette, Malou has an expressionist nightmare vision of herself running through a street of whores, falling into a steaming cauldron of naked men, smashing a stool over the head of a man advancing on her, and screaming as prison bars descend around her in every direction. Fortunately for her this presentiment does not come to pass. The man she has married is no stooge for the syndicate, but a stalwart taxi driver who is able to rustle up an army of cabbies and, after battling with her captors, effect her rescue. Meanwhile, Maria commits suicide, and in revenge Vicki turns on Nick, locking him in a closet, and setting it on fire. Nick breaks out but falls to his death. The *Monthly Film Bulletin* was not impressed by the film's pretensions to social realism, calling it "the most wholeheartedly absurd prostitute drama yet."[15]

West German contributions to the social-problem cycle included *Gefährdete Mädchen/Dolls of Vice* (1958), about two Viennese shopgirls who get caught up in a brutal sex-industry trafficking operation, and *Küsse, die Töten/Kiss the Dead* (1958), in which "a young woman flees from East Germany only to fall into the hands of unscrupulous men who deal in narcotics and prostitution."[16] *Madeleine Tel. 13 62 11,* from the same year, exposes the operations of a Berlin call-girl madam, Frau Clavius, who is ruthless in the control she exerts over her employees. Based on factual

37. Malou (Odile Versois) and Vicki (Diana Dors) in *Passport to Shame*. bfi Collections

journalism, the film asserts its credentials as a social document by incorporating, near the beginning, a lecture by a judicial official about the prostitution problem and using the device of a student researching her thesis on call girls as a narrative axis. The main dramatic focus is on one of the prostitutes, Madeleine (Eva Bartok), who falls in love but is too frightened to break away from Clavius and attempts suicide; the climax comes as the police raid the establishment while a striptease party is in full swing, with one of the dancers about to be raped. At the end, Madeleine and the man she loves are free to start a new life together.

A later handling of similar material, *Sperrbezirk* (West Germany, 1966), is also set in Berlin and has obvious parallels with *Madeleine Tel. 13 62 11* in its superimposition of a social realist, journalistic discourse on a personal romantic drama (although *Sperrbezirk* also attempts, unsuccessfully, to incorporate some heavy-handed comedy). The ingredients are familiar: Bernard Kalman is the kingpin of a gang that lures young women into prostitution — he is able to reinforce his personal charm with the offer of attractive apartments because he is also a real estate agent — and then exerts ruthless control over them through beating and intimidation (a police inspector shows an investigative reporter a file of photographs of women with scarred faces—"the ones who wanted to get out"). As social commentary, the perspective of the film is that the problem has been intensified by a wholesale extension of the *Sperrbezirk*—the area in which prostitutes are prohibited from operating—thus forcing the sex trade out of the inner city and making it more difficult for police to maintain surveillance of it: the effort to clean up the city has backfired. As romantic drama, *Sperrbezirk* traces the redemption of Bernard at the hands of his latest recruit, Ann (Suzanne Roquette), whose preparedness to sacrifice her body to his financial needs out of pure devotion turns him from his misguided ways. But as the inspector comments, "a pimp who falls in love is practically a dead man": Bernard's corruption is too ingrained, his crimes against womanhood too egregious for their memory to be erased. He dies in a gang fracas, and Ann is released from his psychological thrall.

In the United States, *The Phenix City Story* (1955) was a hard-hitting exposé, based on recent events of vice and corruption in Phenix City, Alabama, "the most vicious town in the United States," but there is no indication in the film that the hookers of the infamous Fourteenth Street dives are Captives, working against their will. In *Vice Raid* (1959), however, it is clear that no kid gloves are used, as Carol (Mamie Van Doren), a hustler from Detroit brought in by the New York mob to help frame an honest vice squad detective, discovers when her sister is beaten and raped by the gang boss's henchman. And in *Underworld U.S.A.* (1961), with its highly schematic treatment of organized crime, the prostitution racket is identified as one branch of a nationwide syndicate that uses ruthless strong-arm tactics in its operations, including its current drive to get more teenagers hooked on drugs and schoolgirls recruited as hookers.

International trafficking of women for the purposes of prostitution was a favorite subject of white slave films of the silent era such as *Mädchenhandel*, discussed in chapter 1. The topic was revived in strength in the 1950s and 1960s. The plot most frequently involved European women being lured or abducted to South America—as in *Marchands de filles/ Sellers of Girls* (France, 1957)—or North Africa, especially Tangiers—as in *Schwarze Nylons—heisse Nächte/Indecent* (West Germany, 1958), *Détournement de mineures/The Price of Flesh* (France, 1959), and *La casa de las mil muñecas/ Das Haus der tausend Freuden/House of a Thousand Dolls* (Spain/West Germany, 1967). In *Das Nachtlokal zum Silbermond/Caverns of Vice* (West Germany,

1960), "five German dancing girls go to Turkey to fulfill a contract at the 'Silver Moon' nightclub, only to find that more is expected of them than just dancing."[17] Similarly, exotic dancer Mara in *Acosada/The Pink Pussy* (Argentina, 1963) signs a contract in New York for a supposed job in Caracas, Venezuela, where "her passport and money are stolen, and she is abducted and raped."[18] *Passport to Shame*, as we have seen, depicts a woman being trafficked from Paris to London, and reference is also made to recruits for the British sex trade being procured in Vienna and Zurich. *La Prostitution/The White Slavers/Prostitution* (France, 1963) traces the trajectory of a young woman, Irène, from the provinces who becomes trapped in a vice ring in Paris and is sent to Hamburg, the Netherlands, Mexico, and finally Hong Kong, while in *Girl Smugglers* (USA, 1967), "to meet the demand in New York City for young Puerto Rican prostitutes, a gang is organized to kidnap young women in San Juan and smuggle them into the United States."[19] *Out of the Tiger's Mouth* (USA, 1962) offers a variant in that the victims are two Chinese children who are smuggled from the mainland to Hong Kong and from there, instead of being handed over to their uncle, they are delivered to a whorehouse in Macao.

The woman is typically offered employment in a bar or nightclub, or with a theater company. En route or at the destination, she learns that the job does not exist and is then subjected to violence, and often drugged, with the intention of coercing her into prostitution. Thus in *Marchands de filles*, "Gofferi, a member of a vicious narcotics and white slavery ring . . . soon sells Josette to Mottia, who uses drugs as well as violence to force women into compliance."[20] One of the group of female dancers who are being trafficked from Marseilles to Tangiers in *Schwarze Nylons* suspects the truth and is murdered. Irène of *La Prostitution* "is drugged until she becomes an addict" in Hong Kong.[21] Mara in *Acosada* falls under the control of a "vice lord who lures women to Caracas, drugs them, and forces them into white slavery,"[22] while Diane in the baroque *House of a Thousand Dolls* is kidnapped and held captive in a brothel run by "illusionists who use their magic act to drug and overpower young women for an international ring of white slavers."[23]

Help, however, is at hand. An investigative journalist comes to the rescue (*Schwarze Nylons, Détournement de mineures*), or a friend or lover intervenes. In some cases the local police smashes the ring, in others Interpol does the job (*Marchands de filles, Schwarze Nylons, La Prostitution*). The Captive is liberated.

These films were often quite authentic in depicting the recruitment techniques used by traffickers. Fraudulent offers of employment in the entertainment or hospitality industry in a foreign country, for example, have been resorted to over many decades.[24] The films, however, totally ignored those women — probably the majority — who knowingly migrated for the purposes of working in the sex trade abroad. And in emphasizing violence and constructing a rescue narrative, they considerably underplayed the day-to-day problems of prostitutes working outside their country of origin.[25]

With the social-problem and international trafficking pictures, whatever their proclaimed seriousness of intent, there was always an additional agenda at work. At a time when nudity in the cinema was rare, for example, *Les Compagnes de la nuit* contains a sequence in which prostitutes are treated in a clinic, stripped to the waist with their breasts prominently bared — voyeurism in the guise of documentary realism. And later in the film we are shown Jo seizing, manhandling, and brutally slapping Yvonne, causing her death. In *Madeleine Tél. 13 62 11*, while Madeleine herself is modestly attired throughout, there is a great deal of visual eroticism in the portrayal of other women at Frau Clavius's house, and the sexual assault by an older client on a striptease dancer is explicitly depicted. The opportunities the Captive characterization provided for female bodily display and the depiction of sexual activity and violence, especially against women, were seized upon by filmmakers, and eventually, as censorship relaxed, all pretense at making a socially concerned statement about the evils of prostitution was dropped.

Europe led the way with productions such as *Brigade des moeurs / Paris Vice Patrol* (France, 1959), a *policier* about a Paris prostitution ring described as "offering ready excuses for intermittent . . . striptease acts,"[26] and *Des femmes disparaissent / The Road to Shame* (France, 1959), in which the story of the smashing of a gang of white-slave traffickers in Marseilles provides viewers with a "detailed recital of assaults, murders and whippings" reaching a "bullet-spattered climax."[27]

The films that followed exploited the heightened erotic tension that a narrative of coercion supplies, with the heterosexual male viewer, at least, torn between sympathy for the victim and a pleasurable but consciously disavowed identification with the captor. Such an appeal is evident from the plot synopses: thus *In Frankfurt sind die Nächte Heiss / Call Girls of Frankfurt* (Austria, 1966) features "a gang war between the underworld rivals . . . in which the prostitutes are stripped and humiliated,"[28] and in *Traquenards Érotiques / Érotique* (France, 1969) "Varen and Bob agree to help Georges, a white slave trader, although Varen has misgivings about their involvement, particularly after Leda, a pretty young girl, has been lured into Georges' clutches."[29] Similar dynamics are set up in other films depicting young women at the mercy of ruthless pimps and gangsters, such as *Heisses Pflaster Köln/Walk the Hot Streets* (West Germany, 1967), *Engel der Sünde/Angels of Sin*[30] (West Germany, 1967), *Schamlos/Shameless* (Austria/France/West Germany, 1968), and *Schrei nach Lust/Cry for Lust* (West Germany, 1968).

Nudity and sexual content steadily increased during the 1960s, reaching a climax in a film such as *Die Mädchenhandler/White Slavers* (Switzerland/West Germany, 1972) in which the coerced-prostitution plotline is reduced to little more than a pretext. "In order to assemble a number of attractive girls who will be kidnapped and sold to brothels overseas, a gang of white slavers organize a 'Miss Bosom' contest in Berlin," the story goes. "Each of the nine finalists is seen undressing as she considers entering the contest, is admired naked on stage, and is kidnapped and imprisoned until she learns to accept her fate. The girls are then seen running a brothel."[31]

Simultaneously the quota of violence, particularly of a sadistic nature, was rising. In *L'Amour à la chaîne/Tight Skirts, Loose Pleasures* (France, 1965), for example, "after joining a new brothel managed by Corinne, Pornotropos' mistress, Catherine is brutally assaulted when she refuses the gangster's advances." After she has escaped from the syndicate, "Pornotropos, assisted by his brother Thanatos, a sadistic killer, and by a pair of murderous twins, pursues and recaptures Catherine."[32] *Massacre pour une orgie/Massacre of Pleasure* (Luxembourg, 1966) depicts the activities of a Parisian crime syndicate that drugs and kidnaps young women and sells them off to brothels. The victims are compelled "to submit to sadistic sexual practices," and "the gangsters torture and murder those who refuse to cooperate."[33]

By 1973, with the demented *Dvaergen/The Sinful Dwarf* (Denmark/USA, 1973), the Captive formula in European cinema was fully into its baroque phase, exploited unashamedly for its sadomasochist pleasures, though with a certain element of self-reflexivity. Young women are lured with the aid of a mechanical puppy into a house in London, where they are stripped naked, locked up, and sometimes chained by the vile dwarf of the title in a filthy attic brothel, forcibly addicted to heroin to pacify them, and turned into pure sex objects for the delectation of the clientele. The repulsiveness of proceedings is perhaps mitigated by the invitation held out to sadists in the audience to recognize in the greasy, depraved villain an image of themselves—though the choice of a dwarf for the part may also be a device by means of which violent fantasies can be simultaneously indulged and disowned.

Developments in Europe were paralleled in the United States, with the slackening of censorship constraints and the expansion of the independent sector of the industry resulting in a flood of low-budget Captive sexploitation movies in the 1960s and 1970s. Films taking advantage of the formula to show scenes of rape, captivity, bondage, and torture heavily predominate.

The 1964 *Olga* series starring Audrey Campbell was representative of the trend. In the first, *White Slaves of Chinatown,* Olga is introduced as a syndicate-backed dealer in narcotics and white slavery, "luring young women newly released from prison to her headquarters in New York's Chinatown." Here, in her basement dungeon "filled with medieval torture devices designed to destroy the resistance of the most hardened captives," she uses her sadistic techniques, including forcible drug addiction, to condition the women into becoming pushers and prostitutes, prepared to "do the bidding of the syndicate in cities around the country."[34] The sequel, *Olga's Girls,* again dwells on the condition of her "drug-addicted slaves, brutally tortured for the slightest offense, some of them locked into chastity belts." Olga "punishes an informer discovered in their midst by cutting out her tongue." Her assistant defects to set up a rival call-girl business, "taking many of the best girls with her," but after a battle Olga emerges victorious.[35] *Olga's House of Shame* transposes the setting to a deserted mining shack in upstate New York, where Olga has retreated after having been run out of Chinatown. Here she "operates her School of Torture, forcibly training young girls in prostitution and narcotics peddling. She metes out fiendish punishments for the slightest offense and terrorizes her slaves into complete obedience."[36]

It was not uncommon for the films of this cycle to feature a female torturer, perhaps mirroring the tendency that can be observed in prostitute murder stories of displacing guilt away from the male (see chapter 19). The successor to the *Olga* series, *Mme. Olga's Massage Parlor* (1965), depicts Olga's "health club" being taken over by syndicate gangsters Elaine and Nick, and Elaine, too, enforces "iron discipline" over her "captive, high-priced call girls."[37] In similar vein, *The Devil's Sisters* (1966) shows a young woman, Teresa, lured to a secluded Mexican hacienda owned by the Alvarado sisters, where she is beaten and starved, and eventually forced by Rita Alvarado "to accept the advances of a procession of men"; later, Teresa is sent to a barn in the country where she is tortured, along with other victims, by Marta, "a sadistic, cigar-smoking tyrant."[38] Likewise, Ellie in *Cargo of Love* (1968) becomes prey to the Lupo sisters who run a "white slave racket" to keep their estate, "a playground for wealthy men," supplied with pliable females; Ellie, after being drugged, "awakens to the screams of an inmate being flogged and is alerted to the danger of attempting to escape when another inmate is tortured to death and burned."[39] The theme is reprised in *Invitation to Ruin* (1968), in which Mama Lupo "conditions" young women at her castle for "a syndicate head who supplies women to buyers around the country." One new recruit, Elaine, "is taken to a dungeon where she is tied to a bed and raped"; Mama Lupo then "interrupts the whipping of a favorite 'slave' to administer heroin to Elaine and sexually abuse her."[40] Other films showing young prostitutes under the control of a sadistic lesbian include *And Five Makes Jason* (1969), *Sex Circus* (1969), and *Carny Girl* (1970).

In movies in which the principal malefactors are male, there is characteristically a stronger emphasis on rape and blackmail as prostitution recruitment techniques. In *The Block* (1964), for example, dancer Violet is raped, threatened with exposure by means of pornographic film and photographs, and killed when she tries to go to the police, while fellow entertainer Penny is seduced, coerced into prostitution, and tortured. The use of force is highlighted in *Tortured Females* (1965), in which a traveler, Helen, takes a swim in a creek when she is out in the country and is spotted by a hunter: "He takes her into the woods and rapes her. Then he leaves her at a house used as the center of a white slave ring, and there she is beaten and tortured. Another woman there is beaten to death and secretly buried on the property. During an orgy, Helen is stripped and forced to perform."[41] On the other hand, compromising films and photographs, as in *The Block*, are deployed in *Blackmailed Wives* (1968), *The Wildest!* (1969), and *We Do It!* (1970).

The pattern was amenable to period adaptation: in *Lady Godiva Rides* (1969), for instance, a party of English maidens are trafficked to California in the mid-nineteenth century to service the saloon clientele in a wild frontier mining town, while *House of the Red Dragon*, of the same year, is set in San Francisco's Chinatown in the 1890s ("The enraged father throws Heather into his opium den where she is bound and drugged into gratifying the sexual desires of his customers.").[42] But it is perhaps in venturing into contemporary social comment that the Captive sexploitation formula yielded its most intriguing results. In *The Cycle Savages* (also 1969), a Los Angeles motorcycle gang recruits women against their will for subsequent sale to a Las Vegas prostitution ring. They kidnap Janie —

a high-school-age girl eating ice cream at a bus stop—rape her one by one, and give her a large dose of LSD. The technique is not particularly effective, however; Janie simply goes to the police, and the gang members are arrested. The "white slavery" operation does not convince, and seems dreamed up as just one more crime to lay at the feet of these crazed drug-freak-free-loving-rapist-hippie-motorcycle rebels.

With the social-problem, international trafficking, and sexploitation cycles—and no doubt comparable developments in the cinemas of other countries, notably Japan—the conventions of Captive representation were well and truly established.[43] They were available to be called on whenever it was felt desirable, for whatever reason, to introduce the topic of forced prostitution. In the remainder of this chapter I single out three films that, in being firmly anchored in social reality and rejecting fantasy-fulfillment, have used—and played against—the conventions to powerful effect.

Kei Kumai's *Sandakan hachibanshokan bohkyob / Sandakan No. 8* (Japan, 1974) is the unsensational, experience-based version of the international trafficking narrative. It is structured as a series of flashbacks as Osaki, now an old woman, recounts her life story to the researcher who has come to stay with her in her very modest home in Amakusa. Osaki (played as a young woman by Yoko Takahashi) was a *karayuki-san*, a woman who worked as a prostitute overseas. She is a child when she leaves Japan, in the fond expectation of improving the family's fortunes after her father's death. Her brother had sold her to a brothel owner, and she is smuggled out in a coal vessel, eventually reaching Sandakan in Borneo. There she lives in the brothel and works as a maid until, at the age of fourteen, she is compelled to become a prostitute. Osaki explains that she spent seventeen years there until, with the death of the owner, she was able to get away. She married and lived in Manchuria, but her husband died during the war, and back in Japan she has experienced only poverty and ostracism as a stigmatized *karayuki-san*, rejected even by her own brother (who built his house on the money she sent) and son.

Kumai's treatment is striking for the comparative absence of violence and eroticism. When told she must go to bed with customers, Osaki rebels ("We didn't say we'd be whores! . . . I refuse!") but is brutally slapped and informed of the two-thousand-yen debt she must repay with her body. She makes a run for it, only to be grabbed and dragged into her room. The madam consoles her ("All women have to do it sooner or later—no tears on your first night"), and Osaki—as clearly she must, given the power differential — relents. We see her first client thrusting himself on her, and her face screwed up in pain, tears in her eyes. Thereafter it is work she is compelled to perform, relentlessly ("I couldn't take a rest even though I had a headache"), as bonded labor. A montage sequence depicts the typical experience: the client leans down / his hands / his looming face / his feet pressing against the bed end / his body moving / Osaki's expressionless face. She remains at the brothel not through continued violence and intimidation, but because of debt enslavement and the lack of other options; the one man whom she falls in love with and who promises to redeem her eventually reneges when he sees her lying naked, unattractive, worn out. The film ends with the researcher, a young woman, paying her respects at the graves of the Sandakan *karayuki-san* who did not survive, the markers now almost swallowed up by the Malaysian jungle.

The achievement of *Shirins Hochzeit/Shirin's Wedding* (West Germany, 1976) by Helma Sanders-Brahms is to infuse a bleak social analysis with a vividly realized female subjectivity. Rebelling against poverty and the marriage her uncles have arranged for her, Shirin (Ayten Erten) makes her way from rural Turkey to Germany as a migrant worker, in search of Mahmud, to whom she was betrothed in childhood. She obtains accommodation in a hostel and employment in a factory, but loses both when there is an economic downturn. Raped when she pleads against her dismissal from a cleaning job, she is rendered ineligible in Turkish custom for marriage and will be unwelcome if she returns home. Dispirited, without a work permit, Shirin is powerless to resist the blandishments of the pimp who promises free meals, lodging, a stamp in her passport, and lots of money. "You knew what they would do with you," the director comments, in a voice-over dialogue with her protagonist, which she conducts throughout the film. "Not exactly," Shirin replies. "What I was thinking was, I should go on, not looking left and right." Her words express the hopelessness of her situation and her resigned acceptance of whatever fate may have in store for her. In an action that occurs offscreen, she is immediately burned with a cigarette on her forearm, branded.

She is sent by her pimp through a cellar window into a workers' hostel, instructed to service six clients. Among the men there she finds Mahmud. Turning her head away to avoid recognition, she has sex with him, and as his hands move over her, she imagines the wedding she has dreamed of all her life, with the villagers around them, the fields, and the noise of the wind. Then he nudges her, and she gets out of bed, takes her

38. Shirin (Ayten Erten) with Jannis (Jannis Kyriakidis) in *Shirins Hochzeit*. Stiftung Deutsche Kinemathek — Filmmuseum Berlin.

clothes, and resumes her life of prostitution. Shortly afterwards she will be killed, shot in the back by a pimp when, exhausted, she ignores his order to get back to work. Better than any comparable study, *Shirins Hochzeit* demonstrates how prostitution is imposed on women disempowered by patriarchy and economic imperialism.

The more traditional male perspective of *Les Filles de Grenoble* (France, 1981), is perhaps best illustrated by the fact that when the protagonist, Cora (Zoé Chauveau), receives a cigarette burn from one of her pimps, it is on her breast, which has been exposed by tearing her dress, and the act of torture is shown, albeit briefly, in close-up. A similar voyeuristic camera is at work in an earlier scene, showing her being broken in, scantily dressed, as a prostitute: vehemently objecting that she is not going to be a whore, that taking on clients was not part of the arrangement, she is seized, manhandled onto a table, held down with a belt around her neck as she struggles, injected with a drug, laid out on her back on a bed, and callously assaulted by a pimp who rips off her bra. Nonetheless, if the film, directed by Joël Le Moign', inherits something of the sadistic tendency of the Captive sexploitation cycle, it also develops the social-problem tradition in several significant ways. Based on recent events — the breaking up in 1980 of a brutal gang of pimps in Grenoble, and their conviction on the testimony of four of their prostitute victims — the film benefits from an adherence to fact (at the expense, at times, of narrative tidiness) and a documentary realism in the filming of the bleak locations where the sex work actually takes place — a barren strip of highway, a grim workers' barracks in an industrial wasteland. Moreover, like *Sandakan No. 8*, *Les Filles de Grenoble* invites us to experience the horror of relentless violation of the body from the point of view of the woman concerned: the agony on Cora's face as one of the workers in the barracks thrusts at her, with others standing awaiting their turn, and then a montage of men approaching and looming down over her, one after another (we are told later that there were eighty or so), until she can bear it no more. She screams and races away, only to be caught, struck viciously with a belt, and brought back.

The socially critical stance of *Les Filles de Grenoble* is also strengthened by its suggestion that gangs of pimps are not more frequently prosecuted because of cozy relationships they enjoy with the police and the judiciary: the superintendent admits that usually they don't go after pimps because they're valuable informers, and the prosecutor, who attempts to dissuade the judge from pressing the case (those girls, he says, can lie through their teeth), is shown to be on very friendly terms with one of the defendants. But perhaps the film's most provocative comment on coerced prostitution is reserved for the very end. The credits are rolling over a shot of a street in a red-light district at night, thronged with people, when suddenly the accompanying song about prostitutes being exploited by pimps is interrupted by a voice-over: "There are also three million clients whom one never speaks of. Why?"

11

Business Woman

Keeping her customers happy seems to be the simpler part of the
business for Ann. As a manager of a service business, she must meet a
fixed set of customer needs: to have in stock what he wants, to keep
regular and convenient hours, to be in a convenient location, to keep
prices down, and to give him attention when he wants it.
—BARBARA SHERMAN HEYL, *The Madam as Entrepreneur*[1]

The intrusion of the economic motive into sex is always in a greater or
less degree disastrous.
—BERTRAND RUSSELL[2]

The Business Woman is the prostitute who capitalizes on her assets. She
engages in the trade without any qualms as to its morality, and being in
charge of her own affairs she does not suffer like the Captive or Martyr.
If she is happy enough earning a bit of extra money now and then, she
continues to engage in casual, part-time prostitution, choosing the time,
the place, the customer. If she is ambitious she rises in the social scale
along with the prosperity of her clientele — without ever being able fully
to shake the stigma of the whore — and may well expand her business interests by becoming a madam. As the ultimate variant of the type, the
dominatrix, so clearly demonstrates, the Business Woman is in thrall to
no man, be he pimp or customer, cop or brothel-keeper — though the
marginal legal status of her enterprise curbs her power, and she may be
vulnerable if she overreaches herself.

Business Woman films show prostitution as an integral part of the
capitalist economic system and, to some degree, a symbol of it. The
metaphor operates in two diametrically opposed ways. For critics of capitalism, prostitution is a model of the distortion of interpersonal relationships and the human alienation that occurs in a society in which all
activities become commercialized. But for advocates of free enterprise,

prostitution can become an image of the way a market economy allows for the fulfillment of human desire in all of its diversity.

The metaphoric overtones are explicitly invoked in films of both tendencies. Thus, for example, *Mandi/Marketplace* (India, 1983) centers on a brothel whose rhetorical function is to burlesque middle-class hypocrisy and the corrupt practices of local politicians and businessmen: "Indeed," writes Sumita S. Chakravarty, "a distinct link is made between whoring and the Indian business community."[3] Similarly, *Patul conjugal/The Conjugal Bed* (Romania, 1991) deploys prostitution as a symbol of the venal nature of postcommunist society. "Everybody in *The Conjugal Bed* speaks about starting a business, be it selling balloons or shooting porn," comments Dina Iordanova. "Everything is now called a 'business company.'" Stela (Coca Bloos), cashier in a movie theater, "becomes a prostitute, or rather she enters an 'escort business' run by her husband. . . . Now, in a situation where one's own body is the only capital available for venturing into the new capitalism, her promiscuity is exploited as a business asset."[4]

In other films, however, the prostitution-business connection is cause for comic celebration. In *Anonima cocottes/Petites femmes et haute finance/The Call Girl Business* (Italy/France, 1960), for instance, call girl Jeanne (Anita Ekberg) becomes involved with an honest bank cashier, Paolo, who has been discredited and sacked for blowing the whistle on his embezzling bosses. "She musters her call girl friends, who appoint Paolo their financial adviser and form themselves into a company which, through Paolo's manipulations and their bedroom intrigue, eventually takes over the bank."[5] Although the Copenhagen-based Swedish prostitute (Diana Kjaer) in *Dagmars Heta Trosor/Dagmar's Hot Pants Inc./Dagmar & Co.* (Sweden/USA/Denmark, 1972) is getting out of the business ("I've decided that now's the time to quit, when I'm ahead"), the film stresses her financial independence and ability to support men — she has been bankrolling her fiancé's medical studies — while validating prostitution as a socially worthwhile enterprise. Dagmar winds up her affairs after a farewell visit to her stockbroker . . . during which she sexually initiates his son. In *Catherine et Cie./Un letto in società/Catherine & Co.* (France/Italy, 1975), Manchester girl Catherine (Jane Birkin) arrives in Paris and sets herself up as a prostitute with a regular clientele. Learning from a stockbroker-lover about the mechanisms of corporation ownership, "she then forms Catherine and Company, with herself as the capital investment and all her male friends as stockholders,"[6] and makes her fortune.

While films such as *Marketplace* and *The Conjugal Bed* inherit the mainstream socialist tradition, discussed in chapter 5, of condemning the system that generates prostitution, *Anonima cocottes* and its successors herald the growing normalization of the sex trade, acknowledging capitalism's interest in making it a legitimate business activity like any other. The stark contrast in attitude results in fascinating contradictions in the Business Woman archetype as it evolves. The left-wing version enjoys a snug fit with the "official" patriarchal line of deploring prostitution, whereas the right-wing version, aligned with "unofficial" patriarchal ideology and buttressed by the global expansion of free-market forces, challenges this position head-on.

The left-wing inflexion of the prostitution-capitalism metaphor originates with Marx. In the *Economic and Philosophical Manuscripts* (1844), he describes capitalism as a system in which "*an inhuman power* rules over everything," refers to money as "the universal whore" with "the power to confuse and invert all human and natural qualities," and notes that "since prostitution is a relationship which includes both the one who is prostituted and the one who prostitutes (and the latter is much more base), so the capitalist, etc. comes within this category."[7]

While the analogy is a complex one, it may be seen to have two main aspects. In the first place, both prostitution and capitalism are regarded as corrupting, in that subordinating other goals and concerns, including moral considerations, to the one goal of making money corrodes one's integrity. Second, they are conceived of as alienating, in that converting human interrelationships into commercial transactions turns persons into objects.

Both aspects may be observed, in embryo, in the Rome episode of Roberto Rossellini's *Paisà/Paisan* (Italy, 1946), in which the contours of the left-wing variant of the Business Woman film begin to take shape. This powerful essay on the social impact of the occupation of the city by American troops (as representative of the forces of capitalism) centers on a hardened streetwalker (Maria Michi), who is contrasted in flashback with the demure, innocent young woman of a few months earlier, at the moment of liberation. Here the degradation of the heroine is symbolic of a general social collapse in values: coarseness, brutality, and cynicism supplant gentleness and hope.

The earlier encounter between Francesca and American GI Fred, significantly presented as *his* flashback, is pictured as an occasion for joy overriding the difficulties of communication: laughing, they exchange inapposite expressions from a phrase book. Michi's playing is marked by a delicacy—when Fred places his hand on her wrist, for example, she shyly withdraws it, then turns and walks away—in total contrast to the vulgarity she displays as a prostitute six months later. In the present, drunk and disenchanted and not recognizing her, Fred as a reluctant customer of Francesca recalls the earlier time: "Now, you're all alike. Before, it was different somehow."

The Marxist deployment of prostitution as a political metaphor thus has a Christian women-should-be-virtuous subtext, with the compact narrative structure of the episode drawing upon the entrenched polarity, male-defined in relation to women's bodies, of purity and pollution. Is it any coincidence that on the day of liberation Fred comes to Francesca for water to wash away the grime accumulated in a US Army tank? The soiled woman cannot escape the taint of guilt; in fact, she obliquely condemns herself, saying, in defense of the women of Rome, "There are many decent girls who work, who've *always* worked, who've known how to protect themselves against hunger and misery." Unlike them, Francesca has become the very emblem of corruption and alienation.

For those films focusing on the aspect of corruption in the metaphoric depiction of prostitution, the typical approach was to be that of satire, as a selection of examples from West Germany, Japan, and India may demonstrate. Here sharp dealing and political graft are presented not as aberrations but as endemic to a capitalist society, just as—so it is suggested—prostitution is inevitably compromised.

The classic model is provided by Rolf Thiele's *Das Mädchen Rosemarie* (West Germany, 1958). An excoriating critique of the postwar "Economic Miracle," the film was based on the actual case of a young Frankfurt call girl, Rosemarie Nitribitt, whose client list included men prominent in business, industry, and politics, and whose 1957 murder was never solved.[8] *Das Mädchen Rosemarie* is constantly surprising in its idiosyncratic mix of comedy, musical, and melodrama, and German critics have referred to it as a *Lehrstück* employing alienation techniques.[9]

A close link between the prostitute and the new corporate elite is established in the opening sequence, in which the platinum blonde Rosemarie (Nadja Tiller) joins two street minstrels as they sing an irreverent ditty about the Economic Miracle ("Yes, the blossoms of our Miracle are shining bright in neon light"), and then offers herself suggestively to a bevy of businessmen gathered for a conference. Rosemarie ("from an early age she hiked her skirt above her knee") is to become the very symbol of the mercenary values of the much-heralded business revival.

39. Poster for *Das Mädchen Rosemarie*.

The film's plot follows her spectacular upward mobility, marked in particular by her acquisition of that cachet of German postwar prosperity, a Mercedes SL 190 sports car, as she moves among a circle of building materials magnates, manipulated by a French businessman wishing to penetrate their cartel. Eventually she learns too much for her own good, but the film focuses less on the intrigue, which leads to her death, than on the milieu in which it occurs. The controversial movie's satirical sideswipe at the culture of the Economic Miracle is carried out through the emblematic characterization of Rosemarie who, subordinating everything to the goal of making money, simply apes what the businessmen around her are doing.

In *Anita Drögemöller und die Ruhe an der Ruhr/Peace on the Ruhr* (West Germany, 1976), the target is big business and governmental corruption in the industrial center of the Ruhr. After being raped in high school, Anita (Monique van de Ven) works her way up from streetwalker and barmaid to high-class call girl, acquiring among her clientele a clique of crooked business executives and politicians including, on one occasion, an American vice-president named Spiro Kaizler, who romps with her while attending to his percentage of a Lockheed bribe. Like Rosemarie, however, Anita gets entangled in a surveillance plot and is eventually bumped off. Wavering uncertainly between political drama, vulgar comedy, and erotica, *Anita Drögemöller* lacks the panache of its predecessor but continues the leftist tradition of linking prostitution with the venality of capitalism.

The Japanese cinema draws at times on a similar vein of satire, principally in the work of Shohei Imamura. His *Buta to gunkan/Pigs and Battleships/The Flesh is Hot* (1961), for example, zeroes in on both the Japanese underworld and the US military in its depiction of illegal rackets, including prostitution, flourishing around the American naval base at Yokosuka. Here the rape of the heroine, Haruko, by a group of rowdy and violent American servicemen—filmed with the camera above the bed rotating slowly, then faster and faster—seems to presage her being dragged down into a whirlpool of prostitution. At the end, however, as a large group of Japanese sex workers eagerly rush toward the landing stage at which sailors from an American aircraft carrier are arriving, Haruko determinedly walks in the opposite direction, toward the train that will take her to Nagasaki. Thus, unlike *Paisà, Pigs and Battleships* finally holds out some hope for the retention of personal/national integrity versus surrender to American money/military power.[10] Among Imamura's subsequent films, *Nippon konchuki/The Insect Woman* (1963) corrosively chronicles the career of an ignorant young peasant woman who becomes the proprietor of a call-girl business in Tokyo; *Jinruigaku nyumon: erogotshi yori/ The Pornographers: An Introduction to Anthropology* (1966) comically portrays the activities of an incompetent group of men running a pornography and pandering enterprise (they hire prostitutes and put on an orgy for tired businessmen, declaring "Debauchery is the way to freedom!"); while *Zegen* (1987) satirizes Japanese imperialism in recounting the true adventures of a pimp who, seeing himself as a patriotic entrepreneur, sets up a chain of whorehouses throughout Southeast Asia.

The use of prostitution as an image of the corrupting nature of a profit-hungry society is also evident in Indian cinema, in the films for example of Shyam Benegal (such as *Marketplace*, mentioned earlier) and Satyajit Ray. Of the motivation behind his *Jana Aranya/ The Middleman* (India, 1975), Ray declared: "I felt corruption, rampant corruption all around, and I didn't think there was any solution."[11] The principled young protagonist, Somnath, attempts to enter the business world as a *dalal*, or middleman, but soon discovers to his chagrin that the only way he can pull off a major deal is by employing the services of a call girl to soften up his client. Against his better nature, he succumbs, recognizing it is no coincidence that the other meaning of *dalal* is pimp.

Films that concentrate on the aspect of alienation in the prostitution-capitalism analogy constitute a diverse group whose common thread is the lack of human fulfillment in a society ruled by commercial imperatives. Dimensions include a weakness for illusory satisfactions, an absence of deeply felt emotion, self-objectification, and a forfeiture of individual identity to mass consumerism.

"This is a big concrete box divided into compartments and each compartment is a machine for making money," the brothel madam (Shelley Winters) tells her bookkeeper, in *The Balcony* (USA, 1963), adapted from Jean Genet's play. "We sell dreams! Your job is to keep the overhead down." In the streets of an unnamed city a revolutionary uprising, depicted in recycled newsreel footage, is taking place, but at the "house of illusion" it is business as usual. Here prostitute-client interactions are rigidified by an all-pervasive stereotypical role-playing, such that nothing as earthy as intercourse seems ever to take place. A gas station attendant masquerading as a bishop sweats lewd confessions out of a "penitent" (Joyce Jameson); a milk wagon driver plays a military general riding a whinnying "horse" (Arnette Jens) in black negligee; an accountant taking on the role of a judge hears a recitation of a crime by a "thief" (Ruby Dee) and licks the toe of her shoe. The security situation worsens, but when the fake dignitaries are paraded through the streets by the chief of

40. Ruby Dee in *The Balcony*. David Lascelles Stills Collection.

police, the rebellion is quelled. Satirizing social hierarchies and the ideological glue that holds a society together, *The Balcony* renders absurd a
population's obeisance to the authoritarian structures of the law, the
army, and the church (it is interesting to note that big business is unrep-
resented). At the end, the madam addresses the camera: "You can all go
home now. To your own homes, your own beds, where you can be sure
everything will be even falser than it is here."

The idea of the alienation of prostitution as one manifestation of the
more general alienation of contemporary society pervades the work of
Fassbinder. Here, it may be sufficient to cite *Katzelmacher* (West Germany,
1969), the director's adaptation of his own play about the disruptive impact of a foreign migrant worker on a group of Munich layabouts. The
film is striking for its coolness and detachment, the casualness of sex for
money paralleling the unemotional nature of the interpersonal relationships. The camera does not move in closer to allow us to read the com-
plexity of feeling registered in a face, nor to heighten the erotic charge of
the naked body stripped for sex. Rosy (Elga Sorbas) qualifies as a Business Woman in the sense that she is under no man's control, but she is
little more than an amateur, confining her clientele to her circle of friends
and failing to make anything approaching a decent living from her work.

In this milieu prostitution, as with other forms of mutual exploitation, is so thoroughly engrained that the whole film, as with much of Fassbinder's work, is permeated by a thoroughgoing pessimism.

Barroco, sometimes referred to as *Barocco* (France, 1976) reworks familiar territory in associating prostitution with its disabused study of contemporary capitalism and the dirty dealings it is steeped in: a newspaper editor is publishing embarrassing revelations about a candidate in an upcoming election. But in its representation of the prostitute character, Nelly (Marie-France Pisier), it interestingly explores the notion of alienation as reification. Nelly is first seen displaying herself in a street-level window of the red-light district (the film is shot in Amsterdam, though set in a fictional French city): beautiful, elegant, she poses in glittering low-cut blouse and tight skirt. Director André Téchiné comments: "Shop windows and windows in general have a strong attraction for me, which has to do, I think, with the frame. . . . It is something that greatly fascinates me though I have not been able to theorize it, this form of fixity of everything that is framed."[12] Outside the frame, the character escapes self-alienation. Somewhat apart from the typical Business Woman caught up in the cycle of consumption, Nelly with her baby daughter and male partner has no great material ambitions; she simply wishes to be able to support herself in a less exhausting profession, perhaps one with a cultural side to it, like bookstore assistant. But in the last shot of the film, she is back in the window. As rain washes heavily down the glass, she sits legs spread, a blurred figure by a table lamp, and takes a drag on her cigarette. Crowds scurry past the lighted rectangle.

While shooting *2 ou 3 choses que je sais d'elle/ Two or Three Things I Know About Her* (France, 1967), Jean-Luc Godard famously commented that the idea for the film was sparked off by a newspaper anecdote that "linked up with one of my pet theories, that in order to live in society in Paris today, on no matter what social level, one is forced to prostitute oneself in one way or another — or to put it another way, to live under conditions resembling those of prostitution. . . . In modern industrial society, prostitution is the norm."[13] In his portrait of a housewife-prostitute, Juliette (Marina Vlady), shot and assembled in trademark deconstructionist style, Godard thus makes overt appeal to the Marxian metaphor. With much of the analysis centered on the massive new housing developments on the outskirts of the city, where Juliette's apartment is located, the film establishes the sociopolitical context by means of comments made near the beginning by the director in his whispered voice-over: "I conclude that the Gaullist government under a mask of modernization and reform is merely regularizing the natural tendencies of capitalism. . . . Undoubtedly, the planning of the Paris region will . . . allow the monopolies to shape the economy without reference to the needs of its eight million inhabitants."

An anonymous streetwalker stands against a wall. When she speaks to a man (a pimp, as we discover later) who comes up to her, we do not hear her voice. Instead, we hear the voice of Jean-Luc Godard intoning at some length what purports to be the typical history ("always the same story") of the woman with young children forced on the streets to support her family. It may be this prostitute's story, but if it is, she does not get to tell it. Juliette, inverting this paradigm, speaks for Godard, musing philosophically in direct address to camera on issues particularly to do with communication and meaning, which we know from the voice-over to be the director's concern. Marina Vlady commented: "And then there is this girl, Juliette, to whom I lend my physical presence, because it is difficult, with Godard, to speak of playing a part."[14] Insofar as it is possible to read Juliette as a character in a drama, her alienation is signaled principally in her emotional shallowness and her capitulation to consumerism. She exhibits no strong feelings either way toward her husband, and at one point mulls over the idea of leaving him ("He doesn't want to get ahead in the world, he's content as he is."). She engages in prostitution principally to augment her wardrobe, and mouths advertising language ("Would you like me to wear tights designed to look like kneesocks? They make daring dresses decent, and flatter young, slender legs").

The scenes with clients (a young Métro worker, an American Vietnam War correspondent) are marked by radical dissociation between the thinking subject—Juliette continuing her disjointed philosophical monologue—and the body that mechanically goes through the motions of prostitution; the sex itself is elided. The two do not connect except for the brief moment when Juliette says, in her usual expressionless tone, "He's going to put himself between my legs." With the war correspondent, Juliette and her friend Marianne (Anny Duperey) parade up and down naked at his command—though the framing shows only the airline bags that cover their heads. Meanwhile, in the real world, the atrocities in Vietnam—to which there are several pointed references—continue. For Godard, says Vlady, "prostitution is only a pretext, or rather a limit point, a caricature."[15]

Godard's reflections on the subject continue in *Sauve qui peut (la vie) / Every Man for Himself / Slow Motion* (France / Switzerland / West Germany / Austria, 1980). Juliette in *2 ou 3 choses* twice says no to particular sexual acts, but here the prostitute characters—who appear principally in a section of the film labeled "Commerce"—seem prepared to do virtually anything for money, thus turning themselves into pure instrumentality.[16] In one celebrated scene, Isabelle (Isabelle Huppert) and Nicole (Nicole Wicht) take part in group sex, which becomes, under the control of the businessman client, a parodic series of mechanical interconnections, enacting what one critic has termed the "technocrat's wet dream—the Taylorization of sexual production."[17] During the scenes of prostitution there is frequently a detachment, as in *2 ou 3 choses,* between the subjective experience and the bodily ritual, here signaled by the stratagem of a stream-of-consciousness voice-over. Thus when Isabelle is faking sexual pleasure with one client, Paul (who is not taken in, saying "Don't work so hard, don't pretend"), we hear her thoughts: "It was going to be a long one, but never mind. She could use the time to organize her day. First she'll tidy up her room—impeccably . . ." (The device is paralleled in *Dagmars Heta Trosor* by the comic superimposition of thought balloons—images of a blouse, shoes, and a hot dog—in a shot of Dagmar having sex with a client, saying, "Listen baby, you're driving me out of my mind."[18]) Finally, *Sauve qui peut* suggests by means of montage intercutting that the alienation of its prostitute characters extends more generally into society. Katherine S. Woodward remarks that "the frequent cuts between Isabel's prostitution and the normal-looking people rushing to work keeps the emphasis on the pervasiveness of the exploitation and acquiescence and away from the individual people involved,"[19] while Kristin Thompson avers that "the narration seems to be trying, during Isabelle's portion, to generalize her position as a prostitute to the population as a whole—a sort of intellectual montage to associate the metaphor of prostitution with all sexual and commercial intercourse."[20] Deployment of the Marxian analogy here reaches an apogee.

In stark contrast, Business Woman films that have no quarrel with capitalism become a vehicle for the dissemination of bourgeois ideology and register the twentieth century's interest in determining whether prostitution might emerge from its pariah status and become a business like any other. The films accompany and promote the growing trend toward normalization of the sex industry—one aspect of which is the ability to feature the subject in mainstream media where once the very mention of it was taboo.

At first, the films stressed the links with organized crime that develop when prostitution is illegal. Thus *Frisco Jenny* (USA, 1933) depicts the successful career of San Francisco madam Jenny Sandoval (Ruth Chatterton) as being dependent on her close business and personal relationship with a crooked politician who runs illegal gambling and bootleg liquor operations; in court, they are denounced for "controlling together commercialized vice, on which they mutually fattened." Similarly, the dramatization of the life of notorious New York madam Polly Adler (Shelley Winters), *A House is Not a Home* (USA, 1964), focuses on her ties with a bootlegger attached to Lucky Luciano's gang, and her brothel becomes "an undercover meeting place for corrupt politicians, racketeers, and businessmen."[21] This motif was revisited in period films from a later date, including *Kitty and the Bagman* (Australia, 1982), set in Sydney in the 1920s, in which English immigrant Kitty O'Rourke (Liddy Clark) is put in charge of a high-class brothel by "The Bagman," a corrupt detective who "organizes the illicit vice trade on behalf of unseen political masters,"[22] and *Shakedown on the Sunset Strip* (USA, 1988), a TV movie set in Los Angeles in 1948–49 and supposedly based on fact, in which "Queen of the Hollywood madams" Brenda Allen (Joan Van Ark) manages an elite house of ill repute, which flourishes as a result of payoffs made to police top brass.

The sexual revolution of the 1960s, while not generally resulting in changes to the legal status of prostitution, made female promiscuity more socially acceptable. In doing so it ushered in a new wave of Business Woman movies, which celebrated the entrepreneurial initiative of the woman who turned her freer sex life to her financial advantage. Typical of the changing climate is *Moonlighting Wives* (USA, 1966), in which Joan Rand (Diane Vivienne), an attractive suburban housewife, "hires herself and two friends out as shorthand typists but still cannot make enough money to supplement her husband's small income." After her employer pays her for spending a night with him in a motel, "Joan is fired with the idea of setting up a call-girl business." She organizes a group of housewives to moonlight as prostitutes and builds up a wealthy clientele through contacts at a country club. The success of the operation is such that, "still masquerading as an employment agency, the business grows into a large organization with a fully staffed office, a catalogue of housewives available, and many of the town's most respected citizens on its books."[23] The principals are apprehended by police only when "a frightened newcomer flees from an orgy dressed only in her undergarments."[24] In similar vein, Penny (Gerrie Grant) in *Ready for Anything!* (USA, 1968), a "materialistic young woman," finds employment with "an agency that provides companionship for males, especially vis-

iting businessmen," quickly learns the ropes, is seduced by the proprietress of the company, and becomes a partner in the business;[25] while in
The Corporate Queen (USA, 1970), Crystal Laverne (Renay Claire), a New
York streetwalker down on her luck, teams up with a male hooker to create a highly successful massage service ("Sex was big business and the
money just didn't stop. . . . We were able to build the company into a
$200,000-a-year business.")

Clearly, the formula was readily adaptable to pornographic use.
Films in which the presentation of a flourishing brothel or call-girl business seems principally designed to exploit the opportunities for graphically displaying sexual activity include such titles as *Der nächste Herr,
dieselbe Dame / Next Man, Same Lady* (West Germany, 1968), *Das Freudenhaus /
The Bordello* (West Germany, 1971), *Prostitution clandestine* (France, 1975),
and *Oriental Blue* (USA, 1975)—in which Madame Blue's bordello inmates are turned on by means of an aphrodisiac "love juice." The dura-
bility of the narrative premise is demonstrated by a film such as *Madam
Savant* (USA, 1997), in which twenty-two-year-old Suzy Largo (Kira
Reed) from Fishbite Falls, Arkansas, finds herself taking over an upscale
Los Angeles brothel when the madam is killed during a police raid. Since
she has in her possession the precious Black Book of customer details—
it is in numeric code, but that is no problem for Suzy who is a mathematics whiz—she is able to relaunch the business successfully under new
management, though confining its operations prudently to outcalls. She
shows how the concern can be responsibly run without exploitation: the
girls get 50 percent, 10 percent goes into a health and retirement fund,
and another 10 percent into a legal defense fund. It still makes extraordinary profits for the opportunistic entrepreneur. The story line, however,
is little more than a support structure for the scenes of prostitutes cavorting with their clients, which are lingered on with soft-core relish.

Slightly more serious, though still predominantly milking a vein of
erotic comedy, were those films from the 1970s and '80s that took on the
unofficial task of promoting (though sometimes not without contradiction) the legitimation of prostitution. A number of movies, for the most
part loosely based on fact, followed in the footsteps of *A House is Not a
Home* in chronicling the careers of madams. *The Happy Hooker* (USA,
1975), from Xaviera Hollander's autobiography, traced the young Dutch
woman's rise to become "the most successful madam in New York," her
further (fictional) adventures being recounted in the sequels *The Happy
Hooker Goes to Washington* (1977) and *The Happy Hooker Goes Hollywood* (1980).
Lady of the House (USA, 1978) was an adaptation of the autobiography of

San Francisco madam Sally Stanford, while *The Best Little Whorehouse in Texas* (USA, 1982) was a film version of the Broadway musical dramatizing the closure of the renowned Chicken Ranch brothel, with the character of the madam being partially modeled on her real-life counterpart.[26] In France, Madame Claude's notoriety was celebrated in *Madame Claude/The French Woman* (1977) and *Madame Claude 2/Intimate Moments* (1981); in the UK, the vicissitudes of suburban madam Cynthia Payne became the inspiration for *Personal Services* (1987). Other films, including *Trading Places* (USA, 1983) and *Tricks of the Trade* (USA, 1988), featured the independent, freelance prostitute, while *Bei Anruf Liebe/Call for Love* (West Germany, 1983) used the device of a pseudodocumentary investigation of the prostitution scene, principally in Munich.

These films stress the entrepreneurial aspect of prostitution, the necessity of preventing pimps (described as "leeches and bloodsuckers" in *The Best Little Whorehouse in Texas*) from creaming off the profits, and the business acumen of the women involved. Xaviera (Lynn Redgrave) in *The Happy Hooker* keeps up a boastful voice-over account of her success: "My talents were so in demand and the pay scale so fantastic that in just a few months my personal savings account had grown by leaps and bounds. . . . Pretty soon I was running a tight little business with girls for men of all tastes. . . . Within three months I . . . had so many clients that the demands of my professional life started to get to me. Though I still serviced a few regular customers myself, the enormous cash flow and the job of keeping everything in shape required nearly all my time and attention." Likewise, twenty-four-year-old Ophelia (Jamie Lee Curtis) in *Trading Places* is no slouch: "I've saved forty-two grand and it's in T-bills earning interest. I figure I've got three more years on my back— I'll have enough to retire on." The business sense of this young woman from "a small, miserable-looking mining town you probably never heard of" makes her an appropriate partner for the ill-starred commodities broker with whom she strikes a deal: "I help you get yourself back on your feet and you pay me, in cash, five figures." In *Tricks of the Trade*, Marla (Markie Post) has learned about investing from her regular stockbroker client and is toying with getting certified herself.

The movies emphasize the way their female entrepreneurs supply a commodity that is in public demand. "It's just like a Tupperware party really," explains Christine Painter (Julie Walters) in *Personal Services*, "but I sell sex instead of plastic containers." Sally Stanford's brothel was, in her own words, "a place where gentlemen could relax and unwind in an atmosphere of beauty"—the clients being "bankers, industrialists—the kind of men who were not concerned with price tags, because they got their money's worth in quality." During the war, "like other industries vital to the war effort, we worked in shifts round the clock to meet the needs of our men in uniform." Madame Claude's call girls service a high-class clientele including visiting heads of state, and, in *Madame Claude 2*, assist the French government to secure loans from international bankers by ministering to their carnal desires. Most significantly, this group of films suggest that prostitution should be regarded not as a threat but as a necessary supplement to marriage. "You mean to tell me the cows don't appreciate the time off when a bull goes over to another pasture?" says Mona to Deputy Fred in *The Best Little Whorehouse in Texas*, when he protests that he's a married man. Later, in a vox pop interview, a woman lends support to this view. "My Frank when he was alive used to go up there every Saturday," she tells TV viewers. "I took it as a blessing." In *Tricks of the Trade* a murdered stockbroker's wife, Catherine, and his streetwise prostitute lover, Marla, overcome their initial mutual hostility and team up to solve the mystery of his killing. In reflecting on Donald's behavior toward them, each asks what the other has that she doesn't — and the ad for this TV movie spells it out: "The wife who loved him. The call girl who satisfied him."[27] Christine in *Personal Services* contends that "sex soon goes out of a marriage," arguing that "if the wives were willing, I'd be out of a job."

Christine's business caters, in particular, to clients' kinky tastes, including dressing as a schoolboy and being punished by the governess, dressing as a schoolgirl and poring over lesbian pornography with prostitutes likewise attired, dressing in bra and panties and being piddled on, digging the garden under slave's orders, and being strapped in a box with one's head encased in a rubber mask. The other films, too, feature customers who have a fondness for outré sexual practices, such as the man who requires the presence of a ferocious dog (*The Happy Hooker*), the man who acts out a rescue fantasy decked out as Superman (*The Happy Hooker Goes to Washington*), the man who dresses as Little Bo Peep's sheep (*The Happy Hooker Goes Hollywood*), the man who plays at being a psychiatrist (*Madame Claude 2*), the man who wears a Viking helmet (*Tricks of the Trade*), and so on. Apart from the comedic value, the motif appears calculated to highlight the diversity of human desire, which only a commercial sex industry can accommodate.

The films portray opponents of prostitution as narrow-minded hypocrites. In *The Happy Hooker Goes to Washington*, for example, Xaviera (Joey Heatherton) is summoned before a Senate Select Committee on Sexual

41. Julie Walters (right) as Christine in *Personal Services*, with Shirley Stelfox as Shirley and Anthony Collin as Mr Webb.

Excesses in America. Her lawyer explains to her that "there's a moralistic backlash that's sweeping the country . . . we're heading right into the teeth of the new puritanism." Xaviera responds simply that she has "spoken up against repression and ignorance, and let a little fresh air into a few people's lives," and at the hearing gets the better of her accusers: the vindictive senator running the investigation is himself implicated in white slave trafficking, while his fellow committee members are delighted to have their sexual whims catered to by Xaviera's troupe of happy hookers. Sally Stanford in *Lady of the House* is not as triumphant, being forced to close down her San Francisco bordello when "puritans" take over city hall, but she eventually gets her own back in being elected mayor of Sausalito. The conflict between points of view becomes a full-scale battle in *The Best Little Whorehouse in Texas,* as we will see in chapter 12.

The hassles with the law that the protagonists in this group of films experience are made the subject of comedy. Scenes of gaudy hookers cooped up in a police cell (*The Happy Hooker*) or striking sexy poses for their mug shots (*The Happy Hooker Goes Hollywood*), of the presiding judge in a trial suddenly appearing in the schoolboy uniform he dons at the bordello (*Personal Services*), satirize the system that outlaws prostitution. Certainly, Xaviera Hollander is not to be cowed by a police raid: "When

42. *The Happy Hooker:* Xaviera (Lynn Redgrave), left, in police custody.

things get rough, I just move on" she declares at the end of *The Happy Hooker,* as she and her ladies parade through the dawn streets of Manhattan. But the illegal status of the profession is nonetheless a stubborn fact of life, and only the German *Bei Anruf Liebe,* registering a more liberal social climate, is able to proffer an unrestrained endorsement of the commercial sex trade, presenting it as well scrubbed and unproblematic, a happy experience for all concerned and one of the democratic and gender-balanced delights of the modern open society.

Early in her working life as a prostitute, Eva (Gudrun Landgrebe) in *Die flambierte Frau / A Woman in Flames* (West Germany, 1983) takes orders from a finicky customer, obediently washing dishes in apron, bra, and panties. But halfway through the charade, when he demands that she look at his penis, there is a switch. She breaks off, puts the apron on him, daubs him with lipstick, and is launched on her career as dominatrix.

The essence of the dominatrix characterization is an inversion of patriarchal power relationships, achieved through catering to the bizarre desires inculcated by an extreme masochist psychological formation in the male. In exercising control over her clients and dictating the services that she will supply them, the dominatrix becomes an ideal type of the

Business Woman, an independent entrepreneur engaging in the sex trade very much under her own terms.

Although the visual coding associated with the character type dates from the early years of cinema — thus Blanche d'Estrée in *Die schwarze Natter* (Germany, 1913) is a "dominatrix . . . [who] appears in pants, wearing tightly cut black riding clothes and boots" and carrying a whip[28] — fully fledged characterizations with overt indications of prostitution are rare prior to the sexual revolution of the 1960s. A comic foretaste of what was to come is offered in the fantasticated brothel sequence in *Ulysses* (UK, 1967), in which madam Bella (Anna Manahan) appears as whip-cracking lion tamer in top hat and waxed moustache, puffing her cigar, and discoursing on the price of Guinness preference shares while her massive rump grinds "bondslave" Bloom's head into the dust of the circus ring.

The character of Ariane (Bulle Ogier) in *Maîtresse/Mistress* (France, 1975) was inspired by a "very close friend" of director Barbet Schroeder,[29] and cinematographer Nestor Almendros notes that Schroeder "even got some prostitutes who specialized in sadomasochism to help out." They and their clients were present during shooting, and "the flagellation scenes (and the scenes where people have themselves handcuffed, hung up, etc.) are real, and preserve a specifically documentary tone."[30] In this tale of the difficult romantic relationship that springs up between the petite "mistress" and the bulky thief who stumbles upon her dungeon of consensual torture, what drives the drama is the protagonist's insistence on her personal agency ("I am a whore, I like it, I chose it, it's my life, do you understand?") and the pleasure that she takes in fulfilling her clients' perverted fantasies ("It's wonderful to be able to enter people's madness in such an intimate way").

Domina — Die Last der Lust/Domina (West Germany, 1984) takes the documentary impetus one step farther. Filmed with hidden cameras in her salon, a real-life dominatrix exercises her profession; interspersed are shots of her daily life in Berlin and segments of interview, together with a staged sequence, filmed at night, in which shivering "slaves," their wrists shackled, are marched down a slope by the leather-clad Lady de Winter and mistresses brandishing burning torches. Here the image presented in *Maîtresse* is confirmed: these clients like to think themselves not good enough to lick their mistress's boots, and the extent of their willingness to be degraded, to be shackled, pissed on, whipped, and scorched appears limitless. While Ariane succumbs, finally, to romance, Lady de Winter is presented as a workaholic businesswoman too busy for love (and hence

43. Lady de Winter with slaves in *Domina — Die Last der Lust*. Stiftung Deutsche Kinemathek — Filmmuseum Berlin.

with an emotional life as impoverished as her clients'?), cold (like the snow, the bare stone walls, the industrial canal, the girder bridges), and amoral (what inhibits her from killing, if that is what a customer begs of her? — only the law, she replies, and the size of her rubbish bin). If the setting is the contemporary city, the Domina in this portrait emerges as a figure from the mythical past, a pitiless tyrant.[31]

Lady de Winter does not allow herself to be sexually aroused in her work, she tells us: "To lose control, that would be horrible." But one senses that for Wanda (Mechtild Grossman) in *Verführung: Die grausame Frau/Seduction: The Cruel Woman* (West Germany, 1985), business is intermingled with pleasure. In this impressionistic study, inspired by Sacher-Masoch's *Venus in Furs*, of a Hamburg dominatrix, directors Elfi Mikesch and Monika Treut explore the tangled web of polymorphous dominant-submissive sexuality. The narrative is fragmentary and obscure, the identity of characters unstable, but the imagery is stark and familiar: torsos trussed in leather, chains, cages, spikes, whips. Wanda runs a "gallery" where performance art merges with the consensual inflicting of pain: it is difficult to tell whether the slaves are customers or friends, and whether she makes her money from offering services to individual clients or from

staging shows for spectators. Wanda, addressing the camera in a home-
made video, has the last word in this world of strangeness: "You can offer
your slave no greater punishment and therefore no greater pleasure than
your excrement. But don't spoil him. The best thing for you both is to
keep him in a state of permanent desire."

But even as movies depicting successful madams, freelance hookers, and
dominatrices were celebrating prostitution as a marketplace expression
of the new sexual freedom, doubts were emerging, a backlash growing. A
group of Business Woman films from the 1980s, which show bold new
sex-for-sale enterprises coming to grief of one sort or another, reflect a
resurgence of traditional patriarchal values — with a hint of the left-wing
tradition of social critique — and may also embody the influence of the
antiprostitution wing of the women's movement.

In *Night Shift* (USA, 1982), the combination of ingredients makes for
comedy with a bad conscience, a fidgety tiptoe around the whole subject
of prostitution. Two night-shift morgue workers, one a former Wall Street
financial analyst, set up a call-girl agency employing a hooker they have
become acquainted with (Shelley Long), and her friends. The business
flourishes but eventually succumbs to a combination of the police, the
underworld, and the protagonists' own misgivings. Prostitution, suggests
the film, is good for a belly laugh, as in the scene of a hookers' party in
the morgue, but it's not something you want your girlfriend involved in;
it's a worthwhile and profitable enterprise, but at the same time it's making a living off immoral earnings — they might try to call themselves
"love brokers," but in the end they're just pimps like the rest. The movie
flirts with the notion of the agency as a legitimate business with dental
and medical plans and profit-sharing contracts for the women, but it
eventually pulls back, wheeling in the law and extricating our three
white principals from the trade, leaving it in the end to the mostly non-
white criminal milieu. Similar equivocation marks the following year's
Risky Business, which provocatively presents a high-school student running a call-girl service as a project for his "Future Enterprisers" class, designed to provide practical education in the profit motive, competition,
and free enterprise. The idea comes from his hooker girlfriend (Rebecca
De Mornay), who has a cool head for business ("It was great the way her
mind worked. No guilts, no doubts, no fear. None of my specialties. Just
the shameless pursuit of immediate material gratification. What a capitalist!"). The plan reaps a financial bonanza but is wrecked by a vengeful
pimp, while the film's endorsement of prostitution as the provision of

"human fulfillment" is undercut by hesitations and inconsistencies (most having to do with the central romantic relationship and its validation over venal sex), which were picked up by reviewers commenting on the "damnedest set of mixed messages" conveyed by a film "so confused, so strange, and so openly corrupt."[32]

The conflict of attitude is even more pronounced in the films centered around female protagonists. Thus *Money on the Side* (USA, 1982), a TV movie depicting three California women in financial difficulties who turn to part-time call-girl work to support themselves and their families, seems initially on the side of normalization, with the madam (Susan Flannery) justifying herself by attacking hypocrisy and arguing that she is simply enabling people "to live out their own needs, and their own fantasies." But by the time one of the three women (Linda Purl), having been severely beaten by a pathological client, hangs herself, and the other two (Karen Valentine, Jamie Lee Curtis) lose their menfolk when the truth comes out ("You've sullied your marriage vows, you've brought shame to your husbands and families," a male judge tells the women), the film has swung all the way around to a traditional antiprostitution stance. The structure is similar in *Die flambierte Frau*, mentioned earlier, and *Half Moon Street* (UK/USA, 1986). In the former, disillusioned middle-class wife Eva leaves her husband and asserts her independence, entering the prostitution business with the help of a call-girl madam. In the latter, a young American intellectual in London, Dr. Lauren Slaughter (Sigourney Weaver) augments her meager income by taking up part-time hostessing. Both insist that they are fully in charge, with Eva asserting, "My first rule is to do only what I want," and Lauren laying down her terms for sex: "I decide what I do after dinner — and in your case it's no, definitely no." While their ventures are successful financially (Lauren has been attracted into the profession by watching a news report that refers to the "growing number of young women working in London's newest industry, the escort service, grossing several million pounds monthly" and finds that she is indeed able to command good money for her time), they both run aground on the rock of incompatibility with committed personal relationships. Eva falls in love with a male prostitute and they set up shop together, but she finds one of his regulars coming between them, while he becomes increasingly jealous of her clients, eventually dousing her in liquor and setting her on fire. Lauren discovers that her predilection for "uncomplicated sex" doesn't last when she becomes emotionally involved with one of her clients, and the work becomes an impediment to her love life. She quits the escort agency. The

44. *Beverly Hills Madam:* Lil (Faye Dunaway) surrounded by her "ladies" — Wendy (Donna Dixon), top left; Julie (Terry Farrell), top right; April (Robin Givens), bottom left; and Claudia (Melody Anderson), bottom right.

hypothesis that prostitution might be a viable career option for the modern, independent, sexually liberated woman has been found wanting.

Finally, two further portraits of madams, both TV movies, are notable for the ideological about-face they perform in comparison with the brash endorsement of the sex business contained in *The Happy Hooker* and its sequels. *Beverly Hills Madam* (USA, 1986) depicts a call-girl operation based in a Los Angeles luxury home, from which Lil (Faye Dunaway) dispatches her escorts in limousines and Lear-jets to thousand-dollar dates around town and farther afield — the Bahamas, New York, Acapulco. Only slightly less upscale, the Manhattan agency in *Mayflower Madam* (USA, 1987), set up by Sydney Biddle Barrows (Candice Bergen), employs "ladies, not hookers" catering to an affluent clientele. Both businesses are highly profitable, and both come to a premature end, forcing their owners to ponder on what they have lost for the money they have gained. Lil's security slips and one of her call girls is murdered by an unscreened customer; Sydney is taken to court for "promoting prostitution," and while she beats the rap by threatening to release the names of her clients, her cover has been blown and she is no longer admitted to the social set (Barrows is of distinguished lineage, as the title indicates; the film is loosely based on fact). Earlier, Sydney's blossoming romance with a lawyer has come to an abrupt end on his discovering her profession; while Lil is forced to face the fact that her paramour is never going to marry her. "Whores don't have feelings, Lil," one of her call girls tells her, "That's what we give up when we sell ourselves. That's why they pay us the big money." This pair of TV movies, seemingly taking a stand for liberalization and against hypocrisy ("It's the oldest profession and if you ask me it ought to be legalized," declares Sydney), end up by stepping back: prostitution cannot be sanctioned, since it is a crime against the true female destiny of love and marriage.

As Lil and Sydney take their money and leave their past behind them, the fate of the Business Woman remains up in the air. Torn between conflicting ideological pressures, she remains poised at the intersection of prostitution and capitalism, carrying a burden of metaphoric signification almost too heavy for any fully realized individual to bear.

12

Happy Hooker

Come, Enkidu, to Uruk of the Sheepfold,
where people are resplendent in wide belts,
and every day there's a festival,
and where strings and drums are played
and the holy courtesans beautify their forms,
radiating sexual prowess, filled with sex-joy.
At night they force the great ones into their beds.
—*GILGAMESH*, Tablet 1, column 5[1]

If in "official" patriarchal ideology prostitution has a negative sign attached to it, what I shall call "Happy Hooker" films advance the alternative patriarchal line, that it is a valuable and necessary institution for men's carnal pleasure. The films, which depict prostitutes doing the work voluntarily and with high satisfaction, propose by implication that society be less hypocritical and openly endorse the profession. The position has ties with the sexual revolution of the 1960s and the "philosophy" of sexual freedom promulgated by *Playboy*. The new hypocrisy, opponents might argue, is the fiction that women revel in being prostitutes and are free to prosper in the job.

Following the victory of the purity movements of the late nineteenth and early twentieth centuries in characterizing prostitution as a social evil, the suggestion that women might actually enjoy a life of vice was, in most Western nations, scandalous and, in the cinema, necessarily suppressed. *Das Tagebuch einer Verlorenen/Diary of a Lost Girl* (Germany, 1929), for example, created a censorship crisis on its release, with the Prussian state government filing an application with the Higher Film Censor Board (*Filmoberprüfstelle*) for the approval that had been given by the lower censor authorities to be withdrawn. In granting the application, the board objected especially to the brothel sequences in the film, which showed the heroine (Louise Brooks) taking pleasure in her work as a pros-

45. *Diary of a Lost Girl:* Thymian (Louise Brooks) with Erika (Edith Meinhard), at left, in a brothel sequence.

titute. It observed that the inmates' life was depicted as "easy, attractive, comfortable, and thus desirable." It drew attention to the fact that there was camaraderie between the women and that the madam was shown as a soft-hearted personality, and criticized the impression given by the film that it was easy to move on from a life of prostitution: actually, the board argued, the return of a prostitute to normal life was beset by enormous difficulties, so the film was a lure for the unwary young. The board particularly objected to the dramatic structure of the narrative, in that brothel life was contrasted favorably with the morally poisoned atmosphere of the heroine's home and with the sadistic routine of the reform school from which she escapes. The film was banned.[2]

In the United States, industry censors inserted in the 1930 Production Code particular strictures against making sexual immorality appealing and its frequent corollary, making it comic: "In the case of impure love, the love which society has always regarded as wrong and which has been banned by divine law, the following are important: 1. Impure love must not be presented as attractive and beautiful. 2. It must not be the subject of comedy or farce, or treated as material for laughter."[3] It was particularly the success of Jean Harlow and Mae West in portraying women who enjoyed their promiscuous sexuality, sometimes as prostitutes, in a group of films released in 1932 and 1933— *Red Dust, Red-Headed Woman, Bombshell, She Done Him Wrong, I'm No Angel*—that brought down the wrath of religious groups and led to the creation of the Legion of Decency and the introduction of measures to enforce the Code more rigorously in 1934. From that point on, until the late 1950s, prostitution was virtually blanked out in toto from American screens.

One of the key films eventually instrumental in breaking down the ban was *Pote Tin Kyriaki/Never on Sunday* (1960). The Greek production about a Piraeus prostitute who relishes her work was released successfully in the United States through independent cinemas without a Production Code Administration seal of approval. PCA officials at the time were mindful of the threat it posed to the screen morality they were committed to enforcing. Geoffrey Shurlock, head of the agency, wrote an agonized letter to Eric Johnston of the Motion Picture Association:

> In *Never on Sunday,* our leading lady revels in being a prostitute. She never for a moment seems to think there is anything wrong with it (except on Sunday) although the young American does think so and tries to reform her. By the end of the picture, he has been made a complete fool of. Thus, from the Code standpoint, sinful living is made to seem attractive throughout. The fact that at the very end she is going off to get married (probably) is subject to the same criticism as a "hackneyed" reformation that Mr. Youngstein applies to the death of Gloria in *Butterfield 8.* . . .
>
> What I am about to say presents a real dilemma which comes up quite often in the application of the Code. It is that the great public appears not to like to have its nose rubbed in the fact that adultery and prostitution are fundamentally sordid and should be so presented. In our Code attempt to deglamorize sin, we often end up making it look exactly the way it should, repulsive and degrading. This is a valid and proper moral judgment; but a lot of people don't seem to like pictures with repulsive elements, even when valid. . . .
>
> One last observation about *Never on Sunday.* I have been in terror lest someone decide to submit this picture for a Code seal. I am afraid we would have to reject it. But the horrible part is that, in rejecting it, we would probably have to adduce perforce exactly the same reasons as did the Atlanta censor board. And I shudder at the idea. . . . [4]

Never on Sunday opens with its vivacious protagonist (Melina Mercouri) racing to the lively rhythms of bouzouki music through the dock ship-yard, touching men as she goes, radiating an infectious joie de vivre and stripping down to her bikini before leaping off the jetty into the miracu-lously limpid waters of Piraeus harbor. The dock workers, to prove they are men and not slaves, drop what they are doing and jump in to join her. The idea created here of a sensuous utopia, however unlikely, will never be fully dispelled in this film despite the narrative developments that take place; and Mercouri's promiscuously affectionate prostitute overflowing with erotic energy (she won a Grand Prix at Cannes for her performance) will become a definitive image in the new decade of sexual liberation.

Eagerly embraced by the public — its theme song won an Oscar — *Never on Sunday*, as the censors feared it would, gave credence to a previ-ously submerged, disreputable attitude toward promiscuity and prostitu-tion in particular — that of celebrating rather than condemning it. The attitude gained prominence in popular culture, and the newly emerging Happy Hooker archetype captured the male imagination with its en-dorsement of prostitution as a force for the liberation of the libido. Things, in fact, were not quite as simple as they seemed, but for ideolo-gists of the "unofficial" patriarchal persuasion, the archetype had on the surface the great merit of depicting prostitution as a blameless institution since the women involved so palpably enjoyed it.

Irma La Douce (USA, 1963) was an important milestone in the devel-opment of this theme. The colorful array of Parisian streetwalkers who ply their trade in the vicinity of Les Halles are manifestly contented with their lot ("This isn't just a *job*," Irma insists, "it's a *profession*"), while Mous-tache, the local bistro proprietor, denounces the absurdity of outlawing prostitution. "Love is illegal," he laments, "but not hate. That you can do anywhere, anytime, to anybody. But if you want a little warmth, a little tenderness — a shoulder to cry on, a smile to cuddle up with — you have to hide in dark corners, like a criminal." Moustache's point of view is never effectively refuted, while the one-man campaign of honest cop Nestor Patou to stamp out the vice traffic is gently satirized.

The British film *Tom Jones* of the same year reinforced this attitude, even if we have no proof that its lascivious Mrs. Waters (Joyce Redman) actually takes money for her services. Here the Happy Hooker engages in prostitution from a hyperabundance of sexual energy, and any mate-rial advantage that may come her way from sexual frolicking is strictly a side benefit. Described she may be as a "doxy" and "trollop" — but that by a woman who would be happy to libel her. What we do know is that

46. Shirley MacLaine in *Irma La Douce*.

47. *Tom Jones:* Tom (Albert Finney) with Mrs Waters (Joyce Redman). David Lascelles Stills Collection.

Mrs. Waters's gratitude for the assistance of Tom (Albert Finney) in rescuing her from a hanging is expressed in one of the most famous scenes of tandem gluttony in the cinema, in which the licking, sucking, and gobbling is but foretaste of the carnal delights to follow. After the meal there is a frenzied dash to bed, the lewd details of what there ensues being passed over with a modesty made requisite by the censorship regimes of the time. A little later in the film, the pair is rudely interrupted by a rampaging husband (not hers) fancying himself cuckolded. Tom is forced to flee, while Mrs. Waters, coyly draping herself up to the cheekbones, consoles the hapless Irishman by welcoming him to the vacant place in her bed. Fixing him with her lustrous eyes, she sinks back on to the pillow, her feet under the covers doing a frenetic tap dance in anticipation of licentious pleasures to come.

In *Tom Jones* the sexual revolution of the 1960s is ushered in by a throwback to the more robust values of pre-Victorian England. The advocates of puritanical morality (the miserable Blifil and that disputatious pair of tutors, Square and Thwackum) are delivered up to obloquy. Sexual repression is aligned with avarice and small-mindedness; promiscuity with generosity and adventure. The prostitute, who along with other willing lasses can provide the frequent and variegated erotic experience that is the entitlement of the hero, is enlisted in the cause of (male) liberation. But the idea that she may just be in it for the money might spoil the fun: hence the fantasy of the lusty wench of overabundant appetites.

In a more sentimental vein is Madame Hortense (Lila Kedrova) of *Zormba/Zorba the Greek* (Greece/USA, 1964). Here the former prostitute is a woman overflowing with emotion: she is fun-loving, but tears are ready to spill at a moment's notice (as she spills out of her too-tight dresses). She has too much love to confine it to just the one man: hence her tale of the four admirals, all at the one time, which she relates, brimful of nostalgia. "They undressed me, they filled the bath with champagne and they dropped me in. Then they sit all around . . . and they drunk all the champagne, all from the top to the bottom. And then they put out the lights. When I woke up, I smelt so good — all their perfumes, one on top of the other. But they was gone. Men are so cruel."

Madame Hortense's whole person is given over to amorous affairs, or the memory of them. It is not sex, simply, that she represents, but a total integration of the emotional and the erotic: she is the uninhibited versus the self-denying, aligned here with the impulsive Zorba (Anthony Quinn), as the withdrawn widow (Irene Papas) is aligned with the passionless English writer (Alan Bates). One can speculate that her version of the admirals' story is a romanticization of a somewhat more mundane reality — that the ugliness and alienation of the prostitute's life is being repressed, confined to the subtext. Very possibly the male fantasy of the character as written is both embodied and subtly subverted in Kedrova's Oscar-winning performance.

It was schlockmeister Russ Meyer, working the lower end of the market where censorship and moral restraints were relatively ineffective, who was largely responsible for bringing the Happy Hooker to the American cinema. *Fanny Hill: Memoirs of a Woman of Pleasure* (USA/West Germany, 1964) is built entirely on the conceit that the invincibly innocent Fanny is quite unaware of the true nature of the business being conducted around her by Mrs. Brown and her young companions, while those young companions cannot imagine that Fanny is anything other than a prostitute like them. The film portrays Fanny's escapes from the lascivious clutches of a series of randy old gentlemen — she energetically defends her virtue without understanding it to be endangered — and conservatively celebrates the preservation of her virginity so she can be delivered untouched into the arms of her loved one in marriage, but it does not devalue the prostitutes she dwells among by contrast. Although concerned to turn an honest penny ("Don't let the girls know you don't even belong to the guild!" one warns Fanny), they love the work and won't hear of their madam's talk of reform. This being a comedy, the upbeat mood of the film, not to mention its erotic ambiance, would be quite undercut if the women felt oppressed by their situation. *Fanny Hill* was banned by the British Board of Film Censors, ostensibly because it contained "a scene of flagellation and a joke on erection."[5]

In Meyer's *Finders Keepers, Lovers Weepers!* (USA, 1968), bordello inmate Christiana (Jan Sinclair) pauses in the hallway with a client to study a Hindu painting based on the *Kama Sutra* and waxes eloquent upon the situation of the prostitute in India who, she says, does it "by choice and by love" and "is greatly glorified with a position of respect and admiration that's unequalled in any other society." It is clear that Christiana herself does it by choice, but would welcome a bit more of the respect and admiration. The Happy Hooker archetype is more fully embodied in the same director's *Cherry, Harry and Raquel*, of the following year. This desert fantasia features a prostitute so highly sexed that the money is virtually irrelevant. Raquel (Larissa Ely) spends her time searching out new carnal excitements (which leads among other things to a lesbian encounter with Cherry, a nurse) and is constantly on the edge of exploding with erotic energy. If the sex worker is a nymphomaniac, any patriarchal guilt attaching to prostitution can be plausibly disavowed. Nakedly exploitative, Meyer's visuals flaunt the spectacle of the hyperendowed female body in a way calculated to disarm critics through sheer outrageousness.

Given the propensity toward British period romps (*Tom Jones, Fanny Hill*), it is significant that *Cherry, Harry and Raquel* is self-consciously located within its contemporary US context. An opening text (against a background of explicit sexual images) attacks would-be censors and proclaims the rights of viewers. This is followed by a prologue with a commentary about the evils of dope dealing, in which reference is made to the ever-growing disposable income and leisure time of the American middle class, and their quest to avoid boredom. In a final commentary Raquel and Cherry are referred to as "toys . . . superficial in their makeup, but so necessary to our way of life."

The loosening of censorship controls internationally in the late 1960s and early 1970s was accompanied by the appearance of growing numbers of Happy Hooker movies of an increasingly pornographic tendency.

Symbolic of the trend was *Josefine Mutzenbacher/Naughty Knickers* (West Germany, 1970), based on a long-suppressed erotic novel recounting episodes in the life of a Viennese slum girl who discovers prostitution to be a ladder to the aristocracy. It had great box-office success and was quickly followed by a sequel, *Mutzenbacher — 2. Teil — Meine 365 Liebhaber/Mutzenbacher — Part 2* (West Germany, 1970).

Josefine Mutzenbacher's experience includes a period as a brothel inmate, and the new wave of sexually explicit films frequently portrayed the bordello as an arena for extravagant carnal indulgence, initiated as much by the prostitutes for their personal satisfaction as by the clientele. It figures, for example, in *Brothel* (USA, 1966), *The Notorious Daughter of Fanny Hill* (USA, 1966), *Mennesker mødes og sød musik opstår i hjertet/People Meet and Sweet Music Fills the Heart* (Denmark/Sweden, 1967), *Meeting on 69th Street* (USA, 1969), *Das Freudenhaus* (West Germany, 1971), *Auch Fummeln will gelernt sein* (West Germany, 1972), *Maison close* (France, 1975), and *Zona roja* (Mexico, 1975). In *Games That Lovers Play* (UK, 1971), two brothel madams each insist that her top performer can outdo the other's, while the whorehouse comedy *Bordellet — en Gladespigess Erindringer/The Bordello — Memoirs of a Pleasure Girl* (Denmark, 1972) depicts boundless nudity and copulation amid foolish goings-on.

The nymphomaniac prostitute is featured in *Diary of Knockers McCalla* (USA, 1968), *Back Seat Cabbie* (USA, 1969), *The Bedspread* (USA, 1969), *Moonlighting Secretaries* (USA, 1969), *Turned-On Girl* (USA, 1970), *The Pro Shop* (USA, ca. 1970), and *Harlot* (USA, 1971). Orgies involving prostitutes are portrayed in *Make Out* (USA, 1968) and *I Want You!* (USA, 1969). In *My Sister's Business* (USA, ca. 1970), "'Big Sister,' a prostitute who enjoys masturbation as a prelude to sexual intercourse, instructs 'Little Sister,' a naive virgin, in sex techniques" and "later, at a marijuana party, Little Sister practices what she has learned"[6]; in *Memories Within Miss Aggie* (USA, 1974), the heroine "sees herself as an experienced whore in a brothel, masturbating herself to a climax in front of a taciturn customer and imagining herself engaged in oral congress with him."[7]

By and large these were low-budget exploitation movies, which played in disreputable "grind houses." *The Happy Hooker* (USA, 1975), mentioned in chapter 11, was an attempt to break through with the archetype into mainstream Hollywood cinema. Inverting the symbolic trajectory of the fallen woman, the camera shows sex-hungry Xaviera walking toward a skyscraper, and then tilts up to the penthouse suite as she explains in voice-over her decision to go professional: "Well one thing led to another and before I knew it I had made the transition from office girl to working girl." In a subsequent sequence, Xaviera rides her bicycle around Manhattan in miniskirt and white boots, as she comments: "The word spread about a healthy, active Dutch girl who loved her work, and I got so busy I bought myself a bicycle to pedal around faster. I loved the excitement of meeting new people and seeing different faces every day. It was true, I had gotten into a business that wasn't considered very romantic, but I was able to bring something special to it simply because I loved it." Soon after, though, she finds more fun in organizing others to do the dirty work, and becomes a madam. Toning down the material to make it acceptable to a broader audience did not meet with critical approbation. "Yawns abound," opined *Variety*, arguing that "an X-rated version of Xaviera's climb to the apex of Gotham's call-girl nexus might have resulted in a more interesting effort."[8] Nevertheless, the film's success was such as to spawn two sequels.

The formerly suppressed Happy Hooker thus finally entered the mainstream, becoming a feature even of movies made for network television. But she was seldom the dominating force in a film. She would be tossed in for comic relief, or to supply a dash of erotic spice in otherwise bland concoctions. In *Stand Up Virgin Soldiers* (UK, 1977), Private Brigg has a quiet conversation with his prostitute sweetheart Juicy Lucy (Fiesta Mei Ling) and then tenderly makes love, while alongside him his buddy Jacobs does battle with the voracious Elephant Ethel (Miriam Margolyes), purchased in advance sight unseen, who lunges, wrestles, pins him in a hammerlock, takes flying leaps onto him, and presses her massive bosom in his face ("You'll suffocate me. Blimey!"), while the bamboo dwelling shakes, the floorboards splinter, and chaos reigns down below. There is a play of contrasts also in the TV movie *The Red-Light Sting* (USA, 1984), set in a tastefully decorated high-rise brothel. The star (Farrah Fawcett) is a glamour-puss but modestly attired, and there's some ambiguity as to whether she's actually an active prostitute; there's no doubt, however, about the voluptuous, scantily clad Sonia (Sunny Johnson), who is a running gag as the nymphomaniac whore constantly coming on to men ("It's in my genes or something," she laughs). There is whorehouse action, too, in the deliriously silly *Sex and Zen* (Hong Kong, 1991), in which the wife (Amy Yip) who has been sold into prostitution, in narrative terms a Martyr, registers on her face only the agonies of carnal ecstasy or perhaps, to be fair, the extra difficulties entailed in reaching this state with a partner exhausted by unwilling debauchery and equipped with an inconveniently lengthy male member—a transplanted horse's penis: from the evidence of the performance, she is certainly a Happy Hooker.

Outside the mainstream, blue-movie theaters proliferated following the relaxation of censorship and then, in the 1980s, were largely supplanted with the coming of rental video. A vast undergrowth of pornography was created to meet the burgeoning demand, into which the Happy Hooker archetype made its way. Prostitute characters feature in perhaps 25 percent of hard-core porn, frequently depicted as deriving personal pleasure from the mercenary sex acts they engage in.[9] *Throat—Twelve Years After* (USA, 1984), for example, intercuts a prostitute's fellatio of a shy client with a flashback to her fondly recalled first sexual experience, performing fellatio on a high school boy through a cyclone fence. The males reach orgasm simultaneously and at the end of the scene, "the prostitute's own pleasure is signaled (with great restraint for a hard-core film) by the fact that she has finally stopped chewing her gum."[10] In the slickly produced *New Wave Hookers* (USA, 1985), a fantasized pornotopia features hypersexed hookers turned into copulation machines by new wave music: "the film is a music video-style musical with a big production number in which twelve women are placed on a revolving stage à la Busby Berkeley and photographed from above while four men 'plug' into their various orifices."[11]

Pleasure is My Business (USA?, 1989) has a rudimentary narrative: a night's work at Raven's Escort Service, a combined brothel/call-girl agency. Here the central conceit is that the prostitutes do not *feign* pleasure in their work, they actually get off on it. Their grunts of satisfaction as the johns thrust away at them are genuine, they fondle their own breasts not as a come-on to him but for their own satisfaction, and they willingly enjoin the man to spurt his sperm in their face — the preferred locus of ejaculation for the majority of clients. One employee is required to perform cold and aloof to satisfy the customer's wishes, but her voice-over tells us what she *really* feels, as she strips off her skirt and panties: "I know I'm not supposed to get so excited here in the office, but I can't help myself. God, I can't wait to get him in the sack with me. Ooh! God, I'd like to screw!" The first prostitute is so turned on by her client that she does it to herself all over again after he's gone, and the nymphomania theme is reinforced by the boss, Raven, sitting at her desk frantically masturbating throughout the evening ("I love my work," she says, and every time her customers' desires are satisfied, "I feel it too").

If the unofficial patriarchal line on prostitution reaches an apex in a film such as this, it is also buttressed by comedies that make a deliberate point of deriding the stereotype of the suffering prostitute. In *Gaily, Gaily/Chicago, Chicago* (USA, 1969), for example, the innocent young Ben,

48. *Gaily, Gaily:* Melina Mercouri as Queen Lil.

without realizing he is in a brothel, reads a group of the women a sketch for a play he has written called *Fallen Angel*, set on Skid Row on Christmas Eve. "A heavy snow is coming down. A young fallen girl of the streets appears. She is coughing badly. A wealthy gentleman in silk hat and fur coat passes by. The girl holds out a trembling hand. 'Would you care for a night of joy, sir?' The rich man . . . just hurries on, not recognizing the girl he once took to fashionable places." And so on, until the girl, having seen an angel, dies. The women weep at this pathetic tale, but some can scarcely stifle their laughter, and later Ben admits he has never actually known anyone like the consumptive harlot of his story: "I just use my imagination." The film goes on to recount the adventures of this hero who, out to "change the world — a little," to reform the city, soon succumbs to the lure of big money, accepting the pervasive corruption — even of the nominally "Reform" candidate — as the way of the world. Given that the city is Chicago, there are good grounds for the cynicism. There is a parallel in the depiction of prostitution: it is foolish and naive, so argues this comic parable, to try and keep womanhood pure, and "fallen woman" tragic tales can be told only from a position of woeful ignorance. One of the last images is a freeze frame of brothel madam Queen Lil (Melina Mercouri, the original Happy Hooker from *Never on Sunday*) laughing broadly.

When a prostitute in a comedy herself relates how she "fell," it is likely to be a tissue of lies. The classic example is the titles sequence in *Irma La Douce*, in which a series of clients ask the Parisian gigolette (Shirley MacLaine) how she happened to get into this racket. To one, she says she was studying at the Paris Conservatory (but the night of her first recital the piano cover fell on her hand); to a second, that her parents were missionaries in the Belgian Congo ("So now there's just me and my sister, she's in the hospital"); to a third, that she was brought up in a Cherbourg orphanage that was bombed on D-Day. These tall tales are a way of setting at a distance any truth in the general social validity of the fallen woman scenario: that women become prostitutes through having been mistreated by men. At the same time the extravagance of the stories, coupled with the fact that the mugs actually fall for them and dish out sympathy money, serves to deflect any potential female criticism by making a joke at the expense of males. What is being said here, sotto voce, is that prostitutes telling stories of their lives are not to be trusted, that tales of the victimization of women entering prostitution may be exaggerated or totally false, and that clients of prostitutes tend to be so kindhearted and generous that their bullshit detectors fail to function. These statements all present a strongly male point of view. And yet although Irma is revealed to be a liar ripping off her customers, she is exempted from censure because of her charm (a function particularly of MacLaine's performance) and the outrageousness of her stories, which nobody should be taken in by, proving that anyone obtuse is a legitimate butt of comedy, whether male or female. It is a clever piece of writing.

In *The Best House in London* (UK, 1969), set in the late nineteenth century, a "ruined girl," Phoebe (Marie Rogers), recounts to reformer Josephine Pacefoot how she was "took advantage of while in service." The spectator is treated to a visual flashback of what really happened on the occasion of Phoebe being "brutalized by the young master when he came home on embarkation leave," while her story continues in voice-over. "Loathsome he was to look at — fat, bald, palsied" (he is a comely young officer, to whom she displays her rear end, whereupon he uncovers her breasts). "He clawed the clothes from my very body!" (she undresses him). "He rained violent blows upon my fragile flesh" (he tickles her with a feather duster). "Like a ravening beast of prey he hurled himself upon me" (she falls on him). The consequence, being fired — the young man's father "chucked me out bag and baggage," whereupon "the only life left for me was the mutton market"—seems the only truthful element in Phoebe's story. Likewise not to be trusted is one of Xaviera Hollander's ladies in *The Happy Hooker*. Recounting her painful introduction to sex at the age of fifteen, she speaks at one point of lecherous uncles ("they took turns"), at another of being put on trial by Turks who came by her cell and gave her "what they called an examination." The message, here as elsewhere, is clearly to discredit accounts of sexual abuse in the life history of prostitutes.

The drawback for patriarchal ideology of the Happy Hooker concept is that it opens up a space for female subjectivity, agency, and independence. The figure of the prostitute who engages in the trade willingly and enthusiastically can arouse acute anxieties in the patriarchal mind, both as a woman who initiates and enjoys sex independently of her male partner, and as a woman who, turning sexuality to her financial advantage, slips out of male control and achieves individual autonomy. Hence there is resistance; and mainstream films, in particular, become an ideological battleground in which the unofficial patriarchal line struggles to find expression against the official, antiprostitution position.

Never on Sunday is a case in point. "No one goes by my door," Illia's song goes, "for whom I don't feel love," and for her the fitness of a client is judged not by how much he will pay but by whether he's attractive to her or not. This spirit of independence extends to her living arrangements: she's the only one of the dockside prostitutes who does not live in the rack-rent accommodation owned by the local landlord No Face and who, as discussed in chapter 5, leads her comrades in a rent strike against him.

Illia is, of course, a prototypical Happy Hooker. But the position is not straightforward. The film in fact consists in an extended interrogation of the subversive proposition that a prostitute could be happy in her work. Homer Thrace, a visiting American, attempts to convert her to the life of the mind (subsidized by cash from No Face, who is only too happy to have her off the streets), wheeling in the Athenian philosophers to support his claim that true happiness is not to be found in the life of sensuality and physicality that Illia adheres to. Results are ambiguous: schooled—in two weeks—in the classics, Illia becomes at first more restless and then more serene than she had been in her state of innocent barbarism. But with the claims of monogamous love over promiscuity there is no argument; at least the film advances none. At the end Illia is carried away by a young worker whom she's fallen for. To reject the heterosexual couple as the ultimate destination for womanhood was unthinkable for the popular cinema of 1960.

However much she and the men who form her constant entourage may seem to delight in it, Illia's independent, free-spirited whoring is a scandal, which the patriarchy ultimately cannot tolerate. Hence the coalition of American morality and Greek vice, which keeps her temporarily off the docks, followed by the surefire killer, romantic love, which pairs her off with one man for good. The film illustrates the threat to male-dominated society that may ensue if the prostitute steps out of her objectification and becomes subject, no man's woman, promiscuous, commercial, but determining for herself whom she'll sleep with, and for how much. One such woman could surely be contained—yet on her own she has men dropping work to go swimming and the other streetwalkers becoming troublesomely rebellious. The thing is: what if her example should spread—precisely the effect of her independence, which concerns No Face and which makes him determined to put her out of business. The end credits, as the opening credits, of *Never on Sunday* are superimposed over a shot of the legs of four prostitutes marching together, but Illia is not among them and the indications are strong that for the star of the show her door will be shut seven days of the week from now on.

Zig Zig (France, 1974) features Bernadette Lafont and Catherine Deneuve as Pauline and Marie, singers in a Paris nightclub and prostitutes in partnership together. Working on their backs to build their dream house in the mountains (a model of it under construction adorns their apartment), the pair tackle their task with such energy and gusto (much hinges on the performances) that one is almost persuaded that opening one's legs to all comers is a delightful experience. A montage sequence shows the women with clients of every description—African, bearded, young, older, and the like—all cheerfully parting with their money. Of course, this cannot last. The patriarchy cannot permit this little enterprise to flourish, this little story to have a happy ending. The idea of women *using* men, exploiting their attractiveness to achieve personal goals, is amusing to contemplate, but one wouldn't want it to catch on. So the model house is destroyed (shot by Marie by mistake, it *explodes*), and Pauline is killed by a bullet meant for Marie. "Unfaithful" to her old lover (read: subverting the patriarchy in striking out too much on her own), Marie must now pay the penalty in grieving for her lost *copine*, and for her lost home in the snow.

It is particularly in the American cinema that the battle between official and unofficial patriarchal ideology has been fought. As conflicting cultural traditions vie for expression, representation of the prostitute, especially in comedies, has been caught in a vice between puritan and libertarian tendencies. In some films — especially those set in the past — this conflict has been neatly resolved; in others, confusion has resulted.

Support Your Local Sheriff! (USA, 1969), a simple, archetypal Western story of the *Shane, High Noon, Rio Bravo* variety played for laughs, is a good example of a film in which a satisfying resolution is achieved. Here the bordello and its inmates, none of whom are individualized, have an existence very much on the fringe of the action. Still, they play an important thematic role, and the place of prostitution in the Western myth is perhaps clarified here by the very simplicity and stylization.

In the frontier gold-rush town of Calendar, Madame Orr's House flourishes at the beginning and is accidentally smashed to pieces by a cannonball at the end. In the interim, the town's leading citizens have foreseen the passing of the prostitution phase. As the mayor says: "It has been a lot of fun around here up till now, I mean everything all kind of wide open and relaxed. Nobody looking down their noses at anybody who happened to shoot somebody else. Nobody poking their noses into nobody else's business, without them getting their big noses blasted off in the process. I guess now that we've got law and order, churches'll start moving in. . . . And then the women'll start forming committees and having bazaars. Then they'll chase Madame Orr's girls out of town, or make 'em get married, or something even worse. But what the hell, like you said, the law's the law and we've all got to face up to it sometime."

The brothel is thus associated with the period of pioneering and lawlessness, and there is no place for it once civilization arrives. In another homology, the gunslinger hero stays on as sheriff, and his settling down parallels the process of substituting marriage for prostitution in the male-female relationships in the town. So the libertine fantasy of the Western red-light saloon (here not much indulged) has a built-in expiration date: the moment at which the power balance in town shifts to the representatives of law and order. In a neat double play, prostitution is both endorsed (for the past) and disavowed (for the present).

Closely comparable in thematic terms with *Support Your Local Sheriff!* is the Western musical of the same year, *Paint Your Wagon*, which happens to share the motif of gold being discovered in a grave dug for an itinerant stranger. Here prostitution is explicitly depicted as a service appropriate to that particular historical phenomenon, the gold-rush boomtown, because of the heavy overrepresentation of males in the population. After a popular vote, a stagecoach carrying six French tarts is hijacked to No

Name City in order to provide for the sexual needs of the four hundred "horny gorillas" who live there. The town becomes a hotbed of vice and is denounced by a traveling evangelist, who accurately foretells its demise. Around this character a revealing ideological shift is effected. At first, the preacher with his holier-than-thou attitude ("Shameless harlot!") is ridiculed , and the film sides with the miners and their licentious pleasures ("Come on up, parson," calls a prostitute, "and get some old-time religion!"). But the prophet of doom becomes much more attractive when he breaks into song with a grin on his face, and as the film progresses, the highly sympathetic Elizabeth — the one "respectable" woman in the place, though she does have two husbands — comes to share his views, seeing No Name City as an "ugly" town. When, in the comic climax to the film, it collapses into the labyrinth of tunnels that have been dug underneath it and the saloons and brothels are swallowed up, Elizabeth's relief at the turn of events is a sentiment no doubt designed to be shared by the audience. As with *Support Your Local Sheriff!*, prostitution is depicted favorably only within a specific historical context, and the endorsement is terminated once circumstances change.

The Cheyenne Social Club (USA, 1970) is less equivocal in its stance. The "club" of the title is a busy, gracious Wyoming bordello ringing with mirth, whose decorative inmates take no greater pleasure in life, it would seem, than servicing their clients. Yet a certain uneasiness is conveyed through the attitude of the protagonist, the cowboy John O'Hanlan (James Stewart), who has inherited the concern. Protesting that "my folks were fine, upstanding people" and expressing a desire to run a business as "solid and respectable" as a dry-goods store, he declares that he will close the place down, perhaps turn it into a boarding house. Fortunately for the prostitutes, who are thrown into a state of panic, this proves to be contrary to the provisions of the title deed. The operation survives, transferred to the madam, and O'Hanlon heads on back to cowpunching in Texas, his conscience clean. The filmmakers have it both ways.

The Best Little Whorehouse in Texas (USA, 1982), a musical comedy like *Paint Your Wagon*, also dramatizes conflicting attitudes to prostitution. Here, however, the resolution is far from assured. The bucolic brothel with jolly cavorting prostitutes where there's "nothin' dirty goin' on," whose doors have been opened for generations to "soldiers and presidents and farmers, even governors who can remember what a great institution it is" — not to mention the high-school football team treated by the Alumni Association — is closed down as a result of a crusade conducted by a smarmy television announcer. Set around 1973, the film

49. *The Best Little Whorehouse in Texas:* The establishment of madam Mona (Dolly Parton).

alludes to contemporary debates on the issue, with feminists lining up behind a bill for decriminalization of prostitution in the Texas legislature, being opposed by "traditionalists and fundamentalists." Sheriff Ed Earl (Burt Reynolds), supporter and lover of madam Mona (Dolly Parton) puts the civil-rights argument, which is never effectively refuted: "Let's not confuse crime with committing sin. You can't legislate morality. Those girls out there have never caused any trouble to anybody. They're healthy, tax-paying, law-abiding citizens who supply a demand and provide an economic asset to the community." Hence the success of the television campaign leaves a nasty taste in the mouth and results not only in a faulty comic structure but in a contradictory ideological stance, which would like to consign prostitution to a nostalgic past but is unable to do so. There is a bittersweet song in which the newly unemployed hookers contemplate their future, expressing hopes about settling down but resigned to more of the same, in Las Vegas; Miss Mona, having made her money, marries Ed Earl and becomes a politician's wife.

As these examples attest, the clash between the pro- and antiprostitution wings of patriarchal ideology within the same film may be more or less dramatically viable. The outcome of such conflicts, however, is seldom in doubt, the sequence of events proceeding almost invariably, in mainstream cinema, to the victory of the official line. Fun as it is, many Happy Hooker films suggest, to indulge fantasies of erotic fulfillment with oversexed ladies of the night, one recognizes at the end that this cannot go on: the prostitute leaves the life; the bordellos are shut down, raided by the cops, burned down, blown up. There is some relief in *The Best House in London*, in which the brothel is relocated to an airship over Paris, but this is of scant benefit to the citizens of England. The repressed has returned but for a moment: the pleasure principle again makes way for the reality principle, and the circle once more closes.

In the pornographic undergrowth, for example in Playboy productions, the Happy Hooker archetype, unshackled by ideological constraints, continues to flourish; but above ground, where the iconic performances of Louise Brooks, Jean Harlow, Mae West, and Melina Mercouri still provoke and disturb, where their successors are confined to the margins or subsumed to respectability before the end of the film, where the idea of mercenary sex without guilt tempts and tantalizes but cannot be granted free reign, the contradictions remain firmly entrenched.

13

Adventuress

Sometimes by the Lord God I was thinking would I go around by the quays there some dark evening where nobody'd know me and pick up a sailor off the sea that'd be hot on for it, and not care a pin who I was, only to do it off up in a gate somewhere.
—MOLLY BLOOM in *Ulysses* (UK, 1967)

Throughout my clinical practice I have heard women in all walks of life relate fantasies about prostitution.
—ESTELA V. WELLDON, *Mother, Madonna, Whore*[1]

The "Adventuress," as I have called her, is one of the few character archetypes to focus on the subjective experience of the prostitute, though as often as not she remains a creature of the male imagination. She is the woman who uses prostitution to escape from boredom and frustration, to explore her own psyche, to fulfill her sexual desires and fantasies. The money is of little or no consequence. She is often, outwardly, a respectable woman, and leading a double life provides an added thrill as she ventures out from her comfortable home into the dangerous terrain of the red-light district. Perhaps because of the hypothetical nature of the characterization, the Adventuress is a distinct but rare breed amongst cinematic ladies of the night.

She descends, possibly, from the man-hungry empresses of the past— Messalina, Catherine the Great—exploiting their position of power in order to seek sexual satisfaction with commoners. Going beneath oneself is a recurrent theme in the films in which she appears, as is the drive to promiscuity. The Adventuress flagrantly defies a bourgeois morality that would confine her to a single allotted sexual partner, that would prescribe for her a conventional social life among persons of her own class and keep her locked up in dull domesticity.

In *Little Girls* (France, 1966),[2] "seven teenaged girls from wealthy

Parisian families relieve the boredom of their lives through sexual experimentation. They try everything from lesbianism to prostitution. . . ."[3];
similarly, the seventeen-year-old heroine of *Anita — ur en tonårsflickas dag-
bok / Anita* (Sweden / France, 1973) is compulsively promiscuous with both
youths of her own age and adults. *The Sexploiters* (USA, 1965) tells the
story of Lynn Merrick, a "thrill-seeking suburban housewife," who "goes
to New York City and becomes involved in a call-girl syndicate operating within a model agency. Posing in the nude, the 'models' excite desires
that they later satisfy at a price."[4]

It is often because her relationship with her male partner is unfulfilling that the Adventuress takes the path to promiscuity. Although
Helen in *Sylvia's Girls* (USA, 1965), for example, "enjoys a chaste relationship with her boyfriend, Bob, she cannot accept his marriage proposal
because she secretly enjoys being picked up by strangers." A procurer
convinces her to try prostitution, and "Helen agrees and goes to work
for Sylvia, a madam."[5] Barbara Thomas in *The Agony of Love* (USA, 1966)
is ignored by her husband, who is "preoccupied with business"; as a result, she "maintains a separate apartment where she entertains a suc-
cession of faceless customers."[6] Similarly in *Matinee Wives* (USA, 1970),
"Paul Devlin and Tom Chandler are real estate brokers whose quest for
financial success has made them oblivious to the sexual needs of their
wives"—who thereupon "join a group of prominent housewives in the
employ of Kay Gavin, an ex-hooker who is now a madam."[7] The inadequacies of the businessman husband are again stressed in *I idhiotiki mou
zoe / The Lady is a Whore* (Greece, 1972), in which the "inept sexual groping" of her marriage partner drives Eleana Stavrou to feed "her voracious sexual appetite by plying for trade as the prostitute 'Nitsa' outside
a Piraeus hotel."[8]

The clandestine nature of the activity, and the element of disguise and
playacting, are often evident. Helen in *Sylvia's Girls* keeps her work as a
prostitute secret, as do Barbara in *The Agony of Love*, Linda Devlin and Pat
Chandler in *Matinee Wives*, and Eleana in *The Lady is a Whore*. Having a
strand of her life that is not controlled by boyfriend or husband, which
escapes him completely because he does not know about it, is part of the
appeal, but the constant threat of being exposed creates a tension that
eventually becomes unbearable: *The Lady is a Whore* contains repeated
scenes of Eleana (Anna Fousou) "washing away the evidence of her secret
life as a seafront prostitute."[9]

Eleana takes a young building worker as a lover, and the lure of a sexual partner of lower social status than herself, a working-class stud, is

often what motivates the Adventuress. This Lady Chatterley syndrome is typically associated with fantasies of self-debasement. Barbara in *The Agony of Love*, for instance, "although she has 'everything'—beauty, wealth, a good education, an attractive husband . . . is driven by a compulsion to degrade herself"; she finds a "beatnik lover, who manhandles her."[10] Lynn in *The Sexploiters* services a client who "delights in sadomasochistic rituals,"[11] while the teenage protagonist of *Anita* constantly seeks out situations in which she is sexually humiliated.

The Adventuress characterization has something in common with the Happy Hooker, and the films show a similar penchant for staging scenes of lusty sexuality—"an orgy where wild, exotic dances stimulate the senses" (*The Sexploiters*), "in two adjoining motel rooms, both couples find total sexual satisfaction" (*Matinee Wives*), "lurid orgy sequences" (*The Lady is a Whore*).[12] However the Adventuress parts company sharply from the Happy Hooker in finding only temporary pleasure, and no ultimate fulfillment, in prostitution; indeed, her nymphomaniacal tendencies, far from being celebrated as symptoms of a healthy sex drive, are typically seen as pathological.

Thus in *Sylvia's Girls*, "after a few assignments with older men, Helen begins to have doubts and accepts the advice of her roommate, Wanda, that she seek psychiatric help. Sylvia convinces Helen to try one more customer before quitting, but the man's sexual demands repulse her, and Helen leaves in disgust."[13] Similarly Barbara in *The Agony of Love,* "after a disturbing dream . . . visits her psychiatrist, who tries unsuccessfully to bring her secret compulsions to light. . . . Another bizarre dream sends Barbara back to her psychiatrist, who finally succeeds in making her understand that money is a poor substitute for love."[14] Picking up the theme, *Anita* has the teenager (Christina Lindberg) taken in hand by a psychology student, Erik, who through gently encouraging her to reveal traumatic episodes in her past assists her to realize the self-destructive nature of her compulsive whorish behavior.

Anita ends happily, with Anita falling in love with Erik at the classical-music-playing artists' commune where he has taken her to live; more frequently, however, the Adventuress's problems are not so easily resolved. The promiscuity of the teenagers in *Little Girls* "draws them into a web of blackmail, murder, and suicide."[15] Barbara in *The Agony of Love* has a confrontation with her husband when he discovers her among the call girls at an orgy: "She protests that her infidelity is a result of her search for the love that has been denied her, and she runs off into the night. After a chase through Hollywood with her husband in pursuit, destiny intervenes, and Barbara meets her death."[16] Helen in *Sylvia's Girls* kills herself in an agony of frustration after the psychiatrist's response to her cry for help is to try to make a date with her after hours; likewise Eleana in *The Lady is a Whore* "commits suicide after suffering an hallucination in which she kills all her mocking friends and acquaintances."[17]

After initially endorsing the independent-spirited heroine's quest for fulfillment outside conventional bounds, then, the Adventuress film finally turns around and allows the patriarchy to reap its revenge. The monogamous heterosexual couple is, as ever, represented as normative; a desire for multiple sex partners is portrayed as indicative of mental or emotional instability, and prostitution as a desperate plea for the love that has been lacking. The Adventuress may, possibly, be recuperated within marriage; but the woman who strays too far from the norms of ideologically prescribed good behavior is, like all the hookers discussed in chapter 19 and the others too numerous to mention, condemned to death.

The pattern for many of the Adventuress films to follow was set by *Die Lady/Frustration/Games of Desire* (West Germany/France, 1964). Profiting from the 1960s relaxation of censorship, it depicts the elegant wife (Ingrid Thulin) of the Swedish ambassador to Greece as frustrated because her husband's sexual interests lie exclusively with his male secretary. It is a marriage of convenience: "You're playing the role of devoted wife to perfection," the wealthy Eliot tells Nadine, "and I think I give you a very pleasant life." Athens society hostess by day, Nadine explores other options by surreptitiously plying the nighttime trade of waterfront prostitute.

She rents a room where she plays dress-ups, swapping her chaste white underwear for lacy black, putting on bracelets, letting her hair down. If happily married woman is one role she plays, sexy hooker is another and perhaps the more authentic. We see her bring a customer to her room — a tough sailor, hairy arms, tattooed belly. She strips and has sex with him, gripping and releasing the bars of the bedhead, grunting, writhing. Then it's over: he sits beside her on the bed, satisfied, smiling. She shoves him away. He tosses money down onto her body; the next morning Nadine's maid will ask her where she got it, "because it's so dirty."

Nadine meets Nikos, a powerful, macho dock worker. Alone with her, he roughly pulls down her glistening black dress to inspect her breasts, then draws it back up again. Later, he visits her in her room, waving a

50. Nadine (Ingrid Thulin) in *Die Lady*. Stiftung Deutsche Kinemathek — Film-museum Berlin.

wad of cash. "I don't want your money, you understand?" Nadine says. "No, I don't understand," he replies. "All right, I just don't want to sleep with you," she insists, "Is that plain enough?" Nikos is not convinced. He seizes her and throws her on the bed, and as she struggles, biting his arm, he forces himself on her. Suddenly Nadine is still, and there is a cut to a long shot as he lies on her, kissing. The curtain blows in the breeze and the door slowly closes, blocking the camera's vision.

In masochistic self-abasement, the ambassador's wife has found love. "I don't believe in love," she has earlier told her psychiatrist. Later she will explain to Nikos her resistance: "I was afraid of falling in love with you. That's why I fought so hard." Her love will be reciprocated, but complications inevitably ensue, notably when Nikos's sister Elektra bitchily reveals to him Nadine's true identity: "She likes to go slumming with men like you — strong, healthy, stupid men she drags into her bed to satisfy her." In his anger Nikos accidentally kills Elektra, and Nadine's dreams of a transcendent love affair are over. Even if her husband is gay, there is no way that the excessive desire of this Adventuress — to be both prostitute and wife, to have sex and love on top of a luxurious lifestyle — can be countenanced.

Luis Buñuel's teasing *Belle de Jour* (France, 1967) amplifies the concerns of *Die Lady* by plunging us into the fantasy life of a beautiful young Parisian *bourgeoise* (Catherine Deneuve) who seeks to escape the lifelessness of her marriage by working afternoons at a brothel. It is not that Séverine's husband is neglectful, too tied up with business or with sexual interests elsewhere; on the contrary, he is attentive, very much in love, and only too eager to get in bed with her. Séverine, however, despite her adoration of Pierre, fails to be aroused, keeps herself at a chaste distance, and pleads repeatedly for his patience and forgiveness.

Belle de Jour opens with Pierre and Séverine trotting along in an open landau, exchanging saccharine declarations of affection ("I love you more every day," "So do I, Pierre"). But the mood quickly changes. "If only you were less . . . cold," he says. And suddenly he orders the coachmen the stop. They are in a wooded area. Pierre brutally seizes Séverine, and with the coachmen's assistance drags her out of the vehicle. "Don't be afraid to hurt this little tart," Pierre tells the men, and she is violently hauled across the ground, gagged, tied up, and whipped, before being passed on to one of them for rape: "She's all yours."

A cut takes us to the couple's apartment. "What are you thinking about?" Pierre asks Séverine, who is in bed but not yet asleep. She replies that she was thinking about them driving together in a landau. At a stroke an outrageously vicious assault on a woman has been rendered innocuous, revealed to be the masochistic fantasy of the victim dreaming — not without pleasure, it would seem — of her own violation. The real Pierre appears insufferably pallid by comparison with the fantasized figure: it is no surprise that Séverine fends him off when he ventures to get in bed with her.

The daydream propels Séverine into action. She learns that there are still brothels in Paris, though they operate clandestinely; she discovers that one of her friends is working part-time as a prostitute. The idea repels her ("With strangers it must be horrible"), and yet. . . . An acquaintance, Husson, gives her the address of Madame Anaïs's establishment. "I like the atmosphere," he confesses, "women completely enslaved." Séverine is disturbed, she drops things, has a fleeting childhood memory of what is possibly molestation by a tradesman. But not without hesitation, she finds herself an employee of Madame Anaïs, on the 2–5 PM shift. She is "Belle de Jour."

With her first customer, a jovial candy manufacturer, she is difficult. The madam has to take her in hand, and the client, impatient with her reluctance ("I've had enough of your play-acting . . . It's rough stuff you want?"), slaps her down onto the bed, grabs her hair, and forces a kiss on her. The new recruit to the sex trade succumbs, positioning herself as the unwilling victim, just as in her fantasy. At home, she strips off her stockings and bra, and throws them in the open fire.

She has another daydream. This time, cattle are being herded across a plain, and Pierre and Husson are at a campfire. Séverine is tied to a post, clad in pure white. As Pierre stands idly by, Husson flings sloppy black mud at her, until her dress is spattered and her face completely covered. "Piece of trash!" he calls out. "Feeling all right, slut? Scum! Swill! Rubbish! Dung devourer!" The prostitute's sense of being dirtied and degraded has seldom received a more vividly melodramatic interpretation.

Séverine does not return to the brothel for a week. When she does, Anaïs is reluctant to take her back but is "too kind-hearted." Asked to service an eminent gynecologist with a hankering to be whipped like a naughty manservant, Séverine does not cotton on to the dominatrix routine and has to be replaced. She is assigned, instead, an Asian client of massive proportions. Afterwards, she lies on the bed, Deneuve's face expressing, in the words of critic Michael Wood, "fatigue but also a wonderful, weary, deep delight."[18]

There is, it appears, a positive impact on Séverine's sex life with Pierre: perhaps prostitution as frigidity therapy is working. She now gets into bed with him, although not as a matter of course ("I only wish you'd stay more often," he says), and their embrace is chastely restrained. "More and more I want you," she claims, but Pierre cannot satisfy her, as is evident when, back at the brothel, she encounters the flamboyant, sadistic gangster Marcel, and the two fall for each other.

On vacation with Séverine at the seaside, Pierre speaks of her aloofness and reveals that he suspects she's in love with someone else. Séverine says it's impossible, and at this point, curiously, the film gives us for the first time her thoughts in a voice-over: "I don't understand myself. . . . My feelings for you have nothing to do with pleasure. It's much more than that. You may not believe this—I've never felt so close to you." The remoteness that Pierre correctly discerns in her demeanor is contradicted by the words that by cinematic convention are a straightforward transcription of her mental process: paradoxically Buñuel deepens the enigma that is Séverine by permitting the direct expression of her subjectivity.

51. *Belle de Jour:* Séverine (Catherine Deneuve) with the gynecologist (François Maistre).

Back at the brothel, Marcel demands an explanation for her absence and strikes her with a leather belt; when, in a rare assertion of self-assured defiance, she threatens not to come back if he does it again, he smashes a picture on the wall instead. "Why come here then?" he asks, when she admits she's in love with another man. "I don't know," she replies. "It's something else." As they lie down to have sex, one of the lumpen-proletarian thug's patent-leather boots drops off, revealing a large hole in his sock.

The days of Séverine's double life, as for any Adventuress, are numbered. Marcel, having discovered where she lives, threatens to expose her to Pierre if she does not agree to spend a night with him, but Séverine tells him she had decided to tell her husband everything anyway. In a celebrated ending in which it is impossible to separate with certainty reality from fantasy, Marcel shoots Pierre and is himself killed in a shoot-out with police; Pierre, after hospital treatment, returns home paralyzed and perhaps blind and unable to speak as well; and then Pierre, uninjured or recovered it seems, cheerfully chats to Séverine about taking a vacation in the mountains.[19] Whichever outcome one chooses to believe is the actual one, the film offers us the restoration of the happy married couple, either Séverine dutifully waiting hand and foot on the cripple, or else the two reconciled, pleasurably contemplating a vacation together. The straying wife is back within the patriarchal fold.

The profounder ambiguity of *Belle de Jour* is perhaps not the ending, but the question of whether the images of Séverine whipped, tied, and sexually assaulted are, as the narrative would have us believe, masochistic female fantasies, or more precisely sadistic male ones, conveniently attributed to the female as a way of exculpating the filmmakers from guilt. Are we in the presence of an authentic female subjectivity, or is the depiction of Séverine — and of the Adventuress in general — yet another instance of a prostitute figure being invented and exploited to satisfy male desires? Skepticism is no doubt warranted: both Buñuel's collaborator on the screenplay (Jean-Claude Carrière) and the author of the novel on which the film is based (Joseph Kessel) are also male. And yet, there is the positive response of a feminist critic such as Kathleen Murphy, whom I quoted in chapter 2. The arguments of Ellen Willis, expressed in a contribution to the feminist debates on pornography, are relevant to a consideration of the film: "[T]he view of sex that most often emerges from talk about 'erotica' is as sentimental and euphemistic as the word itself: lovemaking should be beautiful, romantic, soft, nice, and devoid of messiness, vulgarity, impulses to power, or indeed aggression of any sort. Above all, the emphasis should be on *relationships,* not (yuck) *organs.* This goody-goody concept of eroticism is not feminist but feminine. It is precisely sex as an aggressive, unladylike activity, an expression of violent and unpretty emotion, an exercise of erotic power, and a specifically genital experience that has been taboo for women."[20]

Such concerns necessarily again come to the fore when one looks at *Crimes of Passion* (USA, 1984), directed by Ken Russell.[21] In this case, however, the Adventuress is on the inflicting as well as the receiving end of sexual violence. Joanna Crain (Kathleen Turner) is a topflight clothing designer, living alone in a well-appointed apartment. She is also China Blue, a streetwalker in the red-light district specializing, it would seem, in rough-trade clientele. Turner confesses she took the role "because I had the chance to act my ass off."[22]

Joanna's motivation for turning tricks is a matter of speculation. It is certainly not the money. We learn that she is divorced and has no boyfriend, and the strongest clue perhaps is her assertion, when in her apartment, that "I'm never horny here." Plunging into prostitution is thus a quest, as with Séverine, for an elusive sexual fulfillment.

It also enables her to role-play. As Joanna Crain, designer, she is masculinized in appearance, in gray trouser suit and tie, with short hair.[23] As China Blue, in spike heels, tight blue dress, heavy makeup, and platinum blonde wig, she is decidedly female, perhaps excessively so: Cynthia Fuchs argues that she appears as "a cheap reproduction of the stereotypical whore."[24] But this is just the beginning. China Blue herself puts on fantasy guises in collusion with her clients: a patriotic Miss Liberty, a musician ("Would you like to see how Miss Liberty plays the flute? First I unzip the case, then I take out the instrument very carefully. . . ."); a rape victim; an airline hostess; a nun. . . . "This is a fantasy business," she says. "I'm Cinderella, Cleopatra, Goldie Hawn, Eva Braun. I'm Little Miss Muffet, I'm Pocahontas. I'm whoever you want me to be." She can even be nursemaid to a dying man whose wife has bought him some comfort, though this is one occasion when Joanna drops all pretense, taking off her wig and giving back the $100 she has accepted for the job. One suspects that China Blue of the Paradise Isle Hotel is a shield-persona adopted by Joanna to protect her vulnerable personal identity, damaged in the past: she tells stories about being raped by her father, and perhaps there is an element of truth in them. Certainly, at a point in the film when we have reason to believe she is sincere, she observes: "That hotel is the safest place in the world. I can do anything there, I can be anything I can dream of because it's not me, don't you see?"

The fantasies she indulges include violence. She is pursued in the street by one client, gets away to the safety of her hotel room, but then the lights don't work, and she is grabbed from behind, a hand is clapped over her mouth, the chain lock on the door set, and she is thrown down and roughly fucked. After he comes, we learn it is a consensual playacting routine. With a cop from the beat, roles are reversed. His wrists handcuffed to the bed, she sits on him, grinding away, while she jabs his baton into his belly and then thrusts it up his ass, and draws blood with her spike heels digging into his flesh, the whole event building to a frenzied crescendo of frantic zoom shots. When it's over, he spits on her: is this part of the routine, or has she overstepped the mark this time?

If Joanna experiences pleasure in her sexual encounters as China Blue, she doesn't let on. The emotions we can read in her face include only disgust (swilling out her mouth after "playing the flute") and dejection (sobbing as she tries to repair her makeup after the session with the cop). She remains opaque.

In the narrative structure of the film, Joanna is caught between two men who stalk her, spy on her, pursue her. There is "Reverend" Peter Shayne, the cracked evangelist obsessed by carnal sin, who gleefully observes her having sex with clients through a peephole in the wall, and wishes only to "save," i.e., kill her. And there is Bobby Grady, unhappily married electronic repairman, who is employed to run surveillance on Joanna since she is suspected of industrial espionage — she is innocent, as is quickly made clear — and whose motives soon become more personal. Both men are driven by the need to understand this woman who eludes comprehension, who is the very incarnation of the enigma of female sexuality. ("She's a mystery," Joanna's boss tells Bobby. "She gets along fine with the other women, but if you've got a penis you're in trouble — she turns to ice.") For Shayne, what is incomprehensible is the physical stress she puts herself under for personal reaffirmation: "Women, you mystify me. The extremes you go to for a little validation, and still go home alone." Bobby, on the other hand, is torn by the uncertainty of not knowing whether her reactions when he has sex with her are genuine: "You felt it too, didn't you? You weren't just acting?"

For Bobby, in the Adventuress tradition, has fallen in love with her, and in due course — when he bursts into her apartment and confronts her as Joanna rather than China Blue — she will reciprocate the sentiment. Does she accept him because it means putting an end to the exhausting charade? When they make love it is all lyrical and sensual in satin sheets, and as Fuchs points out, "conventional, objectifying shots of Joanna's smiling face show her pleasure for us."[25] The narrative development gives the lie to the sadomasochistic streak in Joanna's psychosexual formation, suggesting (unlike *Belle de Jour*) that nice, nonviolent sex can be fulfilling, and pathologizing her China Blue persona. Shayne has claimed that as a hooker she is suffering from a disease; Bobby, who does a barbecue vaudeville stunt as "the human penis," proves that with the right doctor she can be cured.

Where is Joanna's subjectivity in all of this? Nowhere, if we are to believe Cynthia Fuchs. "Her assimilation of male narratives denies her subjectivity altogether, and she recreates her body on the ground of her own absence," Fuchs contends. "By aligning Bobby's romance plot with Shayne's rescue plot, the film reveals the impossibility of representing Joanna's 'will' within either narrative." A wildly improbable climax, with

Joanna dressed as Shayne leaping on Shayne dressed as China Blue and stabbing him to death, lends support to Fuchs's argument. "China Blue and Joanna are never allowed life outside a male story," she concludes, "and this is precisely the self-conscious crime of this film."[26]

Jenny Nicholson (Wendy Hughes) in *Warm Nights on a Slow Moving Train* (Australia, 1988) is an unlikely blend of Martyr, Nursemaid, and Adventuress. Supplementing her income from teaching by picking up clients on the train to Melbourne on Sunday nights, she is able to help support her morphine-addicted paraplegic brother. She is also, having been a nurse at one time, able to indulge a Florence Nightingale complex ("you can't deny that womanly part of yourself") by massaging the troubled egos of her customers: "Each one wants an image to briefly love. . . . And it can be arranged, and if you listen, really listen, and look, you can know what they want. And you can give them so much very quickly, very cheaply, without hurt, without pain, and happiness can be increased."

As an Adventuress, her pleasure comes from playacting. "I'm as many people as I want to be," she declares. "It's a choice I made." It's a modus operandi that suits the situation, since this is a disguised, discreet prostitution. Unlike China Blue, Jenny (identified only as "The Girl" in the credits) does not advertise her availability; rather, she chats up a passenger in the club car, adopting the persona of private secretary, nurse, social worker, or even in an access of frankness, schoolteacher, before drawing him away down the train corridor and whispering, "You're going to have to pay for this." Wearing a multitude of different outfits and a variety of wigs—jet black, red, chestnut, straight hair and curled—she effects chameleon-like shifts of identity.

But we never see her in the process of donning these disguises, which might serve as a clue to her real feelings about the masquerade she is playing. Jenny seldom radiates enjoyment, and even when she's seemingly lighthearted, for example as a youngster in blouse and jacket and short blue denim skirt, flirting with a callow young soldier, the strain is evident. One can sense a tension between the male-authored script, which proposes a level of illicit pleasure for the part-time whore, and the female interpretation of the role, which tends to negate any such reading. "What's wrong with you?" the soldier asks her. "Why do you do this? Do you get a thrill out of it?" Jenny's reply is heavy with sarcasm: "Yeah, a big thrill." And when she kicks her clients out, coldly, at 3 AM, it may be, as she claims, that she's afraid of getting involved; it may also be because she's really disgusted with them and with herself.

Jenny differs from Séverine and Joanna in that she does not appear to get her kicks from bondage and discipline. It is straight sex that she delivers. But there is no mistaking the masculine forcefulness of the one client she falls for, identified simply as "The Man." Sharply differentiated from the gutted football coach, the milksop soldier, the retired salesman who has lost his wife and found God, and the washed-up entertainer, the Man—a tough, young, and suave secret agent for an unidentified employer—has the macho qualities the Adventuress yearns for. Stationing himself uninvited outside her suite, he reveals he knows all about her, and then, as they enter, he seizes her aggressively around the waist. "You're not going to ask for money are you?" he inquires, fondling her breasts, her crotch, her buttocks, unzipping her dress. Instantly aroused, Jenny is soon engaged in lusty sex with him. Infatuation—apparently mutual—follows, to such an extent that she will consent without qualms to his proposition to bump off an awkward politician by clawing him with a poisoned fingernail. The deed done, she collects her reward—$800,000, which will provide lifelong care for her brother—but not the expected bonus: the Man has been "seconded to Washington" with no personal ties allowed.

Female subjectivity, as in the other Adventuress films, remains elusive. In her weekday existence Jenny is depicted, fleetingly, as painter and sculptor as well as teacher, but these dimensions to her life are never explored. The film concentrates on her activities as a prostitute, yet even here, beyond the male-oriented motivations of helping her brother and becoming the Man's steady lover, we learn little of what it is that drives her; and what the experience of dressing up and selling her body means to her, emotionally, remains shrouded in narrative fog.

It is precisely the subjective experience of prostitution deliberately chosen as an option for exploring one's sexuality that is the preoccupation of female filmmakers who have tackled the topic. The pleasurable but troubling fantasies of self-degradation in mercenary sex expressed by undercover cop Lottie Mason in *Impulse* (USA, 1990), directed by Sondra Locke, have been mentioned in chapter 2. On the job, Lottie (Theresa Russell) dresses up and plays hooker and, with a phalanx of uniformed cops ready to pounce, gets men arrested for solicitation and assault. Questioned by the police department's psychologist, she admits that "sometimes, working vice, strangers, the way they look at you, I feel all that power over them, make them pay, it excites me. . . . I wonder what it would be like just to do it." Later in the film she almost indulges her fantasy, taking money from a man in a bar and going up to his apartment, but in the bathroom she has second thoughts ("What am I doing here? I've got to get out of here"), and — fortunately for her relationship with her boyfriend — she is relieved of the necessity of going through with the charade when the john, a dope dealer, is shot.

It is also chiefly on the fantasy level that Catherine Breillat's controversial *Romance* (France/Spain, 1999) deals with the notion of prostitution as a vehicle for female sexual fulfillment. Remarkable for its hard-core explicitness within an art-house psychological drama, the film depicts the sexual odyssey of a young and beautiful schoolteacher, Marie (Caroline Ducey), securing a powerful alignment with her point of view by means of a first-person voice-over narration that continues throughout.

Marie is very much in love with her partner Paul, an attractive male model. Paul, however, has lost sexual interest in her, and cannot or will not have intercourse. Marie, perforce, looks for satisfaction elsewhere. She has a brief fling with a man, Paolo, whom she picks up in a bar, and enters into a relationship of bondage and domination with her school principal, Robert. But it is in prostitution that she sees the purest realization of her desires, and it is perhaps only her pregnancy that arrests what would be the logical narrative development, having her become a full-fledged Adventuress.

The difficulty for Marie in having affairs with other men is that they lead to attachments, relationships. "In my head, there's Paul," she tells us, and she does not want him dislodged. But there is an excitement, too, about sex with people you do not know — "that miracle, a stranger making love to you." What she is after, in fact, is pure physical sensation. Therefore, when she encounters by chance a man on the stairway to her apartment who offers her 100 francs to go down on her, she accepts. "That's my dream," she says in voice-over. "To know that for some guy, I'm just a pussy he wants to stuff, without sentimental bullshit. Just raw desire." As she splays her legs and he gets to work, she continues, her words suggesting the self-abasement often associated with the Adventuress: "To be taken by a guy, a nobody, a bum with whom you wallow for the joy of wallowing, for the dishonor, the discredit, that's pleasure to a girl."

Suddenly he stops. He orders her to turn over. "Pay me," she says. "You've got no choice, bitch," he retorts, and proceeds to throw her down and brutally rape her. "Whore, bitch, I reamed you good," he declares triumphantly. Marie is left pained, shocked, whimpering, but has the strength to yell out, "I'm not ashamed, asshole!" She lights up a cig-

52. *Romance:* Marie (Caroline Ducey) with Robert (François Berléand). bfi Collections.

arette, trembling, and not the least unsettling part of the sequence is the accompanying voice-over, which gives the impression that the violation was in some sense self-willed: "Is nymphomania destroying yourself, because you choose a man who doesn't love you? I don't want to sleep with men. I want to be opened up all the way. . . . Maybe I really want to meet Jack the Ripper. He'd certainly dissect a woman like me."

Marie's conception of a radical dissociation between body and mind, forced upon her by Paul's intransigence, is strikingly expressed in one, close-up shot. In a mirror held in her hands, an image of her bare crotch is reflected; she then tilts the mirror up to show her face. "Paul is right," she says in voice-over. "You can't love a face if a cunt goes with it. A cunt doesn't go with a face." The idea is developed further in the sequence that follows. "I fantasize about a brothel," Marie says, "where a head is separated from a body by a guillotine-like contraption before the blade comes down." The images show us a curved wall with women positioned in holes at intervals, lying on their backs: on one side, the women exchange tender glances with their loving menfolk (in her case, Paul); on the other, the women's legs dangle down and men insert stiff pricks into the open orifices. Marie wears "a silky red skirt that billows up and rustles. And those silly trappings"—referring, presumably, to her stockings and suspenders — "that give men a hard-on." With anonymity of prostitute and client perfectly preserved, the sexual act is reduced to brute physical friction.

This, perhaps, is the paradoxical ultimate dream of the Adventuress, to become pure female flesh, passivity incarnate, to be penetrated at will, ejaculated in or on, a receptacle for male lust, a cavity, an emptiness. "I don't want to see the men who screw me, or look at them," Marie tells us. "I want to be a hole, a pit. The more gaping, the more obscene it is, the more it's me, my intimacy, the more I surrender. It's metaphysical. I disappear in proportion to the cock taking me. I hollow myself. That's my purity."

Refraining from sexual activity — except for one time with Paul — during her pregnancy, Marie defers acting out the urgings of her fantasy. But for her the rift between sex and love has become irreconcilable. At the moment she gives birth to his child, she will punish her partner, for his indifference, with death: Marie is one Adventuress who, in feminist hands, will not be recuperated by the patriarchy.

14

Junkie

You can say prostitution feeds a drug habit. Which comes first? Perhaps
it's a kind of circle. You need the shit to kill the pain of prostitution;
you need the prostitution to kill the pain of needing the drug.
— "M," in Kate Millett, "Prostitution: A Quartet for Female Voices."[1]

Money, smack, money, smack, money, smack. Mostly that means fuck,
smack, fuck, smack, fuck, smack.
— IDA HALVORSEN, *Hard Asphalt*[2]

Høigård and Finstad found in their study of Norwegian prostitution that
"drug use is a central element in many prostitutes' everyday life."[3] Studies in other parts of the world confirm this finding.[4] Priscilla Alexander
stresses that "prostitution is hard work, both in physical and emotional
terms" and that therefore "it is not surprising that a significant number
of prostitutes use drugs of one kind or another to make the work easier."[5]
The drugs taken, of course, vary, but heroin is relatively common, particularly among streetwalkers. American research published in 1979
found that of the street prostitutes surveyed, 100 percent had used heroin
at one time, and 84 percent were addicted; the figures were significantly
lower for "high-class" prostitutes.[6] Prostitution is often the only available
alternative to crime as a way of making money to feed a drug habit.

If, therefore, a sizable group of films depict the prostitute as a heavy
user of heroin or another hard drug such as cocaine or morphine, they
do no more, in one respect, than reflect reality. In a minor role the addicted hooker is often simply part of the scene, adding to the effect of authenticity: thus in *Too Young, Too Immoral!* (USA, 1962), "Gene's girlfriend
Mary, also addicted to drugs, is living in a hotel for young women who
support their habits by prostitution"[7]; in *Way Out* (USA, 1966), Frankie's
girlfriend, Anita, "has become a prostitute to pay for her drug habit"[8]; in
Spiked Heels and Black Nylons (USA, 1967), "Myrna turns to prostitution to

support her costly drug habit."[9] Beyond simple verisimilitude, however, the addict-prostitute takes on potent symbolic value. The most wretched of the character archetypes, the "Junkie" can represent the depths of despair and desperation; she may appear the most abject and pitiable of human beings, and at the same time the most degraded and corrupt.

As with the fallen woman characterization, the Junkie oscillates in her portrayal between victim and author of her own misfortune. Often the two are indissolubly merged in the one person: she is both innocent and guilty, a slave to her cravings and a free person with the power to kick the habit should she have the will to do so. Typically invoking this ambiguity, the narrator at the start of *Liebe kann wie Gift sein / Girl of Shame* (West Germany, 1958) tells us that the film will show "what it means for a girl who has no self-discipline to grow up without a mother." (Just in case we don't get the point, the life of Magdalena, who becomes a drug addict and prostitute, is contrasted with that of Susanne, her fellow student at art school, who despite being an orphan leads a blameless existence.)

There can be little doubt that the figure of the Junkie in the cinema fuels dark male fantasies of the pliable sex object whose resistance has been so weakened that any form of indignity may be practiced upon her. A subgroup of films depicting pimps deliberately pumping women with drugs to make them more amenable prostitutes caters to such fantasies. At the same time, the figure frequently serves respectable ideological purposes by acting as the pivot of a cautionary tale about the downward slope young women who are loose or rebellious may find themselves embarked upon.

While contradictory characteristics are embodied in most Junkie representations, there have tended to be cycles or waves in film history in which a particular approach to the subject becomes dominant. In this chapter we look at five such groups of films: the American exploitation cycle of the silent and early sound period; the wave of biographical portrait films — occasionally based on fact — that appeared from the 1950s to the 1980s; the roughly contemporaneous cycle of "pimp-victim" movies, which I have mentioned; the cluster of teenage addict pictures that were popular from the 1970s through to the 1990s; and a loose grouping of films in which the figure of the Junkie becomes symptomatic of social decay, coming to particular prominence toward the end of the century.

The exploitation cycle relied, tabloid-style, on making sensational, shocking revelations about drug addiction and the prostitution associated with it. The overt concern with delivering social comment is evident from the generality of the films' titles — *Dope, Cocaine Traffic; or, The Drug Terror, The Pace That Kills, Narcotic, The Cocaine Fiends, Marihuana* — and points are typically hammered home by means of highly colored direct address to the spectator. Thus *The Pace That Kills* (1928, silent) opens with a lengthy preface that proclaims:

> History teaches that each nation, each race, perished miserably when they ignored their problems and failed in their struggles against debauchery and sin.
>
> Today, we — the highest civilization the world has ever known — are faced with the most tragic problem that has ever confronted mankind — a menace so threatening, and all embracing that if we fail to conquer it, our race, our people, our civilization must perish from the face of the earth!
>
> What is this octopus, this hideous monster that clutches at every heart, creeping slowly, silently, inexorably into every nook and corner of the world?
>
> It is the demon
> DOPE!

The film concludes by urging audience members to "write to your Senator and lend your support to the Porter Bill for the segregation and hospitalization of narcotic addicts — the greatest constructive measure ever offered for the abatement of the narcotic evil!"

Drug trafficking and prostitution are customarily presented as interlinked rackets, in which the socially respectable and powerful may well be implicated. In *Cocaine Traffic; or, The Drug Terror* (1914), for example, socialite addict Roger Hastings is both an associate of Andrews, who has "amassed a fortune in cocaine," and a procurer for a gang of white slavers.[10] Likewise in *The Money-Changers* (1920), "Hugh Gordon, the head of a large pharmaceutical and chemical firm . . . is also the ringleader of a powerful drug and white slave operation in the Chinese quarter."[11] The story of *China Slaver* (1929) "deals with the Chinese boss of an island which serves as a base for traffic in narcotics and white slavery,"[12] while *The Cocaine Fiends / The Pace That Kills* (1935 — a loose remake of the 1928 film) exposes the operations of a powerful "dope and girl" racket that "peddles drugs to teenagers."[13] Close connections between prostitution and the supply of drugs are also implied in *Narcotic* (ca. 1933), in which the addicted male protagonist and his gang "have a 'dope' party in a bordello with a number of women, during which participants sniff cocaine and inject heroine."[14]

The Junkie in films of the exploitation cycle typically becomes an exemplar of the inexorable fate that awaits the female hard drug user. In *Dope* (1914), for example, the sister of a morphine addict who has impulsively killed his father herself becomes addicted to cocaine. "To finance her habit," the synopsis tells us, "she becomes a prostitute and leaves her husband, walking the streets with their young son."[15] After being arrested and exiled from New York City, Mrs. Binkley returns to attend a cocaine party, and shortly afterward dies at a drug store that caters to addicts.

The Pace That Kills and its remake lay more stress on the Junkie as a corrupting influence. In the silent film, city slicker Fannie O'Reilly (Virginia Roye) seduces country boy Eddie, who has come to town to search for his lost sister, with "something to fix his headache," and he soon experiences a craving for more of the white powder ("One of the most dangerous features of the dope evil is that each addict has the burning desire to induce all of his — or her — associates to 'try it just once'"); likewise in *The Cocaine Fiends* Fanny (Sheila Manners) introduces Eddie to the "headache powder," telling the naive youth: "I'm gonna take you on a sleigh ride with some snow birds." In both films the pair become lovers and addicts, with the woman resorting to streetwalking at the point at which her boyfriend, no longer able to hold down a job, is desperate for a fix. When she becomes pregnant and Eddie is repulsed at the thought ("God! A baby born to a dope fiend and a ———" he says in the 1928 version), the distraught woman commits suicide, jumping into the harbor in *The Pace That Kills* and gassing herself in *The Cocaine Fiends*.

Marihuana (1935) offers another version of the slippery slope, telling the story of high-school student Burma (Harley Wood) who loses her inhibitions when given reefers to smoke. She becomes pregnant, her boyfriend gets involved in smuggling narcotics and is shot dead, and she gives her baby up for adoption. Subsequently she becomes a dope addict, pusher, and prostitute, eventually taking a deliberate overdose and killing herself.[16]

With liberal borrowings from the fallen woman prostitute narrative, it was in the films of the exploitation cycle that the conventions of the Junkie characterization were forged. The cinema was to see many more of what *The Pace That Kills* termed the "hopeless addicts — chained, helpless, tormented! Willing to pay any price, do anything, just so they get their 'shot!'"

James Robert Parish observes that Harley Wood's acting in *Marihuana* is, "for this type of exploitation item . . . surprisingly good": she is "believable as the heroine who changes from a sweet teenager into a hard-as-nails doper."[17] The process of transformation as registered in the features of the protagonist was to become a touchstone of the biographical portrait films that began to appear in the 1950s. Thus the *Monthly Film Bulletin* remarks in its review of *Liebe kann wie Gift sein* that Sabine Sesselmann, "making her début as Magdalena, drifts from wide-eyed innocence to wide-eyed viciousness."[18] What marks this cycle of films off from its predecessor is less concern with making a sociopolitical statement, and greater psychological depth in the characterization.

The Junkie whose life story is traced is likely to come from a family background deficient in some way. Magdalena in *Liebe kann wie Gift sein* has no mother, and her father turns her out of the house when he sees a nude painting of her in an art dealer's window and finds that she is in love with the artist. In *Wild, Wild Girl* (USA, 1965), "the influence of her overprotective father has caused 22-year-old Beatrice to remain childishly naïve."[19] The troubles for Diane in *Hip, Hot and 21* (USA, 1967) begin when her stepfather agrees to let the unprincipled Nick marry her "in return for a 'loan' of $50 from the prospective bridegroom."[20] *Hard asfalt/Hard Asphalt* (Norway, 1986), based on the published autobiography of Ida Halvorsen, depicts in a series of flashbacks Ida's difficult childhood with an amiable alcoholic father.

Whatever its roots, the young woman's character is typically marked by a restlessness that practiced operators know how to exploit. The unscrupulous artist in *Liebe kann wie Gift sein*, for example, casually squeezes Magdalena's breast while saying things like, "Never forget that I am the first person to have loved you with all my heart."[21] When he quickly tires of her, Magdalena moves on to affairs with two of his friends, before drifting into drug-taking. Beatrice (Krystal Ball) in *Wild, Wild Girl* rejects a young prizefighter who loves her; instead "a longtime friend, Emmy, introduces her to the experienced Joe, to whom she gives herself. She then leaves home, becomes a prostitute, and eventually succumbs to drug addiction."[22] Beatrice and Emmy become lovers. *The Grasshopper* (USA, 1970) is structured around the heroine's restlessness, with nineteen-year-old Christine (Jacqueline Bisset) leaving her home in British Columbia for a boyfriend in California, and from then on flitting impulsively from man to man and back and forth between Los Angeles and Las Vegas. Quitting her job as bank teller, Christine becomes a hotel showgirl, gets married, decides to leave her husband (who at this point is murdered), gets into heavy drug use, and finally becomes a high-priced call girl.

A critical factor in the protagonist's becoming involved in both

53. Sabine Sesselmann as Magdalena in *Liebe kann wie Gift sein*. Stiftung Deutsche Kinemathek—Filmmuseum Berlin.

drug-taking and prostitution is often her contact with a milieu in which these activities are commonplace. Thus in *Hip, Hot and 21,* "Nick brings his naive country bride to live in an apartment in a southern city, and she is seduced, under the influence of alcohol, by their neighbor Marla, a bisexual narcotics-dealing prostitute." Her husband deserts her, and Diane (Diane Darcel) turns to Marla for companionship: "Through their association, Diane meets a number of hoodlums, degenerates, and drug addicts." After Marla's death from an overdose, Diane takes up with another bisexual drug pusher and prostitute and becomes a member of her narcotics and sex gang.[23] Helen (Kitty Winn) in *The Panic in Needle Park* (USA, 1971) comes in contact with the New York drug scene through her relationship with an addicted artist, and when she moves on (after a botched abortion) to his supplier, small-time crook and heroin addict Bobby, it is inevitable that she will become part of the crowd that hangs out at "Needle Park" on Broadway and 72nd Street. Helen soon begins injecting, and becomes a hooker to pay for the habit.

Disappointment in love or a setback in a professional career may be the trigger that sets off the protagonist's drug-taking and prostitution. In *Liebe kann wie Gift sein*, for example, Magdalena "finds temporary conso-

54. Helen (Kitty Winn) with Bobby (Al Pacino) in *The Panic in Needle Park*.

lation in drugs" after the affairs with the artist and his friends do not last. "Her former tutor, Stefan, tries to help her break the habit, but Magdalena, now a prostitute, gives up any effort to help herself once she finds out that Stefan is in love with another woman."[24] In the sex film *The Divine Obsession* (USA, 1975), Julia (Julia Franklin) leaves her home in Cleveland as a teenager to pursue an acting career in New York. Unable to find legitimate opportunities, she accepts a lead role in a pornographic movie and becomes an overnight sensation. However, she is arrested on an obscenity charge, loses the case, and penniless, turns to pills and alcohol. A promising relationship with a university student helps her recover, but she is shattered on discovering his infidelity and, with friends, establishes a high-class brothel.

Stories of enduring love between addicts offer some of the most powerful drama in this group of films. Lighting up a bleak existence with moments of rare affection and tenderness, the relationship is nonetheless constantly torn by the unrelenting quest for the next fix, at whatever cost. In *The Panic in Needle Park*, Helen is strongly drawn to the empathetic if self-deluded Bobby (Al Pacino), who returns her feelings. This does not, however, prevent her from sleeping with his brother in order to score, turning to prostitution when Bobby is briefly in jail, as a result of which he beats her up ("Whore! You were peddling your ass all over the West

Side! . . . I was going to marry you! I was going to marry a whore, you know that?"), and finally betraying him to the police. The relationship in *Eroina/Heroin/The Tunnel* (Italy, 1980) between hippie Pina (Corinne Clery) and teacher dropout Marco is similarly fraught. The *Variety* review comments: "Script underlines the degradation of the ceaseless hunt for money to support their habit that doesn't stop at prostitution, stealing from each other, recruiting child addicts." Living in an abandoned bus in a junkyard, the couple are prey to repeated violence such that they "emerge as more pitiable than despicable, victims of a killing habit impossible to break."[25] In *Hard asfalt* streetwalker Ida (Kristin Kajander), devotedly in love with her charming but violent husband Knut and with a baby daughter, has to contend with his alcoholism and its devastating effects as well as her own unshakable heroin addiction.[26] All three films employ a style of near-documentary realism, intensifying the grueling impact of their tales of a heavily addicted young couple clinging to each other in their misery.

All the biographical portrait films trace a relentless downward spiral, as the Junkie's need for drugs increases at the same time as her capacity to earn the money to pay for them lessens. Magdalena in *Liebe kann wie Gift sein*, exhausted by her lifestyle, dies of heart disease. Beatrice in *Wild, Wild Girl*, caught passing a bad check and refused financial help by her father, throws herself in the path of an oncoming train. The ring of drug peddlers and prostitutes Diane belongs to in *Hip, Hot and 21* is smashed in a raging gun battle with police; while Christine in *The Grasshopper*, after getting stoned and enticing a skywriter to write the word "fuck" in the air, is arrested, now at twenty-two having "the haggard, down-and-out appearance of one who has been through it all."[27] In *The Divine Obsession* Julie, whose brothel operation has been destroyed by mobsters and who has joined a singing group, shoots herself in the head on stage.[28]

The protagonists of the love story films survive, but the endings remain resolutely downbeat. Helen in *The Panic in Needle Park*, reduced to a wreck who lies in bed for days on end, finally succumbs to pressure from an undercover cop and turns Bobby in. "Cunt!" he says, as he is arrested, "I was gonna marry you." In the epilogue, having served his time in jail, Bobby ignores the waiting Helen and walks away, but then, relenting, allows her to join him; one is torn between celebrating the reunion and wondering how long it will be before the next betrayal. In *Eroina*, Marco's robbery of a big-time drug dealer goes disastrously wrong and he is forced on the run, with Pina left on her own with no place to turn; while Ida in *Hard asfalt*, having fled from Knut's beatings to her father, gets no help from him or social agencies, loses custody of her child, and returns to Knut and the pavement.

In the inexorability of the slide into ever-greater despair and degradation that these portrait films depict lies much of their meaning. While for a male protagonist in the cinema, drug addiction may be an adventure and a test of character (one thinks, for example, of *The Basketball Diaries*), for the female, tied as it is so closely to sexuality and the sale of her body (*Eroina* even includes a shot of Pina injecting into her genitals), it is much more likely to be portrayed as the confirmation of an inherent depravity.

Cassie was twelve when she began hustling for a pimp named Big Daddy. After four or five months in the life she was gang-raped and then kidnapped by another pimp, Joe, whom she suspects was in league with Big Daddy. They took her to the ghetto, "a really filthy apartment, and they held me down on a bed and they injected heroin into my arm." She was locked in a room, naked, for a week and a half. "It was really weird. They had tricks set up for me, black men and white men, and they kept me on heroin all the time until near the end." There were maybe seven or eight men a day. "I can't really remember exactly because I'd always be so high. . . . They would constantly come in and beat me." Eventually — with the police closing in, she thinks — she was taken off heroin and released.

Cassie's story, recounted in Gitta Sereny's *The Invisible Children: Child Prostitution in America, Germany and Britain*,[29] is a reminder that the often highly melodramatic "pimp-victim" films, as I have termed them, may have, like other Junkie narratives, a basis in fact. But it is their power to mobilize sadistic male fantasies, through the image of the sexual female subjugated by drugs, that is undoubtedly at the root of their appeal, as the low-budget, sexploitation nature of most of the movies tends to confirm.

I have dealt elsewhere with a number of these films. *Thriller* (Sweden, 1974) is discussed in chapter 6, and *Marchands de filles* (France, 1957), *La Prostitution* (France, 1963), *Acosada* (Argentina, 1963), *White Slaves of Chinatown* (USA, 1964), *Olga's Girls* (USA, 1964), *Olga's House of Shame* (USA, 1964), *House of a Thousand Dolls* (Spain/West Germany, 1967), and *The Sinful Dwarf* (Denmark/USA, 1973) are described in chapter 10. The figure of the forcibly drugged prostitute also crops up in films from Asia: *Hentai/Abnormal* (Japan, 1966) features a large narcotics ring whose members "abduct, rape, and torture young women, addict them to heroin, and force them to work as prostitutes,"[30] while in *Diexie jietou / Bullet in the Head* (Hong Kong, 1990), singer Sally Yan explains to the protagonists that she was lured to Saigon, where the nightclub owner "took my passport, hooked me on drugs and made me his whore."

Two films in particular may demonstrate the sleazy appeal of the pimp-victim narrative. *Ginger* (USA, 1971) flaunts abundant nudity in showing off its Junkie characters and exhibits with relish the power that possession of drugs imparts; *Street Girls* (USA, 1974) follows step by step the process by which the female recruit's resistance to turning tricks is overcome.

Ginger depicts the efforts of a female operative to crack a prostitution-drugs-blackmail ring operating on the resort coast of New Jersey. Ginger discovers that the women working for the gang are customarily recruited into prostitution with the use of drugs: thus good-girl Cathy (Linda Susoeff) explains that she dated one of the men ("I wasn't looking for far-out wild excitement"), he pulled out a joint, one thing led to another, and "before I knew it, I was in so deep I couldn't get out." She is now, she says, a "rotten lousy two-bit whore — go down to the Imperial any night and lay down $125, and you can have Cathy Carson's body any way you want it!" Ginger proceeds to seduce her sexually and pump her for information; the next morning she finds Cathy's dead body, naked, on the beach, tied at the wrists and ankles and with a plastic bag over her head.

Another of the women, Allison (Herndon Ely) is from a wealthy background, now hooked on drugs by the syndicate. A black member of the gang, Jimmy, lusts after her "stuck-up white ass" and is given the go-ahead to proceed by the boss. Delivering her heroin, Jimmy tells her, "You'll screw for it, you white bitch!" Desperate for a fix, Allison can do nothing but bow to his demands. She takes her clothes off. "Panties, white girl! Take off those nice white silk panties. . . . On the floor!" Allison complies. "I'm going to be on top of your warm, soft, white body," Jimmy gloats. "Spread your legs — wide!" There is a crotch shot as she does so, and then he mounts. The command-obey patterning of the action in conjunction with the explicitness of the imagery delivers a punchy message of male power over the erotic female, here made piquant by race and class revenge, for any in the audience inclined to receive it.

Street Girls, shot on location in Eugene, Oregon, tells the story of a go-go dancer, Angel (Chris Souder) pressured into prostitution by the bar owner she works for, Irv, and his confederate, Mario, a drug dealer. Irv's initial strong-arm tactics — he tries to persuade her to "party" by pushing her against the wall, shoving his hand up between her legs, and brutally squeezing her breasts — prove unavailing, and he calls on Mario for assistance. The dealer has fortunately has already begun to win Angel away from her lesbian girlfriend Sally. "She needs a lesson," Irv says. "You're gonna build her up to a big habit real quick."

Angel is eager to have "a little taste." Mario shows her how to do it, tying a tourniquet around her thigh. Before long we see her preparing a fix, naked, while Mario watches, fondles her, then knocks her around until she slumps. "Took her clothes away, just like you said," he reports to Irv. "Got her off on the smack, too. She's nice and edgy." When Irv tells Sally — who also works as a dancer at the bar and isn't fussy about taking on paying customers — that Angel's going to turn a trick, she scoffs. "Mario's got her strung out," Irv assures her, "She'll do what she's told."

Mario doesn't think she's ready. "Let me turn her out slowly," he pleads, but Irv is brooking no delay. "Look, she starts paying her way tomorrow, or I'll ship her to a whorehouse in Detroit, where she can turn thirty tricks a day." Mario acquiesces, inducing Angel to service a garage mechanic who, it turns out, has a penchant for golden showers. Angel is disgusted. Her resistance stiffens. Still kept locked up naked in a room by Mario, she is visited by Irv, who beats her up.

The outlook is grim. Meanwhile, however, Angel's father has been searching for her. With a little help from the bartender, he is able to rescue his daughter before she suffers further depredation. Sally is not so fortunate. Angering Irv by defiantly turning tricks on the side, she is throttled, presumably to death.

Irv and Mario are no more likable than Jimmy: *Street Girls* and *Ginger*, like the pimp-victim films generally, permit the guilty pleasures a male spectator may experience in watching the enforced submission of a sexually attractive and promiscuous woman to be disavowed. The pimp, yet again, is the bad guy. But the recurrence of the theme of coerced heroin addiction indicates that it strikes a responsive chord among some, at least, of the movie audience. As for the Junkie, who is stripped, along with her clothes, of personality and individuality, she is less a character than a lump of flesh with veins and orifices.

The teenage Junkies, on the other hand, tend to be strongly developed characters, whose plight is magnified by their youth and vulnerability. Although the subject of drug use among high school students, with a concomitant drift into prostitution, had been broached before, for example, in *The Cocaine Fiends* and *Marihuana*, it was in the TV film *Go Ask Alice* (USA, 1973) that it first received high-profile, mainstream attention. A cluster of films followed, each in its own way addressing questions of the failure of the nuclear family, the drug subculture, and the vicious circle of prostitution and addiction. While seriousness of purpose and a quasi-sociological approach predominate, particularly with the TV movies, there are also wayward streaks of sexploitation and (largely failed) comedy.

Go Ask Alice was based on the allegedly authentic diary of a high school girl who got heavily into drugs at the age of fifteen. Shy and lonely, oversensitive about her weight, and under pressure to conform to the expectations of her high-achieving parents, Alice (Jamie Smith-Jackson) begins experimenting with drugs, popping pills, and dropping LSD. Before long her appearance and attitude have totally changed, her highs alternate with excruciating lows, and she is hooked on heroin. She runs away from home, becomes a vagrant, and turns to prostitution to survive, becoming tangled up in the grim milieu of pushers and pimps. Reworking *Marihuana* in social-realist mode, *Go Ask Alice* was shot on location in Los Angeles with quasi-cinema-vérité camerawork and impressed, despite a moralistic tinge, with its strong performances and psychological plausibility.

Very different in approach is *Die Schulmädchen vom Treffpunkt Zoo/ Confessions of a Campus Virgin* (West Germany, 1979), which incorporates drugs and prostitution as the sordid underbelly of a Berlin high-school coming-of-age comedy featuring a significant amount of nubile nudity. Not surprisingly, inconsistency of tone results. Peepshow dancer/prostitute Doris,[31] a minor character, appears by virtue of her friendship with schoolgirl protagonist Petra and is seen in three scenes with clients. In the first, played for comedy, she rides the man naked, with a bit in his mouth, whipping him and digging in with spurs until he climaxes. She is next encountered gangbanging—at the behest of her pimp, who promises "prima sex"—a squad of football players: the men line up outside a caravan awaiting their turn, some peering in through the window, as inside Doris endures the thrusting of number one, sobbing and staring upward and then closing her eyes. Finally, in a scene shot for its scopophilic potential, Doris is stripped naked by a client in a brothel, who discovers track marks in her arm as he pours champagne over her voluptuous body. Doris clearly figures in the narrative as an image of Petra's potential destiny—we have earlier seen druggies hanging out at the Zoo Station, and one of them keeling over dead in the lavatory—but the contradictory ways in which she is portrayed result in a highly ambiguous response.

There is no such ambiguity in *Christiane F.—Wir Kinder vom Bahnhof Zoo*

(West Germany, 1981), for which *Schulmädchen* may be seen as a sketch. The druggies move to centre stage, and the prostitute takes over as protagonist: there is no comedy, and no eroticism. Based on the sensational published memoirs of a teenage addict, *Christiane F.* is bathed in sepulchral blue and, picturing Berlin as an urban pit of desolation, pins all on the narrative and spectacle of degradation.[32] Thirteen-year-old Christiane (Natja Brunckhorst) makes a swift downward plunge from discontented schoolgirl, fed up with the filth in her bleak apartment building and losing touch with a mother preoccupied with her new lover, to desolate junkie shooting up in the restroom of the Zoo Station. Along the way she hangs out with her mates at a disco that is awash in drugs, snorts and rapidly advances to injecting heroin, goes to live with a boyfriend who feeds his habit by hustling, begins turning tricks and hates it, experiences agony in going cold turkey, immediately goes back on the needle, finds a roommate dead of a hot dose, and has two other friends die. Relief comes only in an epilogue: over a wide shot of a village under snow, Christiane tells us in voice-over: "I survived it. My mother took me to a village near Hamburg, where my aunt and grandma live. I've lived here, and have been clean for one and a half years."

If the drug-taking is shown in excruciating detail (close-ups of needles jabbed in flesh and hypodermics squeezed), the prostitution is by comparison elided (we do see Christiane giving a hand job, face averted, to a man in a car). It is nonetheless a grueling portrait, enhanced by authentic casting (most of the actors are nonprofessionals aged thirteen to fifteen) and semidocumentary filming at the disco, the Zoo Station (where Christiane, face ravaged, blends in seamlessly with the addicts and hustlers who congregate there), and a David Bowie concert. The strength of *Christiane F.* is its unrelenting yet convincing picture of a netherworld that remorselessly swallows up the teenagers who drift into it.

Hanna D.—La ragazza del Vondel Park/À seize ans dans l'enfer d'Amsterdam/Hanna D.—The Girl from Vondel Park (Italy/France, 1984), while clearly indebted to *Christiane F.*, harks back also to the sexploitation imagery of *Die Schulmädchen vom Treffpunkt Zoo*. The film has a teasing opening, with Hanna (Ann-Gisel Glass) appearing as a schoolgirl in a train compartment, giving a man who enters a provocative glance, baring her thigh and breasts, then revealing her panties and stripping them off. It is not until after the image fades out that we discover she is already a prostitute. *Hanna D.* then shifts register to become a subdued drama of life on the margins. Sixteen-year-old Hanna, caught in an intolerable domestic situation—whoring to support a heavy-drinking mother, whose

55. Natja Brunckhorst in *Christiane F.—Wir Kinder vom Bahnhof Zoo*. Stiftung Deutsche Kinemathek—Filmmuseum Berlin.

boyfriend tries to rape her—takes refuge in hard drugs and becomes a pawn fought over by bad-guy pimp Miguel and good-guy lover Axel. Meanwhile, her condition worsens: after some work in porno films, she is jailed, goes cold turkey, and subsequently reaches a low point of degradation under a bridge "up to her eyes in dope and syphilis" and then smashing an apartment up, desperate for a fix. Eventually, however, Axel wins out, assisted by Miguel's suicidal tendencies, and we end on a radiant Hanna—modestly dressed in long skirt, bulky pullover, and scarf—

running across a square in Amsterdam clutching her man. The Junkie's miraculous recovery becomes a token of patriarchy redeemed.

In later films dramatizing the plight of the addicted teenage prostitute the narrative perspective is more dispersed. Thus *Children of the Night* (USA, TV, 1985) has for protagonist a doctoral student who becomes personally involved with the Hollywood street kids she is researching; *Hollywood Vice Squad* (USA, 1986) adopts the point of view of the police and of the midwestern mother who has come to L.A. searching for her runaway girl; and *Daughter of the Streets* (USA, TV, 1990) centers as much on the social activist divorcee who loses touch with her daughter as on the highschool student who slides off the rails into streetwalking and cocaine.

Children of the Night focuses particularly, among the adolescent prostitutes whom Lois Lee shelters at her apartment, on Valerie (Lar Park-Lincoln), a sixteen-year-old victim of sexual abuse by her stepfather. Lois takes her in after she has been slashed in the stomach with a razor, and attempts unsuccessfully to effect a reconciliation between Valerie and her mother. Already drug-dependent, Valerie quickly reverts to the streets and her pimp. Six months later, after her dissertation is finished, Lois remains concerned about Valerie, but the defiant hooker, still on drugs, scorns her overtures. ("You can't scare me back into your place, Lois. . . . Your place is freaking boring!") Later, after searching fruitlessly for Valerie at an urban hell-hole, a derelict building where destitute addicts and street kids hang out, Lois rescues her once more after a violent attack by a client. This time, hugged by a tearful Lois ("I love you, Valerie"), she is prepared to acknowledge the error of her ways. Like Hanna D., Valerie makes an overnight recovery, although here the discourse is lesbian; she is next seen striding down Hollywood Boulevard in jeans and loose sweater, joining Lois in her mission of saving the child prostitutes.

The locale is the same, but *Hollywood Vice Squad* takes a very different approach to its subject. The tale of teenage runaway Lori (Robin Wright), now an addicted hooker at the mercy of her pimps — who dispose of another troublesome young member of their stable by supplying her with uncut heroin — is told in orthodox dramatic fashion. But her storyline is sandwiched in between burlesque chases and brawls as the movie attempts to raise laughs out of the perennial duel between crooks and cops, and also out of the activities of a sadomasochist child pornographer. The mixture of genres fails to ignite, and the film collapses in confusion of purpose.

Daughter of the Streets reverts to the sober social-problem mode of the

TV movie, with a storyline, like that of *Children of the Streets*, based on fact. Charley (Roxana Zal), neglected by her community-organizing mother Peggy and overburdened with the responsibility of caring for her re-tarded young brother, is sucked onto the streets by a "peculiarly wimpy pimp who never resorts to violence with any of his girls, and apparently really does fall in love with Charley."[33] Foiled by the law in her plan to kidnap Charley back, Peggy then attempts to track her down by going public through the media. Eventually the cocaine-addicted teenager, dis-illusioned with her existence, is reunited with her mother. Faulted for failing to breathe life into the well-worn subject matter (the *Hollywood Reporter* criticized its "lack of credible characters and plausible plot"),[34] *Daughter of the Streets* marked an end, for the time being, of fascination with the teenage Junkie.

Fusing the concepts of addiction and prostitution with all their connota-tions, the Junkie becomes a potent symbolic figure at the disposal of film-makers acting as social critics. On the one hand, there are those films that use the addict's remorseless craving for a fix to critique the soullessness of a money-driven economy. On the other, the prostitute's heedless promiscuity becomes representative of a hedonism destructive of human values.

The first tendency is well exemplified by the East German television miniseries *Wolf unter Wölfen* (1965). The "Valuten-Vamp" (Ingeborg Nass), the cocaine-addicted streetwalker frenziedly banging, demanding schnapps, and screaming of "red ants" in her police cell is suggestive of the hyperinflation, economic collapse, and incipient fascism of Germany in the year in which the episode is set, 1923. The point is reinforced by a voice-over narration that refers to Berlin as a "Sodom and Gomorrah" and titles that exclaim "GELD GELD GELD." Signaling a similar preoccu-pation, *Pretty Woman* (USA, 1990) opens with the image of coins being manipulated in the hands of a man doing tricks with them. While the corporate raiders prepare their next takeover bid, Skinny Marie is found dead in a dumpster on Hollywood Boulevard. She would be "out on these streets day in, day out, trading her sorry self for some crack," the in-vestigating cop is told. Fellow hooker Kit (Laura San Giacomo) is dis-missive. "She was a flake, she was a crackhead," she says. "Dominic was trying to straighten her out for months." This is the woman who has just blown the rent money on some "great shit," since she "needed a little pick-me-up." Here the street Junkie, an unlamented corpse or headed in that direction, is the corrective to all the Wall Street wealth and Beverly

Hills glamour that the rest of the film is awash in, a sharp reminder (see chapter 17) of the rottenness in the system.

El patrullero / Highway Patrolman (Mexico/USA, 1992) is the tale of a newly qualified law enforcement officer who soon discovers that whatever his idealistic aspirations, bribery is a fact of life in his line of work. Meanwhile, the hooker Pedro meets at a roadhouse brothel, who is supporting two young children after her husband walked out on her, has become miserably addicted to cocaine. Thanks to Pedro's intervention ("I don't want to find you dead in this shit-hole"), Maribel (Vanessa Buache) is able to go home and recover. Pedro, who has a wife and child himself, learns to his chagrin that his financial contributions — which have come to date from the proceeds of illicit confiscations from drug runners — will have to be ongoing. The addicted prostitute is here symptomatic of the messy morality of an endemically corrupt society, further compromised by an illegal drug traffic servicing the demand from Mexico's northern neighbor.

The destructive impact of monetarist policies on regional communities is the backdrop to the human tragedies of *My Name is Joe* (UK, 1998) and *La Ville est tranquille / The Town is Quiet* (France, 2000), and in each case the Junkie is a key figure. In *My Name is Joe*, set in Glasgow, the life of recovering alcoholic Joe is blighted, like that of many other working-class men and women in the city, by the all-pervading unemployment. Among Joe's friends are a young couple, Liam and Sabine, with a four-year-old child. They are both heroin addicts, but Liam has managed to kick the habit. Sabine (Annemarie Kennedy) hasn't. She is on the game, to Liam's distress ("back in streets getting shagged by fucking perverts"), and has run up a drug bill with the local gang boss that will eventually result in the destruction of her family (with Liam committing suicide) and very nearly the wrecking of Joe's life as well. The wretchedness of the situation is encapsulated in an excruciating scene in which Sabine begs Joe to hold the tourniquet as she injects into her ankle, while her boy — who has already been lost once to welfare authorities — is uncared for out on the landing. In an equally cheerless vision, the Marseilles of *La Ville est tranquille* is a city decomposing under the impact of globalization, with the National Front on the rise, the docks closing, and a proud tradition of working-class solidarity receding into distant memory. Fish-packer Michèle (Ariane Ascaride) comes home to her bleak apartment building to find her daughter Fiona (Julie-Marie Parmentier) giving a blow job to a client in the lounge. Michèle angrily breaks it up, but from now on it is up to her to find the wherewithal to feed Fiona's heroin habit, which

56. Michèle (Ariane Ascaride) in *La Ville est tranquille*. bfi Collections.

means turning to prostitution — unwillingly and not very successfully — herself. Fiona has a baby, which is being neglected. As things wear on, unbearably, it gets to the point where the daily dose isn't enough, but for Michèle it is the utmost she can manage. Fiona screaming, the baby screaming, Michèle can take no more. She deliberately administers to her daughter a fatal overdose. In both films the human degradation resulting from economic policies driven from elsewhere is graphically symbolized by the figure of an addicted prostitute less concerned with her own child than with her next fix.

The second tendency, to do with the loosening of constraints in the "permissive society" and the implications of ungoverned pleasure-seeking, emerges for example in *Klute* (USA, 1971). The strung-out hooker Arlyn Page (Dorothy Triton), panicked by the arrival of Bree and Klute at her door since she is about to make a connection, is symptomatic of New York's urban decadence in an era that has embraced the tenet of "let it all hang out"—as Bree urges the psychopathic businessman who will become Arlyn's killer. *Hardcore* (USA, 1979) is another reflection on the theme. Here Niki (Season Hubley) is off the hard stuff, though perhaps not for long: her pimp is looking for her and as she is reminded, "He can make life real tough on a working girl—he can get you strung out again . . . sniffin' and snortin' and shootin'. . . ." Her symbolic role in this story of a midwestern businessman come to track down his teenage daughter in the sleazy dives of the Los Angeles sex industry is deceptive. Initially the free-spirited Niki, who claims to be a member of "the Venusian Church — you know, Venus, goddess of love," appears to be much more together than the adherent of the puritan Dutch Reformed Church whom she is assisting in his search. Jake is uptight and violent, and has lost his wife and daughter through not being able to communicate his love for them. On closer inspection, however, Niki's togetherness is just a façade: she is in thrall to her pimp who takes all her money, she has no personal love life, and she is in danger of reverting to drugs ("I guess we're both fucked, hunh?" she says. "At least you get to go to heaven. I don't get shit."). It is Jake's perspective ("It's this culture! It's based on sex, sold on sex") that finally prevails and the upright integrity of Grand Rapids, Michigan (at the beginning we see a montage of churches and children tobogganing in the snow) upheld over the sexual degeneracy of California, of which Niki is ineluctably a part.[35]

Like Skinny Marie in *Pretty Woman,* Anita's mother in *Guncrazy* (USA, 1992) is never seen, a signifying absence. Away in Fresno "out peddling her ass for some shit-skinned pimp so she can earn enough money to shoot heroin in her arm," she has left her sixteen-year-old daughter to fend for herself, living in a trailer in Nevada with the mother's lowlife boyfriend, Rooney. When Rooney rapes her, Anita shoots him and then goes on a killing rampage with a convict on parole. It is evident that the mother, through abandonment of her child, triggers off the relentless chain of violence, but the originating cause can be traced back to the male: to her vicious pimp Soda Pop, whom we encounter; by implication to all the pimps in her past; to Rooney and the men who have sexually abused Anita from the age of nine; and to the totally absent father, never referred to and perhaps not even known. In the larger picture, the Junkie here is less cause of aberrant crime than symptom of a sexist society in which, as traditional family structures break down, men reduce women and girls to instruments of their pleasure.

The Basketball Diaries (USA, 1995) and *Requiem for a Dream* (USA, 2000), both set in New York, offer narratives of descent into the hell of drug addiction. In each case, though she is a subordinate character, the Junkie is crucial to the symbolic patterning. In *The Basketball Diaries,* Diane (Juliette Lewis) is introduced as a young dopehead, desperate for cash and offering head for fifteen dollars. She is strung along by protagonist Jim and his teenage gang of buddies ("What do you say guys? You want to do it, all four of us?") and then rejected, despised. Later, she is seen shambling through a dismal underground addict hangout in forlorn quest of a fix. Marianne (Jennifer Connelly) in *Requiem for a Dream* takes the characterization farther. At the breaking point when her boyfriend fails to score the heroin she is hanging out for — and the money for which she has acquired by sleeping with her therapist ("I fucked that sleazebag for you!")—Marianne in great distaste has oral sex with a pusher/pimp "who likes broads." Several days later she goes back to the man's apartment and performs naked with another woman in a hellish sex-show orgy in front of leering and chanting men tossing dollar bills. The horror is amplified by the montage technique, which intercuts at a frenzied pace her anal intercourse with the treatment of her boyfriend's infected and gangrenous arm (climaxed in the buzz of the electric saw slicing into flesh and bone) and his mother's electro-convulsive shock treatment for diet-pill addiction. Marianne is last seen curling up in temporary peace on her sofa, clutching her precious stash to her breast. In these two films the strung-out young Junkie, in prostituting her body in demeaning situations, offers up an image of the ultimate debasement that lies at the heart of an empty hedonism.

It remains to consider Stanley Kubrick's *Eyes Wide Shut* (UK/USA, 1999). The setting, again, is New York, but the pleasure-seeking here has a new dimension — the riches that multiply its possibilities for the city's elite. "The real pornography in this film is in its lingering, overlit depiction of the shameless, naked wealth of end-of-the-millennium Manhattan," writes Tim Kreider, "and of the obscene effect of that wealth on the human soul, and on society."[36] Haunting the tale is the figure of a prostitute, Mandy (Julienne Davis). At an opulent party, she is a sprawling naked body in the host's bedroom, requiring resuscitation after an adverse reaction to a mix of heroin and cocaine. At a ritualistic masked orgy she is the woman (as we discover later) who offers to redeem the interloper with her life. At the morgue, she is a corpse, officially the victim of an overdose. Perhaps she was killed; perhaps she just "got her brains fucked out." The Junkie is dead, but, as with all the rest, she has served her purpose.

15

Baby Doll

This then was the monster to which my conscientious benefactress, who had long been his purveyor in this way, had doom'd me, and sent for me down purposely for his examination. Accordingly she made me stand up before him, turn'd me round, unpinn'd my handkerchief, remark'd to him the rise and fall, the turn and whiteness of a bosom just beginning to fill; then made me walk, and took even a handle from the rusticity of my gait, to inflame the inventory of my charms: in short, she omitted no point of jockeyship; to which he only answer'd by gracious nods of approbation, whilst he look'd goats and monkies at me: for I sometimes stole a corner glance at him, and encountering his fiery, eager stare, looked another way from pure horror and affright, which he, doubtless in character, attributed to nothing more than maiden modesty, or at least the affectation of it.

—JOHN CLELAND, *Fanny Hill: Memoirs of a Woman of Pleasure* (1749)[1]

Just look at Emma, propped up on the pavement with her mother in the shadows. She stands there for hours, absolutely quiet and still, waiting for her next event. There is something almost serene about the way she stands there. She is a frail creature, small and thin, with a sickly air, the kind of child that would be no good at games. She is not pretty either. She has no figure to speak of, and although her face must once have been pleasant enough in a pale kind of way, it is now hacked up with spots and sores. She is in the wrong place, doing the wrong thing, yet she stands there at the end of Gedling Grove like a rock in a storm, absolutely determined to carry on. Ordinary life sweeps past her—not just the cars on the road and the people on the pavement, but all the everyday feelings of ordinary people. In her position, they might feel pain or shame or loneliness or distress, they might run away in fear or scream in rage or simply go mad from the pain of it all. But not Emma. She is homeless, she is a crack addict, she is a child prostitute, she has been raped, robbed, strangled and whipped, and yet she makes no protest. Something inside her is different.

—NICK DAVIES, *Dark Heart: The Shocking Truth About Hidden Britain* (1997)[2]

There she is, auburn curls cascading down from beneath the wide white brim of her hat, the twelve-year-old in skimpy halter top and red hot pants, long skinny legs raised on platform heels, clutching her sunglasses, cloth bag with tassels slung over her shoulder. Nonchalant, as in the movie. It is Jodie Foster as Iris the child prostitute, one of the iconic images of twentieth-century Hollywood, on the cover of the Collector's Edition DVD of *Taxi Driver* (USA, 1976).[3]

Despite the heavy makeup, there is no mistaking her age. Or her profession. She is a child, available for sex. In the film Sport, her pimp, spells it out. "Fifteen dollars fifteen minutes, twenty-five dollars half an hour. . . . You ain't never had no pussy like that. You can do anything you want with her. You can come on her, fuck her in the mouth, fuck her in the ass, come on her face, man, she'll get your cock so hard she'll make it explode. But no rough stuff."

For Travis Bickle (Robert De Niro), who has it in mind to rescue her, it is inconceivable that Iris should be on the street of her own free will. But she upsets his expectations. When he goes up to her room, she is only too eager to loosen his trousers and get to work; there's astonishment and a hint of disappointment, too, when he repeatedly pushes her off. "Goddammit!" he exclaims. "Don't you want to get out of here?" "I can leave any time I want to," she insists. The next afternoon they talk in a diner. "Why do you want me to go back to my parents?" Iris asks. "I mean they hate me. Why do you think I split in the first place? There ain't nothin' there." Travis presses his case: "Yeah, but you can't live like this. It's a hell. A girl should live at home." Iris is not convinced: "Didn't you ever hear of women's lib?" A few moments later she is giggling like a schoolgirl at Travis's playful assertion that he is a narc: "God, I don't know who's weirder, you or me!"

For Travis, Sport is the typical pimp, "the lowest kind of person in the world . . . the scum of the earth." Iris doesn't see it like that. "Sport never treated me bad," she argues. "I mean he didn't beat me up or anything like that once." The diner scene is followed by one in which Sport gently assures Iris of how much she means to him: he takes her in his arms, caressingly, for a slow dance, and Iris relaxes in his embrace, eyes closed, expression dreamy. The scene was an addition to the script, improvised by the actors. "I thought it was a really important thing in terms of the relationship between her and Sport," director Martin Scorsese explains, "to show that she's not being held there against her will, and to show that this is her family at this point. . . . And to show that he doesn't beat her, he doesn't drug her."[4]

Perhaps Travis's words have had some effect. Iris tells Sport, "I don't like what I'm doing." She has mentioned to Travis that she might head off to a commune in Vermont. Before she has a chance to do so, Travis slaughters Sport and all the other men around her in a ferocious blood-bath, and Iris finds herself back at home in Pittsburgh. "She's back in school and working hard," her father writes to Travis, hailed as a hero, "but the transition has been very hard for her, as you can well imagine."

Taxi Driver powerfully illustrates the transgressive nature of the "Baby Doll" character type — the adolescent prostitute — and its contradictory appeals. As an erotic object the Baby Doll is a beguiling blend of inno-cence and corruption: "It's the shock of the disjunction — a child, sexu-alized, in an adults' world," as B. Ruby Rich writes of Jodie Foster's Iris, "that provides the tone of perversity."[5] Idealized, she is a picture of bud-ding youth, with its freshness and beauty, yet with a carnal undertow. The Baby Doll offers an image of female sexuality stripped of its fright-ening connotations: she is the prostitute who — at least on the surface — proffers no challenge, no threat ("You can do anything you want with her"), and hence there is an association of eroticism with power. The dis-parity between her sexual and physical or emotional maturity is often at the root of her fascination. But the Baby Doll, too, is very often a figure of pathos, a character who evokes a strong sympathy because she is a young person victimized by forces beyond her control.

In the stories that are told about her, the Baby Doll, like the Junkie, is typically from a family background whose deficiencies account for her deviant behavior. She is frequently on a quest for love resulting in at-tachment to a much older man; while her emotional problems, no more than subtextual in *Taxi Driver*, may escalate into obsession and violence.

Films, like *Taxi Driver*, that downplay the Baby Doll's victimhood, sug-gesting that she took up prostitution voluntarily and is suffering no ill consequences from it, make it easier for the male audience to indulge fantasies of sex with a young girl. Guilt is assuaged. This is the dominant tendency in one strand of Baby Doll movies, in which she is first and fore-most an erotic object; the approach shades off into the pornographic, although an exploitative scenario may be given a veneer of legitimacy by a genuflection toward social comment. In the second main strand, in contrast, adolescent prostitution is assumed to be damaging and wrong, the commonly held belief which *Taxi Driver* also plays upon. These are typically social-realist dramas, with a focus on an analysis of the girl's plight, and sometimes the dynamic of a rescue narrative. Eroticism, in keeping with the seriousness of intent, is generally subdued, but on occasion — as with the Captive movies — the social treatise may be spiced up with nudity or sex. A subgroup of this social-realist class is an American cycle of movies about runaway teenagers, which partially overlaps the cluster of teenage Junkie films previously discussed. In this chapter I examine each of these strands and conclude with a look at two films from the 1990s, both within the social-realist tradition, which embody starkly contrasting ideological positions.

> High school honey goes hard-core for the usual results.
> — *Variety* on *Harlot* (USA, 1971)[6]

At her simplest, the Baby Doll is a pure signifier of adolescent promiscuity, her profession heightening the excitement for a heterosexual male audience by signaling her availability. The appeal is encapsulated in the very title of a film such as *Sex und noch nicht sechzehn/Sex and Not Yet Sixteen* (West Germany, 1968), about a girl who runs away from home and starts playing sexual games as an underage prostitute.[7]

The "erotic object" strand of Baby Doll movies use a variety of devices to intensify the aphrodisiac effect. One of these — employed when censorship permits — is to set some of the action in a bordello, with its multiplicity of delights on display and its ambiance dedicated to sensual pleasure. This is a ploy used, for example, in *Moral und Sinnlichkeit* (Germany, 1919), one of the so-called *Aufklärungsfilme* (sex education films) produced in the hiatus between the abolition of censorship after the war and its restoration in 1920. The male protagonist and the teenage girl whom he has deflowered and initiated into sexual game-playing visit a secret brothel with underage girls for "an amusing afternoon together." (The young women playing the prostitutes, clad in sexy underwear — lacy silk vests and stockings — were not in fact underage, we are informed.)[8] Picking up the motif, *Pretty Baby* (USA, 1978), set in 1917, dramatizes the early adolescence of a girl inmate of a brothel in the Storyville quarter of New Orleans, while *Petites filles au bordel* (France, 1980) shows young prostitutes in a Parisian *maison close* of the 1930s.

In Pasolini's controversial *Salò o Le 120 giornate di Sodoma/Salò or The 120 Days of Sodom* (Italy/France, 1975), incidents in a brothel are narrated and reenacted rather than being straightforwardly depicted. Based on the writing of the Marquis de Sade (like *Petites filles au bordel*, which is inspired by *La Philosophie dans le boudoir*), *Salò* is set in 1944 in Northern Italy. Young peasants are rounded up by Republic of Salò soldiers, held prisoner in a villa, and required to act out sexual tales told by female storytellers for the delectation of their Fascist masters. One of the women, Signora Castelli (Caterina Boratto) relates with apparent relish several incidents that occurred after she entered a brothel at the age of nine, involving sodomy and masturbation of the client; straightforward heterosexual intercourse is outlawed under the libertines' regime. Here, though the film is operating as a critique and exposé of the fascist tendencies of the bourgeoisie (reaching a climax, later, with torture and murder), the device of the female autobiographical storyteller gives credence to the notion of the willing participation of the young prostitutes in the sexual acts described — nine-year-old Happy Hookers, as it were.

The adolescent girl's loss of virginity and initiation into the delicate nuances of sexual practice is a characteristic preoccupation of the "erotic object" Baby Doll movie. *The Yellow Teddybears* (UK, 1963), in fact, is named after the teddybear pins that girls at a boarding school proudly wear to indicate that they have "done it." After subtly suggesting that the twelve-year-old protagonist of *Pretty Baby*, Violet (Brooke Shields), has begun turning tricks doing "French," the film reaches a climax with the auctioning off of her maidenhead. "The finest delicacy New Orleans has to offer," she is paraded naked under a filmy gauze wrap before the assembled clientele, and sold, "as fresh as a baby's lips," to the highest bidder. "For her it was like First Communion, the moment when she would enter life," argues the director, Louis Malle.[9] In the hard-core *Petites filles au bordel*, the sexual education of sixteen-year-old Julie,[10] who has previously been kept at arm's length from urban vices, is taken in hand by her mother, a star attraction at the Chat Rose brothel, together with the manager of the establishment and the maid. Finally, when she has become an expert libertine though still a virgin, she is sold at auction, like Violet, to the clientele.

The matter-of-fact way in which the Baby Doll is represented as taking up prostitution, often at a very young age, is a feature of this class of film, again serving to discount any reservations the audience may have about the practice. There is Iris, twelve, of *Taxi Driver*, for whom hustling is an expression of women's lib; Violet, twelve, of *Pretty Baby*, for whom entering the profession means the long-anticipated acquisition of full status at the brothel where she's lived all her life; Molly of *Angel* (USA, 1984), who has been working Hollywood Boulevard since the age of twelve — "It was easy, I just put on some sexy clothes and high heels and went out and made a living"; Mathilde of *Noce blanche / White Wedding* (France, 1989), who began at eleven — "It wasn't

57. Violet (Brooke Shields) in *Pretty Baby.*

rough, or traumatic — we just did it, like that." A similar nonchalance marks the attitude, also, of those who start later, like fifteen-year-old Sofi (Lena Löfström) of *Lämna mej inte ensam / Leave Me Not Alone* (Sweden, 1980) who "starts turning tricks to get quick money for an Ibiza holiday with her amateur boxer boyfriend."[11]

For these precocious, vivacious girls, prostitution significantly appears to have negligible psychological impact; in the case of the emotionally troubled Mathilde of *Noce blanche*, prostitution features more as a symptom than a cause of her problems. Molly (Donna Wilkes) of *Angel*, fifteen at the time of the action of the film, is a particularly noteworthy exemplar of this phenomenon: totally unaffected by having had to work the streets to support herself for the past three years after having been abandoned by her mother, she doesn't drink, doesn't take drugs, continues to be a straight-A honors student, is exceptionally enterprising and brave (she becomes a vigilante hunting down a serial killer), and goes on, in the sequels *Avenging Angel* (USA, 1985) and *Angel III: The Final Chapter* (USA, 1988), to get a law degree and become a professional photographer.

The idea of the schoolgirl prostitute, the stuff of many an erotic fantasy, is frequently stressed. *The Yellow Teddybears* and *Die Schulmädchen vom Treffpunkt Zoo* (West Germany, 1979) flirt with the notion, with the schoolgirl protagonists having close contact with prostitute characters but not actually crossing the line themselves. In other films there is no such reticence. In *The Wild Scene* (USA, 1970), "a doctor and father of a high-

58. Molly (Donna Wilkes) in *Angel*.

school student gives his daughter and her friends birth control pills, essential to their jobs as afternoon prostitutes,"[12] while *Harlot* "tells the sad
tale of Mary (Fran Spector), an eager nymph working her way through
Hollywood High by really putting on a show."[13] *Angel* opens with Molly
tripping off to school with pigtails tied up in white bows; then she's ap-
plying mascara, lipstick, and blusher, and heading down to the strip, hair
down, in spike heels and tight miniskirt, the camera tilting up her petite
adolescent figure as she bends over to speak to a prospective client in a
car. *Noce blanche* has frequent classroom scenes, since the male protagonist, François, gets to know Mathilde in his capacity as teacher.[14] In the
TV real-life drama *Amy Fisher: My Story/Lethal Lolita* (USA, 1992), Amy
(Noëlle Parker) is a high-school senior, and the film includes scenes at
school, such as her boasting to classmates of the hundred dollars an hour
she makes as an "escort."

   The films that depict the Baby Doll principally as an erotic object
may enhance their appeal by having her become romantically involved
with a male character who can serve as a vehicle for spectator identification. In the typical pattern, the girl has been deprived of love as the result of a deficient upbringing and seeks it out in the person of a man

much older than herself whom she seduces and becomes strongly attached to. Scandalously transgressive in nature, the affair cannot last, and may have catastrophic consequences.

Violet in *Pretty Baby* has never known a father and is left behind at the brothel when her mother marries and leaves New Orleans. Angered at being whipped for attempting to seduce a black youngster, she seeks out photographer E. J. Bellocq (who has spent a lot of time photographing the prostitutes without availing himself of their sexual services). Pulling him down on his bed, she asks if she can stay: "Will you sleep with me, and take care of me? . . . I want you to be my lover, and buy me stockings and clothes — I won't even charge you anything at all." (In *Erotic Innocence*, James R. Kincaid observes that in launching herself at Bellocq as audience surrogate figure, the bewitching child is "fulfilling our culture's central pedophile fantasy.")[15] After initial reluctance, Bellocq succumbs, acknowledging, "Some men are different, I'm different." The sex, of course, is elided, but there is considerable footage of Brooke Shields's naked body, particularly that licensed by the convention of the artistic nude when Violet poses for Bellocq's camera.[16] Following predictable vicissitudes in the relationship, the couple are eventually married, but Violet's mother procures an annulment and carries her daughter off to lead a respectable life in St. Louis, Missouri.

St.-Étienne high-school student Mathilde in *Noce blanche*, now seventeen, has apparently left her drug addiction and prostitution in the past, though her frequent absenteeism and other aspects of her behavior leave considerable room for doubt. Feeling neglected by her preoccupied father and emotionally unstable mother, who live in Paris, the highly intelligent but wayward Mathilde is on her own. Concerned about her, middle-aged philosophy teacher François becomes her after-hours mathematics tutor and soon, excited by glimpses of her lissom nudity, her deeply enamored lover. The flowering of the relationship is given a lyrical gloss with sensuous imagery, romantic music, and a glowing performance from Vanessa Paradis as the beautiful, enraptured teenager: "I haven't felt like this since I was a kid," she exults, stripping off her dress on a rustic riverbank and drawing François down to her. Later she declares her unconditional love ("Old, fat, thin, sick, aging, I don't care. . . . You made a woman of me"), but François is reluctant to leave his wife, Catherine, and foresees practical difficulties if they were to live together, since she is still a minor. The relationship breaks up, whereupon Mathilde begins to make vitriolic and violent attacks on Catherine. Still, François cannot resist the girl's pull. When the scandal breaks, he is hastily transferred to Dunkirk, his marriage wrecked. He hears no more from Mathilde. A year later her body is found: she has committed suicide, after having obsessively watched over François's classroom for months.

Having been sexually abused by her father, the Long Island school-girl protagonist of *Amy Fisher* defies her parents by becoming deeply involved with a body-shop mechanic, Joey Buttafuoco, who is twenty years older. It all begins with a flirtatious exchange when the buxom sixteen-year-old asks him to paint "Aimee" on her car in pink. "Hot pink?" he asks. "How hot do you want it?" "As hot as you've got," Amy replies, seductively running her tongue over her lip. They are soon having sex,[17] and Joey treats her to cruises in his power boat and meals at elegant restaurants. (He is certainly living high off the hog for a mechanic; Mafia connections are hinted at.) At Joey's instigation, Amy takes up work for an escort agency. She enjoys the money but has misgivings about being a prostitute. "I thought a shower would just wash it all away," she tells us in voice-over. "I mean what was the big deal? Joey didn't care." But the relationship with Joey founders over his refusal to contemplate divorce from his wife, Mary Jo. Angered, Amy procures a gun and shoots her rival, resulting in Mary Jo's permanent disability. Amy is convicted and sentenced to five to fifteen years.[18]

The movies of the "erotic object" strand thus paint a picture of the Baby Doll as an attractive, seductive adolescent who engages in prostitution voluntarily and on whom it has no identifiable ill effect. She is the cinema's ultimate nymphet, since she is available to any man who pays her price; yet should you become emotionally involved with her, age is no barrier, and she will offer you total devotion spiced with danger. If the Baby Doll love story ends up in a punitive purgatory, as ideologically it must, it will afford for the man of youth-oriented sexual inclination many a glimpse of heaven along the way.

The social-realist Baby Doll movie is very different in approach. It operates on the assumption that prostitution is not something that adolescent girls should have to engage in, and that there is something seriously amiss with a society in which this occurs. The Baby Doll becomes a symptom of social dislocation and malaise: of an ethnic minority community afflicted by poverty and racism, for example, in *The Young Savages* (USA, 1961) and *The Cool World* (USA, 1963); of disenfranchised and alienated youth, in *491* (Sweden, 1964) and *Mouth to Mouth* (Australia, 1978); of rural displacement and urban agglomeration, in *Iracema* (Brazil/France/West Germany, 1975) and *Salaam Bombay!* (India/France, 1988).

This representative group of films — together with others such as *Christiane F.* (West Germany, 1981), discussed in chapter 14 — have much in common stylistically. They have documentary qualities, and several — *The Cool World, Iracema, Salaam Bombay!* — inherit, like *Christiane F.*, the Italian neorealist practice of using nonprofessional actors. There is a tendency for the texture to be deliberately rough, in accord with the subject matter: thus a critic writes of *Iracema* that "the style of the film is gritty,"[19] and *Mouth to Mouth* is said to have a "gritty surface."[20]

For New York Puerto Rican teenager Louisa Escalante (Pilar Seurat) in *The Young Savages*, it is the combination of poverty and family duty that is the determining factor in her being on the streets. A star witness in the trial of three Italian gang members for the murder of her brother, she testifies that she has been a prostitute since the age of fourteen. She was not coerced into it: "I thought of it myself." Asked by the prosecutor why she did it, she explains simply: "We had no money, and my mother was sick. . . . I tried to get a job. They do not give me a working permit." The attorney is anxious to know what her mother thought of her being a prostitute. "She said, why didn't we let her die," the tearful Louisa replies.

If fourteen-year-old Luanne (Yolanda Rodriguez) in *The Cool World* has a family, it is never mentioned. The film, set in the African-American community of Harlem, depicts prostitution as one strand in the nexus of poverty, unemployment, racist oppression, drug addiction, and crime. The resident whore of the Royal Pythons ("she's our property exclusive"), Luanne becomes the lover of "Duke" Custis, who takes over the gang. Under the guiding hand of a female director (Shirley Clarke), Luanne is portrayed without eroticization (compare, for example, *Pretty Baby*), without heroics (*Angel*), and without pathos (*Taxi Driver*). With her warmth toward Duke and her touching naïveté (she dreams of going to San Francisco to see the ocean, unaware that there is ocean at the end of a New York subway ride), Luanne is one of the few bright spots in this dark world of underprivilege and violence. Her disappearance after a happy day at Coney Island plunges Duke into a depressive state of mind from which he will not emerge, turning him from small-time marijuana dealer into killer.

Steva (Lena Nyman) in the much-censored *491* also becomes attached to a male gang, in this case a band of teenage delinquents who are running amok in the context of a misguidedly liberal experiment in rehabilitation, here severely compromised in that the elderly welfare inspector overseeing the project sexually abuses two of his charges.[21] Picked up from a ship where she is raped by one of the sailors, the teenage girl goes to live with the youths, who use her as a prostitute when they need money. Steva's ultimate degradation comes when she is forced perform, in front of the group, a sexual act with a German shepherd ("mercifully off-screen!" comments the British censor).[22] Following this, one of the boys commits suicide. Here the adolescent prostitute is a signifier of the alienation of youth within a society—in contrast to that depicted in *The Young Savages* and *The Cool World*—that is relatively affluent, egalitarian, and ethnically homogeneous but nevertheless deeply sexist and corrupt.

Mouth to Mouth also deals with youth on the margins of an otherwise prosperous society. Set in Melbourne, it follows two teenage girls on the run from a reformatory who set up home in a derelict power station with two country boys who are drifting around unemployed. As relationships develop, the characters receive from one another some fragile emotional solace despite the remorseless pressures of their situation, but one of the girls is recaptured, and the other, Carrie (Kim Kreus) finds herself gravitating into prostitution. As in *491*, the Baby Doll in *Mouth to Mouth* registers the failures of a materialistic system to offer its young people the nourishment they crave, but the tone is not as cynical and the ending not so bleak: "One is left with the impression," as one critic writes, "that, like resilient weeds, the four will survive, perhaps even thrive."[23]

The Third World setting of *Iracema* and *Salaam Bombay!* again shifts the connotative functioning of the Baby Doll characterization. In the former, the teenage Iracema (Edna De Cassia) is a member of a family of exploited fruit-pickers in the Amazonian forest. Patterns of life in the region are being overturned by the construction of the Trans-Amazonic highway and the accompanying deforestation, and Iracema (whose name is an anagram of "America" and who is representative of the indigenous peoples of Brazil) escapes what Patricia Aufderheide terms her "nineteenth-century-style subjection" to become a prostitute in the dives of the port city of Belem. Subsequently, "learning the language of rootless discontent quickly," she hitches a ride with a trucker and becomes an itinerant, blundering from one roadside settlement to the next, until finally, "drunk, despairing, missing a tooth, she's at the end of her road at sixteen."[24] Iracema is a vivid incarnation of the impact on indigenous communities of untrammeled capitalist development.

The protagonist of Mira Nair's *Salaam Bombay!* is a boy from the countryside who winds up, like thousands of others, a homeless street kid in Bombay, and it is his fate that is the principal subject matter of the film. However, prostitution—like drug addiction—is a significant subtheme.

59. Solasaal (Chanda Sharma) in *Salaam Bombay!* Stills Collection, New Zealand Film Archive.

Working as a teaboy, Krishna comes in contact with a prostitute, Rekha (Aneeta Kanwar), along with her charming little daughter, and with a Nepali girl, Solasaal ("Sweet Sixteen"), who is purchased from a trafficker by a malignant madam and prepared for the sale of her virginity and entry to the profession. The powerlessness and vulnerability of Solasaal (Chanda Sharma) parallels that of Krishna: just as the boy is exploited by his employer and ripped off by the hashish addict who befriends him, so the girl (unable to speak a word of Hindi) is helpless to prevent the use of her body for prostitution. The youngsters team up in one gesture of defiance, when Krishna sets fire to Solasaal's bed and the pair run away, but they are quickly recaptured and the act of rebellion snuffed out. Thereafter Solasaal is "tamed" in classic fashion by Rekha's smooth pimp, Baba, who (for a handsome fee from the madam) reconciles Solasaal to her fate by playing the romantic admirer who will rescue her as soon as he gets a chance. Solasaal is last seen, docile, bedecked in finery ("Isn't she a pure bud?"), being driven away by her first client; soon after, Krishna stabs Baba — who is trying to prevent a disillusioned Rekha from leaving him — to death. Resonant with echoes of all the Baby Doll movies that preceded it, *Salaam Bombay!* registers the human impact of social and geographical dislocation in the sorrowful face of a sixteen-year-old girl being taken away by a stranger to be sexually violated for money.

In the cycle of American teenage runaway movies initiated by *Go Ask Alice* (1973), the Baby Doll figures first and foremost as a victim — of parental neglect or abuse, of exploitation by predatory pimps, of drug addiction, of laws that prevent her working underage, of violence, occasionally of corruption within the juvenile penal system. This is particularly so of the TV movies — films such as *Go Ask Alice* itself, *Dawn: Portrait of a Teenage Runaway* (1976), *Alexander: The Other Side of Dawn* (1977), *Little Ladies of the Night* (1977), *Off the Minnesota Strip* (1980), *Children of the Night* (1985), and *Daughter of the Streets* (1990) — which characterize adolescent prostitution as a serious social problem with readily identifiable causes but no easy remedy. The films aimed at cinema release, like *Trackdown* (1976) and *Hollywood Vice Squad* (1986), are less likely to treat the teenage prostitute as pure victim and are more inclined to bring home to her some moral culpability for her plight.

Parents, like those in *Go Ask Alice*, who are loving but just out of touch with their daughter because of the hippie-era generation gap, are the exception. The father is characteristically absent, as in *Dawn* (and its companion piece, *Alexander*), *Children of the Night*, and *Daughter of the Streets;* otherwise, he may be a weakling, like the drunkard in *Off the Minnesota Strip*. The mother is typically forced to shoulder much of the blame for her daughter's waywardness, pictured as being alcoholic, in *Dawn;* insensitive, in *Off the Minnesota Strip;* uncaring, in *Children of the Night;* neglectful, in *Daughter of the Streets*.

The part played by sexual abuse in predisposing a teenager toward prostitution is acknowledged, as we have seen, in *Amy Fisher*. In *Avenging Angel*, Molly asks a young streetwalker if she has ever thought about going home. "Yeah, my father would really love that," the girl retorts, "At least on the streets I get paid for it." In the films of the runaway cycle, perhaps surprisingly, sexual abuse features only infrequently, as in the instance of Valerie and her stepfather in *Children of the Night:* "I learnt to be a prostitute," she explains, "from my mother's boyfriend."

"You know why kids run away in the first place?" social worker Lynn in *Trackdown* asks. "Because their parents are such idiots that it drives them around the bend." But *Trackdown* and *Hollywood Vice Squad* are not willing to lay all the burden of guilt on parental figures. Betsy in *Trackdown* hankers after money and luxury, and tells the prostitute who mentors her, "What the heck do you think I ran away for? I made up my mind a long time ago I wasn't going to end up like my mom." And in *Hollywood Vice Squad,* Lori's mother is portrayed as naive but earnest, loving and plucky, undercutting her daughter's claim that "she didn't care about me—all she thinks about is what other people say."

The pimp is a key figure in nearly all the teenage runaway narratives, easing the girl into prostitution and keeping her there once she has started. "I don't turn anybody into hookers," Valerie's pimp, Roy Spanish, claims in *Children of the Night.* "Their parents do that. By the time I get 'em, they already know the game—I just teach 'em the fine points. And I give 'em loving—their parents never did that." The pimp's archetypal alternation of brutality and tenderness is depicted as being particularly effective with adolescent girls cut off from their families and with no other support mechanisms. Swan in *Dawn* is "as violent as he is winning";[25] in *Off the Minnesota Strip,* Michele is "brutalized by the one person . . . whom she thought she could trust."[26] The pimps in *Trackdown* and *Hollywood Vice Squad* are particularly heavy, adding the manipulation of drugs to their arsenal of control measures. Only rarely, as in *Daughter of the Streets,* is the pimp depicted as getting his way by nonviolent means alone.

Victimized by a parasitical pimp, often trapped as well by a drug habit and the impossibility of making a living any other way, the runaway Baby Doll is unlikely to be able to make a break from prostitution without outside intervention. Several films of the cycle activate a rescue narrative that is reminiscent of the white slave films of the silent era. Thus in *Trackdown,* Betsy's brother Jim arrives in Los Angeles from the family's Montana ranch to try and locate her, gets no help from the police (who claim they have their hands tied),[27] and ends up battling the pimps himself—though he doesn't get to Betsy before she's dead at the hands of a customer. In both *Hollywood Vice Squad* and *Daughter of the Streets* the mother herself ventures into the urban jungle hoping to retrieve her daughter, while in *Children of the Night,* as we saw in chapter 14, the researcher turns social worker and becomes savior. But even if the girl does return home, it is no guarantee that she will leave the life behind her. In fact Dawn in *Alexander* and Michele in *Off the Minnesota Strip* go back on the streets after receiving scant parental sympathy and being taunted by their schoolmates.

Perhaps to engender a sense of crisis, the films tend to emphasize both the intractability and the sheer scale of the problem ("fifty thousand runaways, fifteen police jurisdictions"—*Trackdown;* "The number of teenage kids who run away from home in this country each year numbers close to one million"—*Little Ladies of the Night*), while lauding those who battle against the odds, like Lois of *Children of the Night*. "After taking over 250 children into her own home," the end title of that film informs us, "Dr Lois Lee founded CHILDREN OF THE NIGHT, a non-profit organization that continues to help teenage prostitutes. It operates a hotline, a street outreach program and a walk-in crisis center in the heart of Hollywood."

With its feisty female protagonist, and its rare willingness to point the finger at the clientele ("These streets are a supermarket of sex — I mean every morning around 6 AM the teachers, the lawyers, the judges, the laborers on their way to work, the thing that they're most interested in buying are the kids"), *Children of the Night* embodies a feminist discourse that is ultimately, as previously mentioned, overtly lesbian. More commonly, the runaway Baby Doll movie is firmly entrenched in a male point of view, as consideration of a film that epitomizes the cycle, *Little Ladies of the Night,* may demonstrate.

Little Ladies of the Night is the story of Hailey, a fourteen-year-old Los Angeles runaway who is befriended by a pimp and inevitably ends up streetwalking. She is contrasted with Karen, another juvenile prostitute. Whereas Linda Purl as the petite, blonde Hailey oscillates convincingly between child and adult in appearance, communicating softness, vulnerability, and innocence, Kathleen Quinlan as Karen conveys a toughness and maturity, which suggest that prostitution may be something that the older girls are capable of handling (Karen turns sixteen and thus comes of age, for California, during the course of the film).

Responsibility for the girls' plight is laid squarely at the door of their uncaring mothers. After Karen has been picked up for prostitution, social worker Lyall York calls her mother from the police station and informs her of the situation. "I kinda figured she was doing something like that," Mrs Brodwick tells him; and asked if she would come and collect her daughter, she replies: "Forget it! Oh, ah, one more thing. Don't call me up no more, OK? I don't need no more news bulletins on that kid. She's got her life, I got mine." Hailey, on the other hand, is taken home by her father (who, it is implied, has developed an incestuous crush on her) to a cool reception from her mother. "Was it me?" she asks. "You were picking on me, all the time," Hailey explains. "Everything I did was wrong." Before long, she runs away again. Later, in desperate straits, Hailey begs to be allowed to return home, but her mother, enjoying the lack of competition for her husband's attention, turns her down.

Grim as it is, the mothers' indifference pales in comparison with the active malevolence and corruption of other women Hailey encounters after she enters the prostitution scene, including her pimp Comfort's number-one lady, who sits in the room doing nothing as Hailey painfully endures her first john; the female director of the juvenile detention facility to which she is sent, who forces the girls into pornographic photography; and the bevy of whores who viciously beat up Hailey at Comfort's bidding, to teach her a lesson. It will take a man to rescue the young hooker from the miserable fate to which maternal failure has condemned her.

The climax of the film is a fight between Comfort and York (a reformed pimp himself), with Hailey looking on. There is no chance of the young woman exercising her own existential choice: her future is to be determined by the struggle between two men for possession of her, body and soul. York, who has spent a thousand dollars of his own money to redeem her, is stabbed. Comfort runs off, and Hailey, who has previously declared her intention of sticking with him, now stays with York, her true nature revealed as she becomes nurse to the injured male. York survives; he has arranged for Hailey to move in with the family of a friendly cop.

Little Ladies of the Night thus confirms the runaway Baby Doll in her role as innocent victim of dysfunctional family life and deficiency of mother-love. The damaged inflicted on her by the experience of prostitution at a tender age can possibly be mended—but only if she receives genuine care and affection. And the social problem that she represents will remain, so it is implied, until such time as the family unit is restored to its designated function as a locus of nurturance.

Both *Il ladro di bambini*/*The Stolen Children* (Italy/France/Switzerland/Germany, 1992) and *Stella Does Tricks* (UK, 1997) work within the social-realist tradition in their depiction of underage prostitution as a blight on contemporary society. *Il ladro di bambini* uses children with no previous acting experience in two of the three principal roles, and enhances naturalism and spontaneity by means of semi-improvised performances. *Stella Does Tricks*, director Coky Giedroyc's first feature, draws upon interviews with child prostitutes she conducted for a 1994 documentary series on the homeless. But in their ideological positioning, the two films are poles apart.

Il ladro di bambini opens with eleven-year-old Rosetta Scorella (Valentina Scalici) at home, servicing a middle-aged client at her mother's bidding. The scene is, of course, handled discreetly, comprising a single shot showing the back of Rosetta's head and—as she mutters a prayer to her guardian angel — tilting down her arm to her hand, revealing that she is sitting on a bed. The client's hand enters frame, presses down on Rosetta's hand, and then strokes and fondles it. A police raid follows: both the client and the mother are arrested, and Rosetta and her younger brother Luciano are taken into care. The rest of the film is devoted to a trip that the children make in the custody of a carabiniere, Antonio, from Milan to Rome (where they are refused at a church-run children's home), and thence to Sicily, and is concerned emotionally with the trust and affection that gradually builds up between the characters.

The film acknowledges the culpability of the client, and is unusual in that it shows the man being arrested. It also lays some of the blame for Rosetta's situation on the father's abandonment of the family when Luciano was an infant. In other respects, however, *Il ladro di bambini* functions as a traditional patriarchal text.

With the father being absent, the major guilty party — as in many of the runaway films — is identified as being the mother, who in this case is not simply neglectful but herself acts in the role of pimp. Poverty may be an explanation — the Scorellas live in a rundown-looking apartment building — but is no excuse: there are obviously many other poor women who do not prostitute their daughters. The mother's guilt is insisted on in the scene in which Rosetta receives the client: she observes the man enter the girl's room, turns and walks away with downcast eyes, sits down resignedly, and then picks up the money on the table and counts it. When, a few minutes later, she yells "Let me go! I ain't done nothing!" as she is escorted down the steps by police, the audience's sympathy is not with her.

Il ladro di bambini is in realist mode, but here the Baby Doll is not symptomatic of a society gone awry. On the contrary, Rosetta's case is presented as atypical — so unusual that it becomes the subject of a nation-wide scandal, with a magazine cover declaiming ONLY 11 YEARS OLD AND HER MOTHER MADE HER A PROSTITUTE. The circumscribed nature of the problem is stressed in that there is no mention of any client other than the one we see, and no suggestion of other children being involved; moreover, the authorities take swift and effective action in dealing with it.

On her travels with Luciano and Antonio, Rosetta shows signs of becoming rebellious. She fights with her brother, almost makes a getaway, and when caught threatens to accuse the carabiniere of molestation. But with Antonio's care and understanding the revolt is quickly subdued, and Rosetta reverts to the devout and docile child we saw at the start. By the end of the film she has been set on the correct female path, becoming caregiver to the sickly Luciano, rehearsing for her role to come as nurturing mother.

Thus Italian society is depicted as fundamentally sound. There are blemishes—moral failings of individuals like the client and Rosetta's father and mother, and of institutions like the uncompassionate children's home—but they are more than compensated for by the virtues of the protagonist, a man of integrity and sensitivity who in his social role is representative of authority (the army). The problem of child prostitution is an isolated one and mechanisms to remedy it are readily to hand. Patriarchy is reaffirmed.

In contrast, *Stella Does Tricks* is an uncompromisingly feminist text, in which the Baby Doll turns Avenger. Fifteen-year-old Stella (Kelly MacDonald) is one of several underage London prostitutes under the control of oleaginous middle-aged pimp Mr. Peters—a man who is no societal outcast but an outwardly respectable businessman. Flashing back in memory and fantasy sequences to her Glasgow childhood with her sexually abusive single-parent father, a mediocre stand-up comic, and her authoritarian aunt, the film tracks Stella's life over a period of several weeks as she breaks with Peters (for which she is punished by being brutally gang-raped) and takes up with Eddie, a teenage heroin addict.

Unlike *Il ladro di bambini, Stella Does Tricks* positions the father as the actively guilty party, mercilessly exploiting his daughter's powerlessness and affection for him. The locus of abuse is a pigeon loft, where we see young Stella struggling with him, yelling "Leave me alone!"; later, in another flashback, we witness the girl burning the loft down, ecstatic as it blazes.

Far from being isolated, Stella's case is represented as being typical. This is apparent both in the way that Peters is shown as putting on the market a constantly replenished supply of young flesh, and in the end title that steps outside the fictional narrative to give thanks to "the girls we met in Glasgow, Manchester and London whose lives inspired the making of this film." Moreover—until Stella wreaks her revenge—Peters is clearly able to conduct his teenage prostitution business without fear of intervention by the authorities.

Most significantly, however, the British film differs from the Italian in its characterization of the girl prostitute herself. Stella, of course, is several years older than Rosetta, but more importantly she is an utterly disillusioned rebel, who as the film goes on acquires the strength to pull off

60. *Stella Does Tricks:* Stella (Kelly MacDonald) with Mr Peters (James Bolam). bfi Collections.

ever more effective acts of vengeance against all those who have oppressed her and girls like her. After one portly old client praises Stella saying she's "a really beautiful girl — lovely mover — really grand little fuck," she takes out her disgust and fury on a row of parked cars, ripping off a windscreen wiper, scratching the paint, trashing a side mirror, wrenching off an aerial, and finally, as an afterthought, kicking in a headlight. Other acts of revolt are more directly targeted. Another client, a "nasty bastard," gets something agonizing stuck up his ass that was not the cannabis resin he was promised. A drug-dealing thug who savagely beats up one of Stella's prostitute friends gets his car blown up, courtesy of a lighted match in the gas tank. On a trip back to Glasgow with Eddie, Stella plays a prank on her aunt by wafting inflated condoms into her garden, and

then goes for her father, squirting flammable liquid at his penis and setting it on fire. Finally, observing Peters in the park engaged in one of his
favorite rituals, being jerked off under cover of a newspaper by a young
teenager bearing ice-cream cones (Stella herself does the business in the
opening scene of the film), she has him arrested in flagrante delicto and
publicly humiliated as he is bustled off by police.

There is no doubt about the stance of the film. Underage prostitution
is an oppressive institution exploiting the vulnerabilities of abused children. Moreover, it is no isolated occurrence, but a pervasive evil perpetrated by a significant sector of the community, the mature men who
enjoy purchasing the sexual services of adolescent girls, and those who
pander to them. By its existence British society is radically compromised,
and in the absence of any social measures to rectify the problem, individual action is called for. In the hands of the feminist filmmaker of *Stella
Does Tricks*, the Baby Doll no longer dances dreamily in the arms of her
pimp. From now on, she is an incendiary guerilla.

16

Working Girl

Essentially you're there as a service industry. It doesn't matter whether you're a waitress or a prostitute or a typist — you're still doing things for other people. A secretary uses her hands, and that's considered quite nice and normal. A prostitute uses another part of her anatomy, and "oohh!"

—HILARY, in Jan Jordan, *Working Girls* [1]

Prior to the 1980s there were isolated attempts to strip the prostitute in film of the aura of glamour and pathos that enveloped her, to bring a down-to-earth, factual approach to the depiction of the sex trade. *Girl of the Night* (USA, 1960), for example, "one of the most forthright films ever made on the subject of prostitution," [2] adopted a semidocumentary style in bringing to the screen the case history of a call girl. Eschewing all sensationalism, all lurid detail, it was a failure at the box office. Also deploying documentary techniques, Jean-Luc Godard's *Vivre sa vie* (France, 1962) incorporated a voice-over narration offering facts and statistics on contemporary prostitution in Paris. It was followed by a group of less well-known films, including *Dossier prostitution* (France, 1969), *Bella di giorno, moglie di notte* (Italy, 1971), and *La Punition* (France, 1973), which are described as resulting from serious research and based on authentic memoirs. [3] In 1975 the TV movie *Hustling* presented a well-researched exposé of street prostitution in Manhattan, centering its findings on the system of exploitation that delivered super profits and immunity to the men controlling the business, while the women doing the work were routinely thrown in jail.

But in productions such as these the prostitute remained an object of inquiry, the phenomenon at the center of a psychological or sociological discourse originating from the outside. (*Girl of the Night*, based on a book by Dr. Harold Greenwald, had an approach described as being "along psychiatric lines" [4]; *Vivre sa vie*'s narration was derived from *Où en*

305

est la prostitution? by Marcel Sacotte; while *Hustling* was a dramatization of
the investigative journalism of Gail Sheehy.)

There were only isolated attempts to communicate the perspective of
the women themselves, especially prostitutes who had chosen the work
and intended to keep on at it.[5] *Flamman/Girls Without Rooms/The Flame*
(Sweden, 1956) was a pioneering work in this regard. Based on case material from Stockholm's Langholmen Prison, it tells the story of an intelligent, rebellious seventeen-year-old girl, Fransiska (Catrin Westerlund),
who becomes a prostitute "out of boredom with family life and the
drudgery of a regular job. Eventually arrested by the juvenile authorities,
she defends her profession and attacks the corruption and hypocrisy of
society."[6] Challenging her accusers, Fransiska asks: "What 'crime' have I
committed? I have robbed no one, injured no one, murdered no one."

After the emergence of prostitutes' rights organizations (which date
from the early 1970s) this perspective was bolstered. *Prostitute* (Tony Garnett, UK, 1980) and *Working Girls* (Lizzie Borden, USA, 1986)—both low-
budget productions right at the margin of the commercial cinema—
affirm the female voice, focusing on the subjective experience of their
prostitute characters while rejecting all fantasies centered upon them.
Deromanticized, deglamorized, the prostitute here is an ordinary person
going about her humdrum, banal work, which is obviously unpleasant
in some ways but not necessarily worse (so it is implied) than exploitative
labor in a factory, restaurant, or office.

Prostitute came about in the context of a campaign being waged by
PROS (Programme for Reform of the Law on Soliciting) for the decriminalization of prostitution in Britain. Women working the street
were constantly subject to arrest, and subsequent fines or imprisonment,
under laws against soliciting and loitering. Garnett, who had previously
been associated as producer with director Ken Loach on films and television dramas noted for their left-wing social-realist aesthetic, came to
the project with an open mind. "My starting point," he said, "was simple
curiosity, I had no feelings about prostitutes and the law. But they convinced me. I'm quite certain now that the law should be changed." Researching the subject for four years in close contact with PROS, Garnett
evolved a script that was open to revision up to the last moment: the
method allowed for creative input from the actors, some of whom may
have been prostitutes themselves. "Most of my cast were professionals,"
he explained, "some weren't and I'd rather not say which is which. But
the way I worked was insisting on certain things and then letting them go
their own way afterwards. Then I'd be up half the night rewriting be-

cause of what they'd shown me. That's a helluva way to spend a short six-week shoot."[7]

His approach was applauded by PROS historian Eileen McLeod, who wrote: "Some media personnel have been very ready to lend support because the campaign's aims happened to fit in with their perspective. In this respect PROS' happiest experience of collaboration has been with Tony Garnett in the production of *Prostitute* . . . PROS' position meshed with Garnett's egalitarian approach, which also permeated his method of working."[8]

Prostitute deals with the experiences of a Birmingham prostitute, Sandra (Eleanor Forsythe), over a period of several months. Deciding to quit the streets, she finds employment in a massage parlor and then shifts to London, where she works for a visiting massage agency and subsequently on her own account. A particularly nasty encounter with local detectives induces her to return to Birmingham, where her future remains indefinite. Interspersed with Sandra's story is that of a social worker, Louise, with whom she shares her apartment. Louise gets involved in the prostitutes' campaign for reform of the law and runs into difficulties with her employers, the local council, for this reason. For most of the time-span of the film another prostitute, Rose (Nancy Samuels), is in jail for allegedly soliciting while under probation; it is her release which provides the muted upbeat note on which the film ends.

In keeping with its rejection of the melodrama that so often colors prostitute narratives, Garnett's film has, for the most part, an air of studied neutrality about it, with just an occasional leaning toward lyricism (a country riverside scene in which Sandra and Louise sit in a dinghy and chat) or light comedy (Sandra being forced to endure a German businessman's disquisition on pistons, cylinder blocks, and tool-grinding). But *Prostitute* pursues its political agenda by incorporating within its tapestry of everyday life several scenes designed to elicit from the audience a strong emotional reaction, a sense of outrage. These incidents function as samples of a general, institutionalized injustice, and align the film with the classic tradition of social exposé stretching from the earliest days of cinema through landmarks like *I am a Fugitive from a Chain Gang* and *The Grapes of Wrath*. Rose, for example, is walking home when plainclothes police seize her, drag her into an unmarked car, and subject her to sneering abuse all the way back to the station. "This baggage," they call her, and joke about her education: "Reading in pornography, was it?" The sequel in court demonstrates how the odds are stacked against the woman defined in law as a "common" prostitute: advised by her lawyer to play it

61. *Prostitute:* Sandra (Eleanor Forsythe) and Louise (Kate Crutchley). Stills Collection, New Zealand Film Archive.

cool, to "smile," Rose complies, unwillingly ("How can you smile at the fuckers when you've done nothing?")—and is rewarded with a hefty jail term (the magistrate is female). Sandra's equivalent experience also exposes abuse of power by the police. Having advertised her "massage service" by means of a card in a newspaper shop window, she is visited one morning by two plainclothes officers who pound on her door, burst in, and seize her by the throat. One of them then proceeds to demand a tribute in fellatio ("Don't you bite me you slag!") before confiscating her takings and announcing he'll be back next week.

 Prostitute goes beyond the social exposé tradition in positing a response to the injustice in terms of collective political action. Working committee meetings are shown, distributing leaflets, visiting the local MP, handling publicity in the media. The hurdles met with in such organizing are acknowledged: the reluctance of some streetwalkers to participate, fearing they and their families may become more vulnerable; the suspicion of the working-class prostitute toward the middle-class socialist activist ("Why don't you put your cunt in the bloody street,"

Sandra says to Louise, "You could be one of us then"). The campaign is depicted as making slow progress without any concrete victories to celebrate, a scripting strategy that accurately reflects the political situation of the time while depriving viewers of the conventional emotional experience that would go along with triumph or defeat.

But if *Prostitute*'s intentions are serious and its commitment to the decriminalization campaign such that dramatic considerations can be sacrificed to it, still the film does not become stuffily didactic. For one thing, protagonist Sandra is no heroine of the proletariat, not even of the Birmingham prostitutes, for whose organizing activities she has little time. With her plump figure, rosy complexion and curly red hair, her ready repartee, and her touching shyness, she's an attractive character in many ways, unburdened by the duty of incarnating political correctness (a duty that Louise more plausibly performs). For another thing, *Prostitute* is ready to laugh at an overly theoretical approach to its subject matter, which it does in the satirical characterization of the sociology lecturer from York, Griff. There are "logical problems with the functionalist model," Griff tells Louise. "I personally tend to take a phenomenological point of view . . . how prostitution comes to be seen as a thing in the world." "Have you ever met one?" Louise asks. "Not as far as I know," he bashfully admits.

Despite such light moments *Prostitute* is on the whole a downbeat film, not defeatist but resigned to the idea of the process of getting a law change being a long-drawn-out struggle. It is not exciting, inspiring, or erotic, even in the intimate quasi-lesbian scenes between Sandra and Louise. Its appeal lies in its authenticity, its honesty toward communicating the experience of women working in a not very pleasant job made worse by its social pariah status. It shocks not by its vicious brutality, as so many films exposing the oppression of prostitutes do, but by the very humdrum quality of its violence.

> Prostitution is only a *specific* expression of the *universal* prostitution of the worker.
> —KARL MARX[9]

> It is perhaps a measure of how far contemporary populations have internalized bourgeois values that it is possible for liberals nowadays to use the comparison not to discredit wage labor but rather to rehabilitate prostitution.
> —ALISON M. JAGGAR[10]

62. *Prostitute:* Eleanor Forsythe as Sandra. bfi Collections.

In a similar way to *Prostitute*, but without a specific political agenda, *Working Girls* is devoted to conveying the quotidian experience of New York prostitutes from their point of view. Its director, Lizzie Borden, came to the project from an art-school background and with one experimental — and controversial — feminist feature, *Born in Flames* (1983), behind her. Among the many women who worked collectively on *Born in Flames*

were Flo Kennedy and Margo St. James of the prostitutes' rights organization COYOTE, and their perspective influenced the theoretical position that Borden was to adopt toward prostitution.[11]

In particular, Borden saw the film she was to make as a vehicle for
counteracting the denigration that prostitutes were subject to, not only
from male society but also from certain sections of the feminist movement. She was aware, she stated in an interview, that ". . . groups such as
Women Against Pornography were really putting working women — not
just prostitutes but also other women in the sex industry — in a bind. The
conventional social criticism, of course, says that, 'these are bad women,
fallen women, degraded and victimized.' Then the feminists, who criti-
cize these women for perpetuating the sex industry, also tell them that
they are victims. Many working girls, however, have chosen their jobs
and do not feel like victims. Women in the sex industry have been so re-
viled on both sides that there must be a way in which we can establish a
dialogue which is not against women who work in this way. I wanted to
eliminate that automatic sense of degradation for women who have
worked as prostitutes or done anything like it."[12] She hoped that *Working
Girls* would "help to validate prostitution, or at least to raise some serious
questions about the way it is perceived in our society."[13]

Borden scripted *Working Girls* after having done a good deal of research — "meeting many women who worked, going to houses, hanging
out, talking to different madams, different johns" — and with the deliberate intention of negating prevailing images of the prostitute in the
commercial cinema. "So many films," she explains in the documentary
Calling the Shots, " — and most of them have been by men — about prostitution, even the ones by women, tend to be highly sensational, and the
women in them tend to be highly victimized, or there's a heavy sense of
moralizing about the women — if they're not murdered by the killer
they're saved by the cop — and that was definitely what I wanted to avoid
in *Working Girls.*"[14]

Most of the action in the film takes place in a small, plainly decorated,
middle-class Manhattan brothel, and the narrative covers a working
day — which stretches through a double shift — in the life of one of the
workers, Molly (Louise Smith). A photographer with two college degrees,
Molly is, as Borden argues, "not the stereotype of a prostitute."[15] She
lives with her lover Diane, a black woman, whom we see briefly at the
beginning and end of the film. The stuff of *Working Girls* is Molly's interactions with a widely assorted array of clients, with the other prostitutes,
and with the querulous madam, Lucy.

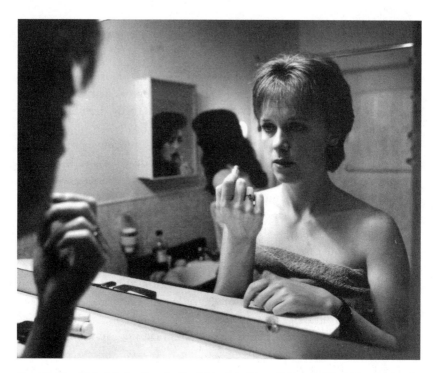

63. *Working Girls:* Molly (Louise Smith) with Gina (Marusia Zach) in the background.

Like *Prostitute, Working Girls* has its moments of lyricism and comedy, but its predominant tone is again one of detached, unemotional observation of the work process. Commenting on her performance, Louise Smith remarks that she "thought about waitressing a lot . . . the way that the room was set up, the Kleenex, the condoms, the bedsheets, the whole thing, you know it's like the table cloth, the matches, the ashtray, it was to me very similar in that sense."[16] More sex scenes are included than in the British film, and a certain sensual quality does float in the air from time to time, although it is undercut by detail shots such as the wrapping of a used condom in a paper napkin. Borden asserts: "In none of the scenes was the female body looked at by the camera in order to titillate the audience. In fact the intention was to make it as unerotic as I could."[17]

The clients are old and young, fat and skinny, overbearing and timorous; one likes being hit on the rear with a Ping-Pong paddle, another induces Molly to play the part of a blind virgin miraculously cured by his penis power, a third goes for light dominance in the "jungle room." One or two are rough or otherwise objectionable (an Asian who refuses to wash), but there is nothing like the parade of ugly aggressive male sexuality that *Broken Mirrors* displays. With them all (except the Asian) Molly is sweetly compliant, and it is understandable that, although she is no stunning beauty, she receives presents and offers of support on the outside.

In both *Working Girls* and *Prostitute* much of the strength of the portrayal comes from their handling of what goes on outside the bedroom—like chatter on the job. Of little or no dramatic import, such idle dialogue could, from a conventional (male) perspective, be readily dismissed: in his *Cineaste* review, for example, Graham Fuller accused *Working Girls* of evasiveness because of "the film's interest in the smooth, empty chitchat that goes on 'downstairs.'"[18] Yet the significance of such scenes from a feminist point of view is readily apparent; it is at these times, in the breathing spaces between clients, that the prostitutes are able to claim a women's place, offer one another mutual support, relax and joke, be themselves and not the phony lover. And it is here, too, that they can say what they think of men. In *Prostitute,* two scantily dressed "visiting masseuses" in the agency run by "Mrs. T" sit together on a sofa and have fits of laughter as they discuss the national characteristics of their clientele: the Japs the best ("tiny pricks . . . whipped in, whipped out, wiped it . . . so quick it was untrue"), the Yanks pretty generous, the Arabs who make you work for your money ("dicks like donkeys . . . got a hard-on it was that big . . . damn rough all right, bang bang bang bang bang"). In *Working Girls* Molly says: "One good thing about this job: I've completely lost my fear of men," and her workmate Gina replies: "You can handle any man so long as you know what his sexual trip is."

Both films adopt a quasi-documentary style. The effect derives in part, of course, from the absence of stars and from the filmic techniques, particularly noticeable in *Prostitute* with its (simulated?) available-light cinematography, its graininess, its noisy sound recording, its out-of-focus foreground intervention that resembles the uncontrolled action of cinema vérité. But just as important is the story construction, which in both movies is episodic and undramatic, tends to stray a little from the major characters, and includes sequences of minimal narrative significance such as going to the drugstore to buy contraceptives. The documentary-like quality is obviously aimed at deromanticizing the image of the prostitute, of strengthening the claims to authenticity that the films make. Against Hollywood gloss and glamour is set drab imagery of everyday working life, and the truth value of the representation is thereby, so it is felt, enhanced. But there may be another, less conscious reason for the leaning toward documentary: it perhaps enabled the film-makers to draw back from their characters whenever, coming too close, they did not like what they saw.

For if documentary is predominantly concerned with people in their working life, then it can be excused for not digging too deeply into their personal psyches. And both *Prostitute* and *Working Girls* exhibit a certain reticence when it comes to revealing the thoughts and feelings of their protagonists.

Working Girls, for example, several times shows Molly adopting erotic or affectionate poses with her client and observing the effect in the mir-ror. Is she trying out the idea of a heterosexual relationship, or perhaps contemplating giving up brothel work and becoming a kept mistress, as several clients urge her to? Or is she simply playing with sexual imagery? Commenting on her performance, Louise Smith suggests: "I think this has to do with this feeling that some women express, and I think this is what the filmmaker was trying to get across with the scenes too, of look-ing at yourself reinvented—wow, I'm a sex object!—making *yourself* a sex object."[19]

In one such scene, Molly and a young musician, Paul, kiss as if pas-sionately and then sink out of frame, like lovers in a movie. A close-up shows him lying on her, tenderly, so it seems; there is a pan as he kisses her breasts and strips off her panties, then a pan back as he leans down over her. Here, not only the gestures but the framing and camera move-ments mimic lovemaking as seen in the commercial cinema—creating a strongly ambivalent effect. Is Molly a very good actress, which would explain her high rate of regulars, and the persistence with which clients urge her to meet them outside the brothel? Is she just playing the game, or does she actually experience some attraction for this man? Since the film is in fact a drama, not a documentary, all is at a level of performance, and it is difficult to determine just which level. Given an absence of in-sight into Molly's feelings here, the seeming complicity of the camera and mise-en-scène with her show of passion complicates and confuses.

No such ambiguity marks the filming of the sex scenes in *Prostitute*. The two explicit sequences—the jerk-off of a client in a massage parlor by a bare-breasted masseuse, and a lesbian sex show at a party of young, upper-class Londoners—are filmed in static medium shot with flat light-ing, depriving the acts of erotic appeal for the spectator and providing an analogue for the evident dreariness of the work for the women. ("All greasy and sexy sliding up and down, making you all randy and excited," says the masseuse, but if the client is getting excited the same can not be said for the viewer.) *Prostitute* is however as cagey as *Working Girls* when it comes to exploring just what the protagonist feels about the work she does. Neither of the overt sex scenes directly involves Sandra, and when we do see her with a customer she is never in bed with him. Nor does she talk about her work with, for example, Louise. (She does confess to feeling "a right berk" when enlisted, with one regressive client, to play a little girl in a lace-frilled dress with ribbons in her hair.)

Neither film confronts the issue of the invasion of personal space by the client, and the tactics that prostitutes adopt to combat it and retain a sense of their own integrity. In the testimony of sex workers this question is frequently at the forefront. As one expresses it: "Each girl has her own rules in terms of what she lets clients do. Like no girls will let clients kiss them; it's too personal. The whole neck up is a taboo area. To have any client even touch your face is incredibly claustrophobic. From your neck up is *your* space. You can switch off to the rest of your body, but you can't switch off to your face."[20]

In recent years this concern has often been acknowledged in the commercial cinema by showing the prostitute deliberately turn her head away from the client when having intercourse with him. It is all the more surprising, then, that the feminist *Working Girls* depicts its nominally lesbian protagonist engaging in extensive kissing with her clientele. One of the other women, Dawn, who never lets her clients kiss her, raises the question with Molly, but the objection she raises, that of it being potentially unhygienic, would seem to be a side issue. Since Molly is insistent on the right of the prostitute not to do anything she doesn't want to, one is forced to ask why she does it, and again the answer is far from clear. Is Molly really attracted to these guys, or perhaps being generous to them? Or is the show of affection all totally feigned, the kissing undertaken simply for monetary gain? And if it *is* all an act, how does Molly retain her dignity — which she does — when her private space is being so consistently violated?

The films steer clear, too, of the question of the extent to which the nature of the work plays havoc with the private emotional lives of the characters. In *Prostitute*, Sandra is shown as living in a fairly stable though not especially affectionate relationship with a black man, Winston, and his son, Michael; whether she is Michael's mother is never made quite clear, which is an indication of the film's vagueness in dealing with this aspect of her life. About to go off to London to try her luck there, Sandra betrays no concern about leaving her partner — "Fuck Winston, I don't give a shit about Winston," she tells Louise, "I've been supporting him for the last four years" — but there are no intimate scenes between Sandra and Winston that would confirm this statement or clarify in other ways the nature of their relationship and the impact, if any, Sandra's profession has upon it. Likewise *Working Girls*, though it starts and ends on an image of Molly in bed with Diane, hardly delves at all into Molly's emotional life outside her workplace. There are some valuable clues: at one point Molly says "I can't stand to be touched when I leave this place," and she keeps the nature of her work secret from Diane, as the young prostitute Dawn — with some difficulty — does from her boyfriend. (The necessity for secrecy is confirmed by Gina, who explains in a poignant and revealing line of dialogue that she doesn't see her boyfriend any more: "When our relationship first started I decided I had to be really straight about this job, and I told him, look, if you really loved me you should be able to deal with my working, and then I thought, if you really loved me, how could you?") But the toll this constant lack of candor exacts, and more fundamentally, the extent to which feigning the gestures of love mechanically, repeatedly, incapacitates one to make the real gestures, is not explored.

The films leave us in little doubt, though, that the work itself is not something from which the women derive much personal fulfillment. It's a grind; even when exercised under comparatively favorable conditions, without pimps, in one's own call-girl business or in a female-run brothel, it's characterized by oppressive routine and constant disparagement. Why do it then? Since the Working Girl films insist that their characters engage in prostitution out of their own free will, the answer can only be money. The work is clearly much better paid than most other jobs open to women, especially without workplace qualifications. But as neither *Prostitute* nor *Working Girls* places much emphasis on the lack of available options, money-in-the-abstract becomes the theme — particularly in the latter with its close-ups of hundred-dollar bills being counted, placed in a wallet, deposited in a bank.[21]

Hence the question that these films keep approaching but then drawing back from: what are the costs of selling oneself? To what extent can one turn one's body into mere instrumentality, the object of desire on which the male client centers his fantasies, into which he pumps his sperm, while still claiming to act as a free, autonomous human being? Is hiring out one's body something that can be done without damage to one's person, without self-alienation, and is the prostitute worthy of the dignity that society accords any other working woman? There is a troubling scene in *Working Girls* in which Paul, having sex with Molly, tells her: "So long as I'm paying for this, we're not equals . . . I can understand you fucking somebody for fifty thousand dollars, but for fifty bucks, you're a whore." The distress this causes Molly — she immediately goes to the basin and washes her face, very upset — is obviously attributable to the change in attitude from a client who had previously seemed tender and affectionate, but may also derive from a feeling that he's right, that in granting access to her body for money she is degraded.[22] Louise Smith comments: "He's more like a peer to her, a kind of reminder of what the world is that she comes from, since she's an artist, he kind of gets inside her more emotionally, and that's why she's affected by him."[23]

Thus the films encounter paradox. They set out to validate, by a process of simple factual description, the work of the prostitute — yet the more they succeed in depicting just what the work entails, the less comfortable the filmmakers become with it. The aim of restoring dignity to women who choose the profession is undercut by the close study of what is involved, which demonstrates just how demeaning the work can be. And the goal of stripping bare the institution of prostitution, of showing it like it is, results also in a stripping bare of the character of the women involved: the greater their involvement in the profession is an act of choice, the less attractive as human beings they appear.

Hence despite their overt agendas, *Prostitute* and *Working Girls* end up portraying prostitution as a trap. The narratives are circular, returning at the end to the point of departure, conveying a sense of repetition and futility. The images of constricted — often windowless — interiors, especially with the tight framing with which the brothel is filmed in *Working Girls,* reinforce this feeling ("The film is purposefully incredibly claustrophobic," says Louise Smith.)[24] There is a scene near the end of *Working Girls,* however, which suggests breaking out. After Molly has told Lucy she's not coming back, she leaves the brothel and the door slams shut. There is a blast of music and a cut to Molly on the exterior, smiling, and then wide tracking shots of the city at night as she rides her bike home. Here the cinematic rhetoric can mean only one thing: release, liberation from confinement.

It's no accident that both films juxtapose their prostitute protagonist with children at play: in *Working Girls,* Molly pauses in a park to watch the kids on her way back from the pharmacy, while in *Prostitute* the last sequence shows Sandra beside a playground as the children sing a sex rhyme, "Carry on my Brother John." Coming dangerously close to a sentimental pathos more appropriate to other archetypes of the prostitute, the scenes confirm the vacillation at the heart of the Working Girl representation. Try as they might, Garnett and Borden cannot convince us that prostitution is a viable option for the woman needing a job; and that is no doubt because they cannot convince themselves.

17

The Love Story

There is a saying that prostitutes make the best wives. This to me is
definitely a myth. Prostitutes either become nymphomaniacs or get to
hate men, and it is almost impossible for them to settle for one man.
—XAVIERA HOLLANDER, *The Happy Hooker*[1]

Sex for hire (multiple partners, money changing hands, temporary) is at
the opposite pole to romantic love (single partner, no financial transaction, permanent). The prostitute love story deals with this opposition,
seeking to resolve it by drawing the prostitute away from her job. If in the
fallen woman narrative the virtuous female loses her innocence, the love
story aims to reverse the process, redeeming the heroine so she is a fit
partner for the man who cherishes her.

This story is heavily reliant upon a Judeo-Christian conception of the
prostitute as a figure of debasement. Prostitute stories containing an element of romance from within Asian cultural and religious traditions tend
to have a differing orientation, with the woman who sells her body accorded an esteem lacking in the West. In Buddhist thought, for instance,
she may even take on the guise of spiritual teacher; a prostitute during the
Buddha's time is reputed to have "used sex to teach Buddhism; all the
men she had sex with became enlightened."[2] The Buddhist tradition is
evident in a film such as *Shinju ten no amijima/Double Suicide* (Japan, 1969),
discussed in chapter 4, which follows a familiar Siren love story pattern,
but whose prostitute protagonist is granted a rare respect by her lover's
wife. In Indian cinema, as Sumita S. Chakravarty argues, Hindu and
Muslim conceptions merge in the enigmatic figure of the courtesan:
"variously described as dancing girl, nautch-girl, prostitute, or harlot,
she appears again and again in Indian cultural texts, at once celebrated
and shunned, used and abused, praised and condemned." Although "socially decentered," she is "the object of respect and admiration because
of her artistic training and musical accomplishments."[3]

319

Within the Western tradition, however, the love story has at its heart a rescue fantasy. For the woman involved, what is at stake is escape from an oppressive milieu and from psychological despondency. Typically, in *Tempi nostri/A Slice of Life* (Italy/France, 1954), "a young girl, forced to resort to prostitution by the war, falls in love with a schoolteacher who persuades her that life is still worth living."[4] Prostitution, necessarily, is portrayed in a negative light. Even in *Klute* (USA, 1971), where the call girl appears in the guise of the independent woman who accepts her profession as a normal part of modern life — "I don't think there's anything wrong with it, morally" — even here there is vulnerability to violence from freak clients, a clear and evident danger of slipping into devastating drug addiction, and a strong emotional alienation. For Bree (Jane Fonda), as for many another prostitute in film, it is a question of getting out of the city and, after so much dead time going mechanically through the motions of lovemaking, of rediscovering the capacity to feel, of finding, precisely, love.

For the man, on the other hand, his desire for a prostitute lover points to a lack, a deficiency in himself, which only she can help him overcome. He may be physically handicapped (Toulouse-Lautrec in John Huston's version of *Moulin Rouge*), professionally unfulfilled (*The World of Suzie Wong*), emotionally alienated (*Pretty Woman*). By "rescuing" the prostitute, he creates for himself — if he is able to pull it off — the ideal love object, in whom are fused the erotic thrill of the woman who flaunts her sexuality with the nurturing care of the woman who is so grateful for being saved that she lavishes all her love on the instrument of her deliverance. The fears of engulfment, of loss of autonomy, of becoming a slave to emotion, of regressing into an infantile dependency, that a man may experience with a respectable woman, a woman on the same level of the social scale as he is, are here allayed; with the (ex-) prostitute, so far beneath him — even if he is only an ordinary working guy — he need not feel beholden. She can make no demands, must be grateful for what she gets, and can be dismissed at will, without guilt. With such a partner, his relational needs can be met while being simultaneously denied.

So it is a utopian fantasy (steeped as it is in patriarchal ideology) that is at play here, a dream of reciprocal liberation. But the narratives in which it is embodied can take different paths: the dream may be tragically denied or triumphantly fulfilled; or it may turn into a nightmare.

The model for tragic denial is *La Dame aux camélias,* the novel and spectacularly successful play (1852) by Alexandre Dumas fils. First adapted for the screen in 1907 as the Danish production *Kameliadamen,*

64. *Klute:* Jane Fonda (center) as Bree, with Donald Sutherland as Klute.

the Dumas tale was filmed at least eleven more times in the silent era alone, and despite changing social mores it has continued to appeal to movie audiences in new versions over the years.[5] Situated on the margins of this study because its heroine is courtesan rather than prostitute proper, the romantic drama of passion doomed because of the rigidity of class hierarchies and the social stigmatization of the woman who trades her sexual favors for a living nevertheless provides the basis for one strand—what might be thought of as the European version—of the prostitute love story.

The American version, in contrast, asserts that such class barriers shall not prevail: the younger generation will tear them down. In an upwardly mobile society, the happy ending supplants tragedy. *The Overcoat* (USA, 1916) sets the pattern: Maurice Norton's millionaire father insists that he choose between his family and his prostitute sweetheart Belle, who urges him to relinquish her; but Maurice defies his father and marries Belle. An optimism pervades the standard Hollywood treatment of the story, embodying a belief that the travail of prostitution is but a phase in life's journey and not an ineluctable fate from which deliverance comes only in death.

A happy ending is not possible when the love between the principals is unreciprocated, a story that is told—reflecting cinema's patriarchal bias — almost exclusively from the male point of view. If — as in *Moulin Rouge*, for example — the fallen woman is unworthy of the affection the hero bestows upon her and cannot be redeemed, the dream becomes a nightmare expressed in a bitter little tale of obsession and betrayal. Reflecting upon masculine folly with more than a streak of misogyny, such films cast the love object in the role of Siren or Gold Digger and have been discussed in chapters 4 and 8.

The stories of reciprocated passion, whether finally unfulfilled or triumphant, fall into two main categories depending on the class origin of the male protagonist. On the one hand, there are those films in which he is significantly better off than the prostitute, usually wealthy or from a social elite. By falling in love with a woman of much lower social station than himself, the man rebels against his class and the rigid stratification that it imposes. These films tend to be fish-out-of-water stories, deriving drama and sometimes comedy as well from the vividly contrasting backgrounds of the lovers. The second type of story is that in which the male protagonist comes from within or close to the woman's own lumpenproletarian milieu; he's often a sailor, a criminal, a drifter, a man of no fixed abode. The dramatic dynamic here deals with overcoming the loneliness of being one of society's outsiders, by becoming part of a couple and settling down.

Over the course of film history the two types have been produced in roughly equivalent numbers, but an initial favoring of the class-contrast narrative has given way in recent decades to the proletarian story. Moreover, the division between the types has itself begun to break down, with the emergence of figures such as the unemployed intellectual whose income is significantly less than that of the prostitute he is in love with, as in *Cuori al verde* (Italy, 1996), and the ordinary working-class guy who discovers he is dissatisfied with his humdrum bourgeois lifestyle, featured for example in *My Son the Fanatic* (UK, 1997). These developments perhaps reflect a gradual loosening of social hierarchies under the impact of contemporary capitalism, and with it a slight weakening of the whore stigma.

In the class-contrast stories, the male lead is typically well connected and well-to-do. If he is from Europe, there is a strong tendency for him to be a member of the titled aristocracy, like the Russian Prince Dmitri Nekhludov of the many versions of *Resurrection*, discussed in chapter 1, and the French Chevalier des Grieux of the *Manon Lescaut* adaptations (see chapter 4). The protagonist of *Lady of the Pavements* (USA, 1929) is

Ruritanian nobleman Count Karl von Arnim; of *The Lady Refuses* (USA, 1931) the English Sir Gerald Courtney; of *Divina Creatura* (Italy, 1976) the Italian Duke Daniele di Bagnasco. Alternatively, he may simply move in gentlemanly circles, like Armand Duval in the *Dame aux camélias* adaptations, or Philip Carey in the various versions (USA, 1934, 1946; UK, 1964) of W. Somerset Maugham's *Of Human Bondage*. If American, he is likely to be wealthy, a millionaire, or at least the son of one, as in *The Overcoat*, *The Waiting Soul* (USA, 1917) and *Go Naked in the World* (USA, 1961); in *Trading Places* (USA, 1983), he is an exceedingly rich and pampered commodities broker. Whatever his nationality, he is typically in business or the professions, and may have political ties.

Inevitably, this male protagonist, from a privileged background or in a position of power, will be suffering from some psychological deficiency: simply bored, or lacking inspiration, repressed, frustrated, emasculated by an overbearing father, the victim of a drinking problem perhaps. The savior of prostitute Miriam (Ann Murdock) in *Outcast* (USA, 1917) is a "wealthy but alcoholic" London barrister.[6] In Frank Capra's *Ladies of Leisure* (USA, 1930), upper-crust artist Jerry Strange leaves a wild party being thrown at his Manhattan penthouse studio and drives alone to the waterfront, where he meets by chance disaffected "party girl" Kay (Barbara Stanwyck): the dissipated life style he has been leading with his frivolous fiancée and an alcoholic pal is clearly unfulfilling. Bo Gillis, guitar-playing candidate for governor of a southern state in *Ada* (USA, 1961), is riding high on a popular campaign, but his nervous fidgeting in the presence of prostitute Ada Dallas (Susan Hayward) betrays his embarrassment at being unsure as to just why he is running for office.

Part of the protagonist's ennui has to do, in many cases, with his well-bred but unexciting girlfriend, fiancée or (infrequently) wife: the "suitable" woman who is sometimes domineering, occasionally scheming, and nearly always devoid of passion, generosity, and imagination. In *Penthouse* (USA, 1933), for example, attorney Durant's socialite fiancée breaks their engagement off when, after having defended a mobster, he is forced to quit his prestigious law firm. In *Mifune* (Denmark/Sweden, 1999), businessman Kresten's new wife, the boss's daughter, abandons him when she discovers he has a mentally deficient brother that he has not told her about. Even if she decides to persevere, the respectable woman will be no match for her bad-girl rival, and sooner or later the relationship will come to an end.

The attraction of the woman the protagonist falls in love with is, generally, her seductive sensuality. Whether she is at this stage of the

65. *The World of Suzie Wong:* Nancy Kwan as Suzie, with William Holden as Robert Lomax.

narrative a prostitute — and if she is, whether he is aware of it — it is her erotic beauty (sometimes fused with an exotic otherness, as in *The World of Suzie Wong*) that draws him to her, turns his head. It may be enough to derail his life completely, as in the Siren and Gold Digger tales told elsewhere; in *La viaccia/The Love Makers* (Italy/France, 1961), a young man falls desperately in love with a stunning Florence prostitute (Claudia Cardinale) and neglects his wine business to become bouncer at her brothel, only to be fatally stabbed by a customer.

Generally, though, her influence is positive, certainly at the start. If he is an artist — as he is in *Ladies of Leisure, The Song of Songs* (USA, 1933), *Die Sünderin* (West Germany, 1951), *Moulin Rouge* (UK, 1952), and *The World of Suzie Wong* (UK/USA, 1960) — she will model for him, become his muse. It is not without significance that the subject of Jerry's allegorical painting in *Ladies of Leisure,* for which Kay poses, is "Hope": she must gaze upwards, and they talk of how in Arizona, where they plan to go and live, you can reach up for the stars and grab them. Similarly, the prostitute restores a demoralized doctor's self-esteem in *Mandalay* (USA,

1934), induces an unscrupulous attorney to admit his wrongdoing in *Criminal Lawyer* (USA, 1937), awakens in the politician a social conscience in *Ada* — and, in a comic mode debunking of the theme, makes an aspiring writer realize he has no talent and that he might as well remain a bookstore clerk, in *The Owl and the Pussycat* (USA, 1970).

While it is her sensual allure that normally attracts the male protagonist to the woman who is to become his lover, there is often a significant insistence on the absence of sexual relations, at the start, between the couple. In *Ladies of Leisure*, for instance, Kay spends the night at Jerry's studio, but it is made very clear that she sleeps on the sofa while he remains in his bedroom. It is a Love Story convention, normally observed, that the two cannot have sex while she is sleeping with other men, or while the memory of her clients is still fresh. The obligatory period of abstinence is to mark a distinct break between the prostitute and the wife-to-be, to make sure that there can be no confusion between the disreputable woman of the past and the respectable woman of the future. Of course, this period should not be too prolonged: in *Chinese Box* (France/ Japan/USA, 1997), set in Hong Kong, the British journalist's love for the Chinese prostitute (Gong Li) he has never slept with becomes a debilitating and doomed obsession.

Complementing the comparative chasteness of the relationship there is likely to be a breakfast scene or its equivalent, signaling the wild woman's willingness to be domesticated and presaging a future of conventional connubial routine. The heroine fixes her lover fried eggs, in *Ladies of Leisure;* scrambled eggs, in *Night Shift* (USA, 1982); orange juice, in *Risky Business* (USA, 1983).

The relationship, nonetheless, is bound to be rocky. Frequently this entails the male protagonist's coming to terms with his lover's (former) existence as a whore and adjusting to the notion of marrying her, something that is especially difficult for the man of some social standing. For the woman, the propensity of her potential savior to keep thinking of her as a creature of the gutter is ineluctably galling. What is more, as in *La Dame aux camélias*, she may be prevailed upon to relinquish her lover for the sake of his family and career, or she may let him go on her own initiative, in a spirit of self-sacrifice. Conflicts ensue, and sometimes tragic outcomes — the heroine commits suicide in *Go Naked in the World*.

But in the usual happy ending, man of substance and woman of the streets are united in triumphant defiance of an old-fashioned caste-system morality that would keep them apart. She has found a way of escaping her oppressive past; he has overcome the psychological handicap that has prevented him living life to the full. They will head together to a new horizon, be it Buenos Aires (*Outcast*), Arizona (*Ladies of Leisure*), or Princeton University (*Risky Business*); on a liner bound for Paris (*Penthouse*) or aboard a yacht in tropical seas (*Trading Places*). Or they might just decide to stay on the rundown farm in Lolland together, rejecting the city that has unhappy associations for both of them (*Mifune*).

The conventions of the class-contrast Love Story are fully, and self-consciously, embodied in *Pretty Woman* (USA, 1990), a film that provides an excellent example of the mechanisms at work. Set in the western precincts of Los Angeles, *Pretty Woman* casts its class differences in terms of a geographical opposition between the heights of Beverly Hills and the flat stretches of downtown Hollywood, a symbolic divide between wealth and poverty, power and powerlessness, glitz and sleaze. It makes the dream of the Hollywood Boulevard hooker (Julia Roberts) come true in transporting her to the penthouse suite of the Regent Beverly Wilshire Hotel. One moment scratching to find the unpaid rent on her modest lodgings, the next she is earning $3,000 for a week keeping company with a fabulously wealthy and highly attractive businessman (Richard Gere). The vulgarity of Vivian's hooker's outfit is out of place alongside the refinement of Ed's stylish dark suits — and yet appropriately the prostitute's flesh-revealing halter top and mini is the marker of a person who is upfront and honest, her motives blatantly commercial, while Ed, conservatively dressed, goes in for underhand dealing in his bid to take over a ship-building company. Class distinctions are further pushed in the disparity between Ed's penchant for high art (*La Traviata*) and Vivian's love of popular culture (*I Love Lucy* reruns).

The oppositions are stark but beneath them lies a fundamental commonality. "You and I are such similar creatures, Vivian," Ed tells her. "We both screw people for money." Coming after a discussion in which they agree about not getting emotional in their line of work ("When I'm with a guy I'm like a robot," says Vivian), the line posits prostitution as a metaphor for the general corruption of human values in a money-driven society. The Beverly Hills/Hollywood Boulevard class rift simply distinguishes those who sell their souls from those who sell their bodies. Despite his money, Ed is alienated and unfulfilled, emotionally starved. Despite her poverty and her profession, Vivian has human qualities that Ed, out of touch with ordinary Americans, lacks.

Striking a populist chord, *Pretty Woman* thus suggests that US capitalism has produced an obscene inequity of income and power between the

66. *Pretty Woman:* Vivian (Julia Roberts) and Ed (Richard Gere).

elite and the masses, and that the engine of material prosperity has delivered a spiritual vacuum. In this bipartite schema, the rich are condemned to an artificial, predatory existence in the business world, and the poor to prostitution, with its related drug addiction and violence.

It is in crossing the boundary between these two equally deracinated worlds that redemption is — or may be — possible. Ed gets lost and strays into downtown Hollywood; Vivian shows him the way back to Beverly Hills and is invited to stay. Their interaction is positive: Ed becomes aware of the destructive nature of his asset-stripping corporate raiding and drops the original objectives of his takeover bid, choosing to save the failing ship-building company and keep it intact rather than dismember it; Vivian, having broken her rules and kissed a client on the mouth, has tasted love and can no longer go through with its simulacrum. And then there is, of course, the fairy-tale ending: the knight on his white charger (white limo, in this case) comes to rescue the princess, and she, as Vivian confidently asserts, "rescues him right back." With a reciprocity that is more of a subtext in the traditional version, the princess-prostitute redeems her savior from his alienation, and while she quits the streets and goes back to school (no immediate slide into domesticity for her), he will henceforth no doubt become a founding member of Businesses for Social Responsibility. This is a feminist-inflected postmodern *Pygmalion* in which the patriarchal possessive has been dropped: *Pretty Woman* not *My Fair Lady*.

By scandalous border-crossing, then, by uniting the Wall Street magnate and the streetwalker, the failure of American society to deliver equity and emotional fulfillment can be overcome. Possibly. Lest *Pretty Woman* lose its credibility with the more skeptical among us, it tacks on a self-referential ending sardonically commenting on the movie industry's manufacture of romance. As the couple kiss on the fire escape of Vivian's downscale hotel, a black passerby calls out: "Welcome to Hollywood! What's your dream? Everybody comes here. This is Hollywood, land of dreams. Some dreams come true, some don't. But keep on dreamin'!"

The proletarian Love Story does not have an equivalent obstacle of social disparity to surmount. Here there is no societal taboo to contend with, and although the male protagonist may occasionally, like his higher-class analogue, have difficulty accepting the notion of a prostitute for his wife, it is more often only his macho reluctance to be tied down — coupled with outside forces — that impedes the flourishing of the romance. Generally there is an oppressive situation to contend with, and

67. *Red Dust:* Jean Harlow (right) as Vantine, with Mary Astor as Barbara.

whether the emphasis falls more heavily on his problems or on hers, the fact that the two constitute a natural couple practically guarantees that they will make a good fighting partnership and find refuge in each other's arms.

The male lead's working-class background is communicated first and foremost by the connotations of the star who plays the role — typically the kind of stocky, muscular, roughneck figure epitomized by a George Bancroft or James Cagney, Burt Reynolds or Bob Hoskins. At times such connotations overwhelm the actual class status of the character being portrayed, as with Clark Gable's rough-and-ready rubber-plantation manager in *Red Dust* (USA, 1932), who is clearly marked as lower-class — and as such an appropriate partner for Jean Harlow's Saigon prostitute — in contrast to the refined, educated survey engineer who works for him.

If this character has problems beyond those of staying alive in a dangerous environment, they are typically emotional or psychological in nature. Dennis Carson in *Red Dust* is, at the beginning of the film, a bad-tempered slave-driver of his coolie labor: something is obviously eating him. Percy in *Rattle of a Simple Man* (UK, 1964) is a mother's boy, a thirty-nine-year-old virginal bachelor. In *Hot Boarding House* (USA, 1970), "an emotionally troubled man suffers from nightmares in which his sexual encounters culminate in murder."[7] Tony Church of *Rent-a-Cop* (USA, 1988) is emotionally scarred after being fired from the police force when a drug raid goes wrong. Deep-rooted difficulties may include being an alcoholic, as, for example, in *Driftwood* (USA, 1928) or *8 Million Ways to Die* (USA, 1986); a drug addict, as in *Man With the Golden Arm* (USA, 1955); or the sufferer of a psychiatric disability, as in *The Million Dollar Hotel* (Germany/USA/UK, 2000).

The female lead's problems, on the other hand, nearly always relate to her situation as a prostitute and the desperate straits that led to her taking up the profession: poverty, sexual abuse, abandonment, personal tragedy of one sort or another. In this respect she differs little from the love objects of the class-contrast movies, though she may be more matter-of-fact about her calling. She puts a brave face on things, may be brazen or bitter, wise-cracking or scathing, but in unguarded moments will admit to loneliness, unhappiness, failure to cope. Maggie (Barbro Kollberg) of Ingmar Bergman's *Det regnar på vår kärlek/It Rains on Our Love* (Sweden, 1946), giving up aspirations to be an actress, heads out of town alone and pregnant, not knowing who the father is; another Maggie (Marsha Mason), in *Cinderella Liberty* (USA, 1973), hustles sailors at a Seattle red-light bar, is single mother to an eleven-year-old boy who is running wild, and is pregnant again. Tired of the life, the hooker may well harbor dreams of marriage and thus become impatient with admirers who fail to pop the question, like Corrie in *The Reivers* (USA, 1969); here, her friend Boon responds, "All I want to do is just spend a dollar and have some fun — any crime in that?" Dallas in *Stagecoach* (USA, 1986) admits that she "finally realized once and for all no one was going to find a million-dollar dream in a two-dollar room."

The man who teams up with a prostitute sweetheart is very frequently an ordinary worker, particularly one who is footloose or who has a nomadic job such as a prospector or seaman. Alternatively, he may be on the wrong side of the law as a criminal, gangster, deserter, prison escapee, or ex-convict. In contrast, he may be a cop — but if so, he is likely to be on the outs with his department, a loner with his own conception of justice.

As worker, the male protagonist may be miner (*Il cammino della speranza*, Italy, 1950) or carpenter (*Casque d'Or*, France, 1952); bus conductor (*Turn the Key Softly*, UK, 1953) or railroad worker (*Tragovi crne devojke*, Yugoslavia, 1972); bath attendant (*L'Acrobate*, France, 1975) or cleaner (*Stormy Monday*, UK/USA, 1988); taxi driver (*Virtue*, USA, 1932), truck driver (*Thieves' Highway*, USA, 1949), or pedicab driver (*Qun long hu feng*, Hong Kong, 1989). But it is frequently the stories set on the waterfront, when he is a longshoreman or seaman, that carry the most conviction. There is typically a poetic realism (associated with location filming) in the depiction of the milieu of docks and bars where sad whores hustle sex-hungry seafarers, which helps anchor the melodrama in a solid, authentic setting. Moreover, the development of affectionate relationships between prostitutes and sailors, rare with other classes of clients, has a basis in sociological fact.[8]

This strand of the proletarian love story is well exemplified by films such as the New York-based *Anna Christie*, in its silent and sound versions (USA, 1923, 1930)[9] and *The Docks of New York* (USA, 1928); *Razzia in St. Pauli* (Germany, 1932), for which the Hamburg port area is the locale; and *Dédée d'Anvers* (France, 1948), set in Antwerp. As in other versions of the prostitute romance, the American movies, with their customary happy endings, tend to celebrate the triumph of love over adversity, while the European films are bathed in a pessimistic pathos.

In *Anna Christie*, for example, the love of seaman Matt Burke (after he has overcome his revulsion) offers the potential of delivering Anna from the bitter world-weariness and hatred of men that she has acquired following an abusive childhood and two years in a St. Paul whorehouse; in Josef von Sternberg's *The Docks of New York*, stoker Bill Roberts's rescue of waterfront floozy Sadie[10] from a suicide attempt is the prelude to an edgy one-night stand that incorporates a mock marriage ("Why get serious about it, anyway?") but ends with the prospect of the real thing. On the other hand, in *Razzia in St. Pauli*, Ballhaus-Else falls head over heels in love with Matrosen-Karl, the boisterous sailor who breaks into her room while on the run from the police for a burglary, but their relationship scarcely has a moment to flourish before Karl is arrested and Else returns to her deadening nightly routine — an outcome that strongly recalls that of *Jenseits der Strasse* (1929), discussed in chapter 5. Similarly in *Dédée*, the star attraction at the Big Moon nightclub sees a hope of escaping the thralldom of prostitution when she falls in love with an Italian sailor, Francesco, but her sadistic pimp destroys her dreams by gunning him down. Although Dédée exacts her revenge, she cannot liberate herself from the profession in which she is trapped.

An equivalent empathy for characters down on their luck is appealed to in the films in which the hero is on the wrong side of the law. If he is a loner, sympathy for his plight is generated by the oppressive weight of the societal forces bearing down on him, and is often heightened by the fact that he is innocent of the crime of which he is accused. Forming a relationship with a prostitute affords him the solace and nurturing he is desperately in need of, while she as a fellow social outcast discovers a warmth lacking in her other interactions with men.

Thus in *The Red Lily* (USA, 1924), the lovers are a couple from a French provincial town now adrift in Paris, she a streetwalker, he a thief; in *Wild Oats Lane* (USA, 1926) they are a young woman reduced to prostitution in Manhattan and a criminal recently discharged from Sing Sing, now with a drug problem. Similarly, in *He Was Her Man* (USA, 1934), a former prostitute falls in love with an ex-convict intent on gaining revenge on gangsters who betrayed him; in *Stagecoach* (USA, 1939, 1966, 1986), a whore being driven out of town teams up with an outlaw on the run; in *Strange Cargo* (USA, 1940), a tough chanteuse finds herself hooking up in the jungle with a bunch of escapees from a French penal colony and becoming romantically involved with one of them; and in *It Rains on Our Love*, Maggie becomes the partner of a recently released prisoner trying to go straight. The examples could be multiplied, with the pattern retaining its popularity up to the present day.[11]

The marginalization of the outsiders who discover affection for each other in films of this nature hovers between the two poles of social victimization and psychological alienation. The former is highlighted in *Senza pietà* (Italy, 1948). In the port of Livorno, corruption and racketeering are rife in the aftermath of World War II. A young woman, Angela (Carla del Poggio), who has been disowned by her family after having an illegitimate child, is pressured by gangsters into prostitution; meanwhile a black GI, Jerry (John Kitzmiller), who has encountered racism and been injured in a desertion attempt, escapes from a military compound. The couple fall in love and plan to get away to America. However, their scheme gets them entangled in the criminal activities of the underworld; Angela is shot, and Jerry drives over a cliff with her body.

Miami Blues (USA, 1990), in contrast, illustrates the pole of mental disturbance. Like other nihilist American movies of its period — see also, for example, *True Romance* (1994) — it yokes brutality and humor in an unsettling way in its tale of a relationship between Junior (Alec Baldwin), a kooky psychopathic killer, and Susie (Jennifer Jason Leigh), an introverted part-time hooker working her way through college. Susie is of course the soothing balm, the oasis in the desert, for this violent lost loner; but perhaps reflecting an influx of European pessimism, she has no psychological effect on him: he carries on with his murderous ways. They talk of her quitting the life, him quitting crime, but as in *Senza pietà* it doesn't happen, and Junior is killed resisting arrest. We are a long way from the sentimental happy ending of a silent movie like *The Red Lily*, in which the thief, having done his time in jail, and the streetwalker, having reformed, leave the corrupting influences of the city behind and return together to the country.

As a final group in the proletarian Love Story category, we may consider those films in which the male protagonist is on the side of the law, as a policeman, private detective, or secret service agent. The titles include *The Treasure of San Teresa/Rhapsodei in Blei* (UK/West Germany, 1959), *Irma La Douce* (USA, 1963), *Sylvia* (USA, 1965), *Klute* (USA, 1971), *Hustle* (USA, 1975), *The Gauntlet* (USA, 1977), *Clean-Up Squad/Chiens chauds* (Canada, 1980), *Sharky's Machine* (USA, 1981), *The Best Little Whorehouse in Texas* (USA, 1982), *The Red-Light Sting* (USA, 1984), *8 Million Ways to Die* (USA, 1986), *PrettyKill* (USA, 1987), *Rent-a-Cop* (USA, 1988), and *Heart Condition* (USA, 1990).

Accepting that the conjunction of policeman (particularly) and prostitute is immediately useful for creating dramatic conflict—something that *Irma La Douce* plays on to strong comic effect—there are a number of reasons why the pair are paradoxically so well suited to each other, prime contenders for the coupling routine.

They are both, for a start, disabused and cynical (if we leave *Irma La Douce*'s idealistic Nestor Patou out of the reckoning for the moment). They've been around and they know human nature inside out, and they're not greatly impressed. They live on the margins of respectable society, and mix in with a brutal criminal subculture whose values brush off on them. Typically, the cop hasn't found the woman of his dreams, and the prostitute hasn't found the man; just because they don't believe in love any more, they're ripe for each other.

The happily married family-man cop has too much stake in society to take chances (or his partner won't let him). The hero is the loner, and either his dedication to work or his addiction to liquor (often both) make ordinary girlfriend relationships impossible for him. Suffering, besides, from a bad case of macho, he is not noted for his sensitivity toward women. Only the prostitute, equally marginalized, can relate to him; used to abuse, verbal and physical, she can handle him, can see through the hard exterior to the suffering soul inside.

Then again the prostitute is physically tough, unlike other women. Hence she can truly team up with the cop in his escapades. There is a scene in *The Gauntlet* in which Gus (Sondra Locke) and Ben (Clint East-wood) jointly deal with a bunch of nasty bikers on a train: Gus uses both strength and seductive guile, luring the bad guys off Ben by baring her breasts and daring them to show what they've got between their legs. In *Rent-a-Cop,* Della (Liza Minelli) and Tony (Burt Reynolds) outwit and outdrive their corrupt police adversaries, and Della kills the mob hit man and saves Tony's life.

Finally, in some of these movies (*The Gauntlet, 8 Million Ways to Die*) the cop's in the gutter, a drunk; and so a hooker, who's also at the bottom of the social scale, is an appropriate partner for him. Of course, he's not really a bum, he's kept his integrity intact, just as she's not really a pros-titute, not at heart (Gus even has a college degree to prove it). They can, therefore, haul themselves out of the muck together. Reciprocity again rules: the policeman is saved from his self-destructiveness by the nurtur-ing ministrations of the hooker, who is in the process herself rescued from her less than salubrious life and transformed into blissful housewife.

At the core of many a prostitute love story is a regressive male fantasy of instant attraction and total devotion. She is the supercharged erotic beauty who concentrates all her energies and affections on the one lucky man who is at the center of the narrative, who reconciles through the unfolding of the plot the desirability of the sexually available woman with the fidelity of the wife-to-be. In *Stormy Monday,* for instance, Kate (Melanie Griffith) is a gorgeous hooker who, in an early image, displays her legs up to the crotch, and later wears a low-cut top to show off her ample breasts; she stumbles on down-and-out Brendan in the street—he's getting a job as a cleaner—and within hours is madly in love with him. Likewise in *True Romance,* nerdy bookstore assistant Clarence is as-sailed in a movie theater by a kooky young blonde (Patricia Arquette) re-vealing lots of boob, and shortly afterward they are in his pad having sex. She confesses the next day she's a call girl who'd been hired by his boss as a birthday treat for him—but she's never had as much fun in her life as last night, and she's fallen in love.

This beautiful woman, overflowing with libido, is accepting of the protagonist whatever his limitations. In *Gros Câlin* (France, 1979) a lonely unemployed man in his fifties with a pet python falls in love with a stun-ning black hooker (Véronique Mucret) thirty years his junior, and mir-acle of miracles, the feeling is reciprocated. Shortly before the end she leaves him, citing her need for company, but finally the power of love proves too strong. Similarly Doc of *Cannery Row* (USA, 1982) is a deadbeat marine biologist whose squalid way of life attractive young prostitute Suzy (Debra Winger) pours scorn on, but this does not prevent love between them springing up and flourishing.

The prostitute, in such stories, has no complicating ties to a past life (family responsibilities, for instance) that might interfere with her total commitment to her lover—unless it is enslavement to an underworld pimp, something which her new possessor can easily overcome *(8 Million Ways to Die, Stormy Monday, True Romance)*. Her background is generally kept vague, and even though she's been around, she's not psychologically damaged or hardened.

In fictions of this nature, the love story is sketchy: the principals need go through no stages of getting to know each other and building a relationship. The prostitute is a love object whose devotion does not have to be won (by means of actually communicating with her) but is simply gifted—or, as in *8 Million Ways to Die,* bought. In that film, ownership of Sarah (Rosanna Arquette) is traded by sacked cop Matt (Jeff Bridges) in a dangerous drug transaction with her pimp-boyfriend Angel. The woman who sells sex as a commodity becomes herself commodified, harking back to the white slave films in which the prostitute is traded as a going concern. Neatly avoiding the difficulty of having to work through with his wife the marital problems caused by his alcoholism, the script offers Matt another woman instead: Sarah, whose availability to the man with cunning and daring enough to wrest her from her current keeper is a dream come true. Being "owned" by Matt, she idolizes him. She can make no demands, as a wife might, and is totally his, body and soul. Her desires, of course, do not come into it. The only choice Sarah has is to renounce tainted luxury—Angel lives in a Gaudí-designed house, a pinnacle of decadence—and endorse Matt's choice of her, and the film sets it up so that we're not supposed to imagine her wanting anything else. Unlike Matt's wife, Sarah *understands* his drinking problem (her father is an alcoholic, and she has a problem herself) and is able to prevent his relapse by the love she proffers as a substitute for booze.

Many prostitute love stories indulge their dream romance only so far, before cutting it short in an unhappy ending. A handful resist both easy pleasure and unearned pathos, in grappling with the representation of a relationship that might believably take place between a sex worker and a male lover in real life.

John Cassavetes' *Faces* (USA, 1968) presents us with the image of a beguiling, nurturing call girl (Gena Rowlands) who turns out to have a life of her own which she's not about to bestow on our hero. For Richard (John Marley), unlike Matt of *8 Million Ways to Die*, there is no magical escape: he must go home and face again the truth of a disintegrating marriage.

Unusually, *Hustle* (directed by Robert Aldrich) forces its policeman protagonist (Burt Reynolds) to confront the day-to-day implications of living with a woman who is an active hooker. Recently unhappily divorced, Phil is clearly emotionally reliant on the company of Nicole (Catherine Deneuve), with whom he has made an arrangement: "I do what I do and you do what you do." But the strain is evident from the start, when he tells her he was planning to take her to a football match: "Have you wear those tight white pants and . . . that sexy blouse . . . watch all those guys looking at you, say to myself, 'She's for sale.'" Overhearing her erotic phone calls to clients, enduring the jibes of his colleagues at work ("I think I'll have Vice bust her on Christmas Eve — yeah, I'll put her in with all the penned-up bull dykes"), starting in his mind to "draw dirty pictures" about what she does, he finally snaps. They fight, make love, acknowledge their affection for each other, but cannot sort out their differences. She will not quit working until he agrees to marry her, which he is not yet ready to do.

Tellingly, Nicole points out that Phil broke up with his wife because he found her in bed with another man. "I'm a whore, so it's all right," she remarks, "but she's your wife, so it's not all right." The conflicted emotions that their relationship generates are not easily resolved; they continue to simmer until Phil, at the end, is killed in the line of duty.

In Werner Herzog's *Stroszek* (West Germany, 1977), Bruno (played by Bruno S.) is the "moron," just released from prison, whom Eva (Eva Mattes) clings to in attempting to get away from her violent pimps. Gentle and passive, Bruno is no help whatever when the bad guys beat her up and wreck their apartment. But he provides companionship; together (along with an old man, Scheitz) they quit Berlin and make it to the United States, the trip financed by Eva's turning tricks with immigrant workers. In Wisconsin they purchase a mobile home, but Eva's wages as a waitress and Bruno's as a mechanic are insufficient to keep up the payments; she returns to hooking. There is a sad dialogue exchange when Eva tells him not to be bitter. "You don't want me to be bitter?" he replies. "When somebody despises me? When I'm grown up enough, to need to be loved? When I get shut out of the bedroom, and can't sleep with you any more, and have to sleep by myself in another room, like in a cage?" She enfolds him in her arms, like a big lost child; but shortly af-

68. Simone (Cathy Tyson) in *Mona Lisa.*

terwards, the situation unviable, she sends Bruno packing and knuckles down to the job in the cab of a truck heading for Vancouver.

The story is of a search for freedom, escape from captivity, a journey from the Old World to the New; and a discovery that freedom proves illusory. Eva gets beyond the reach of her pimps; but is the sacrifice of human warmth, of her love for Bruno, worth it? In the United States, alienation and the values of the marketplace prevail. *Stroszek* is a tart antidote to the saccharine Love Story.

Finally, it is worth considering *Mona Lisa* (UK, 1986), directed by Neil Jordan. Just out of jail, George (Bob Hoskins) is hired by his gangster contacts to chauffeur Simone (Cathy Tyson) to assignations with her high-class clientele. They're an odd couple, social outcasts, working-class crim and black whore. He falls in love; will she? Simone tells him she has a friend, a teenage hooker on drugs, under the thumb of her old pimp. There are sadists who like young girls, she says, find her for me. George, the patsy, finds her, retrieves her. In the operation Simone uses a pistol to lethal effect, almost adding George to her casualty list. And then he discovers she's in love all right—with the girl they've rescued.

Here the prostitute is a figure of mystery, a dark continent (the black woman), the enigma and threat of female sexuality. Mona Lisa, how deceptive that smile. Simone is to be demystified, slapped around a bit till the truth comes out, and what is the truth? That her interest in Cathy is as object of her lust. The phallic woman, possessor of the gun, is not victim of a cruel male underworld but aggressor, destroyer, definer of her own desires which don't include men. The slim and angular hooker, frizzy hair teased out at the back, sequined outfits glistening in the moonlight, swivels from dream to nightmare in the masculine imagination. The portrait is drenched in disillusionment, but it has more claim on a sociological authenticity than the starry-eyed romantic image more typical of the Love Story.

Klute was praised by feminist critics at the time of its release for its incorporation, within a prostitute love story, of a female point of view. Michelle Citron, for example, wrote: "What made *Klute* a good film was not only its intellectual precision, but that it was the first film that made me cry in five years. I understood what it was in Bree Daniels' socialization that made her confront the present existence of the other two call girls as her own possible future. I recognized similar elements of our common socialization." For Citron, Bree was "not a stereotype, but a person shaped by real forces."[12] Similarly Diane Giddis, contending that the film was told from the "highly subjective viewpoint" of Bree Daniels, argued that "in her tormented journey she succeeds in embodying one of the greatest of contemporary female concerns: the conflict between the claims of love and the claims of autonomy."[13]

Much attention was focused on Jane Fonda's performance (including the celebrated moment in which she glances at her watch while faking orgasm with a client), and on the scenes, improvised by Fonda, in which Bree discusses her life with her psychiatrist.[14] In one of these, Bree talks of how, for example, in having sex with Klute, she has feelings that are new to her: "I feel different. My body feels different. I enjoy making love with him. Baffling. All the time, I keep feeling the need to destroy it, to go back to the comfort of being numb again. It's a new thing, it's so strange."

This expression of female subjectivity was nevertheless contained within a conventional patriarchal structure, as other feminist critics subsequently pointed out.[15] The prostitute love story told unequivocally from the point of view of the female protagonist is very rare, but it is appropriate to conclude this chapter with a discussion of one such film, Dagmar Beiersdorf's *Dirty Daughters — Die Hure und der Hurensohn* (West Germany, 1981).

69. Betty (Lothar Lambert) and Rita (Dagmar Beiersdorf) in *Dirty Daughters —
Die Hure und der Hurensohn*. Dagmar Beiersdorf.

A low-budget Berlin underground production, *Dirty Daughters* features Beiersdorf herself as Rita, a streetwalker who forms a relationship
with Hossein (Mustafa Iskandarani), a Lebanese émigré unable to find
employment in Germany as he does not have a work permit. The film is
notable, for a start, for the rigor with which the relationship is stripped
of all glamour. On their first night together, Hossein collapses drunk on
Rita, and then gets up and spews: Rita comments in voice-over that the
only reason she let him stay was that he was so drunk he wouldn't have
been able to find his way home. Though, later, they enjoy tender moments together, when they have sex only pain and resignation can be
read in Rita's face. And he is violent: when he catches her in a lie, he
beats her with his belt and then forces her to suck him off.

Rita's background and daily life are much more fully described than
would be the case in a male-fantasy film. She tells, in extensive voice-
over, of her childhood as the daughter of a prostitute, culminating in a
suicide attempt at the age of eighteen. She relates what the experience of
prostitution means to her ("I've really only known men since I've been a
prostitute. They do with us what they want. All the things they don't dare
to do at home with their wives, they practice on us. For them we're not
human beings.") There are scenes of Rita with her own daughter, who is
in a children's home; with her close friend Betty, a flamboyant transvestite; and with clients, one of whom rapes her.

The customary rescue dynamic is inverted: it is her lifting *him* out of
a miserable situation, not vice versa. The power resides with Rita — she
has the sporty car, the nice apartment. But when Hossein insists on her
quitting sex work, financial problems set in; he has no income, cannot get
the papers he needs to be legally employed, and is a failure in an attempt
to be a male prostitute. Their talk of marriage comes to nothing; Rita
goes back to the streets, while Hossein is arrested on an assault charge
and deported.

Beiersdorf made the film, she says, "because it annoyed me that those
two broke up. They needed each other more than virtually any other
couple — in fact you can equate loving and needing." Rita was based on
a woman she knew. "Can you imagine what it means for a prostitute to
find a partner who loves her, who stays with her?"[16] *Dirty Daughters* asks
the question that haunts all the Love Story films, slanted as they are
towards the male perspective, and answers it with a rare conviction.

18

Prostitute and Pimp

The same sort of devotion and self-sacrifice is often poured out upon the miserable man who in the beginning was responsible for the girl's entrance into the life and who constantly receives her earnings. She supports him in the luxurious life he may be living in another part of the town, takes an almost maternal pride in his good clothes and general prosperity, and regards him as the one person in all the world who understands her plight.

—JANE ADDAMS, *A New Conscience and an Ancient Evil* (1913)[1]

I just can't get it into my head how a bitch can walk the street every night, I mean even in the rain, you know, and take a chance on maybe gettin' robbed or sent to jail, or maybe even gettin' her arm broke by some sadistic fool out of the suburbs, right? And then she gets all that money and then she takes it and gives it to some dude. I mean I just can't figure that shit out.

—pimp in *The Mack* (USA, 1973)

Madeleine Bastille (France, 1946) is an amateur film (8mm), silent, only seven minutes long. While an elegant Parisienne sits at a cafe terrace and window-shops in the chic Place de la Madeleine, a *souteneur* drinks in a small working-class dance-hall in the Bastille district and then goes on the prowl. Shortly the man introduces himself to the woman and they start a conversation. They stroll together, and he puts on the charm. They enter a bar. There is a pan to a sign reading Hôtel. Next we see the same woman standing against the wall of a building with rooms to rent, cigarette in her mouth, importuning a man who passes. The film ends on the pimp sitting down at a cafe table, eyeing approvingly another woman walking by.

This miniature drama reprises in highly compressed, abbreviated form the archetypal narrative of the woman lured into prostitution by an attractive pimp. It is a tale told over and over in the cinema, beginning as far back as *The Downward Path* (1900), if not earlier. Without access to this archetype, audiences would find the film incomprehensible — as it is, the ease with which the pimp picks up the fashionable woman, and the speed with which she is transformed into a street whore, seem implausible.

But even when it is filled out at great length, there is always a knot at the center of the prostitute and pimp narrative that defies understanding, and it is this that accounts for its perennial fascination. This is to do with the psychological hold that the pimp has over his female partner, even if he inflicts violence on her. That a spirited woman can be suckered into going on the street to prove her love for the man who's so clearly exploiting her; that she should hand over all her earnings to this person who treats her despicably; that she will not seize the opportunity to escape his power when her misery becomes acute; that, above all, she can respond to his brutality with expressions of devotion; all this, to the outside onlooker, beggars belief.

Paradoxically, however, this tale rings true in a way that so many prostitute love stories, discussed in the previous chapter, do not. There is a weight of sociological evidence demonstrating the widespread, inveterate existence of codependent prostitute-pimp relationships of this kind.[2] Thus the Chicago vice commission, reporting on prostitution in the city in 1911, described the role of the "cadet" (as the pimp was then known) in these terms: "The cadet is the go-between, he is the agent through whom business is directed toward his own women, or the house in which she works. He looks after her when apprehended by the law, and either uses some political influence in her behalf, or sees after her fine or bail. In many cases, he is the lover or 'sweetheart,' and by some power so attaches his girl to himself that she will never betray him no matter if he has beaten and abused her. This strange paradox often prevents justice being meted out to this outcast of society, for in many cases he can be convicted only on her testimony."[3]

Likewise researchers Cecilie Høigård and Liv Finstad, examining Norwegian police documents for the 1960s to the 1980s, discovered endemic violence in a large number of prostitute-pimp relationships, tied to the woman's occupation and the man's dependence on her money: "The woman relates that her husband/partner threatens or beats her to get her out on the street to earn money, or to get her earnings when she comes home from the street. Police investigations uncovered instances of brutal and grotesque acts of violence: beating, kicking, wounds inflicted with a knife or broken glass, broken noses, and internal bleeding have been reported. One of the women was dangled from the balcony of a tenth-floor apartment by her husband, who threatened to drop her if she wouldn't go out on the street. Another woman's husband ran into her with a car. The man typically becomes increasingly violent if she threatens to leave him. In most instances it is the woman who reports her violent boyfriend. Most of them later withdraw the complaint. . . ."[4]

If it were merely a question of violence and intimidation, the phenomenon would be more readily understandable. The pimp is simply a vicious criminal who must be dealt with, by legal means or otherwise. This is the angle taken in films such as *Les Filles de Grenoble* (France, 1981), discussed in chapter 10, which depict prostitution as an underworld racket.

But it is more than this. "The relationship between the woman and the pimp is far too complex to be reduced to a question of physical force," contend Høigård and Finstad. The couple are "intertwined as sweethearts, lovers, enemies and friends, supporters and adversaries, close to each other through the shifting emotions and their shifting roles. For him, she is not just a whore. For her, he is anything but a pimp." Høigård and Finstad go on to argue that "physical coercion often plays a completely subordinate role. . . . *The pimp's foundation of power rests solely on the fact that she feels that she needs him.*"[5]

This perception of need may derive from the practical services that the pimp provides, such as that of a bodyguard or, in jurisdictions where the prostitute is subject to arrest, protection from the law. But it may also be emotional. "Outside, a world that looks at her with contempt; outside, a world that treats her as a hole surrounded by flesh; outside, a world that has caused her pain and defeat — is it so strange, in this freezing cold, that love warms?"[6] If this love often appears sadomasochistic in nature, it is likely that it is related to what has recently been labeled battered-woman syndrome, and that it has its origins in childhood physical and sexual abuse, of which there is a high incidence among prostitutes.[7]

In using the term "sadomasochistic," I am not suggesting that the prostitute derives physical pleasure from the beatings she receives. Rather, I am deploying the expression more in Erich Fromm's understanding of it: "The sadistic person is as dependent on the submissive person as the latter is on the former; neither can live without the other. The difference is only that the sadistic person commands, exploits, hurts, humiliates, and that the masochistic person is commanded, exploited, hurt, humiliated."[8]

Gail Sheehy, investigating New York prostitution, concluded that most of her subjects were searching for a strong father figure: "By choosing the biggest, baddest, most brutish and dictatorial man they can find — the pimp — they are assured of remaining helpless little girls." She recounts: "To Valerie (as to most street girls), the pimp is still sacred, a superbeing created in her own desperate brain in whom she is investing all hopes, dreams and goals for the future. She wears his beatings proudly as symbols of affection. He is the father-substitute; he disciplines, he cares. She submits gladly to his sadistic lovemaking. The pimp as lover takes her money, tricks her, gives her raw sex but denies her an ounce of emotion, and drops her ten minutes later for another woman — exactly reversing the sadomasochistic process she must play with her own tricks."[9]

On the other hand, there is the nonviolent boyfriend-pimp: the man who may not be planning to entrap the woman when he meets her, may be genuinely in love with her, may support himself to some extent financially, and may have a relationship only with her. Though not as numerous as those conforming more to the violent pimp stereotype, Høigård and Finstad discovered that pimps displaying one or more of these characteristics did indeed exist, but were seldom acknowledged in discourses about prostitution.[10]

Prostitute and pimp stories in the cinema draw on this factual background to create fictions of highly charged emotional drama. Predominantly, continuing traditions established in the silent era with the fallen woman and white slave films, they retell the archetypal tale of seduction, betrayal, and exploitation — followed perhaps by escape and vengeance. But sometimes, often in interesting ways, they depart from this mold, depicting pimps who are closer to the nonviolent boyfriend model. The small sample of films selected for discussion in this chapter are representative of both tendencies.

Telling its story from the point of view of the pimp, *Der Mädchenhirt* (Germany, 1919) works an important variation on the evil seducer/ innocent victim pattern. As I have argued earlier, within patriarchal ideology the pimp is the convenient scapegoat figure on to whom all male guilt for the existence of prostitution is displaced. He is thus typically demonized, and movies in which he is a sympathetic figure are the exception. Hence a film like *Der Mädchenhirt*, which places at its center a seventeen-year-old "herdsman of girls" who is the product of a difficult upbringing and who eventually repents of his calling, is particularly interesting.

Though there is considerable allusion to a downward path — "The first step toward ruin," "And so Jarda slides still deeper" — here it is the soul of the male protagonist rather than the fallen woman that is at stake. And in a significant gender switch, it is Jarda's girlfriend who promotes the idea that she go on the game (so that she can buy him a fashionable cane and patent-leather shoes). Jarda only half-heartedly assents, and when Betka (Lo Bergner) carries through with an assignation, his "better self" comes to the fore and he unsuccessfully tries to prevent it. He becomes distraught, overcome with revulsion and jealousy.

Jarda is nonetheless corrupted. While becoming involved in an affair with a singer at a nightclub, he offers up Betka for the lascivious entertainment of his male friends there. (A title states that "he now gives away the girl — for whom several months earlier he would have shed his heart's blood — out of vanity, to prove his power over women.") Meanwhile, he is instrumental in introducing another young woman, Luise (Roma Bahn), to the business. The two prostitutes under Jarda's wing offer a simple contrast: Betka, who slips into the sex trade out of peer pressure and for the easy money, and Luise, who takes on the work reluctantly since her family is on the verge of starvation.

Following the film's moral patterning, it is appropriately Betka who abandons Jarda after his arrest for theft and confinement to a VD hospital, while Luise takes him in hand. They fall in love, and on his release, Jarda refuses to allow Luise to continue whoring, thus doing his bit to restore the damaged patriarchal fabric and his own integrity.

There will not be a happy ending, however. Jarda finds himself in conflict with the police inspector Duschnitz, whom he now discovers is his real father, and in a robbery attempt stabs him to death. Unable to bear the guilt, Jarda and his faithful lover wade into the river together.

Never inflicting brutality on his women, and not shown as exploiting them financially, Jarda is clearly the nonviolent-boyfriend type of pimp. His eventual rejection of prostitution as morally wrong reinforces the stance taken overtly by the film — though the merry-making of the happy gang of prostitutes and pimps on Kampainsel, mentioned earlier, is an unassimilated element. Where *Der Mädchenhirt* differs ideologically from the norm is in its assigning responsibility for societal corruption not to the pimp but to the representative of respectable patriarchal authority, his father. Unloving and uncaring, Duschnitz who has refused to openly acknowledge Jarda as his son, who hasn't even laid eyes on him since he was seven years old, is held to blame for the boy's youthful waywardness — and as a doctor declares, Jarda's fate "is that of thousands of illegitimate children whose fathers do not look after them." Based on a novel by left-wing author Egon Erwin Kisch, *Der Mädchenhirt* connects with those films, discussed in chapter 5, which portray the evil of prostitution as endemic to capitalist society.

In Pier Paolo Pasolini's *Accattone* (Italy, 1961), the narrative perspective is again that of the pimp. Sunk in an abyss of self-pity, Vittorio (known as "Accattone") internalizes the shame heaped on men of his type by society at large and embraces a self-willed martyrdom.

Accattone is one of a group of pimps who hang out in a desolate district on the fringes of Rome, layabouts who treat prostitutes with disdain. On learning that the woman who currently works for him, Maddalena (Silvana Corsini), has been hit by a motorcycle, he rushes home, only to berate her coldly for carelessness and then to order her back on the streets, despite her broken leg.

There are indications, however, that in spite of his macho posturing Accattone may not share the values and psychological formation of his peers. He listens despondently to a tale gleefully told by a fellow pimp of how several of them took a streetwalker to a field and hit and kicked her till she cried for mercy. And despite promising to punish Maddalena for her crime in informing on her previous pimp, Ciccio, in Naples, he does not do so, and it is left to members of Ciccio's gang to give her a thrashing.

Maddalena ends up in jail, convicted for making a false accusation as to her attacker. Accattone seeks to replace her with Stella (Franca Pasut), an attractive young blonde he comes across working in a bottle yard. He makes the customary moves—sweet-talking, a show of affection, and, with the help of a friend, presents of a new dress and jewelry. She responds, becoming submissively devoted and, despite her sexual inexperience and shyness, prepared to go whoring for him.

But when Stella finds she can't go through with the act with her first client, a sexton, Accattone's life moves toward a crisis. He does not have it in him to use the necessary force, does not fit the mold of the brutish tyrant. He is too soft, may even have genuinely fallen in love, though there is no visible evidence of desire in his interaction with her.[11] With no cash resources, he is immediately in desperate financial straits. He is a failure as a pimp, and he knows it.

In a partial inversion of the archetypal pimp-prostitute relationship, the suffering—at least as he conceives the situation—is all his: he is a masochist, not a sadist. "You've ruined me, wrecked my life," he complains to Maddalena. "I could have been an honest worker, an honest thief, at least." Likewise in Pasolini's next film, *Mamma Roma,* the

70. *Accattone:* Vittorio (Franco Citti) and Stella (Franca Pasut). bfi Collections.

pimp Carmine—again played by Franco Citti—will accuse his partner in prostitution: "I knew nothing of women like you—you ruined me, you made me a pimp."[12]

At the root of Accattone's affliction is a bad conscience about his occupation, and the humiliation he feels as a result ("Even in jail they despise pimps. . . . We'd be better off stealing than in this stinking racket"). The perspective, of course, is male, and patriarchal to the extent that it devalues the working and living experience of the women. Only one client, the sexton, is shown, and his dumping of Stella is laughingly accepted by the other prostitutes. Resigned to their lot or not (and Maddalena's denunciations to the authorities of a series of pimps, including finally Accattone, are indicative of her rebellion), it is not the women's fate, but Accattone's, that the narrative is concerned with.

Since Accattone's sense of identity is so tied up with being a pimp, when he ceases to be one he is as good as dead. He tries being a manual laborer, but one day of heaving scrap metal is too much for him. Then he gets involved in petty theft, but when stopped by police (who have had him under surveillance since Maddalena's accusation) he makes a run for it, steals a motorcycle, crashes, and is killed. It is a death that has long been anticipated, from the moment near the beginning when he jokingly discusses the sort of funeral he would like (he would leave his woman, he says, to the Salvation Army), to the insistent presence of Bach's *St. Matthew Passion* on the soundtrack, to the sequence in which Accattone, after angrily rejecting Stella's offer to go back on the streets, dreams of his own burial service.

This is a milieu in which the gendered division of labor is rigid, the exploitation of female by male intensive. Accattone's struggle can be seen as an intuitively grasped effort to mediate this opposition. Hence his oscillation between harsh and yielding behavior with women, his (perhaps overplayed?) relinquishing of the macho facade in breaking down and crying when he is with the pimps from Naples, his acknowledgement of shame in his characteristic downcast glances. There can be little doubt that Accattone is an author surrogate, and that his status as mediator between male and female is equivalent to that of the gay male artist, Pasolini, in an unremittingly harsh social and cultural environment.[13]

The identification of the homosexual filmmaker with the figure of the pimp is even stronger in the case of Rainer Werner Fassbinder. Alfred Döblin's novel *Berlin Alexanderplatz* had had a powerful influence on him in his adolescence,[14] and his identification with the central character, the pimp Franz Biberkopf, was so all-engulfing that at the time of the screening of his fourteen-part television serial based on the novel, in 1980, Fassbinder declared, simply: "I am Biberkopf."[15]

In his first feature film, *Liebe ist kälter als der Tod/Love is Colder Than Death* (West Germany, 1969), Fassbinder himself plays a pimp. He does so again in *Schatten der Engel/Shadows of Angels* (Switzerland/West Germany, 1976), Daniel Schmid's adaptation of Fassbinder's controversial play *Der Müll, die Stadt und der Tod* (*Garbage, the City and Death*). The two films offer a vivid depiction of the prostitute-pimp relationship as a paradigm for human interaction in a bleak world of exploitation and violence.

Both productions are characterized by a heavy theatrical stylization, which marks them off strikingly from the neorealist-influenced *Accattone*. The rhythm is relentlessly slow and oppressive, the dialogue very sparse (*Love is Colder Than Death*) or mesmerizingly intoned (*Shadows of Angels*), the compositions heraldic. In *Shadows of Angels*, prostitutes on the beat sing spontaneously in *a capella* harmonies.

Love is Colder Than Death offers a sketch of the dominant-submissive sadomasochist bond that is at the heart of the prostitute-pimp scenario. Franz (Fassbinder), a small-time gangster, lives with Joanna (Hanna Schygulla), a prostitute who expresses a desire to settle down with a quiet life, a secure apartment, and a child. Their routine is disturbed when Bruno, an elegant cold-blooded killer, enters their lives. Franz, evidently attracted, becomes servile toward him, while remaining coldly domineering in his interaction with Joanna. There is a moment, for example, when she giggles as Bruno kisses her on the breast and face, and Franz viciously slaps her ("You laughed at Bruno, and Bruno is my friend"). As always, Joanna remains passively compliant, though later, like Maddalena in *Accattone*, she will get her own back by becoming a police informer. In this film, the casual lethal violence of the criminal underworld backgrounds the absence of warmth in the domestic situation of Franz and Joanna.

As events unfold there is a shift in Franz, though whether it is toward a more openly acknowledged homoeroticism or toward greater acceptance of Joanna's dream of a normal family life is difficult, in this oblique, enigmatic film, to determine. The latter is perhaps signaled in his beating up of one of Joanna's would-be clients, brutality being his only mode of expressing emotion. *Love is Colder Than Death* certainly embodies that persistent male fantasy of the woman (her function for Fassbinder being that of nurturer rather than sex object) who loves you whatever you do to her, who can be despised because she is herself degraded in the eyes of society. Franz's last word to Joanna, as they speed off together having dumped the body of Bruno, shot by police, from their car, is "Whore!"

Shadows of Angels yokes prostitution, crooked political/business scheming, and violence together in schematic form. The corruption of the rich and powerful is exposed (dishonest city councilors bending the rules for the Jew, the defenestration from police headquarters of an awkward witness, the trumping up of a case against the pimp Raoul), but unlike the "Comrade" films discussed in chapter 5, the film cannot be called left-wing, since there is no anger, no prospect of an alternative, only cynicism. (Fassbinder's later *Lola* reworks, in a more conventional realist style, much of the same basic material — a building speculator's relationship with a prostitute — giving it a different inflection, omitting the pimp and the violence, and with more of a political bite. For a thorough discussion, see chapter 4.)

Shot in Vienna (though set, according to Schmid, "at the end of the century in a nameless city"),[16] *Shadows of Angels* highlights again the sadomasochist nexus in its handling of the relationship between streetwalker Lily (Ingrid Caven) and her pimp Raoul (Fassbinder).[17] Consumptive, freezing cold, Lily returns empty-handed to their apartment one bitter morning and is ordered back on to the streets immediately: Raoul is short of cash for gambling. Submissive, without a hint of protest (in an emblematic image, she leans over backwards in his arms, knees bent, supported on the tips of her toes), Lily does his bidding.[18] And then, when she returns later with a fistful of money, he is cruelly unappreciative, seizing her violently, demanding to know what she had to do to get it ("Did you lick his arse, whore?").

But in this avant-garde work there is a self-conscious analysis that amounts almost to a deconstruction. Dialogue repeatedly returns to the mutually understood terms of a relationship built on cruelty. "Don't beat me up!" are Lily's opening words when she returns to Raoul the first time. "Who's beating you?" he asks. "Beating means love. So who's going to beat you?" "You love me," she objects. "So I beat you if I love you," he replies, "But I can't love you all day and all night." Later, Lily comments to another prostitute: "I keep thinking if I'd learnt to enjoy pain I'd enjoy the blows, and love would be love, which it isn't."

Despite the ties binding them, the prostitute-pimp relationship in this film does not survive. Finding that the city's bourgeoisie will pay her well simply to listen to them talk, Lily experiences a bettering of her material circumstances—such that Raoul is no longer able to love her ("My feelings don't match up to luxury"). He has in the interim, echoing the development in *Love is Colder Than Death*, discovered homosexual desire and now decides to act on it. He leaves Lily to immerse himself in the downtown milieu and is severely beaten up in a gay bar. Meanwhile Lily, bereft, decides she no longer wants to live and, on a strip of wasteland on the outskirts of the city, induces her client the Jew to kill her.

The sociopolitical paralysis is thus matched on the personal level. If, as is the case for Raoul, love can only emerge in the mire, then there is no way out: Lily's death and the framing of the pimp for her murder are symbolically appropriate. Prostitution may be an image of corruption in the Fassbinder world, but the opposite pole of innocence is absent. The fallen woman films trace the process from an initial state of purity, but in Fassbinder the fall took place so long ago that the memory of an Edenic origin has been lost; there is simply a pervasive pessimism, an obscure recognition that human potential has been dashed.

Hollywood's blaxploitation cycle of the early to mid-1970s made a familiar figure of the flashy black pimp running a stable of sexy women slavishly devoted to him. In films such as *Coffy* (1973), *Willie Dynamite* (1973), *Truck Turner* (1974), and *Dolemite* (1975) he struts his stuff, outfitted with his gaudy flared suit, tinted shades, fur coat, omnipresent hat and gold-tipped cane, prowling his turf in his Cadillac or stretch limo. If he is a bad guy it is because he is dealing, as well, in drugs; no opprobrium is attached to his dealing in human flesh. The members of his stable lounge around seminaked in glitzy interiors or beside luxurious swimming pools, offering scopophilic delights that plot developments are often designed to enhance — in *Coffy*, for example, King George's women get their gowns systematically ripped off, exposing their breasts, in the catfight that ensues when the entry of "Mystique" (Pam Grier) to the stable upsets the pecking order.

Key to the fantasy of power, wealth, and sexual fulfillment that such portrayals of the pimp supply is the notion that his prostitutes not only do not resent the control that he exerts over them, but that they actively adore him. "What I need is some real action, honey, the kind I can only get from my old man," coos Meg (Linda Haynes) in *Coffy*. Such devotion is taken to baroque excess in *Dolemite*, which features a poetry-spouting, ass-kicking pimp (Rudy Ray Moore) and his retinue of doting hookers who not only provide sartorial services, chauffeuring, and erotic ambiance — not to mention a sizable cash flow — but who form a mean kung fu fighting force aiding him to regain control of his club from a rival.

Of this cycle, perhaps the most interesting is *The Mack* (1973), both for its attempt to situate the action within an authentic milieu, and for the strategies it adopts to make the pimp acceptable as a fantasized hero.

The Mack was written by Robert J. Poole, who had served time in jail for pimping. It was filmed on location in Oakland, California, and its scenes include footage of a real Bay Area Players Ball, the gaudy annual highlight of the prostitution scene. Its action-genre storyline of a pimp getting his business up and running from scratch after being released from prison, and the battles he is forced to wage against rivals and corrupt law enforcement officers, is given a social-realist backdrop with the characterization of his brother as an activist whose black-rights organization is committed to ridding the community not only of drug dealers but also of pimps and prostitutes.

Despite a sympathetic portrayal of the activist group, the film's rhetoric suggests that prostitution is a comparatively harmless activity alongside drug pushing, and a justified survival tactic in an oppressive socioeconomic environment created by white racism. Thus the protagonist Goldie (Max Julien) is surprised to find that his friend Lulu (Carol Speed) has become a hooker — he had imagined her as a nurse or a lawyer. "Yeah man, that would be righteously together if I was white," she

71. *The Mack:* Goldie (Max Julien) and Diane (Sandra Brown).

explains. "Shit, I don't have to tell you how hard it is for a nigger to earn a decent living." Later, Goldie and Lulu reminisce about how when they were kids there was never food for lunch, and Goldie does his bit to make sure this generation is better off by distributing largesse to boys in the ghetto.

There is nothing coercive about Goldie's tactics in getting Lulu to work for him. In fact, wearied of being an "outlaw," she begs him to take her on: "Goldie, you know, I need a man, somebody in my corner, man. . . . Somebody to be there. Do you think I'm wrong? Help me then Goldie, I'm tired of bein' by myself. Man, you'll never regret it. Man, I'd do anything, d'you hear me, anything, everything that you ask me to do." Lulu gives Goldie's business a kick start.

Still, Goldie is the stereotypical pimp. In pursuit of his dream of being "the meanest mack who ever lived," of getting "the hottest bitches I can find, with a whole boatload of money," he seduces a young white woman, Diane (Sandra Brown), the daughter of corporate lawyers, into joining his stable. She is overwhelmed by his magnetism ("there's an incredible excitement about you, being very powerful") and falls for his pitch ("I'm gonna be your father, I'm gonna be your friend, I'm gonna be your lover, but you got to believe in me"). And when Lulu approaches him in hysterics, distressed about a client who robbed her and tried to kill her, Goldie can only respond by saying, "I don't give a shit about what happened to you" and ordering her back on the street: "Get yourself together and get back out there and get me my money!"

But whatever Goldie does pales in comparison with the evil done by the white pusher/pimp Fatso ("You won't be satisfied till every ten-month-old kid has a needle stuck in his arm") who, it is suggested, is responsible for Diane's death by heroin overdose; or by the bigoted, bent white cops who shoot the honest black policeman who is onto their game. Gang rivalries eventually result in the death of Goldie's mother, and he is forced to leave town, but not before he has made sure that Fatso and the white cops get what they deserve. The pimp here becomes the antiracist avenging hero of the oppressed black community.

In *La Dérobade / The Getaway / The Life* (France, 1979), the pimp reverts to his more usual negative image. The film offers up once more the familiar sadomasochist scenario, retold with the visual explicitness of the 1970s. What is permitted, now, is an eroticization of the subject, not only of the sexual encounters but partially also of the violence. Based on the autobiographical novel of Jeanne Cordelier (who collaborated on the screenplay), *La Dérobade* chronicles the bitter experiences of a young woman from the provinces who falls for the wiles of a Parisian *souteneur* and who escapes his hold only after a series of horrific ordeals.

Marie (Miou-Miou), like her forebears, has a steadfast belief in the love that her seducer has for her, this man in the flashy red sports car who lures her away from her dull boyfriend and shoe-store job and installs her as a prostitute in a series of gang-connected bars and brothels. The torture she suffers, much of it from Gérard (Daniel Duval) himself, cannot shake her blind trust in him, which she clings to in the face of all evidence to the contrary. Toward the end, after all she has been through, she unsuspectingly allows herself to be taken by Gérard away from a happy family meal back to her apartment, where he abruptly attacks her viciously. In despair, resigned to annihilation, she says "Kill me, I don't care," but in a characteristic switch of mood he sobs at her feet. It is only now that she can make a decisive break.

In the performance of Miou-Miou, with her small but wiry body a combination of fragility and toughness, there is an ingenue quality, above all, a naive delight in life that surges up despite the horror of her existence. Her guileless smile that keeps flashing unexpectedly sustains the film at a level somewhat above the sordid, to which it would be condemned if the machinations of brutal pimps and gangsters were to brutalize Marie as well. She is a punching bag for male violence, but her softness can take the blows; she is not broken, she can endure and survive. There is a streak of the sentimental here, to which the diffuse lighting and soft music contribute. Marie is an archetypal Martyr (see chapter 7), whose spirit soars high no matter the degradation and violation of the flesh to which she is subjected.

At the end, she goes to take her name off the police register of prostitutes. Her pimp will expect a lot as his payoff, the official suggests. Marie turns to face the camera and says, with apparent sincerity: "A pimp? I've never had a pimp."

The pimp as bad guy moves to the brutal limit in the exceptionally violent *Vice Squad* (USA, 1982),[19] a portrait of a psychopath on the loose. Set on the streets of downtown Hollywood, the movie depicts a hellish world ("a river of neon slime" as the theme song has it) populated by battered prostitutes, freak clients, teenage addicts, savage pimps, and ruthless cops.

The paradigmatic sadomasochistic bond yoking pimp and prostitute is explored particularly in the film's compressed depiction of the relationship between supervillain Ramrod (Wings Hauser) and his victim Ginger (Nina Blackwood). Ginger appears in only two scenes. In the first, having been beaten up by Ramrod, she is hiding out at the Hollywood Sunset Motel. Ramrod tracks her down and, apologizing for his treatment of her, induces her to unbolt the door. Immediately he is in the room, he says scornfully, "I cannot believe how stupid you are," and grabs her. "Ungrateful fucking bitch! I took care of you, didn't I?" he yells, seizing her by the throat and slamming her head against the wall. Then he stuffs a handkerchief in her mouth and binds her wrists with wire. "You bet your sweet ass you ain't leaving me!" he tells her, "You ain't gonna be able to give my money-maker away for quite a while." Shaping a metal coat hanger into a weapon, he starts hitting her with it.

In the second scene, Ginger is on life support in a hospital. Her face is horribly bruised, and the doctor speaks of vaginal mutilation. A detective urges her to identify Ramrod as her attacker. Ginger declines to do so, saying only, "He loves me." She dies. In this melodramatically heightened picture of the archetypal hooker-pimp relationship, Ginger's psychological attachment to her tormentor is so unyielding that she seems almost as pathological as Ramrod.

The rest of *Vice Squad* is concerned with attempts by the police to place Ramrod in custody and keep him there. In the course of these at-

72. *Vice Squad:* Princess (Season Hubley) and Ramrod (Wings Hauser).

tempts, Princess (Season Hubley), a streetwalker with a three-year-old daughter, is used as bait. Her cover blown, she becomes a target for Ramrod's revenge and very nearly ends up another of his murder victims. The vicious pimp takes on the attributes of the monstrous, almost indestructible antagonist, repeatedly evading the cops who outnumber him many times over.

Ramrod's violence toward prostitutes, whether his "own" or others who cross his path, exceeds that normally shown in the cinema by a factor of several times: it is, precisely, pathological. But because the film offers no counterbalancing portraits of "good"—or at least sane—pimps, Ramrod comes to stand for the pimp in general. This impression is reinforced by details such as his torture instrument fashioned from a coat hanger having a name known to police: it's the "pimp stick," and vaginal injuries received from it are, the doctor says, not uncommon.

Thus the prostitute-pimp relationship becomes an image for the exploitation and cruelty of the commercialized sex industry. Were it not for the glimmer of hope provided by the apparent decision of Princess at the end to quit the profession and revert to her real name ("Once the sun comes up, it's Karla"), it would be a very bleak picture indeed.

In stark contrast to Ramrod, Dédé (Philippe Léotard) of *La Balance/The Nark* (France, 1982) is the very model of the nonviolent boyfriend-pimp. He and Nicole (Nathalie Baye) have been in a steady relationship for several years, continually harassed because the law against *proxénétisme* makes it virtually illegal for a prostitute to live with her lover. It's even risky to kiss in public, something alluded to in a touching moment in the film.

Dédé is gentle and affectionate. The first time we see him, he meets Nicole in a bakery and presents her with a red rose. They are playful, clearly enjoying each other's company. This is a real working partnership: he supplies the charm, she supplies the cash.

The police unit charged with controlling crime in the tough Paris district of Belleville is not about to let this happy idyll to continue. Inspector Palouzi has lost his most valuable informer, wiped out by the gang boss of Belleville, Roger Massina, and now must urgently replace him. His choice falls on Dédé, once a confederate of Massina, but who had a falling out with him over Nicole. Palouzi puts the squeeze on the couple both together and singly, threatening to put Dédé back behind bars if they do not turn stool pigeon. They are caught in an ever-tightening vice between the remorseless law-enforcement machine and the ruthless Belleville underworld.

Under pressure, the transgressive nature of the comradely prostitute-pimp relationship is exposed. It is like a marriage, but only in some respects. Violating patriarchal norms, it positions the female as earner, the male as kept partner. Asked by police if she would like to put her occupation down as "housekeeper," Nicole defiantly says no, she is a whore;

it is Dédé who does the shopping and the cooking. There is an underlying tension to this arrangement, which becomes clear at one point when Dédé complains that he is tired and Nicole comments tartly, "Really? Been working have you?"

Palouzi successfully plays off one against the other so that eventually Dédé snaps, slapping Nicole forcefully during a quarrel and throwing her down on the bed. It is totally uncharacteristic behavior for Dédé, but stereotypical for the man in his situation. Shocked, Nicole sobs: "Are you playing the pimp now?"

That Dédé does not forfeit audience sympathy either for his parasitic ways or for his momentary lapse into violence is a function of the empathetic performance by Léotard (he won a César for best actor),[20] but particularly of the narrative structure, which insures that the violence to which he is subjected is much greater than his own. Dédé is in fact on the receiving end of police brutality on no less than four occasions; in this film it is the pimp, and not the prostitute, who is the punching bag.

It is Dédé's genuine affection for Nicole, however, that is his major redeeming feature. *La Balance* tells the story of a relationship replete with moments of intimacy, sadness, and tenderness; of anger that is rapidly subsumed by remorse; of nurturing care and—what is especially unusual between prostitute and pimp on screen—strong, reciprocal, sexual desire. It is a relationship, of course, that will see more vicissitudes—Nicole turns Dédé in to the police for his own protection, after he has killed Massina. But it stands as a rare instance of a—no doubt overly romanticized—prostitute-pimp love affair in film that is mutual and free of sadomasochistic tendencies.

Streetwalkin' (USA, 1985), on the other hand, is yet another reworking of the tale of the bad guy pimp and his prostitute victims. The interest in this case lies in the feminist spin given to the material by welding to the familiar story an Avenger scenario.

Cowritten and directed by Joan Freeman, *Streetwalkin'* recounts traumatic events in the life of Cookie (Melissa Leo), a teenage girl who arrives in New York City with her kid brother Tim, escaping from a drunken mother and abusive stepfather. She is quickly enticed into prostitution by good-looking pimp Duke (Dale Midkiff), whom she falls in love with. Cookie and Tim share an apartment with another of Duke's girls, Heather (Deborah Offner). When Duke viciously beats Heather up for threatening to leave him, Cookie is terrified and puts herself in the hands of another pimp, Jason. Warfare between rival gangs of pimps ensues. Eventually, after learning of Heather's death, Cookie is able to mete out the prostitutes' revenge on Duke.

A marker of female authorship is perhaps the less-than-totally-mesmeric hold that Duke has over his women. As soon as Heather starts being roughed up by him, she makes the decision to move out, and Duke's aggressive behavior when he comes upon her with her bag packed will not deter her. Demanding that he take his "slimy hands" off her, she struggles, getting away from his grip and insisting, "I am not your woman any more!" Only then does Duke overpower her, subjecting her to a heavy, sadistic beating, shown in explicit detail. Likewise Cookie, renouncing her love for him, will become a rebel, despite the very great danger that places her in.

Even more indicative of a female perspective is the ending. Duke's vicious reign of terror is halted, firstly by an older, independent hustler, Queen Bee (Julie Newmar), who injures him, and finally by Cookie herself. Seemingly as indestructible as Ramrod, Duke attacks the stalled car in which Queen Bee and Tim are cowering, smashing the windshield with a steel bar. Cookie comes to the rescue, putting a bullet in his back. He spins around in shock, facing Cookie. The teenager is fragile and vulnerable-looking in her skimpy streetwalker's getup of diaphanous mauve top and short pink skirt, but the hands on her gun do not waver. Disregarding his pleading ("You can't kill me, baby. . . . You know you love me!"), perhaps aware that he is sneakily taking out a knife behind his back, ignoring his frenzied command to put the gun down, Cookie blasts him away, firing four shots into his chest. She then crumples up in horror and agony.

The predominant emotion generated by this version of the prostitute-and-pimp scenario is thus not pathos—the woman as victim of brutal forces beyond her control—but relief and silent rejoicing in rightful revenge. The motif is not new—the prostitute guns down her procurer in *The Red Kimona* (USA, 1925), as has been mentioned; in *The Wages of Sin* (USA, ca. 1938), an obscure, low-budget exploitation movie; in *Thriller—en Grym Film/Thriller* (Sweden, 1974); and in *The City Girl* (Canada/USA, 1983), for example. But it is significant that in this mainstream American movie of the 1980s there is no longer any hesitation about putting high-powered weaponry in the hands of women, illustrating a weakening in the hegemony of patriarchy. Whereas in the past—in *Vice Squad*, for instance—justice would typically be meted out to the rampaging pimp by the forces of law and order, here the cops are nowhere in sight and it's the pros themselves who dispose.

In Heather and Cookie's awakening to oppression and subsequent rebellion against the man they love there is a strong analogue to the consciousness-raising of the women's movement of the 1970s, and an implicit gesture of solidarity with all battered women. *Streetwalkin'* betrays a feminist influence that will inform many other representations of prostitutes on screen, particularly those in the Avenger category. From now on the tale of the prostitute and the pimp will no longer be the same, and the male fantasy of a compliant female slave will be haunted by visions of violent retribution. Still, there will be little letup in the screen hooker's inveterate vulnerability to male violence, which I examine in the next chapter.

19

Condemned to Death

It was agreed that . . . the lead, to be played by Miss Vivian [*sic*] Leigh, would not be killed in an airplane raid, but, rather, would be run over by a combination of motor trucks and tractors on the streets of London.
—JOSEPH I. BREEN, Production Code Administration file memo on *Waterloo Bridge* screenplay, 1940

Nadia's murder by Simone is very beautiful yet horrible, meticulously staged yet sensuous, symbolically rich but so palpable that the feel of the knife piercing Nadia's flesh can be precisely measured; her writhings, however artificial, are delicious, however posed, excruciatingly real.
—SAM ROHDIE, *Rocco and His Brothers*[1]

Josef von Sternberg's *Dishonored* (USA, 1931) starts with the suicide of one prostitute and ends with the execution of another. The story pivots on which death Magda (Marlene Dietrich) will choose: self-annihilation through depression and desperation, or being gunned down in action, with the attached excitement. "I've had an inglorious life," she tells her recruiting agent, "It may become my good fortune to have a glorious death."

It is Vienna, 1915. Magda the streetwalker is transformed into glamorous Austrian agent X-27. Committed to her country's cause, she nevertheless becomes fatally involved romantically with an agent for the other side. X-27 elects to face her executioners in a "uniform of my own choosing"—which includes a feather boa that forms a spectacular headdress. In front of the firing squad, she refuses the blindfold, crosses herself, lifts her veil to apply lipstick, and then, in an exact repetition of her gesture at the start of the film, when she was loitering under a street lamp in the rain, she leans down to tug on her stocking. There is a shot. She topples over in the snow.

For the woman who can wear the garb of the streetwalker as a badge of honor there is only one possible fate. X-27 joins that select band of prostitute characters who are condemned to death by judicial authority, and the legions who are killed off by other means. Whatever their ostensible crime, it is their excess, their status as women who do not know their place, that draws down upon them the severity of patriarchal law.

The prostitute in the films considered in this chapter is the very paradigm of the unruly female character Teresa de Lauretis speaks of, who is not simply the "love interest" for the hero, and who resists confinement in the symbolic space allotted to her by "disturbing it, perverting it, making trouble, seeking to exceed the boundary — visually as well as narratively."[2] And for that transgression she must pay the penalty.

Again and again the films go through the ritual of targeting for death the woman who creates trouble for the patriarchal order: slovenly and insolent, perhaps, defiant and scornful, or not content with her lowly place in the scheme of things. One senses, for example, at the point in Jean Renoir's *Nana* (France, 1926) at which the heroine spits out her disgust at the departing Count Muffat — "Mufe, dirty Mufe, to think that I almost loved that!" — that this woman must be destroyed. Despite the lively satiric tone of the film, such lèse-majesté — the Count is an attendant to the Emperor, after all — cannot be allowed to pass unpunished. And so it is: what better than a sudden outbreak of smallpox to strike her down? Or in *Cat People* (USA, 1982), for instance, one feels that retribution is in store for the hooker who arrives forty-five minutes late for work at her massage parlor and tells the manager to "fuck off" when he reprimands her. Due reckoning is, in fact, not long in coming: she is attacked and very nearly torn to shreds by her customer, who has unexpectedly metamorphosed into a panther. The uppity whore in a matter of minutes has been reduced to a hysterical blubbering wreck; it is only by chance that she has escaped this time the ultimate fate of other victims of the wild beast, prostitutes who have been half-eaten, their genitals torn out.

Yet the imperative of making an ideological point hardly explains the sheer volume of films in which prostitute characters meet an untimely death. It is undoubtedly because it allows for the venting of an aggressive fantasy that the motif is so persistent. As I have suggested in chapter 2, the Condemned to Death scenario is resorted to because it permits the cultural expression of a deeply rooted male hostility toward women.

Thus with the killing off of the prostitute the interests of patriarchal ideology dovetail neatly with those of male fantasy. She is to be put to death because of the disturbance she causes: socially, by defying patriarchal authority; psychologically, by arousing male anxiety about the

female as a threatening Other. Unlike the Love Story, the Condemned to
Death scenario is unforgiving. If this troublesome woman succumbs to
fatal accident, mortal illness, or suicide, that is all to the good; otherwise,
the Ripper's knife awaits.

She asked for it. The prostitute's transgression in movies in which she
meets a grim fate is to constitute an erotic excess or to violate the male-
defined boundaries in gender-power relationships.

Of course, it may not always be serious. In the female-directed comedy *In the Spirit* (USA, 1990), the misdemeanor of Crystal (Jeannie Berlin)
is to talk blithely at polite dinner parties of sucking cock, jerking off, and
dildos. Her punishment is to be crushed to death beneath her waterbed.
But generally, there is nothing funny about the prostitute's crime against
patriarchy or the fate to which it consigns her.

By her very existence, the prostitute symbolizes unbridled sexuality,
an immediate flashpoint in societies with a heritage of puritanical Christianity that aims to extirpate the passions. There is some variation here
between Protestant and Catholic attitudes: in the Protestant tradition
there is a belief in the possibility of sexual restraint (and hence the prostitute is more liable to be viewed as an evil temptress leading men astray),
whereas Catholicism tends to regard sex as an ineradicable human
(male) need, and to look on the prostitute favorably for catering to it.[3]
Still, the danger that the figure of the prostitute, with her suggestive attire and provocative gestures, can pose by inflaming male desires, and the
need for that reason to hold her in check, has been felt very strongly in
all societies with a Christian heritage.

In the cinema, the puritan tradition has practically guaranteed that
for female characters in general, being ostentatiously sexual and behav-
ing promiscuously is an open invitation to violence. In *Magnum Force*
(USA, 1973) — to take just one example among myriads — topless women
in a swimming pool are gunned down by a killer with an automatic rifle
in a scene cut so fast that nothing is individualized, and everything becomes a confused blur of erotic and violent imagery. The prostitute, especially if she is brazen, becomes a particular target for such aggression.
In a typical serial-killer scenario such as that of *Hard Vice/Vegas Vice* (USA,
1994), the modest hookers survive, while those who flaunt their bodies are
murdered. The paradigmatic *Dressed to Kill* (USA, 1980) insists on the archetypal interpenetration of sexuality and aggression, the one as provocation for the other. The female is pictured as sensual naked flesh,

temptress, voluptuary; the male as instiller of order, eliminator of the licentious. The figure of the prostitute, the very incarnation of promiscuity, is indispensable to this configuration, especially when, as here, she has a strong sexual drive — asked if she ever has sex except for money, Liz (Nancy Allen) replies yes, with men who turn her on. Although Liz suffers the ultimate fate only in a nightmare, she exists in this film solely as a target, a vulnerable woman to be stalked and slashed. Her promiscuity condemns her to this, the revenge wreaked upon the fornicating female by the razor gangs of patriarchy.

The hooker in film may trespass fatally against the patriarchal regime by sexual insubordination. In not making her body available on demand, for example, she defies male definition of her role. The prostitute in *Evangeliemandens Liv/John Redmond, the Evangelist* (Denmark, 1914) "undresses in silhouette behind a curtain" in order to excite Redmond, but then rejects him after he has been expelled from home and no longer has an income from his parents.[4] Katusha in *A Woman's Resurrection* (USA, 1915) "assumes the gay life and becomes known for her loose morals," but later "refuses to grant sexual privileges" to her prison officer in Siberia in return for an easing of the harsh conditions in which she is held.[5] Rosário of *La mujer del puerto* (Mexico, 1933), the "prostitute queen" of a tropical cabaret, is "a sort of untouchable priestess," disdainfully turning down clients who do not take her fancy,[6] likewise Bebe of *Sweet Smell of Sex* (USA, 1965) "rejects the advances of Joe, who has been following her, because he appears too upright and ordinary."[7]

Or it may be a case of deceptively toying with her clients, playing one man off against another. In *Tianming/Daybreak* (China, 1933), Ling Ling is found at a nightclub table "with four customers, flirting with each of them individually through furtive glances and gestures, behind the others' backs or under the table, and convincing each that he's the one."[8] Lulu of *La Chienne* (France, 1931) lets a middle-aged cashier believe she is in love with him, while remaining emotionally attached to her pimp; Yvette of *En cas de malheur* (France, 1958) duplicitously oscillates between a wealthy lawyer and an impoverished medical student.

For the hooker to become involved in a lesbian relationship at the expense of her relationships with men is obviously an insult to the patriarchy, to be dealt with accordingly. Beatrice in *Wild, Wild Girl* (USA, 1965), who rejects the prizefighter who loves her; Grear in *The Big Doll House* (USA, 1971), who declares all men off limits from now on ("I'm not goin' to let a man's filthy hands touch me again!"); and Rosa in

Marcados para Viver/Branded for Life (Brazil, 1976), who defiantly asserts her solidarity with other marginalized women — all meet their death.

As a provider of extramarital sex the prostitute is frequently seen as a threat to the cornerstone of patriarchal power, the family. Films reflect this belief in showing hookers in the role of endangering the institution of marriage. In *Virtue* (USA, 1932), Gert's financial scheming almost causes her friend Mae to break up with her husband; in *Ánimas Trujano/The Important Man* (Mexico, 1961) Catania leads the drunken, philandering protagonist astray, with the result that his wife is forced to support him and his family; while in *Money on the Side* (USA, 1982), Annie resorts to part-time prostitution, without her husband's knowledge, to buy herself luxuries. Characters like Myra in *Waterloo Bridge* (USA, 1931, 1940) and Julia in *Strictement personnel* (France, 1985) who do not let their fiancé know of their disreputable occupation are clearly begging for trouble.

The prostitute may create a disturbance in gender-power relationships by, for example, being a corrupting influence on an honest man. Thus Auguste in *Dirnentragödie* (Germany, 1927) induces her boyfriend-pimp Anton to commit murder for her, while Aurora in *Sensualidad* (Mexico, 1951) seduces a judge into becoming a criminal. Or her crime may be to discover too much about the dubious workings of the male power structure, since her profession may well place her in intimate contact with the movers and shakers of society. The eponymous heroines of *Das Mädchen Rosemarie* (West Germany, 1958) and *Anita Drögemöller und die Ruhe an der Ruhr* (West Germany, 1976) become too aware for their own good of corrupt ties between business and politics in the Federal Republic, while Lily in *Shadows of Angels* (Switzerland/West Germany, 1976), as touched on in chapter 18, becomes privy to the compromising secrets of the town's morally bankrupt elite. Other ill-fated hookers who know too much include Helen in *Beyond Soho* (UK, 1988), Connie in *Full Exposure: The Sex Tapes Scandal* (USA, 1989), Rose in *The Last Tattoo* (New Zealand/USA, 1994), and Patrice in *Jade* (USA, 1995).

But the prostitute's ultimate transgression, for which she is predisposed as an outcast character already beyond the law, is to be responsible for a man's death. As a killer she may be one of two types, virtuous (in spite of her vocation) or ineluctably debased. The model for the first type is provided by Madame X, the heroine of many film versions of the play, beginning in 1909 (see chapter 1). Her self-sacrificial murder of a blackmailer is matched by Helen Smith's shooting of a brothel client trying to harm her daughter, in *The Governor's Ghost* (USA, 1914), and Jenny Sandoval's shooting of her underworld business partner to protect her son, in *Frisco Jenny* (USA, 1933). Gilda in *Safe in Hell* (USA, 1931), who kills a man assaulting her, and Ella in *Heaven's Gate* (USA, 1980), who shoots a gunman belonging to the vicious ranchers association, are also women of integrity. On the other hand, a prostitute's act of murder may be the ultimate mark of her corrupt nature. Maria in *Chair de poule* (France/Italy, 1963), who has married her husband for his money, kills him in an argument. Laura in *Antônio das Mortes* (Brazil/France, 1969) is an amalgam of devious calculation and primitive passion, urging the politician Mattos to kill the man whose mistress she is, the landowner Horácio, so that they will inherit his wealth, stabbing Mattos to death when he misses his chance, and abandoning herself to lust with another lover, the teacher, over Mattos's body. And the drug-crazed hooker Charlotte in *Fort Apache, the Bronx* (USA, 1981) shoots two policemen without provocation at point-blank range, and slashes the throat of a customer with a razor blade gripped between her teeth.

But whether justifiably or not, all these women have strayed into masculine territory and killed a man. A power imbalance has resulted that can only be righted, as in the case of other offences, by the forfeiting of the guilty woman's life — sometimes in fact by judicial execution, as in *Safe in Hell* and *Frisco Jenny*.

It is noteworthy however that both Gilda and Jenny go to the gallows *of their own volition*. In *Safe in Hell*, Gilda is about to be rightfully acquitted on grounds of self-defense when she incriminates herself ("I killed him in cold blood!"), in order to keep a vow of fidelity to her fiancé and escape, by death, the sexual slavery threatened by the island's jailer. In *Frisco Jenny*, the protagonist — a financial force in the San Francisco prostitution racket — refuses to take the stand on her own behalf or reveal her motive for the shooting, which might have granted her a reprieve: she is determined to prevent her son — who is the prosecuting district attorney — from learning that she is his mother.

The execution of a member of the weaker sex, if she has redeeming qualities, has the potential to reflect badly on the patriarchal system. *I Want to Live!* (USA, 1958), which recounts the true story of a prostitute, Barbara Graham, sent to the gas chamber for alleged participation in a homicide, is a case in point. The same difficulty applies, in some respects, to murder. Hence in the cinema it has frequently been found ideologically preferable to dispose of the prostitute by gentler means.

Having her die accidentally is a convenient way of exempting the male power structure of blame for her demise. Thus Fifty-Fifty Mamie of

Children of Eve (USA, 1915) dies after being injured in a cannery fire, Liz of *The Promiscuous Sex* (USA, 1967) is run over, and Annie of *Foxes* (USA, 1979) is killed in a car crash. In a common configuration in which the female is caught between male adversaries, the prostitute in *John Redmond, the Evangelist* is unintentionally shot in a struggle between Redmond and a friend of hers, Maria in *Il bandito / The Bandit* (Italy, 1946) dies in a brawl between her pimp and her brother, and Laura in *Antônio das Mortes* is caught in crossfire during a gunfight. And there are those who are victims of manslaughter: in *Virtue*, Gert is killed when bad guy Toots "pushes her to the ground, which causes a fatal blow when her head hits the radiator,"[9] while Mamie Adams in *Primrose Path* (USA, 1940) is accidentally killed by her drunken husband.

Illness may also strike down the woman who is surplus to requirements. Helen in *The Governor's Ghost* dies, presumably of shock, before she can be executed for her crime. Annette in *The Supreme Temptation* (USA, 1916) expires from a cataleptic seizure, while Mayda in *The Courtesan*, of the same year, suffers a fatal heart attack. Camille, of course, in the many adaptations of *La Dame aux camélias* (see chapter 17), dies of tuberculosis, while Nana, at least in the 1926 version of Zola's tale, is stricken with smallpox. Disease is directly linked to the prostitute's way of life in *Orizuru Osen* (Japan, 1935), whose protagonist becomes insane and dies from syphilis, and *Liebe kann wie Gift sein* (West Germany, 1958), in which "worn out by debauchery, Magdalena dies of coronary thrombosis in hospital."[10]

The prostitute ennobles herself at the last, in a few films, by an act of self-sacrifice. In *A Woman's Resurrection*, Katusha is killed when she jumps in front of Prince Nekhludoff to shield him in a duel. "Lucky Legs" from Saigon in *China Gate* (USA, 1957) atones for her dubious past by killing herself in the act of blowing up a Communist ammunition dump. Similarly though less spectacularly, Natalie in *55 Days at Peking* (USA, 1963) is killed while on a mission to obtain opiates for the wounded, during the Boxer Rebellion.

But it is by the device of suicide that the objectives of patriarchal ideology are most fully achieved. The unruly woman — whose wish to define *herself*, to reject any reification, is an intolerable provocation to the male order — is killed off, and all guilt for this act displaced from the system on to the victim herself. The prostitute character internalizes the shame that the whore stigma attaches to her, and validates society's moral condemnation by the self-infliction of her punishment.

Suicide is often the ultimate outcome of a fallen woman narrative, for which *The Downward Path,* discussed in chapter 1, provides the prototype. The progressive demoralization of the innocent young woman who strays from the path of virtue provides an object lesson to any who might be tempted to follow her lead, with her suicide clinching the case. *Kungsgatan* (Sweden, 1943) offers a typical later example of the scenario. Country girl Dolly (Marianne Löfgren) comes to Stockholm seeking work, cannot find a job, drifts into prostitution, and becomes so depressed that she kills herself.

Whether in a fallen woman story of this type or not, male violence may well be a factor in the decision to commit suicide. In *Trädgårdsmästaren / The Gardener / The Broken Spring Rose* (Sweden, 1912), the effect is long-term: the female protagonist, raped by her boyfriend's father, is reduced to prostitution and many years later returns to where it happened to end her life. *Captain Salvation* (USA, 1927) depicts a prostitute who, sexually assaulted by a ship's captain, kills herself rather than submit. Former Bronx hooker Margie in *Quelli che contano / Cry of a Prostitute* (Italy, 1974), now the wife of a Mafia boss, is raped twice and beaten so severely that in despair she takes a lethal overdose of pills. Manhattan streetwalker Dee Dee in *Hustling* (USA, 1975) slits her wrists after being attacked by her pimp and by a violent client. In *Money on the Side,* Annie is beaten to a pulp by a prostitute-basher, following which she hangs herself in a police cell. Sixteen-year-old Lilya in *Lilja 4-Ever / Lilya 4-Ever* (Sweden/Denmark, 2002), trafficked to Sweden from the former Soviet Union, coerced into prostitution, and repeatedly brutalized, finally escapes and jumps to her death from a highway overpass. While such films clearly indict individual male wrongdoers for their violence, guilt for the ultimate crime of taking a life is conveniently deflected back on to the woman herself.

When the suicide takes on sacrificial overtones, as it does very clearly, for example, in *Fängelse* (Sweden, 1949), *WUSA* (USA, 1970), *Édes Emma, drága Böbe* (Hungary, 1992), and *Farewell My Concubine* (China/Hong Kong, 1993), the prostitute becomes a Martyr to the patriarchal cause (see chapter 7), her death a sad but necessary offering for the renewal of (male-dominated) society.

"Well, we haven't had a good juicy series of sex murders since Christie. And they're so good for the tourist trade. Foreigners somehow expect the squares of London to be fog-wreathed, full of hansom cabs and littered with ripped whores, don't you think?"
—pub customer in Hitchcock's *Frenzy* (1972)

If misogyny is restrained in those films in which the prostitute meets her death through accident, illness, or suicide, it is unleashed when she becomes the victim of murder. Particularly since the 1960s—perhaps as a backlash against the women's liberation movement—hookers have been targeted for gory demise in an unending torrent of movies that have made of the serial killer an icon of popular culture.

In images catering to an aggressive fantasy, the victim is typically dispatched with sadistic relish. She may be shot, stabbed, slashed, battered, or strangled. She may be run over. She may be poisoned with drain cleaner or injected with a hot dose of heroin. In *Street Angel* (China, 1937) the prostitute is killed with a knife thrown at her; in *Trackdown* (USA, 1976) she is gassed; in *Blow Out* (USA, 1981) she is garroted; in *The Banker* (USA, 1989) she is shot with a crossbow; in *Shotgun* (USA, 1989) she is attacked with a bullwhip before being beaten to death. The call girl in *Kamikaze Taxi* (Japan, 1995) who sticks up for a face-gouged colleague is silenced for good by a gangster grinding his foot down on her throat as she's sprawled on the floor.

Nor do the indignities cease at the point of death. In *Welcome to Arrow Beach* (USA, 1974) a hooker is hacked up with a meat clever and eaten. In Bergman's *Aus dem Leben der Marionetten / From the Life of the Marionettes* (West Germany, 1980) the murderer has anal intercourse with the corpse. In *True Confessions* (USA, 1981) the body is sliced in two, with a candle stuck up the vagina. Prostitutes are converted into sausages, in *Bilbao* (Spain, 1978); fried up into fritters in *Motel Hell* (USA, 1980); disemboweled in *The Ripper* (USA, 1985); skinned in *Skinner* (USA, 1995); and dismembered in *Very Bad Things* (USA, 1998).

The prostitute may be treated in such a fashion, whether on screen or in the real world, because society permits it. Such is the contempt that the woman who sells her body is held in that she may be regarded as scarcely human, her demise of no significance. In *True Confessions,* two detectives examine the hooker's nude corpse, which has been found on a grassy slope. "Nice pair of charlies," remarks one. The lower half of the body is some little distance away. As the policemen wander over to it, they chat about a fight the previous night and make wisecracks. The scene uncannily mirrors an episode described by an American sex worker, who in scrutinizing "society's feelings that hookers' deaths— and lives—are unimportant," recalls: "When I was in a crummy New York hotel, I remember overhearing the police discussing the death of a hooker with the hotel manager. All three men were laughing, and making jokes about the parts of her body that had been found in garbage cans."[11]

The woman of the streets is thus an easy target for male aggression. *The Night of the Generals* (UK/France, 1966) depicts a fanatical Nazi officer responsible for the brutal killing of prostitutes in Warsaw, Paris, and Hamburg. "I'm assuming of course a dead body like this will attract a certain amount of attention — unjustifiably in my view," he remarks, after one of his attacks. "After all, who was she? A whore." Similarly, the sadistic Los Angeles lawyer of *Shotgun*, who counts two dead prostitutes among his victims, says simply, "Those weren't people, Jones, they were hookers!" The words of these fictional constructs echo those of the "Yorkshire Ripper," Peter Sutcliffe, who declared: "The women I killed were filth, bastard prostitutes who were just standing round littering the streets."[12]

Historian Nickie Roberts has argued that in the Sutcliffe case, statements by the attorney general and a senior police officer involved in the investigation point to "actual complicity" with the murderer: "Behind the apparently civilized façade of the law, its spirit still decrees that whores . . . are 'guilty' of their stigma, and that a hideous and barbaric death is a fitting punishment for their guilt."[13] *La Vie, l'amour, la mort/ Life Love Death* (France/Italy, 1969) is pertinent in this regard. Allegedly based on fact, it is a provocation against the death penalty, not by chance in the case of a man convicted of murdering three prostitutes. Despite the film's liberal pretensions, a subtext that asserts that a woman's death is not worth a man's life is clearly evident — especially when she's a hooker who has humiliated her client by commenting on his sexual inadequacy. In this instance there is possibly a certain racism in the sentencing — the offender is a North African immigrant — which overcomes the indulgence within the justice system toward the slighted male that would normally operate. The film, then, redresses the balance: in taking up cudgels for the murderer it inevitably, by implication, condones the crime.

Much of the excitement generated in movies by aggression against the prostitute is associated with the idea that she can be murdered with impunity. In *Henry: Portrait of a Serial Killer* (USA, 1986), Henry and Otis kill two hookers and dump them by the roadside. "What's going to happen when they find those bodies?" Otis asks. "Nothing," replies Henry. And he's right: the police do not come after them. Later, Henry advises Otis not to kill a college student, because they'll put him away for sure. To take another example, Laimi in *Nan yang shi da xie shu/Eternal Evil of*

Asia (Hong Kong, 1995) becomes fixated on a woman hairdresser and in the grip of his obsession brutally rapes and murders a prostitute. The anonymous victim's sole function is to demonstrate the ferocity of Laimi's lust that, unheeding of the woman's cries of protest, tips over readily from sex to murderous violence. The killing is perfunctory—although there is plenty of blood—and there is no narrative conse- quence: the prospect of Laimi facing any penalty for his crime does not come into it at all. Uninhibited violence extends to mass murder in *Heaven* (New Zealand/USA, 1998), in which the strippers and hookers in a nightclub are offhandedly gunned down, purely for the gory spectacle, by arsonists who are torching the joint for the insurance money.

The thrill for the (male) viewer may be heightened in murder se- quences by the device of subjective camerawork, positioning him as the killer witnessing the terror of his female victim as he closes in on her. In the opening sequence of *They Call Me MISTER Tibbs!* (USA, 1970), for example, the naked prostitute, defiantly telling her client to get out, steps toward the camera looking directly into the lens, before male hands en- ter frame and grip her around the neck. In another opening sequence, that of *Jack's Back* (USA, 1988), a streetwalker runs terrified toward the camera in a back alley at night. She takes shelter behind a broken picket fence, and a shot of her hand covered in blood indicates that she has been slashed. As she glances back down the alley, the camera moves slowly in on her in a handheld track; she spins around, a flash of light illuminates her face very briefly, and she screams.

In both of these sequences the face of the killer remains unseen, and for most of the film he remains unidentified: this has the important effect of absolving the spectator of guilt for the crime. The famous prototypical sequence, in *Peeping Tom* (UK, 1969), on the other hand, shows the mur- derer before depicting his action (seen from the perspective of the movie camera held at waist-height with which he is filming it) of picking up a streetwalker, following her up the stairs to her room, watching her begin to undress, and then closing in on her with an unseen weapon as she starts screaming. As I have discussed earlier (see chapter 2), the tech- nique and narrative structure in this case forces an identification with the serial-killer protagonist, which many viewers of the film—as with the later *Henry: Portrait of a Serial Killer*—found most unsettling. More con- ventionally, a direct appeal to sadistic impulses in the audience is averted by making of the killer a shady or openly repulsive figure: a monster, not a man; Mr. Hyde, not Dr. Jekyll.

73. Streetwalker victim Dora (Brenda Bruce) in *Peeping Tom*. Stills Collection, New Zealand Film Archive.

Male feelings of hostility toward women that find expression in the perpetration of violence against a prostitute may have their roots in resentment against the mother for the emotional power she is able to wield over her dependent child. Any retaliatory physical aggression against the mother is, of course, taboo, and in this configuration the prostitute, because of her marginalized social status, becomes an acceptable substitute. A number of films make such a link explicit, often in melodramatic terms.

Thus the killer's mother may herself be characterized as a whore. The disturbing impact that this has on the protagonist is explored in *Love — My Way* (USA, 1966), in which Steve tells a psychiatrist his life story: "As a little boy, he watches his mother, a prostitute, service her customers. She discovers him and beats him with a belt. Grown older, he derives sexual pleasure as a voyeur." Having served a jail term, "he persuades two prostitutes to let him watch them make love. One of the women, Capri . . . joins with him in mutual flagellation. Steve becomes overwrought and, believing Capri to be his mother, kills her."[14] Henry in *Henry: Portrait of a Serial Killer* describes similar abuse from his prostitute mother ("She made me watch it, she beat me a lot too"), while brutal pimp Sharkey in *Uncaged* (USA, 1991), as previously mentioned, confuses the hooker he beats to death with his mother, saying to her, "Which man are you going to bring home tonight, Mom? The one who beats me? Are you going to lock me in a closet again?" In both *Aroused* (USA, 1966) and *Jack the Ripper* (West Germany/Switzerland, 1976) the protagonist murders hookers as a deliberate way of gaining revenge for the abuse he has suffered from his prostitute mother. As a variant, the killer's mother may be associated with prostitution in an indirect way: in *Dr. Black, Mr. Hyde* (USA, 1976), for example, Henry's murderous propensities are traced to his traumatic experience as a child, seeing his mother die as the whorehouse inmates she does the cleaning for fail to respond to her anguished cries for help.

Mother fixation, not linked to prostitution, is part of the rampaging killer's psychopathology in, for example, *My Body Hungers* (USA, 1967), *No Way to Treat a Lady* (USA, 1967), and *No Tears for the Damned* (USA, 1968). In *Sweet Kill/The Arousers* (USA, 1972), serial killer Eddie acts out a ritual performance with a call girl, undressing her and masturbating as she plays dead on a table wearing his mother's clothes, but he does not add her to his list of victims.

Peter Egermann, the murderer in *From the Life of the Marionettes*, also has problems with the maternal figure. His psychological formation has been affected, according to the forensic psychiatrist's report, by a "dominating mother"—whose influence has induced in him a latent homosexuality triggering impotence — and by the fact that the "fear caused by aggressiveness toward his mother did not find a natural outlet in Egermann's social environment, in which any form of emotional outburst is considered almost obscene." Despite this, the substitution mechanism operates, overtly at least, in relation not to his mother but to his wife, who (coincidentally?) has the same name, Katarina, as the hooker

74. *From the Life of the Marionettes:* Ka (Rita Russek). Stiftung Deutsche Kinemathek — Filmmuseum Berlin.

he encounters. Peter dreams of murdering his wife, but it is the prostitute who becomes the victim, choked to death and sodomized in an underground porno theater. The psychiatrist does not question why this transference takes place; by his silence he makes it seem natural that tensions arising within a marital relationship should explode in violence against an outsider. The prostitute is in fact subtly blamed for provoking her own murder: "Nothing would have happened," he concludes, "had he remained in his milieu. The disaster was inevitable from the moment he contacted the prostitute."

Sexual dysfunction is a factor in Egermann's crisis. His wife tells a friend of an episode in which Peter "wanted to fuck me from behind. But he couldn't get his prick in. Probably he was too drunk. I started to laugh and he lost his temper and shouted at me." This aligns Bergman's film with many others in which this motif occurs. Significantly, in what is possibly Jack the Ripper's first cinematic appearance as killer, in *Pandora's Box* (Germany, 1929),[15] there is strong reason to believe that he is impotent. The prostitute ill-advisedly comments on the sexual inadequacy of

her client in *La Vie, l'amour, la mort* ("It's not a whore you need, it's a doctor") and in *They Call Me MISTER Tibbs!* ("I'm sick of you and your lousy
hangup!"), and in both instances very quickly pays the penalty. *Heat*
(USA, 1995) shows the hooker commending trigger-happy crook Wain-
gro on his screwing abilities, but it's a mistake: he castigates her for lying
and, evidently troubled by a possible ironic reference to deficiencies in
his manhood, batters her to death.

In general, in films on the Jack the Ripper model the element of threat
posed by the prostitute is uppermost. For the disturbed male she is an intolerable reminder that women are carnal, that by arousing him she
can evoke also his own castration fear. The hooker becomes the victim
of the stabber/slasher (less frequently, strangler) whose usual weapon,
the knife, substitutes for the penis he is too traumatized to deploy.[16] This
more or less deliberately Freudian scenario is played out, for example, in
an early sequence of *Edge of Sanity* (UK, 1989), a film in which the Jekyll/
Hyde myth merges with that of Jack the Ripper.[17] Hyde, having received
an evidently highly disturbing glimpse of female genitals at a brothel,
goes back with a streetwalker to her attic, examines her bared buttocks
while brandishing a knife but does not take up her invitation to sex, and
eventually slashes her throat with a surgical scalpel.

"Representations of murders committed against women frequently
end on this peculiar note of satisfaction ('—and there was peace again in
the land')," writes Theweleit in *Male Fantasies*. "It pushes feelings of dis-
orientation and horror that also surround the event into the background.
The dominant emotion is a passionate rage that will not leave its object
until the object lies dead on the ground."[18] His observation applies to
those many films in which the camera lingers on the image of the
butchered prostitute, lying on a bed whose linen is drenched with blood,
or stretched out, naked and cold, on a mortuary slab. After the paroxysm
of violence, explicitly depicted or off-screen, imagined—emotion is
stilled, passion spent. The troubling figure of the whore has been erased
from consciousness.

Yet guilt lingers. Before the 1960s, extreme brutality against women
(such as that I have described) by and large did not reach the screen:
censorship mechanisms saw to that. With the floodgates lowered, narrative devices permitting the disavowal of the sadistic fantasies being
regularly placed before audiences had to be developed. The patriarchal
mind could not accept responsibility for the misogynist violence it had
conjured up. Hence the common tactic of making the killer not quite
human, a monster. And hence, perhaps, the many films (such as those I

have described) that blame the mother for the killer's mental instability. Hence those films that show the prostitute being killed at the behest of a woman: in *Sin You Sinners* (USA, 1961), the culprit is a striptease dancer who hypnotizes the cabaret owner, causing him to murder; in *The Man From O.R.G.Y.* (USA, 1970), the real instigator of a series of killings is herself a prostitute; in *Angel III: The Final Chapter* (USA, 1988), the evil boss of a white slavery gang who has a rebellious call girl murdered is a woman; and so on. Hence, very possibly, the surprising number of films in which the killer herself is a woman, a motif that crops up across a range of genres but is most noticeable in movies featuring deliberate gender-bending, such as *Hands of the Ripper* (UK, 1971), in which the homicidal maniac turns out not to be Jack himself but his daughter, or *Las Poquianchis* (Mexico, 1976), based on an actual case, which portrays three sisters who run a brothel with inmates who are tortured, starved, and, when they are no longer useful, killed. Perhaps most telling of all, *PrettyKill* (USA, 1987) uses the devious ideological ploy of making its chameleonic serial killer, herself a prostitute, a patriarchal avenger, eradicating hookers as her gesture against the urban chaos (the city is pictured as being saturated in sleaze and overrun with blacks, gays, and kooks): let the deviants, the film seems to be suggesting, clean up their own mess. Whatever the plausibility of such narrative tactics, and in many cases it is very slim (serial killing in the real world being an almost exclusively male occupation), the psychological and ideological effect is clear: to deflect guilt for the indulgence of misogynist fantasies on to women.

In Luchino Visconti's *Rocco and His Brothers* (Italy/France, 1960), the prostitute Nadia (Annie Girardot) enters the lives of members of the Parondi family, recently arrived migrants to Milan from the south of Italy. She has a brief relationship with Simone, a boxer, but calls it off when she realizes that he has been stealing in order to afford her services. Some two years later, after she has done a stint in jail, she takes up with Simone's younger brother Rocco, who has also become a boxer. The couple fall in love, and Nadia gives up the game, taking a shorthand course. On hearing the news, Simone is enraged ("She was my girl! Nobody fools around with my girls! Get that?"). One night he gets a gang of his mates together and they jump the pair: Rocco is held down while Simone rapes Nadia. Afterward, Nadia staggers off alone while Rocco fights with Simone, getting badly beaten up. Meeting her again, Rocco tells Nadia that Simone acted as he did "only in desperation" and that she must go back to him. Demoralized, Nadia reverts to prostitution and later goes to live at the

Parondi family home with Simone, who is now washed up as a fighter. Simone sinks deeper into crime, and his mother Rosaria blames it on Nadia's influence and orders her out of the house. Nadia goes, telling Rosaria, "I'm through with the lot of you!" Locating her in a park at night, Simone suggests that they get together again. When Nadia tells him it's not possible, saying "You're repulsive! I hate your guts!," he stabs her to death.

The prostitute, stigmatized, excluded, despised, desired, is here the focus for all the emotions the tormented failed macho can't control or even understand. Does she deserve to die? Critical responses to *Rocco* indicate that when it comes to violence against hookers, blame-the-victim mentality runs deep.

Geoffrey Nowell-Smith argues that "the source of corruption, in so far as it can be made particular, is Nadia."[19] Claretta Tonetti agrees: "The boys, in effect, meet corruption because of Rosaria's ambition and Nadia's sexuality. . . . Nadia brings degradation with her seductiveness and the power of her femininity."[20] But it is in Sam Rohdie's monograph on the film that a patriarchal denigration of the prostitute character and connivance at her murder is most pronounced.[21]

"Women, at least in *Rocco*, are socially disruptive forces," Rohdie writes, "and however they may destroy men they release in that destruction depths of feeling, which is the place where real liberation in *Rocco* is located." Simone and Rocco — "who box, who shout, who groan, who fight, who murder, who rape, who suffer and gesticulate, whose instinctual and physical sounds become music"—are, according to Rohdie, "victims of the new modern North . . . their grandeur is in their victimization: purer, better values destroyed by vulgar, instrumental, lesser ones." The "purer, better" Simone "destroyed" by the "lesser" Nadia, whom he rapes and murders? Somehow, the female victim has slipped from view.[22]

But how is it that Nadia destroys Simone and Rocco? "It is she who produces an eroticism in both brothers which causes them each in their way to destroy her: Rocco's rejection of her (for Simone), Simone's degrading and violation of her (directed to Rocco), and finally a murder which both brothers participate in through the instrument of a parallel cross-cutting which places each symbolically in the space of the other; behind Simone's knife is Rocco, both brothers together dealing with an erotic and psychic force that overcomes and destroys them."[23] Strange thinking this: she is to blame because they get excited by her? And a warped interpretation indeed, to make the "saintly" Rocco equally guilty of her murder because what he's doing at the same time is intercut.

As suggested in the quote at the beginning of this chapter, Rohdie delights in the staging of the murder scene, which he describes somewhat deliriously: "Nadia writhes in the exquisitely rendered pleasures of sadistic pain and masochistic eroticism." With the prostitute dead, Simone and Rocco are released from travail: "They may have lost their worlds but . . . the loss ennobles them."[24]

Nadia has "doomed Simone and herself": it's her fault she's a target of his violence.[25] But what has she done? First, declined to become Simone's mistress and, much later, taken up with his brother; second, left Simone after a dispute with his mother. In the extraordinary convolution of patriarchal thought of which this is a revealing example, to exercise free will as a woman in not submitting to a male demand for a relationship is a crime for which she will be *justly* raped and killed. Certainly, *Rocco* presents Nadia as disrupting the solidarity of the all-male sibling group (there are also three other brothers), which generates pathos about the breakup of the family and some sympathy for Simone, but one does not need to read against the grain to see in him not an ennobled hero but a vicious thug, in Nadia not a destructive force but a woman of vitality and independence. In a not unusual rhetorical gesture, a male criticism here amplifies misogynist tendencies of the text in occluding the voice, the point of view, the very presence of the female victim. Like so many prostitutes in patriarchal cinema, Nadia dies unlamented, her murder an occasion for rejoicing.

In a quirky piece of feminist subversion, "Niedrig gilt das Geld auf dieser Erde" (Episode 17 of *Geschichten vom Kübelkind* by Ula Stöckl and Edgar Reitz, West Germany, 1970), the prostitute refuses to submit to her preordained fate. Having run through the list of services she offers, for a price ranging from 50 DM to 600 DM, the "Dustbin Kid" (Kristine de Loup) is nonplused when her client[26] throws down 1,000 DM and more. "What do you want?" she asks. "Do you want to beat me?" He laughs. "I just wanted to know if I could kill you for so much money." They play around, but he is not joking. He takes out a razor blade. She pushes him off the bed: "Take your money! Go away! I've got to work." He attacks her, pins her down on the bed, and strangles her.

But "money is of little worth on this earth." In a surrealist resurrection, the customer's purchasing power is nullified. The prostitute laughs at herself: "I'm dead!" Daubed in red paint under the nose as a stylized mark of blood, she gets up, collects her money, and goes outside in the winter daylight. Then she runs through the woods and buries the money under the snow. On the final freeze frame image of her, there is a superimposed speech bubble: "Once you're dead, life becomes beautiful again!" Irrepressible, this prostitute escapes the stereotyped role she's been assigned to.

Just as subversive, but considerably less cheerful, is Marleen Gorris's searing study of brothel life, *Broken Mirrors* (Netherlands, 1984). The film sets up a double-plot structure, one following a group of prostitutes at the "Happy House" in Amsterdam, the other a serial killer who kidnaps a housewife, chains her to a bed in a dungeon, and starves her to death. A powerful montage effect operates so that the lusts of the clients at the brothel become equated with the twisted aggression of the killer, women in each case being the victim. Events reinforce this: one depressed young prostitute, Linda (Anke Van't Hoff), keeps trying to commit suicide and eventually succeeds in hanging herself, while Irma (Carla Hardy), a single mother, gets stabbed in the stomach and slashed in the face by a client (she'll pull through, it is expected, but she'll be disfigured for life and probably blind in one eye). Eventually we learn that the killer (whose face we have not seen) is in fact a regular customer at the brothel, one of the "well-behaved" ones.

Broken Mirrors turns conventions on their head so that the freak psychopath targets "respectable" women, while what kills the prostitutes is not so much the violence of their clientele (though that of course is a factor) as their subjection to the relentless, demeaning objectification of sex for money. "*Broken Mirrors* thus engages the viewer emotionally with the women as subjects and then makes the spectator experience almost physically the pain of woman's continuous objectification: the pain when she is deprived of her voice, her body, her desires, her freedom," writes Anneke Smelik.[27] One of the women, Jacky (Hedda Tabet), is hassled by a client who wishes to touch her breasts and refuses to take no for an answer; another, Francine (Marijke Veugelers), is required by her customer, as he is banging her from behind, to recite all the names she can think of by which the vagina is commonly known. At the end of one ferociously busy night, the women are shown dropping with fatigue. Following on a shot of a used condom being discarded in a rubbish bin, one of the two principal characters, Dora (Henriette Tol), says simply, "I feel like a public toilet."

75. *Broken Mirrors:* Diane (Lineke Rijxman). bfi Collections.

Gorris's film has no truck with any suggestion that the prostitute's death is occasioned by her guilt; on the contrary, it pins the blame squarely where it belongs, with men and the patriarchal mentality. Toward the end, when the killer in his guise as friendly client returns to the Happy House after having driven Irma to the hospital, he stands facing the devastated group of hookers, expecting to be serviced. Told to come back another time, he simply withdraws more money from his wallet. Diane (Lineke Rijxman), the newcomer at the brothel and the other main character, takes the madam's revolver and calmly fires it into the wall next to the man, shattering a mirror. The killer, his face cut by broken glass, finally gets the message. Diane fires the gun into all the other mirrors, then, with Dora, leaves. They will not be coming back. There can be no doubt that those who are left, for whom the daily grind recommences next morning, are condemned to death, of one sort or another.

20

The Paradigm and Its Challengers

I would argue that a man *can't* make a film about a woman now. I don't think they *should* and I don't think they *can*. It's dishonest. Those films are really about themselves, not women, yet they never acknowledge that.

—MICHELLE CITRON[1]

A new language is needed.

—JULIETTE (Marina Vlady) in *2 ou 3 choses que je sais d'elle*

When the all-too-human Jesus of *The Last Temptation of Christ* (USA, 1988) goes into the desert, loneliness eventually takes its toll. A serpent appears to him, speaking in the voice of the prostitute Mary Magdalene. "Why are you trying to save the world?" she asks him. "The world doesn't have to be saved. Save yourself. Find love." He protests: "I have love." But the serpent is persistent: "Look in my eyes. Look at my breasts. Do you recognize them? Just nod your head and we'll be in my bed together."

Suffering mankind — bereft, alone, abandoned — conjures up an image that is all too familiar: the tempting, comforting, alluring female. The prostitute. Elisabeth Shue in *Leaving Las Vegas,* pouring whisky on her bare nipples for Nicolas Cage to lick it off. Stella Stevens in *The Ballad of Cable Hogue,* being sponged by Jason Robards in his desert oasis bathtub. Cordelia González, the Mexican whore tending to bitter paraplegic Vietnam vet Tom Cruise in *Born on the Fourth of July.* Or in a desert that is metaphorical rather than real: vivacious but suicidal Betty Compson in *Docks of New York,* giving meaning to stoker George Bancroft's life; nubile schoolgirl Vanessa Paradis in *Noce blanche* providing her middle-aged teacher Bruno Cremer with all the bliss he ever dreamed of; beguiling call girl Jeanne Moreau in *Eve,* holding out to writer Stanley Baker the promise of erotic fulfillment far beyond what his respectable bride can

offer; sex kitten Brigitte Bardot in *En cas de malheur* pleasurably derailing
lawyer Jean Gabin's comfortable bourgeois life.

Even if there is no male protagonist in the fiction to whom she becomes attached, this fantasized figure is there for the man in the audience. She is the nurturer who succors without demanding or infantil-
izing; the sexually available female who imparts an erotic charge to the
atmosphere simply by putting herself on display; the sensual companion
in struggle. She is the precocious adolescent hungry for sex; the woman
who serves God's purpose by sacrificing herself to men's lusts; the voluptuous hooker who loves her work; the beautiful piece of merchandise under the control of men who may do with her body what they will. She is,
too, the woman with whom illicit sex is perfectly legitimate because she
makes a business of it; the addict whose craving for a fix reduces her to
pure carnality; the explorer of sexuality whose taste for masochism li-
censes the sadistic acts performed upon her. But if there is desire in these
representations, there is also fear: she is the woman whose magnetism is
such that she may draw you into the abyss; the lover who is only after
your money; the deceptively amorous creature whose true motive is to
wreak revenge for all the harm that men have inflicted on her and her
sisters.

Invested with all the longing and anxiety projected on her by the male
imagination, this prostitute of the movies is, as I have argued, a potent
figure, with the capacity to disconcert as well as excite. It is then the task
of the narrative to bring her under control, to negate her autonomy. The
fallen woman is redeemed or comes to a sad end. In a love story the prostitute's promiscuity is curbed, her supercharged sexuality henceforth reserved for the one man who will hold her in his arms. In another scenario, enslaved to a pimp by sadomasochistic emotional ties, she will be
subjected to violence if ever she tries to step out of line. Or ultimately, in
the discharge of an aggressive misogynist fantasy that serves so well the
need to dispose of the disturbing specter of the sexual female, she may be
killed off.

In texts adopting what I have called the "official" patriarchal line, the
existence of prostitution will be deplored, the blame for any suffering the
woman experiences being her own responsibility or that of evil individuals (pimps, criminals) unrepresentative of respectable society. The left-
wing variant of this stance will use prostitution as a metaphor for the corruption and alienation of capitalism, inevitably indicting the woman
herself in the process. Those advancing the contrasting "unofficial" position will deny that the institution of prostitution entails any suffering,

that it may even be a mark of a flourishing, liberal society. In neither case will any guilt be assigned to that large sector of the male population, which, in real life, guarantees the prevalence of prostitution by creating a demand for the services it provides; nor will society be condemned for the stigmatization and criminalization of the woman who does the work.

The prostitute character who appears in these films, a figment of the male imagination, resembles the prostitute of real life only insofar as it is necessary to sustain a semblance of verisimilitude. The fantasy itself is occasionally lively, especially given a radiant performance from the female lead (Louise Brooks in *Pandora's Box*, Simone Signoret in *Casque d'Or*, Melina Mercouri in *Never on Sunday*). But much more often it is regressive, deadening, reactionary. Stretching from the pathetic to the pathological, resorting over and over to arid cliché, the representation is an expression of the profound malaise that has so often afflicted relationships between the sexes in male-dominated society. Undoubtedly rooted in the troubled processes of male psychological development analyzed by Nancy Chodorow and Dorothy Dinnerstein, and given force by the power men wield within the motion picture industry, this is the patriarchal paradigm.

Fortunately, thanks to filmmakers — predominantly female — who have resisted the paradigm, the representation of prostitutes and prostitution in the cinema is richer than this. There are movies that mix archetypal elements such that the prostitute character eludes pigeonholing, and others in which the archetypes are deliberately subverted. There are studies of prostitutes' lives that tell it like it is, building their representation on a base of research, observation, and personal testimony. There are films that expose the oppression and exploitation of women in the sex industry, and those which are particularly concerned with exploring female subjectivity among those engaged in the work. And there are the films, finally, that contest the exercise of patriarchal power in society by celebrating the prostitute's defiance.

Exemplifying the mixture of opposed types, the character Djin (or Gina) in Luis Buñuel's *La Mort en ce jardin/La muerte en este jardín/Evil Eden/Gina* (France/Mexico, 1956) is impossible to pin down. In the role, Simone Signoret retains some of the softness that marked her performance in *Casque d'Or*, but she is tougher and more mature. Oscillating between Gold Digger, Gigolette, and Nursemaid, the subject of two nascent Love Stories as she skips town and treks through the South American jungle with a desperate band of fugitives fleeing from the military, Djin embodies an ambiguity that remains unresolved to the end. Finally, bedecked in jewels looted from the dead in a plane wreck, she declares her love for one of her admirers ("It took me time to realize, but it's true") and is then shot to death by his delirious rival. Refusing both cynicism and sentimentality, Buñuel's prostitute portrait evades categorization in the very process of evoking the familiar archetypal attributes.

Even more destabilizing is the depiction of Nana in Jean-Luc Godard's *Vivre sa vie* (France, 1962). The philosophizing prostitute who sheds tears of empathy watching Joan of Arc's martyrdom on screen, is a fictionalized case study in a sociological documentation of the Paris sex trade, is bought and sold by underworld pimps, and who finally falls victim to gang rivalry, is a character construct that violates realist convention and defies any attempt at classification (Nana is "beautifully acted by Anna Karina but remains totally unconvincing," complains Roy Armes).[2] Unburdened with the mission shouldered by Godard's later prostitute characters of symbolizing the venality of capitalism, Nana becomes a complex, enigmatic figure (appropriately shot in silhouette in the credits sequence, and from behind her shoulder in the first tableau of the film) who quickly exceeds any archetypal delimitation placed upon her.

The archetypes are not so much mixed as purposefully subverted in feminist provocations, discussed earlier, such as *La Fiancée du pirate* (France, 1969), *Geschichten vom Kübelkind* (West Germany, 1970), *Blush* (China/Hong Kong, 1994), and *Purge* (New Zealand, 1994). Nelly Kaplan's *La Fiancée du pirate* demystifies the Siren in its comic exposé of rural patriarchy and permits its heroine to pull off a highly appropriate act of vengeance. Episode 17 of *Geschichten vom Kübelkind* by Ula Stöckl and Edgar Reitz pokes fun at the "Condemned to Death" scenario by means of the quirky surrealist resurrection of its strangled protagonist. In Li Shaohong's *Blush*, the negative Gold Digger archetype is deconstructed to reveal the insecurity and lack of alternative employment opportunities that are at the root of the prostitutes' seemingly avaricious behavior. Finally, the short film *Purge* (by Rachel Anderson and Bridget Lyon) is a savage portrait of the Martyr as victim of sexual abuse.

The social realist aesthetic is powerfully deployed in a number of movies that, although they are under male direction, offer a cheerless depiction of the sex trade far removed from the fond fantasies of the patriarchal paradigm. Whether based on historical research (*Sandakan No. 8*, Japan, 1974), reconstruction of recent events (*Les Filles de Grenoble*, France, 1981), autobiographical memoirs (*Christiane F.*, West Germany,

76. Anna Karina as Nana in *Vivre sa vie*.

1981; *Hard asfalt,* Norway, 1986), involvement with prostitutes' rights organizations (*Prostitute,* UK, 1980), or simply close observation of the contemporary scene (*The Panic in Needle Park,* USA, 1971; *My Name is Joe,* UK, 1998; *La Ville est tranquille,* France, 2000), the films vividly depict the bleakness of an existence devoted to selling one's body, whether as a form of indentured labor, under the brutal control of pimps, subjected to stigmatization and abuse by corrupt police, or in the desperate compulsion for a heroin fix.

In addition there are those films, generally bearing the mark of female authorship, which identify the use of women's bodies in prostitution as a form of gender oppression. Among other white slave productions, *The Lure* (USA, 1914), directed by Alice Guy-Blaché, and *Little Lost Sister* (USA, 1917), based on a novel by Virginia Brooks, expose the dangers young women then faced of being trapped in brothels. Mrs. Wallace Reid's *The Red Kimona* (USA, 1925) goes farther in actually depicting coerced prostitution, showing the protagonist in her New Orleans crib and the desolation of spirit that leads to her act of revenge against her procurer. Decades later, Mira Nair's *Salaam Bombay!* (India/France, 1988) portrays a similar situation in chronicling the miserable fate of a young Nepalese girl sold into prostitution in Bombay. *Hustling* (USA, 1975), derived from investigative journalism by Gail Sheehy, reveals the brutality from both pimps and clients to which Manhattan streetwalkers are subject, and uncovers a system of ruthless economic exploitation of the women by their pimps and the flea-pit hotel owners who together control the illicit sex business. Most powerfully of all, Marleen Gorris's *Broken Mirrors* (Netherlands, 1984), discussed in chapter 19, conveys the unbearable inhumanity of working life in an Amsterdam brothel.

If one of the projects of the patriarchal paradigm is to reduce the prostitute on screen to an object of male desire, a vital feminist response has been to insist on the representation of female subjectivity. The improvised scenes of Bree (Jane Fonda) discussing her feelings with her psychiatrist in *Klute* (USA, 1971) were celebrated as a breakthrough in this regard. By means of subjective imagery and the strikingly original device of a voice-over dialogue between the protagonist and the film's director (Helma Sanders-Brahms), *Shirins Hochzeit* (West Germany, 1976) succeeds in conveying with unparalleled power the experience of a Turkish immigrant worker in Germany forced into prostitution when other options run out. Dagmar Beiersdorf's *Dirty Daughters* (West Germany, 1981) uses a conventional first-person narration in its depiction of a love affair between a Berlin streetwalker and a Lebanese immigrant, but the very extent of the voice-over and its description of the protagonist's painful intimate experience as a child and as a sex worker mean that the film goes much farther than most in suggesting what the life is like from the woman's perspective. Lizzie Borden's *Working Girls* (USA, 1986) takes a contrasting position in rejecting the characterization of the prostitute as victim but is equally committed to communicating — via a frank, quasi-documentary approach — the subjective experience of its central character, a woman doing a hard day's work in a Manhattan brothel. Finally, we might cite Catherine Breillat's *Romance* (France/ Spain, 1999), remarkable for its blunt expression — again through extensive voice-over — of ironically unromantic female sexual desire, the fulfillment of which is pursued through prostitution.

Most subversively of all, feminist movies have celebrated their heroines' defiance of the patriarchal order. Gabriel Darley in *The Red Kimona* guns down her treacherous procurer and gets away with it. Marie in *La Fiancée du pirate* publicly humiliates the men who have abused and denigrated her, and then jauntily takes to the highway. Chantal Akerman's *Jeanne Dielman* (Belgium/France, 1975) unflinchingly portrays a woman who rebels against her condition in male-dominated society by killing one of her clients, a plot motif amplified in Barbara Linkevitch's short *Chinamoon* (USA, 1975), featuring oppressed brothel inmates who wreak their revenge on their customers in an act of ritual murder. In *Streetwalkin'* (USA, 1985), directed by Joan Freeman, and its remake *Uncaged* (USA, 1991), directed by Lisa Hunt, the streetwalker metes out well-merited vigilante justice to her savagely brutal pimp. The Barbra Streisand production *Nuts* (USA, 1987) depicts a call girl who kills a client in self-defense, and then defiantly and successfully fights an attempt to declare her mentally unfit to stand trial. In *Stella Does Tricks* (UK, 1997), directed by Coky Giedroyc, the teenage prostitute gets her own back on her sexually abusive father by setting light to his penis, while in Coralie Trinh Thi and Virginie Despentes' *Baise-moi* (France, 2000), the devastated prostitute and her raped porn-actress companion go on an indiscriminate killing rampage.

The patriarchal paradigm thus finds itself under attack, increasingly so as more women gain access to positions of creative power in the motion picture industry. It is not surprising that the male treatment of prostitutes, in cinema as in life, has generated an angry response. Battles of representation will continue to be waged so long as the blatant oppression and injustice of the sex worker's lot prevails. Whether prostitution, as some feminists demand, ceases to exist, or whether, as others advocate, it becomes a profession like any other, the struggle to be fought is for a society in which men no longer have the power to mark off one class of women from the rest, to be debased, degraded, bought, used, discarded; a society without the need to serve up for entertainment the sight of a hooker with her throat slashed.

NOTES

INDEX

NOTES

1. The Sex Trade and the Cinema

1. Bernard Shaw, *Plays Unpleasant* (Harmondsworth: Penguin, 1946), 248.

2. Gerda Lerner, *The Creation of Patriarchy* (New York: Oxford University Press, 1986), 139. In D. W. Griffith's *Broken Blossoms* (USA, 1919) there is a pertinent sequence in which two possible destinies for the virginal child-woman (Lillian Gish) are visualized: poverty-stricken marriage and motherhood, and stigmatized streetwalking, both unappealing.

3. Frederick Engels, "The Origin of the Family, Private Property and the State," in *Selected Works in Two Volumes*, by Karl Marx and Frederick Engels (Moscow: Foreign Languages Publishing House, 1962), vol. 2, 226. To be precise, Engels is referring to what he calls "hetaerism," or extramarital sexual intercourse between men and unmarried women in general, of which prostitution is the "most extreme form."

4. Sheila Jeffreys prefers, instead of "prostitute," the term "prostituted woman," in line with her belief that prostitution is a form of violence against women, and her formulation "brings the perpetrator into the picture." Sheila Jeffreys, *The Idea of Prostitution* (Melbourne: Spinifex, 1997), 5.

5. The literature on prostitution is extensive. The sociological and historical works I have found most helpful are: Kathleen Barry, *Female Sexual Slavery* (Englewood Cliffs, NJ: Prentice-Hall, 1979) and *The Prostitution of Sexuality* (New York: New York University Press, 1995); Shannon Bell, *Reading, Writing and Rewriting the Prostitute Body* (Bloomington: Indiana University Press, 1994); Deborah R. Brock, *Making Work, Making Trouble: Prostitution as a Social Problem* (Toronto: University of Toronto Press, 1998); Alain Corbin, *Women For Hire: Prostitution and Sexuality in France after 1850* (Cambridge, MA: Harvard University Press, 1990); Frédérique Delacoste and Priscilla Alexander, eds., *Sex Work: Writings by Women in the Sex Industry* (London: Virago, 1988); Cecilie Høigard and Liv Finstad, *Backstreets: Prostitution, Money and Love* (University Park, PA: Pennsylvania State University Press, 1992); Sheila Jeffreys, *The Idea of Prostitution;* Valerie Jenness, *Making It Work: The Prostitutes' Rights Movement in Perspective* (New York: Aldine de Gruyter, 1993); Jan Jordan, *Working Girls* (Auckland: Penguin, 1991); Eileen McLeod, *Women Working: Prostitution Now* (London: Croom Helm, 1982); Jill Nagle, ed., *Whores and Other Feminists* (New York: Routledge, 1997); Roberta Perkins and Garry Bennett, *Being a Prostitute* (Winchester, MA: Allen & Unwin, 1985); Gail Pheterson, *A Vindication of the Rights of Whores* (Seattle: Seal Press, 1989); Nickie Roberts, *Whores in History: Prostitution in Western Society* (London: Grafton [Harper-Collins], 1992); Ruth Rosen, *The Lost Sisterhood: Prostitution in America, 1900–1918* (Baltimore: Johns Hopkins University Press, 1982); Gail Sheehy, *Hustling: Prostitution in Our Wide Open Society* (New York: Delacorte, 1973). Among the autobiographical accounts I have

consulted are Jean Cordelier, *"The Life": Memoirs of a French Hooker* (New York: Viking, 1976); Paulette D., *Les Allées du Bois de Boulogne: les souvenirs d'une professionnelle* (Paris: Presses de la Cité, 1985); Gloria Lovatt and Pam Cockerill, *A Nice Girl Like Me: The Autobiography of Gloria Lovatt* (London: Columbus, 1988); and Marianne Wood, *Just a Prostitute* (St. Lucia: University of Queensland Press, 1995).

6. Mary Ann Doane, *Femmes Fatales: Feminism, Film Theory, Psychoanalysis* (New York: Routledge, 1991), 262–63.

7. James L. Limbacher, *Sexuality in World Cinema, vol 1: A–K, vol 2: L–Z* (Metuchen, NJ: Scarecrow, 1983).

8. See Russell Campbell, "Prostitution and Film Censorship in the USA," *Screening the Past* 2 (1997) http://www.latrobe.edu.au/www/screeningthepast/firstrelease/firdec/ Campbell.html (version current May 4, 2004).

9. The breakdown into character types was inspired by Erik Barnouw's classification of documentary filmmakers in *Documentary: A History of the Non-Fiction Film* (New York: Oxford University Press, 1974). A categorization of prostitute types in literature is given in *The Image of the Prostitute in Modern Literature*, ed. Pierre L. Horn and Mary Beth Pringle (New York: Frederick Ungar, 1984), 3–6: the list comprises "the bitch-witch," "the femme fatale," "the weak-but-wonderful prostitute," "the saved prostitute," "the sinner-but-survivor," "the seduced-and-abandoned prostitute," "the hapless harlot," "the proud pro," and "the cast-of-thousands."

10. A useful table of distinctions between the prostitute and the courtesan is given in Sheehy, 35–36.

11. The film was based on the 1936 prosecution and conviction of mobster Charles "Lucky" Luciano in a New York court on charges of compulsory prostitution. The star witnesses against him were prostitutes in his organization, but because of censorship pressures their movie counterparts were designated "nightclub hostesses." The pioneering feminist study of the film is Karyn Kay, "Sisters of the Night: *Marked Woman* (1937)," *The Velvet Light Trap* 6 (1972), 20–25. Carlos Clarens notes that the prostitute witnesses recanted their testimony two years later in Paris, "signing affidavits to the effect that they had perjured themselves in exchange for protection, immunity, and financial gain." *Crime Movies: From Griffith to the Godfather and Beyond* (New York: Norton, 1980), 157. *Marked Woman* is discussed in chapter 10.

12. See Yuri Tsivian, "Charles Aumont" in *Silent Witnesses: Russian Films 1908–1919*, ed. Paolo Cherchi Usai et al. (London: BFI, 1989), 544–46.

13. See Gertrud Koch, "The Body's Shadow Realm," *October* 50 (Fall 1989): 3–29.

14. See Patrice Petro, *Joyless Streets: Women and Melodramatic Representation in Weimar Germany* (Princeton: Princeton University Press, 1989), 7–8.

15. *International Photographic Films Catalog*, Winter 1897–98. (Microfilm copy available at Margaret Herrick Library, Academy of Motion Picture Arts & Sciences.)

16. The discussion of the fallen woman story here is based on Russell Campbell, "'Fallen Woman' Prostitute Narratives in the Cinema," *Screening the Past* 8 (1999), http:// www.latrobe.edu.au/www/screeningthepast/firstrelease/fr1199/rcfr8b.htm (version current May 4, 2004), in which considerably more detail may be found.

17. See Charles Musser, *The Emergence of Cinema: The American Screen to 1907* (New York: Charles Scribner's Sons, 1990), 267–71. Musser gives the production date as May 1900, which is confirmed in Elias Savada, ed., *The American Film Institute Catalog of Motion Pic-*

tures Produced in the United States: Film Beginnings, 1893–1910. A Work in Progress. Film Entries (Metuchen, NJ : Scarecrow, 1995), 282. Kevin Brownlow, in *Behind the Mask of Innocence* (New York: Knopf, 1990), gives the film's date as 1902, and asserts that it was "intended primarily for peep-show Mutoscope machines" (71, 518). A print of the film is held at the Library of Congress.

18. Quoted in Musser, *The Emergence of Cinema*, 267.

19. Nina Auerbach, *Woman and the Demon: The Life of a Victorian Myth* (Cambridge, MA: Harvard University Press, 1982), 155.

20. Later versions include: *Resurrection* and a Spanish-language version, *Resurrección* (USA, 1931), *We Live Again* (USA, 1934), *Aien kyo* (Japan, 1937), *Duniya kya hai* (India, 1938), *Resurrezione* (Italy, 1944), *Fukkatsu* (Japan, 1950), *Auferstehung* (West Germany/France/Italy, 1958), and *Voskreseniye* (2 parts, USSR, 1960/62). The list is undoubtedly incomplete, and versions of the story are known to have been produced in France, Mexico, and China. Marcel l'Herbier's ambitious *Résurrection*, which began filming in France in 1923, was left incomplete when the director fell ill. There are also several TV adaptations.

21. Tolstoy's Katusha, while a victim of misfortune, is guilty of not knowing her place in class society. She turns down proposals of marriage — "She saw that the life she would be obliged to lead with the labouring men who offered marriage would be too hard for her" — and as a servant is not always obedient — "One day, before she knew what she was saying, she had spoken insolently to her mistresses." See Leo Tolstoy, *Resurrection*, trans. Vera Traill (New York: New American Library, 1961), 13.

22. Auerbach, *Woman and the Demon*, 168.

23. Other films from the silent period featuring an innocent young woman reduced to prostitution include, for example: *Trädgårdsmästaren/The Gardener/The Broken Spring Rose* (Sweden, 1912), *Protect Us* (USA, 1914), *The Wages of Sin* (USA, 1914), *The Painted Madonna* (USA, 1917), *And the Children Pay* (USA, 1918), *Der Mädchenhirt* (Germany, 1919), *Damaged Goods* (UK, 1919), *The Amazing Woman* (USA, 1920), *Anna Christie* (USA, 1923), *The Red Kimona* (USA, 1925), *The Road to Ruin* (USA, 1928), *Trial Marriage* (USA, 1928), and *Das Tagebuch einer Verlorenen/Diary of a Lost Girl* (Germany, 1929).

24. The other versions were: *Madame X* (USA, 1916), *Madame X* (USA, 1920), *Madame X* (USA, 1929), *Madame X* (USA, 1937), *A Woman is the Judge* (USA, 1939), and *Madame X* (USA, 1966). There is also a 1981 American TV version. The play was staged on Broadway in 1910.

25. Silent films with story lines similar in nature to *Madame X* include: *The Governor's Ghost* (USA, 1914), *The Courtesan* (USA, 1916), *The Scarlet Woman* (USA, 1916), *A Mother's Ordeal* (USA, 1917), *Outcast* (USA, 1917), *The Waiting Soul* (USA, 1917), *Out of the Night* (USA, 1918), *The Woman Thou Gavest Me* (USA, 1919), *The Painted Lady* (USA, 1924), *The Red Lily* (USA, 1924), *The Lady* (USA, 1925), and *The Enemy* (USA, 1927).

26. Auerbach, *Woman and the Demon*, 150.

27. Approximately fifty white slave films were produced in the United States alone between 1904 and 1929, about half of which appeared in the four years 1913-16 inclusive.

28. O. Edward Janney, MD., *The White Slave Traffic in America* (New York: National Vigilance Committee, 1911), 13.

29. See in particular Corbin, *Women For Hire*, 275–98, and Rosen, *The Lost Sisterhood*.

30. Rosen, *The Lost Sisterhood*, 133.

31. See for example Jane Addams, *A New Conscience and an Ancient Evil* (New York:

Macmillan, 1913); Maude E. Miner, *Slavery of Prostitution: A Plea for Emancipation* (New York: Garland, 1987, reprint of original 1916 edition); Janney, *The White Slave Traffic in America;* Edwin R. A. Seligman, ed., *The Social Evil, With Reference to Conditions Existing in the City of New York* 2nd ed. (1912) in *Prostitution in America: Three Investigations, 1902–1914* (New York: Arno, 1976); *Importing Women for Immoral Purposes: A Partial Report from the Immigration Commission on the Importation and Harboring of Women for Immoral Purposes* (Washington, 1909), reprinted in Francesco Cordasco with Thomas Monroe Pitkin, *The White Slave Trade and the Immigrants: A Chapter in American Social History* (Detroit: Blaine Ethridge, 1981); and *The Social Evil in Chicago: A Study of Existing Conditions* (Chicago: Vice Commission of the City of Chicago, 1911).

32. Several of these films survive and have been restored by Det Danske Filmmuseum. It is unclear how much distribution any of them received in the United States. Ron Mottram, in *The Danish Cinema Before Dreyer* (Metuchen, NJ: Scarecrow, 1988), asserts: "In the United States the Danish white slavery films were not even shown, at least at the time of their initial release, although copies of *Den hvide Slavehandel I* and *Den hvide Slavehandel II* were sent to the Nordisk agent in New York" (p 97).

33. Frederick K. Grittner, *White Slavery: Myth, Ideology, and American Law* (New York: Garland, 1990), 133.

34. For further commentary on these films, see Mottram, 14, 20, 90–97.

35. On *Traffic in Souls,* see: Kay Sloan, *The Loud Silents: Origins of the Social Problem Film* (Urbana: University of Illinois Press, 1988), 82–84; Brownlow, *Behind the Mask of Innocence,* 71–80; Janet Staiger, *Bad Women: Regulating Sexuality in Early American Cinema* (Minneapolis: University of Minnesota Press, 1995), 120–21, 130–44; Robert C. Allen, '*Traffic in Souls*', *Sight and Sound* 44, no. 1 (Winter 1974/75): 50–52; Shelley Stamp Lindsey, "Wages and Sin: *Traffic in Souls* and the White Slavery Scare," *Persistence of Vision,* no. 9 (1991): 90–102; Ben Brewster, "*Traffic in Souls:* An Experiment in Feature-Length Narrative Construction," *Cinema Journal* 31, no. 1 (Fall 1991): 37–55; Frank Thompson, "George Loane Tucker: The First of the Immortals," *Film Comment* 32, no. 2 (Mar–Apr 1996): 42–45; and Shelley Stamp, *Movie-Struck Girls: Women and Motion Picture Culture After the Nickelodeon* (Princeton: Princeton University Press, 2000), 70–82, 98–99. On *The Inside of the White Slave Traffic,* see Brownlow, 81–84; Staiger, 144–46; Shelley Stamp Lindsay, "Is Any Girl Safe? Female Spectators at the White Slave Films," *Screen* 37, no. 1 (Spring 1996): 1–15; and Stamp, 82–89, 97–100.

36. There are at least two versions of *Traffic in Souls* extant. One, thought to be the English release version, is held at the National Film Archive in London; another, derived from a print purchased and restored by the Blackhawk Film Company, is distributed on 16mm and video in the United States. In the US version, some characters are not identified by name.

37. See e.g. *Chinese Slave Smuggling* (1907), *The Fatal Hour* (1908), and *Chinatown Slavery* (1909). *The Fatal Hour,* which was directed by D. W. Griffith, is usefully discussed in Grittner, 108–9, and in Staiger, *Bad Women,* 129.

38. See Staiger, *Bad Women,* 136.

39. London had recently worked for the US Justice Department, and was on the staff of the Rockefeller white slavery investigation. At one time, however, he had been chief legal counsel for procurers in the Southwest. See Richard Maltby, "The Social Evil, the Moral Order and the Melodramatic Imagination, 1890–1915," in *Melodrama: Stage,*

Picture, Screen, ed. Jacky Bratton, Jim Cook, and Christine Gledhill (London: BFI, 1994), 229, n61.

40. See Staiger, *Bad Women,* 145.

41. Patricia King Hanson, ed., *The American Film Institute Catalog of Motion Pictures Produced in the United States: Feature Films, 1911–1920* (Berkeley: University of California Press, 1988), 526.

42. *Photoplay,* July 1917, quoted in Brownlow, *Behind the Mask of Innocence,* 212.

43. W. L. Shallenberger, distributor of the film, quoted in Brownlow, 87. Despite its reformist stance, *The Finger of Justice* did encounter censorship difficulties. See Campbell, "Prostitution and Film Censorship in the USA."

44. Alice Guy, *Autobiographie d'une pionnière du cinéma, 1873–1968* (Paris: Denoël/Gonthier, 1976), 143 (translation by RC). Guy does not identify the censorship body she is referring to, but it is most likely the National Board of Censorship.

45. Shelley Stamp contends that in the film, "prostitution becomes an apt metaphor for the potentially devastating effects of industrial society in the contemporary imagination." *Movie-Struck Girls,* 92.

46. *Moving Picture World,* December 23, 1916, 1792.

47. See Campbell, "Prostitution and Film Censorship in the USA."

2. Depicting Prostitution under Patriarchy

1. Sheila Rowbotham, *Woman's Consciousness, Man's World* (Harmondsworth: Penguin, 1973), 43.

2. Teresa de Lauretis has commented that it is "precisely the feminist critique of representation that has conclusively demonstrated how any image in our culture — let alone any image of woman — is placed within, and read from, the encompassing context of patriarchal ideologies, whose values and effects are social and subjective, aesthetic and affective, and obviously permeate the entire social fabric and hence all social subjects, women as well as men." *Alice Doesn't: Feminism, Semiotics, Cinema* (Bloomington: Indiana University Press, 1984), 38–39.

3. See Charles Bernheimer, *Figures of Ill Repute: Representing Prostitution in Nineteenth-Century France* (Cambridge, MA: Harvard University Press, 1989), 2, and Alain Corbin, *Women for Hire: Prostitution and Sexuality in France after 1850* (Cambridge, MA: Harvard University Press, 1990), vii, 251–52. Much of the writing was highly colored. Bernheimer, for example, cites the passage in Zola's *Nana* in which the prostitute heroine is described as a fly "flown up out of the dung, a fly that absorbed death from the carrion left by the roadside," poisoning anyone on whom it settled (202).

4. Klaus Theweleit, *Male Fantasies, I: Women, Floods, Bodies, History* (Cambridge: Polity, 1987), 142.

5. Theweleit, *Male Fantasies,* 167.

6. Nancy Chodorow, *The Reproduction of Mothering: Psychoanalysis and the Sociology of Gender* (Berkeley: University of California Press, 1978); Nancy J. Chodorow, *Feminism and Psychoanalytic Theory* (New Haven: Yale University Press, 1989), parts 1 and 2; Dorothy Dinnerstein, *The Mermaid and the Minotaur: Sexual Arrangements and Human Malaise* (New York: Harper & Row, 1976). Chodorow and Dinnerstein are cited by Barbara Ehrenreich in her foreword to Theweleit, *Male Fantasies,* xvi.

7. The references to the mother in this sequence are a baroque embroidery upon the equivalent scene in *Streetwalkin'* (1985), of which *Uncaged* is a generally faithful remake. The directors of the films are Joan Freeman and Lisa Hunt (as William Duprey), respectively.

8. Chodorow, *Feminism,* 6.

9. Dinnerstein, *The Mermaid and the Minotaur,* 66–67, 70.

10. Sigmund Freud, "The Most Prevalent Form of Degradation in Erotic Life" in *Sexuality and the Psychology of Love,* ed. Philip Rieff (New York: Collier, 1963), 64.

11. Freud, "The Most Prevalent Form," 61–62.

12. Freud, "A Special Type of Object Choice Made by Men" (1910) in *Sexuality and the Psychology of Love,* 50–51, 54–55.

13. Shulamith Firestone, *The Dialectic of Sex: The Case for Feminist Revolution* (New York: Bantam, 1971), 59. On mother/whore images in the male heterosexual imagination, see also Jonathan Rutherford, "Who's That Man?" in *Male Order: Unwrapping Masculinity,* ed. Rowena Chapman and Jonathan Rutherford (London: Lawrence & Wishart, 1988), 49–51.

14. Dinnerstein, *The Mermaid and the Minotaur,* 70.

15. See Chodorow, *Feminism,* 108.

16. Freud, "A Special Type," 55.

17. Karen Horney, "The Dread of Women" (1932), in *Feminine Psychology* (London: Routledge & Kegan Paul, 1967), 134–35. The essay is cited by Chodorow in *Mothering,* 183, and *Feminism,* 35.

18. Ibid., 146.

19. Bernheimer, *Figures of Ill Repute,* 2.

20. Freud, "A Special Type," 52.

21. See Russell Campbell, "Prostitution and Film Censorship in the USA," *Screening the Past* 2 (1997) http://www.latrobe.edu.au/www/screeningthepast/firstrelease/firdec/Campbell.html (version current May 4, 2004).

22. This narrative device did not, however, succeed in deterring copycat killers. In 1974 in Ogden, Utah, three murders using the same technique were committed by men who watched the movie several times in one day. See Russell G. Geen, *Human Aggression* (Milton Keynes: Open University Press, 1990), 82.

23. "I had been sent the script and had thought that the film would contribute to a public understanding of mental illness, but the film seemed to be totally different. Having accepted the project at script stage we did not feel able to reject the film, so we made extensive cuts and hoped for the best." John Trevelyan, *What the Censor Saw* (London: Michael Joseph, 1973), 159.

24. These reviews are quoted in Ian Christie, "The Scandal of *Peeping Tom*" in *Powell, Pressburger and Others,* ed. Ian Christie (London: BFI, 1978), 54–56.

25. *Henry: Portrait of a Serial Killer* was screened at the Chicago Film Festival in 1986 but did not attain general release until 1990.

26. The most contentious sequence was one in which the murders were viewed, as in *Peeping Tom,* through a camera viewfinder. See Tom Dewe Mathews, *Censored* (London: Chatto & Windus, 1994), 264–68. The issues are analyzed in W. K. Hastings, "The Cutting and Banning of *Henry: Portrait of a Serial Killer:* A Portrait of Censorship in New Zealand" (paper, 1994).

27. See Alison M. Jaggar, "Prostitution," in *Philosophy of Sex: Contemporary Readings,* ed. Alan Soble (Totowa, NJ: Littlefield, Adams, 1980), 349–53.

28. For a discussion of the extent of female attendance at motion pictures in the United States in the 1910s, in relation particularly to white slave films, see Shelley Stamp, *Movie-Struck Girls: Women and Motion Picture Culture After the Nickelodeon* (Princeton: Princeton University Press, 2000), 7–8.

29. Chodorow, *Mothering*, 167, 169.

30. For an account of women filmgoers' identification with female performers see Jackie Stacey, *Star Gazing: Hollywood Cinema and Female Spectatorship* (London: Routledge, 1994).

31. Patrice Petro, *Joyless Streets: Women and Melodramatic Representation in Weimar Germany* (Princeton: Princeton University Press, 1989), xxi, 174.

32. Quoted in Thomas G. Plummer et al., *Film and Politics in the Weimar Republic* (New York: Holmes & Meier, 1982), 53.

33. Molly Haskell, *From Reverence to Rape: The Treatment of Women in the Movies* (Harmondsworth: Penguin, 1974), 52.

34. Quoted in Stacey, *Star Gazing*, 146.

35. Lea Jacobs, *The Wages of Sin: Censorship and the Fallen Woman Film, 1928–1942* (Madison: University of Wisconsin Press, 1991), 15.

36. Heide Fehrenbach, "*Die Sünderin* or Who Killed the German Male: Early Postwar Cinema and the Betrayal of Fatherland," in *Gender and German Cinema: Feminist Interventions, vol 2: German Film History/German History on Film*, ed. Sandra Frieden et al. (Providence: Berg, 1993), 148, 150. Fehrenbach quotes one such woman as saying: "I was fed up with marriage . . . I am not the type of person who likes so terribly to subordinate herself to others."

37. Kathleen Rowe, *The Unruly Woman: Gender and the Genres of Laughter* (Austin: University of Texas Press, 1995), 200.

38. Nickie Roberts, *Whores in History: Prostitution in Western Society* (London: Harper Collins, 1992), 354.

39. Stamp, *Movie-Struck Girls*, 8.

40. Mary Ann Doane, *Femmes Fatales: Feminism, Film Theory, Psychoanalysis* (New York: Routledge, 1991), 153.

41. Quoted in Gail Peterson, *A Vindication of the Rights of Whores* (Seattle: Seal Press, 1989), 189.

42. Linda Williams, *Hard Core: Power, Pleasure, and the "Frenzy of the Visible"* (Berkeley and Los Angeles: University of California Press, 1989), 231.

43. Kathleen Murphy, "*Belle de Jour*," in *Women and the Cinema: A Critical Anthology*, ed. Karyn Kay and Gerald Peary (New York: Dutton, 1977), 38.

44. Karyn Kay, "The Revenge of Pirate Jenny," *The Velvet Light Trap* 9 (1973): 49.

45. Actually, Jeanne Dielman does have an orgasm with one of her clients, prior to killing him with a pair of scissors. "This orgasm-bit is bound to strike the serious-minded as an unfortunate bow to crass commercialism on Ms. Akerman's part," commented John Coleman in the *New Statesman*.

46. COYOTE has received support from the Playboy Foundation and the American Civil Liberties Union. See Valerie Jenness, *Making It Work: The Prostitutes' Rights Movement in Perspective* (New York: Aldine de Gruyter, 1993), 42, 46, 54. On the prostitutes' rights movement, see also Pheterson, *A Vindication of the Rights of Whores* and Shannon Bell, *Reading, Writing and Rewriting the Prostitute Body* (Bloomington: Indiana University Press, 1994).

47. See Jenness, *Making It Work*, 76–81, and Bell, 97–99, 129. See also Kathleen Barry,

Female Sexual Slavery (Englewood Cliffs, NJ: Prentice-Hall, 1979) and *The Prostitution of Sexuality* (New York: New York University Press, 1995), and Sheila Jeffreys, *The Idea of Prostitution* (Melbourne: Spinifex, 1997).

3. Gigolette

1. Henry Miller, *Quiet Days in Clichy* (London: New English Library, 1969), 8–9.

2. The "lady barbers" in the Western *5 Card Stud* (USA, 1968) offer the following services: "Shave, $1.00; Haircut, $2.50; Shampoo, $3.00; Miscellaneous, $20.00."

3. *Variety*, June 18, 1930, quoted in James Robert Parish, *Prostitution in Hollywood Films: Plots, Critiques, Casts and Credits for 389 Theatrical and Made-for-Television Releases* (Jefferson, NC, and London: McFarland, 1992), 34.

4. James Robert Parish makes this point in his entry on *The Bad One*. See Parish, 34.

5. Douglas Riplet, "The Keystone Film Company and the Historiography of Early Slapstick" in *Classical Hollywood Comedy*, ed. Kristine Brunovska Karnick and Henry Jenkins (New York: Routledge, 1995), 177.

6. See e.g. Marcel Tariol, *Louis Delluc*, quoted in René Prédal, *La Société française (1914–1945) à travers le cinéma* (Paris: Armand Colin, 1972), 91, and Léon Moussinac, quoted in Richard Abel, *French Cinema: The First Wave, 1915–1929* (Princeton: Princeton University Press, 1984), 317.

7. The film was shot in Monterey, California.

8. Jorge Ayala Blanco, *Aventura del Cine Mexicano* (México DF: Ediciones Era, 1968), 132.

9. Though a German production, *l'Étrange M. Victor* was a French-language film with French director and cast, and was shot partially on location in Toulon. See John W. Martin, *The Golden Age of French Cinema 1929–1939* (London: Columbus, 1987), 90–92.

10. *Berlin—Alexanderplatz* was directed by Phil [Piel] Jutzi, who was previously responsible for the left-wing *Mutter Krausens Fahrt ins Glück* (see chapter 5) and *Hunger in Waldenburg*.

11. Edward Baron Turk, *Child of Paradise: Marcel Carné and the Golden Age of French Cinema* (Cambridge, MA: Harvard University Press, 1989), 144.

12. Raymond Durgnat, *Eros in the Cinema* (London: Calder & Boyars, 1966), 177–78.

13. Simone Signoret, *Nostalgia Isn't What It Used to Be* (London: Granada, 1979), 127–28.

14. Ibid., 128.

15. *Monthly Film Bulletin*, June 1967, 95.

4. Siren

1. In *Cony-Catchers and Bawdy Baskets: An Anthology of Elizabethan Low Life*, ed. Gamini Salgado (Harmondsworth: Penguin, 1972), 336.

2. James Robert Parish, *Prostitution in Hollywood Films: Plots, Critiques, Casts and Credits for 389 Theatrical and Made-for-Television Releases* (Jefferson, NC, and London: McFarland, 1992), 419.

3. Robert Murphy, *Sixties British Cinema* (London: BFI, 1972), 89.

4. A curious variant on the Siren narrative is *Alraune* (Germany, 1928), in which the protagonist is the biological outcome of a scientific experiment involving a prostitute be-

ing impregnated with the sperm of a hanged man. Alraune grows up to be a thief's accomplice and circus performer with a coldly destructive attitude to life, who manipulates her sexuality to bring about the downfall of her many male admirers. She directs her attentions particularly at her "creator," who has become obsessed with her, and for whom she has developed an engulfing hatred. The scientist is driven mad with desire and ruins herself for her at the gambling table. One assumes an influence from the contemporaneous eugenics movement; because she has been brought up in a Catholic convent, it is clearly her prostitute inheritance that makes Alraune a monster (as her larcenous tendencies can be put down to her father, presumably a criminal). The film was remade in 1930 and 1952.

5. See Patricia King Hanson, ed., *The American Film Institute Catalog of Motion Pictures Produced in the United States: Feature Films, 1911–1920* (Berkeley: University of California Press, 1988), 570.

6. I deal with the Manon Lescaut story, principally in the version titled *Manon* (France, 1949), in chapter 8. In this study I concentrate on the Renoir and Pabst interpretations of the Zola and Wedekind texts, respectively. Later cinema versions of *Nana* include *Nana* (USA, 1934), *Nana* (Mexico, 1944), *Nana* (France, 1955), *Tag mej—älska mej. . . / Nana 70/Nana/Poupée d'amour/Take Me, Love Me* (Sweden/France, 1970), and *Nana* (Italy, 1982). The Wedekind plays were subsequently adapted as *Lulu* (Austria, 1962), *Lulu* (?, directed by Ronald Chase, 1978), *Lulu* (West Germany/France/Italy, 1980), and *Lulú de noche/Lulu by Night* (Spain, 1985); there is also at least one television version of the Alban Berg opera.

7. See e.g., Günther Dahlke and Günter Karl, *Deutsche Spielfilme von dem Anfängen bis 1933: Ein Filmführer* (Berlin: Herschel Verlag, 1993), 93.

8. Jean Renoir, *My Life and My Films* (London: Collins, 1974), 84.

9. The lap dancer works an intermediate territory here. See *Showgirls* (USA, 1995).

10. "[N]obody who was connected with the film dreamed that Pabst was risking commercial failure with the story of an 'immoral' prostitute who wasn't crazy about her work. . . . [B]esides daring to show the prostitute as the victim, Mr. Pabst went on to the final, damning immorality of making his Lulu as 'sweetly innocent' as the flowers that adorned her costumes and filled the scenes of the play." Louise Brooks, *Lulu in Hollywood* (London: Hamish Hamilton, 1982), 94.

11. *Pandora's Box*, and this scene in particular, have been subjected to extensive analysis. See e.g., Thomas Elsaesser, "Lulu and the Meter Man: Louise Brooks, Pabst and *Pandora's Box*," *Screen* 24 (Jul–Oct 1983): 4–36 (especially 31–32) and Mary Ann Doane, "The Erotic Barter: *Pandora's Box* (1929)" in *The Films of G. W. Pabst: An Extraterritorial Cinema*, ed. Eric Rentschler (New Brunswick: Rutgers University Press, 1990), 62–79 (especially 76–78), reprinted in Mary Ann Doane, *Femmes Fatales: Feminism, Film Theory, Psychoanalysis* (New York: Routledge, 1991), 142–62.

12. Mary Ann Doane comments: "Lulu . . . is oblivious to class distinctions. . . . She is able to travel comfortably through all social spaces and, not recognizing or acknowledging these distinctions herself, is situated in a realm somewhere beyond or outside of social hierarchy." In Rentschler, *The Films of G. W. Pabst*, 70.

13. See Russell Campbell, "Prostitution and Film Censorship in the USA," *Screening the Past* 2 (1997) http://www.latrobe.edu.au/www/screeningthepast/firstrelease/firdec/Campbell.html (version current May 4, 2004).

14. Quoted in Parish, *Prostitution in Hollywood Films*, 348.

15. Changed to "Atkinson" in some release versions.

16. ". . . ce que la plupart des gens ne veulent pas voir et qui est très désagréable à examiner: ce qui détruit l'homme et la femme"—Joseph Losey, quoted in Pierre Rissient, *Losey* (Paris: Éditions Universitaires, 1966), 140.

17. "If you are dealing with a subject which is harsh and cruel, and to many people repugnant as in the case of *Eve* . . . and if you are going to handle it, as I have tried to, so that people can see what beauty is there, what anguish, and have compassion and some understanding, then rhythm of music and rhythm of cutting, and the relationship of one to the other as well as performances, is essential. . . . An essential thing was the lyricism and the poetry and the compassion—the intended compassion, anyway."—Losey in *Losey on Losey*, ed. Tom Milne (Garden City, NY: Doubleday, 1968), 31, 37.

18. See e.g. Milne, *Losey on Losey*, 30–31; James Leahy, *The Cinema of Joseph Losey* (London: Zwemmer, 1967), 109–10, and David Caute, *Joseph Losey: A Revenge on Life* (London: Faber & Faber, 1994), 157–58.

19. Caute, *Joseph Losey*, 162.

20. Losey in Milne, *Losey on Losey*, 29.

21. "Au contraire de Tyvian, Eve est complètement indépendante. Il se sent coupable de faire ce qu'il fait, pas elle. . . . Elle a plus de lucidité et aussi plus d'honnêteté. . . . Elle sait qu'elle donne du plaisir et que cela mérite un salaire. Elle ne se prostitue pas. Elle domine son sexe, parce qu'elle est franche et logique; elle profite des hommes. Mais les relations qu'elle entretient avec eux excluent toute idée de péché."—Losey in Rissient, *Losey*, 134, 136.

22. Losey in Leahy, *The Cinema of Joseph Losey*, 114.

23. Losey in Milne, *Losey on Losey*, 37.

24. Ibid., 27.

25. Caute, *Joseph Losey*, 309.

26. My comments on this film draw upon my review of it, published in *Monthly Film Bulletin*, August 1970, 159–60.

27. See Fassbinder's remarks in *Kino 81/82: Bundesdeutsche Filme auf der Leinwand*, ed. Robert Fischer (Munich: Verlag Monika Nüchtern, 1981), 94.

28. There is an *hommage* to Buñuel in the film: one of the movies that the traveling exhibitor advertises on his van is *Belle de Jour.*

5. Comrade

1. Alain Corbin, *Women for Hire: Prostitution and Sexuality in France after 1850*, trans. Alan Sheridan (Cambridge, MA: Harvard University Press, 1990), 330.

2. Ibid., 234–40.

3. *Libertad*, October 25, 1906, quoted in Corbin, *Women for Hire*, 242.

4. See Corbin, *Women for Hire*, 242–46.

5. Patricia King Hanson, ed., *The American Film Institute Catalog of Motion Pictures Produced in the United States: Feature Films, 1911–1920* (University of California Press, Berkeley, 1988), 481.

6. A French version of the film, *l'Opéra de quat'sous*, was shot simultaneously by Pabst with a different cast. The film was remade as *Die Dreigroschenoper/l'Opéra de quat'sous/Three Penny Opera* (West Germany/France, 1962) and as *Mack the Knife* (USA, 1989). *Liu mang yi*

sheng /Mack the Knife (Hong Kong, 1995) is about a doctor practicing in a red-light district and is not derived from the Brecht/Weill text.

7. Eileen Bowser, *The Transformation of Cinema, 1907–1915* (New York: Charles Scribner's Sons, 1990), 189.

8. See Janet Staiger, *Bad Women: Regulating Sexuality in Early American Cinema* (Minneapolis: University of Minnesota Press, 1995), 130.

9. Hanson, *1911–1920,* 749.

10. *Die freudlose Gasse* was subjected to heavy censorship on its original release, and was recut, virtually eliminating Asta Nielsen's role, for distribution in the United States. My comments are based on the print held in the Bundesfilmarchiv, Berlin, and on the reconstituted version released by the Munich Filmmuseum in 1989. For detailed discussion of the film's different versions and an account of the latest reconstruction, see Jan-Christopher Horak, "Film History and Film Preservation: Reconstructing the Text of *The Joyless Street* (1925)," *Screening the Past* 5, http://www.latrobe.edu.au/www/screeningthepast/firstrelease/fir1298/jhfr5b.html (version current May 7, 2004).

11. Filmoberprüfstelle report, Berlin, March 29, 1926, quoted in Patrice Petro, "Film Censorship and the Female Spectator: *The Joyless Street* (1925)," in *The Films of G. W. Pabst: An Extraterritorial Cinema,* ed. Eric Rentschler (New Brunswick: Rutgers University Press, 1990), 38.

12. Siegfried Kracauer reports that the film was banned in Britain and mutilated in Italy, France, Austria, and elsewhere. *From Caligari to Hitler: A Psychological History of the German Film* (Princeton: Princeton University Press, 1947), 167.

13. On Prometheus, see Bruce Murray, *Film and the German Left in the Weimar Republic: from Caligari to Kuhle Wampe* (Austin: University of Texas Press, 1990). *Jenseits der Strasse* and *Mutter Krausens Fahrt ins Glück* were both scripted by the Prometheus writing team of Willi Döll and Jan Fethke.

14. Paul Willemen and Ashish Rajadhyaksha, *Encyclopaedia of Indian Cinema* (London: BFI, and New Delhi: Oxford University Press, 1994), 285. See also Shampa Banerjee and Anil Srivastava, *One Hundred Indian Feature Films: An Annotated Filmography* (New York: Garland, 1988), 74–75, and Sumita S. Chakravarty, *National Identity in Indian Popular Cinema 1947–1987* (Austin: University of Texas Press, 1993), 92–94.

15. Willemen and Rajadhyaksha, *Encyclopaedia of Indian Cinema,* 305–6.

16. See Graham Roberts, *Forward Soviet! History and Non-fiction Film in the USSR* (London: I. B. Tauris, 1999), 36.

17. Ibid., 43.

18. Ibid., 123.

19. He is named Horst Wessel, though there is some doubt as to the whether this is an authentic portrayal of the historical martyr to the Nazi cause.

20. Robert Stam speaks of "a series of inversions of the sacred and the profane: the church becomes a brothel: the Virgin Mary, a whore; and the Eucharist, LSD." *Subversive Pleasures: Bakhtin, Cultural Criticism and Film* (Baltimore: Johns Hopkins University Press, 1989), 113.

21. See James Robert Parish, *Prostitution in Hollywood Films: Plots, Critiques, Casts and Credits for 389 Theatrical and Made-for-Television Releases* (Jefferson, NC, and London: McFarland, 1992), 418. Vincent Canby wrote in the *New York Times:* "It may be because Miss Fonda's and Sutherland's soberly humanitarian left-wing political views are so well

known that they lend a heaviness to *Steelyard Blues* that it would not have if we were not so aware" (quoted in Parish, *Prostitution in Hollywood Films*).

22. Hanson, *1911–1920*, 632.

23. Lina Wertmüller, in *The Cineaste Interviews: On the Art and Politics of the Cinema* by Dan Georgakas and Lenny Rubinstein (Chicago: Lake View Press, 1983), 136.

24. Another version of the Sartre play is the TV film *Den respektfulla skökan* (Sweden, 1960).

25. That the ending is not more upbeat is perhaps explained in a comment by Fassbinder: "I find it OK for him to murder his oppressor, but it is not OK for him then to go into the desert, since with that he accepts the superior power of others. If he had really believed in what he was doing, then he would have acted in solidarity with other oppressed people, would have acted together with them and then they could have engaged in a joint action. The solo action at the end of the film is no solution and so the film at the end is aimed also against the black man." Quoted in *Rainer Werner Fassbinder Werkschau*, ed. Ernst-Christian Neisel (Berlin: Rainer Werner Fassbinder Foundation, 1992), 19 (translation by RC).

26. Hanson, *1911–1920*, 481.

27. Reviewing the film on its release, André Bazin called it "the first film on the Resistance." See André Bazin, *French Cinema of the Occupation and Resistance: The Birth of a Critical Esthetic*, ed. François Truffaut (New York: Frederick Ungar, 1981), 119.

28. Stephen Teo, *Hong Kong Cinema: The Extra Dimensions* (London: BFI, 1997), 32.

29. The poster is reproduced in Martha Ackelsberg, *Mujeres Libres: Organizing Women During the Spanish Revolution* (pamphlet, London: Brixton DAM, 1987), 14.

30. Mujeres Libres policy was to provide prostitutes with the opportunity to remake their lives in rehabilitation centers named *liberatorios de prostitución*. Wartime conditions meant that this initiative did not get much past the drawing board, despite having some official support from the Republican Government. Prostitution in Barcelona was rife during the Civil War and many of the clientele were indeed militiamen and antifascist soldiers. See Mary Nash, *Defying Male Civilization: Women in the Spanish Civil War* (Denver: Arden, 1995), 157, 163–65. In *Film and the Anarchist Imagination* (London: Verso, 1999), Richard Porton describes *Libertarias* as a "heavily fictionalized tale," contending that "instead of engaging in melodramatic raids on brothels, the Mujeres Libres set up *liberatorios de prostitución*" (96, 274, n89).

31. Carmen Huaco-Nuzum, "Matilde Landeta: An Introduction to the Work of a Pioneer Mexican Film-Maker," *Screen* 28, no. 4 (Autumn 1987): 104.

32. Daniel J. Goulding, "Makavejev," in *Five Filmmakers: Tarkovsky, Forman, Polanski, Szabó, Makavejev*, ed. D. J. Goulding (Bloomington: Indiana University Press, 1994), 240. Goulding also describes Anna as a "militant Marxist prostitute" (239). Much of the imagery—Anna in white lace underwear stripping and seducing the schoolboys, Anna arrested being dragged kicking and screaming, scantily dressed, to the paddy wagon—does connote the prostitute iconographically.

33. Makavejev was a highly motivated member of the Communist youth organization in Yugoslavia from the age of fourteen, became a leader, and was accepted into the party at sixteen. Expelled at twenty-two, he was later readmitted and again expelled at the time of *WR: Mysteries of the Organism*. Conversation with author, October 28, 1977.

6. Avenger

1. Alexander Kuprin, *Yama: The Pit*, in *The Prostitute in Literature*, ed. Harold Greenwald and Aron Krich (New York: Ballantine, 1960), 192.

2. Carol J. Clover, *Men, Women, and Chainsaws* (London: BFI, 1992). Clover describes the films of the cycle — including titles such as *Lipstick* (1976), *I Spit on Your Grave* (1977), *Ms. 45* (1981), and *The Accused* (1988) — as follows: "Women seek their own revenge — usually on their own behalf, but sometimes on behalf of a sister (literal or figurative) who has been murdered or disabled in an act of sexual violence. . . . They share a set of premises that, while not entirely unprecedented, are conspicuously conditioned by changes in social attitudes of the two decades in question: that rape deserves full-scale revenge; that a rape-and-revenge story constitutes sufficient drama for a feature film and that having the victim survive to be her own avenger makes that drama even better; and (more directly politically) that we live in a 'rape culture' in which *all* males — husbands, boyfriends, lawyers, politicians — are directly or indirectly complicit and that men are thus not just individually but corporately liable." (138–39)

3. The credits state that the film was produced "under the personal supervision" of Mrs. Reid. The director was Walter Lang, whose first film it was. Priscilla Bonner reports that "he was very anxious, but she [Mrs. Reid] was a great help to him. . . . She was always on the set, always." Quoted in Anthony Slide, *The Idols of Silence* (South Brunswick: NJ: A. S. Barnes, 1976), 72.

4. Bonner attests: "The truth was so dramatic it needed no changes. They told it as it happened. The only fiction was the chauffeur. . . ." Quoted in Kevin Brownlow, *Behind the Mask of Innocence* (New York: Knopf, 1990), 91. Names were not changed and Gabrielle Darley subsequently successfully sued Mrs. Reid. See Slide, *The Idols of Silence*, 72, and *Early Women Directors* (South Brunswick: NJ: A. S. Barnes, 1977), 78–79.

5. See Russell Campbell, "Prostitution and Film Censorship in the USA," *Screening the Past* 2 (1997) http://www.latrobe.edu.au/www/screeningthepast/firstrelease/firdec/Campbell.html (version current May 4, 2004).

6. Brownlow, *Behind the Mask of Innocence*, 92.

7. Mordaunt Hall, in the *New York Times*, February 3, 1926, 23:1, wrote: "There have been a number of wretched pictures on Broadway during the last year, but none seemed to have quite reached the low level of *The Red Kimono*, a production evidently intended to cause weeping, wailing and gnashing of teeth. Possibly it might accomplish its purpose if the theatre doors were locked, but so long as one knows one can get out of the building, it is another matter." *Variety*, conceding that the picture was "rather well directed," argued that "Mrs. Reid . . . may believe she is doing something for the fallen women in turning out a picture of this sort, but the chances are that she will do tremendous harm to the picture industry as a whole and to herself in particular because she sponsors it [white slavery?] by permitting it [the depiction of white slavery?] to continue." Fred., in *Variety*, February 3, 1926. Both reviews are quoted by Brownlow.

8. See Heide Schlüpmann, "The Brothel as an Arcadian Space? *Diary of a Lost Girl* (1929)," in *The Films of G. W. Pabst: An Extraterritorial Cinema*, ed. Eric Rentschler (New Brunswick: Rutgers University Press, 1990), 80.

9. Pabst's original ending, which he was forced to cut by the distributors, was even more provocative, with Thymian becoming the mistress of a brothel. See R. Borde, F. Buache, and F. Courtade, *Le cinéma réaliste allemand* (Lyon: Serdoc, 1965), 125.

10. See John Trevelyan, *What the Censor Saw* (London: Michael Joseph, 1973), 187–88, and Guy Phelps, *Film Censorship* (London: Gollancz, 1975), 155. Trevelyan's account is inaccurate in detail and vague as to just what the grounds for rejection were. It is significant, however, that he describes Kelly as a thief ("stole his money"), when the film indicates strongly that she took no more than was rightly hers.

11. Patricia King Hanson, ed., *The American Film Institute Catalog of Motion Pictures Produced in the United States: Feature Films, 1911–1920* (Berkeley: University of California Press, 1988), 183. See also Brownlow, *Behind the Mask of Innocence*, 58–59.

12. Gitta Sereny records a similar revenge taken by a Hamburg child prostitute on the gang of pimps who had exploited and raped her: "What Annette made up her mind to do — and this happened just before we met — was a very curious kind of vengeance. She was deliberately going to get herself infected with VD and then she was going to give it to all of them. 'Every one of them was going to get it in the arse, right where it hits them hardest,' she said, viciously. And it worked." Gitta Sereny, *The Invisible Children: Child Prostitution in America, West Germany and Great Britain* (London: André Deutsch, 1984), 144.

13. Linda Provinzano, Howard Besser, Stephanie Boris, and Frank Motofuji, *Films in the Collection of the Pacific Film Archive, vol 1: Daiei Motion Picture Co. Ltd., Japan* (Berkeley: University Art Museum, 1979), 42.

14. Richard P. Krafsur, ed., *The American Film Institute Catalog of Motion Pictures: Feature Films 1961–1970* (New York: Bowker, 1976), 407.

15. The director is Bo Arne Vibenius (credited as Alex Fridolinski), who also wrote the script.

16. Delphine Seyrig, quoted in Marsha Kinder, "Reflections on *Jeanne Dielman*," in *Sexual Stratagems: The World of Women in Film*, ed. Patricia Erens (New York: Horizon, 1979), 249.

17. Kinder, "Reflections," 248.

18. Chantal Akerman, quoted in Kinder, "Reflections," 256.

19. See e.g. Jayne Loader, "*Jeanne Dielman:* Death in Instalments," *Jump Cut* 16 (1977): 10–12. Loader argues: "I find Akerman's film . . . self-defeating in its depiction of the housewife's role and her so-called regeneration through violence at the film's end. . . . Akerman's solution to the fact of female oppression is unfortunately a common one, which is offered not only in several other contemporary films by women but in a significant number of women's novels as well: it is violence, directed at the first male who comes to hand. By his sex rather than his person, he is forced to stand for the oppressors of all the rest. . . . If we are to make real changes in our lives and in our cinema, we must offer not only new cinematic structures but serious solutions to the social problems that persist."

20. Kaye Sullivan, *Films For, By and About Women* (Metuchen, NJ: Scarecrow, 1980), 56.

21. *Utopie* was coscripted and directed by Iranian filmmaker Sohrab Shahid Saless.

22. *Nuts,* based on a stage play by Tom Topor, was scripted by Topor, Darryl Ponicsan, and Alvin Sargent, and directed by Martin Ritt.

23. Tom Milne, in the *Monthly Film Bulletin,* quoted in James Robert Parish, *Prostitution in Hollywood Films: Plots, Critiques, Casts and Credits for 389 Theatrical and Made-for-Television Releases* (Jefferson, NC and London: McFarland, 1992), 308.

24. "We wanted them to kill everybody," Despentes has said, describing the potential victims as "people in the wrong place at the wrong time." See Gavin Smith and Gerald Peary, "Toronto 3," *Film Comment* 36, no. 6 (Nov–Dec 2000): 67.

25. Patricia King Hanson, ed., *The American Film Institute Catalog of Motion Pictures Produced in the United States: Feature Films, 1931–1940* (Berkeley: University of California Press, 1993), 2345. The catalogue entry notes that "at the end of the film, just after the jury takes another vote, a picture of 'Marjorie' is shown on the screen and the following appears, superimposed over her face: 'The jury is still out. What will the verdict be? What would *your* verdict be? $100.00 in cash prizes will be given for the best answer — contest open to all. Win a prize. Mail your opinion in not over 300 words to Real Life Dramas, 4376 Sunset Drive, Hollywood California.' No information was been uncovered to determine if there was a winner to the Real Life Drama contest."

26. See Alix Kirsta, *Deadlier Than the Male: Violence and Aggression in Women* (London: HarperCollins, 1994), 152–53.

27. Wuornos's last victim, Walter Antonio, was in fact a truck driver who was a reserve police officer.

28. "I wish I never woulda got that gun. I wish to God, I never was a hooker. And I just wish I never woulda done what I did."

29. *Dateline NBC*, August 25, 1992, quoted in Lynda Hart, *Fatal Women: Lesbian Sexuality and the Mark of Aggression* (Princeton: Princeton University Press, 1994), 143.

30. Statement of Lee Wuornos at a court hearing, incorporated in the documentary *Aileen Wuornos: The Selling of a Serial Killer.*

31. The documentary *Aileen: Life and Death of a Serial Killer* (UK/USA, 2003) — a sequel to the earlier documentary by the same director, Nick Broomfield, in collaboration with Joan Churchill — contains a 2001 interview with Wuornos in which she asserts "there was no self-defense," and claims that she was lying in her detailed account of the Mallory killing at her trial. The circumstances of the interview and an apparent later retraction, however, cast doubt on the veracity of this statement.

32. A title at the end of the film states: "While this film is inspired by real events in the life of Aileen Wuornos, many characters are composites or inventions, and a number of incidents depicted in this film are fictional."

33. Patty Jenkins explains that she did extensive research into Aileen Wuornos's life, and that she and Charlize Theron studied documentary footage and "got to know such intimate details about her," especially after Wuornos opened up to them the personal archive of letters that she had written on death row. See Phillip Williams, "Killer Movie, Killer Moviemaking: Writer-Director Patty Jenkins on *Monster*," http://www.moviemaker.com/hop/vo14/01/directing.html (version current May 10, 2004).

7. Martyr

1. James K. Baxter, *Collected Poems*, ed. J. E. Weir (Wellington: Oxford University Press, 1979), 243.

2. Blaise Cendrars, from *The Detonated Man* (*l'Homme foudroyé*) in *Selected Writings*, ed. Walter Albert (New York: New Directions, 1966), 273–74.

3. Eric Trudgill, *Madonnas and Magdalens: The Origins and Development of Victorian Sexual Attitudes* (London: Heinemann, 1976), 279.

4. J. M. Murtagh, "Prostitution," *New Catholic Encyclopedia*, vol 11 (New York: McGraw-Hill, 1967), 879, 881.

5. Sumita S. Chakravarty, *National Identity in Indian Popular Cinema 1947–1987* (Austin: University of Texas Press, 1993), 293.

6. Jeanne Cordelier describes abuse by her father in her autobiographical narrative *La Dérobade*, translated as *"The Life": Memoirs of a French Hooker* (New York: Viking, 1976)— "for seven long years I kept smelling his cock under my nose" (p 328)—but this aspect of her background is omitted from the film based on the book.

7. Arturo Ripstein's remake of the 1933 *La mujer del puerto*, with a screenplay by Paz Alicia Garcíadiego, considerably revises the storyline. The film was unreleased in Mexico during the 1990s.

8. Richard P. Krafsur, ed., *The American Film Institute Catalog of Motion Pictures: Feature Films, 1961–1970* (New York: Bowker, 1976), 64.

9. Patricia King Hanson, ed., *The American Film Institute Catalog of Motion Pictures Produced in the United States: Feature Films, 1911–1920* (Berkeley: University of California Press, 1988), 695.

10. In the earlier (1931) version of the Robert E. Sherwood play, Myra relents and promises to marry Roy, only to be killed in an air raid.

11. Bryan Burns, *World Cinema: Hungary* (Trowbridge, Wiltshire: Flicks Books, 1996), 8.

12. That the cadaverous effect is intentional is clear from a planned later scene (included in the published script) in which the prostitute offers herself to Paul. "Paul turns on the light. She didn't expect it, and is shocked. She and Paul look at each other. It is a death mask there, not a face, and this body isn't a body but a skeleton. So Paul thinks. And the woman senses it." Bernardo Bertolucci and Franco Arcalli, *Bernardo Bertolucci's Last Tango in Paris* (New York: Delta, 1973), 174.

13. Hanson, *1911–1920*, 246.

14. Hugo Haas, writer-director of *Hold Back Tomorrow*, was active in the Czechoslovak film industry at the time *Tonka of the Gallows* was made. Like *Der Mädchenhirt*, *Tonka of the Gallows* was based on a novel by Egon Erwin Kisch.

15. Peter Hames, *The Czechoslovak New Wave* (Berkeley: University of California Press, 1985), 16–17.

16. Jorge Ayala Blanco, *Aventura del cine mexicano* (México DF: Ediciones Era, 1968), 130. Federico Gamboa's novel *Santa* was first filmed in 1918.

17. Hanson, *1911–1920*, 645.

18. Keiko McDonald, *Mizoguchi* (Boston: Twayne, 1984), 34.

19. Ibid., 83.

20. Rafael Ma. Guerrero, ed., *Readings in Philippine Cinema* (Manila: Experimental Cinema of the Philippines, 1983), 229.

21. *Variety*, October 3, 1973.

22. Existentialist Godard inadvertently answers the question in *Vivre sa vie*, of the same year. "I think we're always responsible for our actions," declares Nana. "We're free. I raise my hand—I'm responsible. I turn my head—I'm responsible. I am unhappy— I'm responsible."

23. Naomi Greene, *Pier Paolo Pasolini: Cinema as Heresy* (Princeton: Princeton University Press, 1990), 27.

24. Ibid., 26.

25. Chris Chang, "Disordinately Absolute: Pasolini's *Mamma Roma*," *Film Comment* 31, no. 1 (Jan–Feb 1995): 10.

26. Burns, *World Cinema: Hungary*, 8.

27. In 1947, Fellini suggested to Rossellini for the second part of *La voce umana* "the pathetic story of a prostitute from the city's outskirts who, despised by her high-ranking

colleagues, has a magical adventure with the actor Amadeo Nazzari." Angelo Solmi, *Fellini* (London: Merlin, 1967), 126.

28. Federico Fellini, "Letter to a Jesuit Priest," in Fellini, *Fellini on Fellini* (London: Eyre Methuen, 1976), 66.

29. Birgitta Steene, *Ingmar Bergman* (New York: St. Martin's, 1968), 45.

30. As Rachel Douglas, Anderson later wrote and directed the feature *Blessed* (New Zealand, 2002), partially set in a brothel.

8. Gold Digger

1. Catullus, *The Poems of Catullus*, trans. Peter Whigham (Harmondsworth: Penguin, 1966), 222.

2. The line is spoken by her character Ruby Carter in *Belle of the Nineties* (USA, 1934).

3. Quoted in James Robert Parish, *Prostitution in Hollywood Films: Plots, Critiques, Casts and Credits for 389 Theatrical and Made-for-Television Releases* (Jefferson, NC and London: McFarland, 1992), 451.

4. My use of the term "Gold Digger" is of course related to, and derived from, the "gold diggers" who populated American screens in the 1920s and, particularly, the early 1930s, and were saluted in films such as *The Gold Diggers* (1923) and its successors. These characters, however, tended not to be outright prostitutes — partly because of censorship pressures — and, often portrayed in comic mode, they were considerably more sympathetic than the avaricious hooker I describe in this chapter. See chap. 3, "Glamour and Gold Diggers," in Lea Jacobs, *The Wages of Sin: Censorship and the Fallen Woman Film, 1928–1942* (Madison: University of Wisconsin Press, 1991), 52–84.

5. Patricia King Hanson, ed., *The American Film Institute Catalog of Motion Pictures Produced in the United States: Feature Films, 1931–1940* (Berkeley: University of California Press, 1993), 628.

6. Ibid., 728.

7. Stephen Teo, *Hong Kong Cinema: The Extra Dimensions* (London: BFI, 1997), 31.

8. Richard P. Krafsur, ed., *The American Film Institute Catalog of Motion Pictures: Feature Films, 1961–1970* (New York: Bowker, 1976), 110.

9. Ibid., 494.

10. Ibid., 893.

11. Ibid., 685.

12. Isolde Standish, "Korean Cinema and the New Realism: Text and Context" in *Colonialism and Nationalism in Asian Cinema*, ed. Wimal Dissanayake (Bloomington: Indiana University Press, 1994), 81.

13. Andrew Horton and Michael Brashinsky, *The Zero Hour: Glasnost and Soviet Cinema in Transition* (Princeton, NJ: Princeton University Press, 1992), 119.

14. Hanson, *1931–1940*, 1314.

15. Paulo Antonio Paranaguá, ed., *Mexican Cinema* (London: BFI, 1995), 232.

16. Jacobs, *The Wages of Sin*, 68.

17. An employee of the MPPDA protested to industry censor Will Hays about *Bed of Roses*, "which again is the story of a criminal prostitute's methods of wangling luxury out of rich men." She complained that "the constant flow of these pictures leaves me with mental nausea." Alice Ames Winter, quoted in Jacobs, *The Wages of Sin*, 16.

18. Patricia King Hanson, ed., *The American Film Institute Catalog of Motion Pictures*

Produced in the United States: Feature Films, 1911–1920 (Berkeley: University of California Press, 1988), 1033.

19. Aevys Keel, *Monthly Film Bulletin,* July 1971, 148.

20. Hanson, *1931–1940,* 1401.

21. Krafsur, *1961–1970,* 1055.

22. The film is also known under the title of *La storia vera della signora delle camelie.*

23. Charles Bernheimer, *Figures of Ill Repute: Representing Prostitution in Nineteenth-Century France* (Cambridge: Harvard University Press, 1989), 95.

24. Tom Milne, "Intimidades de una prostituta (Sex is the Name of the Game)," *Monthly Film Bulletin,* November 1973, 228.

9. Nursemaid

1. Kenneth Munden, ed., *The American Film Institute Catalog of Motion Pictures Produced in the United States: Feature Films, 1921–1930* (New York: Bowker, 1971), 801.

2. See e.g. Eileen McLeod, *Women Working: Prostitution Now* (London: Croom Helm, 1982). McLeod writes of her British research: "Nearly all the men I interviewed complained about the emotional coldness and mercenary approach of many prostitutes they had had contact with" (84). In *Backstreets: Prostitution, Money and Love* (University Park, PA: Pennsylvania State University Press, 1992), Cecilie Høigård and Liv Finstad report from their Norwegian study that though the majority of customers "say that they go to a prostitute among other reasons because it is noncommittal, they also say that they want warm girls, increased intimacy, and understanding. They complain that prostitution is cold or say that they get an empty or negative feeling when they realize that it is only money that lies behind it" (95). The following comments by women working in the New Zealand sex industry on what clients want from prostitutes are included in Jan Jordan, *Working Girls* (Auckland: Penguin, 1991): "Some of them want nursing; some want to be treated badly; some want to be cuddled and loved" (23); "Some clients want someone to listen to their problems — they're good, because they just sit and talk" (38); "I became close to some of my clients — not serious relationships, more like relaxed friendships. They discussed business, their hang-ups and marital problems" (71); "Most of all I think they wanted substitute wives — someone they could talk to" (75).

3. Ibid., 676.

4. Jorge Ayala Blanco, *Aventura del Cine Mexicano* (México DF: Ediciones Era, 1968), 160–61.

5. Richard P. Krafsur, ed., *The American Film Institute Catalog of Motion Pictures: Feature Films, 1961–1970* (New York: Bowker, 1976), 1079.

6. Ibid., 265.

7. Ibid., 604.

8. The film was twice reedited and rereleased by its director, William Richert, in 1981 as *American Success* and in 1983 as *Success.*

9. Linda Williams, *Hard Core: Power, Pleasure, and the "Frenzy of the Visible"* (Berkeley: University of California Press, 1989), 236.

10. Paul Willemen and Ashish Rajadhyaksha, *Encyclopaedia of Indian Cinema* (London: BFI and New Delhi: Oxford University Press, 1994), 284.

11. Ibid., 396.

12. Typically for a film produced under the regime of the Production Code Administration, Katie's identity as prostitute is alternately affirmed and denied. In the first scene in which she appears, for instance, she is seemingly a streetwalker attracting custom, but then (when Gypo intervenes) a good girl rescued from this fate by her boyfriend. Gypo's friend Terry takes him to Madame Betty's establishment (a brothel?) in the expectation of finding her there — but she's not. (Gypo drunkenly hallucinates her presence, suggesting that the idea that Katie has become a prostitute is simply a product of his fearful imaginings.) But later, talking to good girl Mary McPhillip, Katie says: "I'm not the kind of girl you are. There was a time when I was. And I love Gypo no less for being what I am." (Here, though, "what I am" may mean simply someone who has lost her virginity rather than a prostitute.) The prevarication serves the film's fusion of biblical references, in which Katie is both Virgin Mary and Mary Magdalene, just as Gypo is both Jesus and Judas.

13. James Robert Parish, *Prostitution in Hollywood Films: Plots, Critiques, Casts and Credits for 389 Theatrical and Made-for-Television Releases* (Jefferson, NC and London: McFarland, 1992), 180.

14. The full title of the episode in French version of the film is "Anticipation ou l'amour en l'an 2000," but in the German version it is "Ein Wochenende auf der Erde im Jahre 3000"

15. See Günther Dahlke and Günter Karl, *Deutsche Spielfilme von dem Anfängen bis 1933: Ein Filmführer* (Berlin: Herschel Verlag, 1993), 118.

16. Munden, *1921–1930*, 107.

17. Krafsur, *1961–1970*, 388–89.

18. Munden, *1921–1930*, 723. See also Parish, *Prostitution in Hollywood Films*, 406–7.

19. Truffaut's Clarisse is in stark contrast to the Clarice of the David Goodis novel on which the film is based, who is slim, muscular (a former acrobat), and flat-chested. See Goodis, *Shoot the Piano Player* (New York: Grove, 1956), 43–44.

20. Willemen and Rajadhyaksha, *Encyclopaedia of Indian Cinema*, 363.

21. See Heide Fehrenbach, "*Die Sünderin* or Who Killed the German Male: Early Postwar Cinema and the Betrayal of Fatherland," in *Gender and German Cinema: Feminist Interventions, vol 2: German Film History / German History on Film*, ed. Sandra Frieden and others (Providence, Rhode Island and Oxford: Berg, 1993), 135–60.

22. Dutt subsequently made *Kaghaz ke Phool* (1959), about a creative filmmaker (played by Dutt himself) struggling to make a new version of *Devdas* — the classic story, first filmed in 1935, of a narcissistic and indecisive hero loved by a warm-hearted prostitute — and his subsequent decline into alcoholism when the film is not a success. *Kaghaz ke Phool* failed at the box office and Dutt never directed another film; he committed suicide at the age of thirty-nine. See Shampa Banerjee and Anil Srivastava, *One Hundred Indian Feature Films: An Annotated Filmography* (New York: Garland, 1988), 154, and Jean-Loup Passek, ed., *Le Cinéma indien* (Paris: Centre Georges Pompidou/l'Équerre, 1983), 57.

10. Captive

1. Nuj, in Siriporn Skrobanek, Nataya Boonpakdee, and Chutima Jantateero, *The Traffic in Women: Human Realities of the International Sex Trade* (London: Zed Books, 1997), 2.

2. Films depicting actual sexual slavery under racist or fascist regimes, such as *Behind*

the Rising Sun (USA, 1943), *Hitler's Children* (USA, 1943), *Addio zio Tom* (Italy, 1971), *Ilsa, She Wolf of the S.S.* (USA, 1974), and *Salò o Le 120 giornate di Sodoma* (Italy/France, 1975), go beyond the commercial prostitution that is the subject of this book, though the thematics are obviously related.

3. James C. Robertson, *The Hidden Cinema: British Film Censorship in Action, 1913–1972* (London: Routledge, 1989), 16.

4. Patricia King Hanson, ed., *The American Film Institute Catalog of Motion Pictures Produced in the United States: Feature Films, 1931–1940* (Berkeley: University of California Press, 1993), 1604.

5. Ibid., 1972. *Slaves in Bondage* (pp 1971–972) and *Crusade Against Rackets* (p 432) have separate entries in the *Catalog*, but it is clear from the credits and synopses that the same film is being referred to.

6. Ibid., 2344.

7. Ibid., 1275.

8. Ibid., 728.

9. Ibid., 1979.

10. Warners negotiated with *Liberty* magazine for the screen rights to the stories that it had published of two of the prostitute witnesses, and contracted screenwriters Robert Rossen and Abem Finkel to develop a screenplay based on the trial, with special emphasis on the role of the prostitutes. See Karyn Kay, "Sisters of the Night: *Marked Woman* (1937)," *The Velvet Light Trap* 6 (1972): 20.

11. Kay, "Sisters of the Night," 24.

12. Hanson, *1931–1940*, 1398.

13. *Monthly Film Bulletin*, September 1957, 114, quoted in John Hill, *Sex, Class and Realism: British Cinema 1956–1963* (London: BFI, 1986), 187.

14. Lest it be inferred that the British made a habit of blaming Italians for their social problems, it should be noted that Nick "Biaggi" is a kid from London's East End, something he does not like to be reminded of.

15. *Monthly Film Bulletin*, March 1959, 35, quoted in Hill, *Sex, Class and Realism*, 192.

16. Richard P. Krafsur, ed., *The American Film Institute Catalog of Motion Pictures: Feature Films 1961–1970* (New York: Bowker, 1976), 582.

17. *Monthly Film Bulletin*, September 1960, 130.

18. Krafsur, *1961–1970*, 845.

19. Ibid., 403.

20. Ibid., 958.

21. Ibid., 871.

22. Ibid., 845.

23. Ibid., 498.

24. Thus Skrobanek et al. note that "most recently there have been reports of women sex workers in Bangkok from Eastern Europe. One account spoke of seven young women from Romania, who had been hired to do a cabaret act in Bangkok, but who had been coerced into prostitution by their Turkish agent." Skrobanek, *The Traffic in Women*, 51.

25. Such problems include being forced to work in bonded labor to repay debt, having little control over one's conditions of employment and often being overworked, having one's freedom of movement curtailed, being cut off from family support networks,

encountering language barriers, being subject to arrest as an illegal immigrant, having no right to social services, and being the target of racial discrimination. See Skrobanek et al., *The Traffic in Women*, 66–67.

26. *Monthly Film Bulletin*, April 1962, 50.

27. *Monthly Film Bulletin*, November 1959, 150.

28. Krafsur, *1961–1970*, 139.

29. Ibid., 307.

30. Also known as *69 Liebesspiele / 69 Love Games*.

31. Scott Meek, *Monthly Film Bulletin*, July 1974, 150.

32. Krafsur, *1961–1970*, 1110.

33. Ibid., 692. The film was cut from ninety-one to sixty-seven minutes for its American release.

34. Ibid., 1218.

35. Ibid., 793.

36. Ibid., 793.

37. Ibid., 658.

38. Ibid., 257.

39. Ibid., 148.

40. Ibid., 541.

41. Ibid., 1125.

42. Ibid., 500.

43. Particularly significant in Japanese cinema was the origination of an analysis of coerced prostitution in an historical context, in films such as Mizoguchi's *Saikaku ichidai onna / The Life of Oharu* (1952) and *Sansho dayu / Sansho the Bailiff* (1954).

11. Business Woman

1. Barbara Sherman Heyl, *The Madam as Entrepreneur: Career Management in House Prostitution* (New Brunswick, NJ: Transaction, 1979), 104.

2. Bertrand Russell, *Marriage and Morals* (1929; reprint, New York: Bantam, 1959), 103.

3. Sumita S. Chakravarty, *National Identity in Indian Popular Cinema 1947–1987* (Austin: University of Texas Press, 1993), 302.

4. Dina Iordanova, "Women in the New Balkan Cinema: Surviving on the Margins," *Film Criticism* 21, no 2 (Winter 1996–97): 33–34.

5. *Monthly Film Bulletin*, September 1961, 127.

6. Geoff Brown, *Monthly Film Bulletin*, August 1978, 154.

7. Karl Marx, *Economic and Philosophical Manuscripts*, in *Early Writings*, ed. T. B. Bottomore (New York: McGraw-Hill, 1964), 178, 192, 156n.

8. *Das Mädchen Rosemarie* was coscripted by the left-wing journalist Erich Kuby, who had covered the case in the press. A second film, *Die Wahrheit über Rosemarie*, appeared in 1959. *Das Mädchen Rosemarie* was remade as a television film in 1996.

9. ". . . ein Werk von kühler, scharfer Intelligenz und unverwechselbaren Stil, ein die bundesrepublikanische Wirklichkeit virtuos verfremdendes und mittels dieser Verfremdung analysierendes Lehrstück." Christa Bandmann and Joe Hembus, *Klassiker des Deutschen Tonfilms 1930–1960* (Munich: Goldmann Verlag, 1980), 184.

10. It is not uncommon in the cinema for the US government and its agents to be

associated with prostitution. Apart from *Paisà* and *Anita Drögemoller,* one might consider, for example, *La Putain respectueuse,* in which a corrupt US senator attempts to pressure a prostitute into giving false evidence (see chapter 5); *Nada* (France/Italy, 1974), in which the US ambassador to France is kidnapped by anarchists while indulging himself at his favorite brothel; and *Warm Nights on a Slow Moving Train,* in which the intelligence agent (nationality undisclosed, but next posting Washington) employs an Australian prostitute to commit a political assassination (see chapter 13).

11. Satyajit Ray, quoted in Andrew Robinson, *Satyajit Ray: The Inner Eye* (Berkeley: University of California Press, 1989), 207.

12. André Téchiné, in "Entretien avec André Téchiné *(Barroco),"* *Cahiers du Cinéma* 279–80 (August–September 1977): 62. Translation by RC.

13. Jean-Luc Godard, "One or Two Things," *Sight and Sound* 36, no 1 (Winter 1966–67): 4.

14. "Et puis il y a cette fille, Juliette, à qui je prête mon physique, car on peut difficilement, avec Godard, parler d'interprétation." Marina Vlady, "Du *Nouvel Observateur . . .* à Godard," in *2 ou 3 choses que je sais d'elle,* by Jean-Luc Godard (Paris: Seuil/Avant-Scène, 1971), 120.

15. "La prostitution n'est pour lui qu'un prétexte, ou plutôt qu'un point limite, une caricature." Vlady, "Du *Nouvel Observateur,"* 120.

16. When Isabelle's sister tells her that she would like to earn some money by prostitution, Isabelle asks, "Have you ever licked a bloke's arse?" When the sister replies no, Isabelle says, "Well, you may have to." It is true that she goes on to remark: "But don't say yes to everything."

17. Robert Stam, *Subversive Pleasures: Bakhtin, Cultural Criticism and Film* (Baltimore: Johns Hopkins University Press, 1989), 175.

18. The scene is also reminiscent of Bree (Jane Fonda) glancing at her watch while simulating orgasm in *Klute* (USA, 1971). See chapter 17.

19. Katherine S. Woodward, "European Anti-Melodrama: Godard, Truffaut, and Fassbinder," in *Imitations of Life: A Reader of Film and Television Melodrama,* ed. Marcia Landy (Detroit: Wayne State University Press, 1991), 590.

20. Kristin Thompson, *Breaking the Glass Armor: Neoformalist Film Analysis* (Princeton: Princeton University Press, 1988), 281–82.

21. Richard P. Krafsur, ed., *The American Film Institute Catalog of Motion Pictures: Feature Films, 1961–1970* (New York: Bowker, 1976), 497.

22. Geoff Gardner, *"Kitty and the Bagman,"* in *Australian Film 1978–1994: A Survey of Theatrical Features,* ed. Scott Murray (Melbourne: Oxford University Press, 1995), 130.

23. David McGillivray, *"Moonlighting Wives,"* in *Monthly Film Bulletin,* January 1971, 10.

24. Krafsur, *1961–1970,* 727.

25. Ibid., 891.

26. The Chicken Ranch was run from the early 1950s until its closure by Edna Milton, who played a silent role in the Broadway musical production. See the entry in *The Handbook of Texas Online,* http://www.tsha.utexas.edu/handbook/online/articles/print/CC/ysc1.html (version current May 13, 2004).

27. The advertisement is reproduced in James Robert Parish, *Prostitution in Hollywood Films: Plots, Critiques, Casts and Credits for 389 Theatrical and Made-for-Television Releases* (Jefferson, NC, and London: McFarland, 1992), 460.

28. Heide Schlüpmann, "The Sinister Gaze: Three Films by Franz Hofer from 1913," in *Prima di Caligari: Cinema Tedesco, 1895–1920 / Before Caligari: German Cinema, 1895–1920*, ed. Paolo Cherchi Usai and Lorenzo Codelli (Pordenone: Edizioni Biblioteca dell'Imagine, 1990), 464.

29. Barbet Schroeder, quoted in Gavin Smith, "The Joyous Pessimism of Barbet Schroeder" *Film Comment* 31, no 2 (March–April 1995): 71.

30. Nestor Almendros, *A Man with a Camera* (New York: Farrar, Strauss, Giroux, 1984), 147. Almendros adds: "[T]he flagellation sequences, difficult by their very nature, had to be authentic. We shot them in the following way. We showed Bulle Ogier in her dominatrix outfit, with the client chained to the wall; then Bulle stepped offstage to the right to fetch her whip, and returned almost at once to beat the man furiously. However, now it was not Bulle but a specialized prostitute of the same build, with a similar wig and costume." (151).

31. The dominatrix by arrangement with whom the film had been shot later changed her mind and took out a lawsuit in a bid to prevent its release. According to director Klaus Tuschen, the faces of the clients (whose permission to appear had been gained only after they had been filmed) were optically masked, except for two who were unrecognizable because of distance from the camera. An injunction was taken out based on these two clients, and their faces had to be painted out by hand. Interview with author, August 3, 1992.

32. Sheila Benson, *Los Angeles Times*, and David Denby, *New York*, respectively, quoted in James Robert Parish, *Prostitution in Hollywood Films: Plots, Critiques, Casts and Credits for 389 Theatrical and Made-for-Television Releases* (Jefferson, NC and London: McFarland, 1992), 366, 368.

12. Happy Hooker

1. John Gardner and John Maier, *Gilgamesh: Translated from the Sîn-leqi-unninnī Version* (New York: Knopf, 1984), 81.

2. Filmoberprüfstelle report no. 596, dated Berlin, December 5, 1929, in the collection of the Deutsches Institut für Filmkunden, Wiesbaden. See also Hans-Michael Bock, "Georg Wilhelm Pabst: Documenting a Life and a Career," in *The Films of G. W. Pabst: An Extraterritorial Cinema*, ed. Eric Rentschler (New Brunswick: Rutgers University Press, 1990), 223.

3. "Reasons Underlying Particular Applications," The Motion Picture Production Code, as given in *The Dame in the Kimono: Hollywood, Censorship and the Production Code from the 1920s to the 1960s*, by Leonard J. Leff and Jerold L. Simmons (New York: Doubleday, 1990), 291.

4. Geoffrey Shurlock, letter to Eric Johnston, May 25, 1961, in *Butterfield 8* PCA File. (The Production Code Administration Files are held in the Margaret Herrick Library, Academy of Motion Picture Arts and Sciences, Beverly Hills, California.) The Atlanta Public Library Board of Trustees, the city's board of censors, ruled that *Never on Sunday* would not be licensed for exhibition with or without deletions, declaring that the film "would be harmful to the average child" and that it presented "an unacceptable idea." See Edward de Grazia and Roger K. Newman, *Banned Films: Movies, Censors and the First Amendment* (New York: Bowker, 1982), 267.

5. John Trevelyan, *What the Censor Saw* (London: Michael Joseph, 1973), 110.

6. Richard P. Krafsur, ed., *The American Film Institute Catalog of Motion Pictures: Feature Films, 1961–1970* (New York: Bowker, 1976), 748.

7. Tony Rayns, "*Memories Within Miss Aggie,*" *Monthly Film Bulletin*, August 1978, 162.

8. Sege, *Variety*, May 14,1975. An earlier, soft-core version of the story starring Hollander herself met with a similar critical response. *My Pleasure is My Business* (Canada, 1974) has been described as a "witless comedy" and Hollander's performance "expressionless." See Leonard Maltin, ed., *Leonard Maltin's Movie and Video Guide 1994 Edition* (New York: Signet, 1993), 877.

9. This is an estimate given by Libby Hogg, a video censor, in conversation with the author, Wellington, New Zealand, 1994.

10. Linda Williams, *Hard Core: Power, Pleasure, and the "Frenzy of the Visible"* (Berkeley: University of California Press, 1989), 237.

11. Ibid., 163.

13. Adventuress

1. Estela V. Welldon, *Mother, Madonna, Whore: The Idealization and Denigration of Motherhood* (London: Free Association Books, 1988 [New York: Guilford Press, 1991]), 127.

2. I have been unable to determine if this film, directed by Gilbert Wolmark, had a French title.

3. Richard P. Krafsur, ed., *The American Film Institute Catalog of Motion Pictures: Feature Films, 1961–1970* (New York: Bowker, 1976), 619.

4. Ibid., 971.

5. Ibid., 1060.

6. Ibid., 14.

7. Ibid., 694.

8. John Pym, *Monthly Film Bulletin,* January 1977, 125.

9. Ibid., 125.

10. Krafsur, *1961–1970*, 14.

11. Ibid., 971.

12. Ibid., 971, 694; Pym, *Monthly Film Bulletin*, 125.

13. Krafsur, *1961–1970*, 1060.

14. Ibid., 14.

15. Ibid., 619.

16. Ibid., 14.

17. Pym, *Monthly Film Bulletin*, 125.

18. Michael Wood, *Belle de Jour* (London: BFI, 2000), 19.

19. For a discussion of the various interpretive possibilities, see Michael Wood, "Double Lives," *Sight and Sound,* January 1992, 21–23, and Wood, *Belle de Jour,* 59–69.

20. Ellen Willis, "Feminism, Moralism, and Pornography," in *Powers of Desire: The Politics of Sexuality,* ed. Ann Snitow, Christine Stansell, and Sharon Thompson (New York: Monthly Review, 1983), 464.

21. My comments are based on the full-length version released in the cinema in Europe, and on video. The film was heavily cut for theatrical release in the United States to avoid an X-rating.

22. Quoted in Kerry Segrave and Linda Martin, *The Post-Feminist Hollywood Actress:*

Biographies and Filmographies of Stars Born After 1939 (Jefferson, NC and London: McFarland, 1990), 183.

23. See Cynthia J. Fuchs, *Gazing: Gender, Performance and Representation in Film* (PhD diss., University of Pennsylvania, 1990), 143. Fuchs notes that in the office she seems "'unnatural,' too efficient and aggressive."

24. Ibid., 136.

25. Ibid., 151.

26. Ibid., 136, 152, 154.

14. Junkie

1. Kate Millett, "Prostitution: A Quartet for Female Voices" in *Woman in Sexist Society: Studies in Power and Powerlessness*, ed. Vivian Gornick and Barbara K. Moran (New York: Basic Books, 1971), 29.

2. Ida Halvorsen, *Harter Asphalt: Autobiographie* (Munich: Verlag Frauenoffensive, 1987), 232 [German edition of *Hard Asfalt* (Oslo: Pax Forlag, 1982)], quoted in Cecilie Høigård and Liv Finstad, *Backstreets: Prostitution, Money and Love* (University Park, PA: Pennsylvania State University Press, 1992), 45.

3. Høigård and Finstad, *Backstreets*, 24.

4. A number of studies are cited in Priscilla Alexander, "Prostitution: A Difficult Issue for Feminists," in *Sex Work: Writings by Women in the Sex Industry*, ed. Frédérique Delacoste and Priscilla Alexander (London: Virago, 1988), 202. See also Roberta Perkins and Garry Bennett, *Being a Prostitute* (Sydney: Allen & Unwin, 1985), 243.

5. Alexander, "Prostitution," 202. Alex Adams, "Beverly Hills Madam" in the 1970s and '80s, writes: "And the drugs. Did they fuck for coke, or did they coke to fuck? What a vicious circle. Most of them said they needed the drugs to anesthetize themselves so they could do sex for money, yet the main reason a lot of them became hookers was because they wanted money for drugs." Alex Adams and William Stadiem, *Madam 90210: My Life as Madam to the Rich and Famous* (New York: Villard Books, 1993), 148.

6. Paul J. Goldstein, *Prostitution and Drugs* (Lexington, MA: Lexington Books, 1979), cited in Alexander, "Prostitution," 202. Some authors nevertheless contend that the incidence of drug use may be overstated, especially in relation to teenage prostitution. Thus Gitta Sereny argues: "The fact that child prostitution in Germany appears — quite erroneously — to be almost entirely associated with drug addiction is the result of a vicious circle. Police tend to concentrate their limited resources on pushers. It is these cases which get into the newspapers. The press, anyway — quite understandably — finds the drama of drug addicted youngsters easier to demonstrate than that of young girls and boys who voluntarily choose to be prostitutes." Gitta Sereny, *The Invisible Children: Child Prostitution in America, Germany and Britain* (London: André Deutsch, 1984), xix.

7. Richard P. Krafsur, ed., *The American Film Institute Catalog of Motion Pictures: Feature Films, 1961–1970* (New York: Bowker, 1976), 1122.

8. Ibid., 1198.

9. Ibid., 1019.

10. Patricia King Hanson, ed., *The American Film Institute Catalog of Motion Pictures Produced in the United States: Feature Films, 1911–1920* (Berkeley: University of California Press, 1988), 153.

11. Ibid., 631.

12. *Variety*, May 22, 1929, 24, quoted in Kenneth Munden, ed., *The American Film Institute Catalog of Motion Pictures Produced in the United States: Feature Films, 1921–1930* (New York: Bowker, 1971), 125.

13. Patricia King Hanson, ed., *The American Film Institute Catalog of Motion Pictures Produced in the United States: Feature Films, 1931–1940* (Berkeley: University of California Press, 1993), 1604.

14. Ibid., 1483.

15. Hanson, *1911–1920*, 224.

16. See James Robert Parish, *Prostitution in Hollywood Films: Plots, Critiques, Casts and Credits for 389 Theatrical and Made-for-Television Releases* (Jefferson, NC and London: McFarland, 1992), 273.

17. Ibid., 273.

18. *Monthly Film Bulletin*, January 1960, 9.

19. Krafsur, *1961–1970*, 1228.

20. Ibid., 479.

21. See the entry on the film at http://www.metamovie.de/film/deutsch/liebe.html (version current May 15, 2004).

22. Krafsur, *1961–1970*, 1228.

23. Ibid., 479.

24. *Monthly Film Bulletin*, January 1960, 9.

25. Yung., *Variety*, October 15, 1980.

26. In her book, Halvorsen writes: ". . . the most important thing was that Knut gave me the feeling that I meant something for someone. A strange contrast maybe to all the beatings. But he beat me because he was so insanely jealous. I think that jealousy comes from being unsure of yourself, afraid of losing what you have. When he was beside himself from fear of losing me, I *had* to mean everything to him. Me, an old junkie! For the first time what I did was important to another person." Halvorsen, *Harter Asphalt*, 156–57, quoted in Høigård and Finstad, *Backstreets*, 171.

27. Krafsur, *1961–1970*, 425.

28. Bizarrely, the film also offers a second ending: a closing title states that she died at the age of eighty-three. See Colin Pahlow, *"The Divine Obsession,"* *Monthly Film Bulletin*, July 1977, 145–46.

29. Sereny, *The Invisible Children*, 49–50.

30. Krafsur, 471.

31. The actor appears to be uncredited.

32. The director is Uli Edel, who later made *Last Exit to Brooklyn*.

33. Henry Sheehan, *Hollywood Reporter*, quoted in Parish, *Prostitution in Hollywood Films*, 98.

34. Sheehan in Parish, *Prostitution in Hollywood Films*, 98.

35. In conversation with writer/director Paul Schrader, Kevin Jackson commented that the film "has a strange and extremist moral stance, as if the only two options which existed were the extreme rectitude of the George C. Scott character [Jake] or the extreme depravity of the pornographers." Schrader replied: "Yes, that's a kind of adolescent hyperbole I'm not very happy with." Kevin Jackson, ed., *Schrader on Schrader* (London: Faber & Faber, 1990), 149.

36. Tim Kreider, *"Eyes Wide Shut,"* *Film Quarterly* 43, no 3 (Spring 2000): 41.

15. Baby Doll

1. John Cleland, *Fanny Hill: Memoirs of a Woman of Pleasure* (London: Mayflower-Dell, 1964), 30.

2. Nick Davies, *Dark Heart: The Shocking Truth about Hidden Britain* (London: Chatto & Windus, 1997), 31–32.

3. Columbia Tristar Home Video, 1999.

4. Martin Scorsese, audio commentary, Voyager Criterion *Taxi Driver* laserdisc, 1991.

5. B. Ruby Rich, "Never a Victim: Jodie Foster, a New Kind of Female Hero," in *Women and Film: A Sight and Sound Reader,* ed. Pam Cook and Philip Dodd (London: Scarlet Press, [1993]), 55.

6. *Variety,* March 10, 1971.

7. *Sex und noch nicht sechzehn* was banned in the state of Vorarlberg, Austria, because of its potential to exert a "brutalizing and demoralizing effect on spectators." Decree published March 17, 1969. http://voris.vorarlberg.at/voris/chronik/1969/6_1969.doc (version current May 18, 2004).

8. Alexandre Alexandre, *"Moral und Sinnlichkeit:* Der erste — damals noch — thematisch sehr heikle Sexualfilm" (1919), "Sex im Kino," *Cinema* (Hamburg) *Sonderband Nr. 4* [ca. 1980]: 55, 56.

9. Louis Malle in *Malle on Malle,* ed. Philip French (London: Faber & Faber, 1993), 118. The character is based on an actual Storyville prostitute, "Violet," who recounts her brothel childhood in Al Rose, *Storyville, New Orleans: Being an Authentic, Illustrated Account of the Notorious Red-Light District* (Tuscaloosa: University of Alabama Press, 1974), 148–50.

10. The part is presumably played by Dominique Troyes, who stars in the film.

11. *Variety,* June 4, 1980.

12. Richard P. Krafsur, ed., *The American Film Institute Catalog of Motion Pictures: Feature Films, 1961–1970* (New York: Bowker, 1976), 1227.

13. *Variety,* March 10, 1971.

14. François is clearly an author surrogate for the film's writer-director, Jean-Claude Brisseau, formerly a teacher of literature.

15. James R. Kincaid, *Erotic Innocence: The Culture of Child Molesting* (Durham, NC: Duke University Press, 1998), 126. Kincaid contends that "a country that regards children as erotic and also regards an erotic response to children not merely as criminal but as criminally unimaginable has a problem on its hands." (21).

16. Prior to selecting her for the role of Violet, Malle had seen the *Woman in the Child* series of nude photographs of ten-year-old Brooke Shields by Garry Gross. "I was especially happy with the casting of Brooke Shields," Malle says. "There was something about her astonishing beauty that in the context of the story was both very disturbing and incredibly moving." Malle in *Malle on Malle,* 120, 121. The photographs have been marketed over the Internet by the photographer (http://www.thewomaninthechild.com, version current February 15, 2002).

17. The original film is TV-modest in its handling of sex and nudity, but the version released on video contains additional sex scenes.

18. The film notes that Joey Buttafuoco denied having had a sexual relationship with Amy, but in 1993 he was convicted of her statutory rape. He later became a film actor.

19. Patricia Aufderheide, "Cross-Cultural Film Guide: *Iracema*," http://www.library. american.edu/subject/media/aufderheide/iracema.html (version current May 18, 2004).

20. Raffaele Caputo, "*Mouth to Mouth*,'" in *Australian Film 1978–1994: A Survey of Theatrical Features*, ed. Scott Murray (Melbourne: Oxford University, 1995), 19.

21. *491* was initially rejected by the Swedish censors but eventually passed with cuts. It was banned in Norway and the United Kingdom. In the United States it was seized by Customs, but released by court order. See John Trevelyan, *What the Censor Saw* (London: Michael Joseph, 1973), 157–58; Guy Phelps, *Film Censorship* (London: Gollancz, 1975), 132, 158, 243; and Gillian Hanson, *Original Skin: Nudity and Sex in Cinema and Theatre* (London: Tom Stacey, 1970), 101–2.

22. Trevelyan, *What the Censor Saw*, 158.

23. Keith Connolly, "Social Realism," in *The New Australian Cinema*, ed. Scott Murray (Melbourne: Nelson, 1980), 32.

24. Aufderheide, "Cross-Cultural Film Guide: *Iracema*."

25. James Robert Parish, *Prostitution in Hollywood Films: Plots, Critiques, Casts and Credits for 389 Theatrical and Made-for-Television Releases* (Jefferson, NC and London: McFarland, 1992), 99.

26. Ibid., 317.

27. "You know how we used to handle somebody like Johnny Dee?" the sergeant asks. "We would go in there and bust heads. We would run his pimps out of town, we would roust his joints, hassle his broads, and every time we saw the sonofabitch we would throw him in jail, and by the time he made it around the precinct a few times his face wouldn't be so pretty. It had its bad side but I tell you one thing, the pukes did not run this city."

16. Working Girl

1. Hilary, in Jan Jordan, *Working Girls* (Auckland: Penguin Books [NZ], 1991), 112.

2. Michael Milner, *Sex on Celluloid* (New York: MacFadden, 1964), 88.

3. See Jacques Zimmer, ed., *Cinéma érotique* (Paris: Edilig, 1982), 31. The French title of *Bella di giorno, moglie di notte* is *Prostituée le jour, épouse la nuit*. Zimmer also mentions a film titled *Confessions d'une prostituée*, which I have not been able to identify.

4. Milner, *Sex on Celluloid*, 180.

5. This is the position adopted by Nickie Roberts in *Whores in History:* "From any point of view, in a society which worships money and material achievements to the extent that ours does, becoming a prostitute is a rational decision for a woman to make. Living standards may have risen since the 19th century, but so have expectations; and women are still in the business of refusing poverty when they take up sex work—particularly those disadvantaged women who form the majority of prostitutes. How else are they supposed to give themselves and their families the kind of lifestyle promoted by the Western media as the norm—a life of security, comfort and consumerism? Faced with the choice between drudging for a pittance—with no guarantee that they can keep their heads above water—and making real money through prostitution, these women are making a responsible decision when they turn to the sex trade." Nickie Roberts, *Whores in History: Prostitution in Western Society* (London: Grafton [HarperCollins], 1992), 331–32.

6. Richard P. Krafsur, ed., *The American Film Institute Catalog of Motion Pictures: Feature Films, 1961–1970* (New York: Bowker, 1976), 407.

7. Tony Garnett, in Arts Guardian, *Guardian,* Feb. 10, 1981, quoted in Eileen McLeod, *Women Working: Prostitution Now* (London: Croom Helm, 1982), 139.

8. McLeod, *Women Working,* 139.

9. Karl Marx, *Economic and Philosophical Manuscripts,* in *Early Writings,* ed. T. B. Bottomore (New York: McGraw-Hill, 1964), 156n.

10. Alison M. Jaggar, "Prostitution," in *The Philosophy of Sex: Contemporary Readings,* ed. Alan Soble (Totowa, NJ: Littlefield, Adams, 1980), 358.

11. *Working Girls* premiered at a COYOTE event in San Francisco. Louise Smith, the leading actor in the film, recalls that prostitutes in the audience were "thrilled, because finally there was this film that was more realistic, and the people didn't look like bimbos or drug addicts . . . they were sympathetic, and I was really happy that prostitutes liked the film, that was very important to me." Interview with author, New York City, January 7, 1993.

12. Lizzie Borden, quoted in Lynne Jackson, "Labor Relations: An Interview with Lizzie Borden," *Cineaste* 15, no 3 (1987): 4.

13. Ibid., 9.

14. *Calling the Shots* (Canada, 1989), directed by Janis Cole and Holly Dale.

15. Ibid.

16. Smith, interview with author.

17. Borden, in Jackson, "Labor Relations," 8.

18. Graham Fuller, "*Working Girls,*" *Cineaste* 15, no 3 (1987): 43.

19. Smith, interview with author.

20. Sarah, in Jan Jordan, *Working Girls: Women in the New Zealand Sex Industry* (Auckland: Penguin, 1991), 24.

21. On this subject, see Annette Brauerhoch, "Auf's Geld gekommen: Lizzie Bordens *Working Girls,*" *Frauen und Film* 43 (December 1987): 102–6.

22. Fuller makes this point in his review of the film (43). In her PhD dissertation, *Gazing: Gender, Performance and Representation in Film* (University of Pennsylvania, 1990), Cynthia J. Fuchs interprets the scene in terms of the film's exploration of language as "'oppressive cultural determinant'" (173).

23. Smith, interview with author.

24. Ibid.

17. The Love Story

1. Xaviera Hollander, with Robin Moore and Yvonne Dunleavy, *The Happy Hooker* (New York: Dell, 1972), 189.

2. David E. James, "Im Kwon-Taek: Korean National Cinema and Buddhism," *Film Quarterly* 54, no. 3 (Spring 2001): 31 n26.

3. Sumita S. Chakravarty, *National Identity in Indian Popular Cinema 1947–1987* (Austin: University of Texas Press, 1993), 269–70.

4. *Monthly Film Bulletin* (December 1955), 178.

5. Subsequent silent versions include *La signora delle camelie* (Italy, 1909), *La Dame aux camélias* (France, 1912), *La signora dalle camelie* (Italy, 1915), *Camille* (USA, 1915), *Prima Vera* (Germany, 1917), *Camille* (USA, 1917), *La dama de las camelias* (Mexico, 1919), *Arme Violetta* (Germany, 1920), *Camille* (USA, 1921), *Damen med kameliorna* (Sweden, 1925), and *Camille* (USA, 1927). In the sound era, the story has been filmed as *La Dame aux camélias* (France,

1934), *Camille* (USA, 1936), *La dama de las camelias* (Mexico, 1944), *La dama de las camelias* (Chile, 1947), *La Dame aux camélias* (France/Italy, 1953), *La mujer de las camelias* (Argentina, 1954), *La bella Lola/Une dame aux camélias/Quel nostro impossible amore* (Spain/France/Italy, 1962), *Crónica de un amor* (Mexico, 1972), *Camille* (USA, TV, 1984), and *La dame aux camélias* (France, TV, 1998). Variations on the Dumas original include *The Lover of Camille* (USA, 1924), *Traviata '53* (Italy, 1953), *Camille 2000* (Italy, 1969)—in which Marguerite is a drug addict who dies of an overdose—and *La dama delle camelie/La Dame aux camélias/Die Kameliendama/The True Story of Camille* (Italy/France/West Germany, 1981), discussed in chapter 8. In addition, there are screen versions of the Verdi opera including *La Traviata* (Italy, 1967), *La Traviata* (Italy, 1982), and sundry television productions.

6. James Robert Parish, *Prostitution in Hollywood Films: Plots, Critiques, Casts and Credits for 389 Theatrical and Made-for-Television Releases* (Jefferson, NC and London: McFarland, 1992), 319.

7. Richard P. Krafsur, ed., *The American Film Institute Catalog of Motion Pictures: Feature Films, 1961–1970* (New York: Bowker, 1976), 491.

8. See for example Cecilie Høigård and Liv Finstad, *Backstreets: Prostitution, Money and Love* (University Park, PA: Pennsylvania State University Press, 1992), 29–30.

9. An adaptation of the Eugene O'Neill play was also released in Japan in 1923 under the title *Kiri no minato/Harbor in the Fog.*

10. Referred to in some prints as "Nell," as noted in chapter 3.

11. Later films that could be cited include, with a lone criminal protagonist, *Abhijan* (India, 1962), *Sansar Simantey* (India, 1975), *Zona roja* (Mexico, 1975), *The Great Scout and Cathouse Thursday* (USA, 1976), *Grand Frère* (France, 1982), *Some Kind of Hero* (USA, 1982), *Clinton and Nadine* (USA, 1988); with a gangster, *The Cool World* (USA, 1963), *Hussy* (UK, 1979), *Casino* (USA, 1995); with an ex-prisoner, *Les Clandestines* (France, 1954), *Stroszek* (West Germany, 1977), *Sheng gang qi bing III/Long Arm of the Law III* (Hong Kong, 1989); and so on.

12. Michelle Citron, "Feminist Criticism: What It is Now; What It Must Become," *The Velvet Light Trap* 6 (Fall 1972): 43.

13. Diane Giddis, "The Divided Woman: Bree Daniels in *Klute*," in *Women and the Cinema: A Critical Anthology*, ed. Karyn Kay and Gerald Peary (New York: Dutton, 1977), 27–28.

14. The interview was shot as one scene, which was later cut into several segments and dispersed through the film. Fonda comments: "That was the last scene we shot and by that time I knew the character very well. You find areas in yourself that relate to the character and then learn how those things are expressed differently than you would express them. . . . I think it worked real well." Dan Georgakas and Lenny Rubinstein, *The Cineaste Interviews: On the Art and Politics of the Cinema* (Chicago: Lake View, 1983), 113.

15. See e.g. Christine Gledhill, "*Klute* Part 1: A Contemporary Film Noir and Feminist Criticism" and "*Klute* Part 2: Feminism and *Klute*" in *Women in Film Noir*, ed. E. Ann Kaplan (London: BFI, 1978), 6–21, 112–28; Maggie Humm, "Is the Gaze Feminist? Pornography, Film and Feminism," in *Perspectives on Pornography: Sexuality in Film and Literature.* ed. Gary Day and Clive Bloom (London: Macmillan, 1988), 74–77; Kaja Silverman, *The Acoustic Voice: The Female Voice in Psychoanalysis and Cinema* (Bloomington: Indiana University, 1988), 81–84; Cynthia J. Fuchs, *Gazing: Gender, Performance and Representation in Film* (PhD diss., University of Pennsylvania, 1990), 119–36, 138; and Humm, *Feminism and Film* (Edinburgh: Edinburgh University Press, 1997), 47–52.

16. Dagmar Beiersdorf, in conversation with Judith Kuckart, in *Kino 82 / 83: Bundesdeutsche Filme auf der Leinwand,* ed. Robert Fischer (Munich: Verlag Monika Nüchtern, 1982), 45.

18. Prostitute and Pimp

1. Jane Addams, *A New Conscience and an Ancient Evil* (New York: Macmillan, 1913), 60–61.

2. In *City of Eros: New York City, Prostitution, and the Commercialization of Sex, 1790–1920* (New York: W. W. Norton, 1992), Timothy J. Gilfoyle discusses the emergence of pimps as protectors of brothels and of streetwalkers in the 1830s (see 88–89). According to Jacques Rossiaud, cited by Gilfoyle (358 n37), prostitutes were attached to pimps in fifteenth-century France.

3. Chicago Vice Commission, *The Social Evil in Chicago: A Study of Existing Conditions* (Chicago: Vice Commission of the City of Chicago, 1911), 184.

4. Cecilie Høigård and Liv Finstad, *Backstreets: Prostitution, Money, and Love* (University Park, PA: Pennsylvania State University Press, 1992), 149 (originally published in Norway, 1986).

5. Ibid., 161 (emphasis in the original).

6. Ibid., 170–71.

7. See e.g. Sheila Jeffreys, *The Idea of Prostitution* (Melbourne: Spinifex, 1997), 256–59.

8. Erich Fromm, *The Art of Loving* (New York: Bantam, 1963), 16–17. A similar argument is also made by Simone de Beauvoir in *The Second Sex,* as Jessica Benjamin notes: "De Beauvoir has pointed out that masochism is essentially a desire for subordination to another person, rather than for the experience of pain as such." Benjamin goes on to suggest that "masochism is a search for recognition of the self by an other who alone is powerful enough to bestow this recognition." "Master and Slave: The Fantasy of Erotic Domination," in *Powers of Desire: The Politics of Sexuality,* ed. Ann Snitow, Christine Stansell, and Sharon Thompson (New York: Monthly Review, 1983), 286.

9. Gail Sheehy, *Hustling: Prostitution in Our Wide-Open Society* (New York: Delacorte, 1973), 24–25, 105–6. A more positive picture of the New York pimp is given in Arlene Carmen and Howard Moody, *Working Women: The Subterranean World of Street Prostitution* (New York: Harper & Row, 1985), chap. 5.

10. Høigård and Finstad, *Backstreets,* 168. Their discussion cites a model of four continua — "degree of planning when meeting the woman," "the relationship's emotional content," "economy," and "number of women" — developed by Sven-Axel Månsson. They point out that "because each dimension is independent of the others, a number of different pimp-profiles exist."

11. Naomi Greene remarks: "Although the hero of *Accattone* is supposedly in love with Stella, the camera caresses not Stella, the object of *his* desire, but Accattone himself." *Pier Paolo Pasolini: Cinema as Heresy* (Princeton: Princeton University Press, 1990), 50.

12. The subproletarian milieu on the outskirts of Rome provided the material for Pasolini's first novels and for much of his early screenwriting, including episodes involving prostitutes in *Le notti di Cabiria / The Nights of Cabiria* (Federico Fellini, 1957), *La notte brava* (Mauro Bolognini, 1959), *La giornata balorda* (Mauro Bolognini, 1960), and *La commare secca / The Grim Reaper* (Bernardo Bertolucci, 1962). Franco Citti, a nonprofessional actor, was from the milieu, and Pasolini had known him since he was a small boy. See Oswald

Stack, *Pasolini on Pasolini* (Bloomington: Indiana University Press, 1969), 8, 31–32, 38. *Accattone* and *Mamma Roma* (1962) were Pasolini's first two films as director.

13. For a discussion of the gay sensibility in Pasolini's approach to film, see e.g. Greene, 50–52. For accounts of the attacks to which Pasolini was repeatedly subjected because of his homosexuality, see Enzo Siciliano, *Pasolini: A Biography* (London: Bloomsbury, 1987), 134, 243–48, 356.

14. See e.g. Christian Braad Thomsen, *Fassbinder: The Life and Work of a Provocative Genius* (London: Faber, 1997), 6.

15. See "Fassbinder: 'Der Biberkopf, das bin ich,'" *Der Spiegel*, October 1, 1980, 224–47. The autobiographical investment of Fassbinder in the television version of *Berlin Alexanderplatz* has been much discussed. See e.g. Thomas Elsaesser, *"Berlin Alexanderplatz: Franz Biberkopf/s/Exchange," Wide Angle* 12, no. 1 (1990): 30–33; Achim Haag, *"Deine Sehnsucht kann keiner stillen": Rainer Werner Fassbinders Berlin Alexanderplatz* (Munich: Trickster, 1992); Kaja Silverman, *Male Subjectivity at the Margins* (London: Routledge, 1992), 214–96; and Jane Shattuc, *Television, Tabloids and Tears* (Minneapolis: University of Minnesota Press, 1995), 134–62.

16. Daniel Schmid, in *Chaos as Usual: Conversations About Rainer Werner Fassbinder*, ed. Julian Lorenz (New York: Applause, 1997), 7.

17. Caven and Fassbinder were once married in real life. On their wedding night Caven was locked out of the bedroom while Fassbinder disported with his male lover of the time. Braad Thomsen, *Fassbinder*, 21. Caven later noted: "Rainer was a homosexual who also needed a woman. It's that simple, and that complex." In Lorenz, *Chaos as Usual*, 45.

18. "How are you going to fight back against something that's been done to women for a thousand years?" Fassbinder remarked, in relation to his film *Martha*. "And while this has been going on, they've become much too weak to fight back anyway, even if they wanted to try." "Talking About Oppression with Margit Carstensen" in *West German Filmmakers on Film: Visions and Voices*, ed. Eric Rentschler (New York: Holmes & Meier, 1988), 168.

19. The French title of the film is *Descente aux enfers*.

20. Nathalie Baye also won a César as best actress, and *La Balance* as best film. The movie was an enormous popular success, with four million viewers in its year of release.

19. Condemned to Death

1. Sam Rohdie, *Rocco and His Brothers (Rocco e i suoi fratelli)* (London: BFI, 1992), 30.

2. Teresa de Lauretis, *Alice Doesn't: Feminism, Semiotics, Cinema* (Bloomington: Indiana University Press, 1984), 139.

3. The Catholic Church's position has been strongly influenced by St. Augustine, who declared: "Suppress prostitution, and capricious lusts will overthrow society." Quoted in Nickie Roberts, *Whores in History: Prostitution in Western Society* (London: HarperCollins, 1992), 61. The Church's accommodation with prostitution came under fire during the Reformation. In *Beyond Power: of Women, Men and Morals* (New York: Summit, 1985), Marilyn French notes that early Protestants opposed the system of clerical concubinage whereby priests paid a tax to the Church for their traditional right to maintain concubines and prostitutes (173). Hookers come under attack from deranged religious fanatics

in such films as *Le Puritain/The Puritan* (France, 1938), *Crimes of Passion* (USA, 1984), and *Edge of Sanity* (UK, 1989).

4. Ron Mottram, *The Danish Cinema Before Dreyer* (Metuchen, NJ: Scarecrow, 1988), 186.

5. Patricia King Hanson, ed., *The American Film Institute Catalog of Motion Pictures Produced in the United States: Feature Films, 1911–1920* (Berkeley: University of California Press, 1988), 1065.

6. Jorge Ayala Blanco, *Aventura del Cine Mexicano* (México DF: Ediciones Era, 1968), 131.

7. Richard P. Krafsur, ed., *The American Film Institute Catalog of Motion Pictures: Feature Films, 1961–1970* (New York: Bowker, 1976), 1054.

8. Miriam Bratu Hansen, "Falling Women, Rising Stars, New Horizons: Shanghai Silent Film as Vernacular Modernism," *Film Quarterly* 54, no. 1 (Fall 2000): 19.

9. Patricia King Hanson, ed., *The American Film Institute Catalog of Motion Pictures Produced in the United States: Feature Films, 1931–1940* (Berkeley: University of California Press, 1993), 2338.

10. *Monthly Film Bulletin,* January 1960, 9.

11. Rosie Summers, "Prostitution", in *Sex Work: Writings by Women in the Sex Industry,* ed. Frédérique Delacoste and Priscilla Alexander (London: Virago, 1988), 117.

12. Quoted in Roberts, *Whores in History,* 304.

13. Ibid., 303–4. British Attorney-General Sir Michael Havers said of Sutcliffe's victims that "some were prostitutes, but perhaps the saddest part of this case is that some were not." The statement was published in *The Times,* July 18, 1982. Jim Hobson, acting assistant police chief constable of West Yorkshire during the Ripper hunt, said of the killer: "He has made it clear that he hates prostitutes. Many people do. We, as a police force, will continue to arrest prostitutes." Hobson went on to say: "But the Ripper is now killing innocent girls." See also Roberta Perkins and Garry Bennett, *Being a Prostitute* (Sydney: Allen & Unwin, 1985), 240.

14. Krafsur, *1961–1970,* 642.

15. Jack the Ripper appears as a character (alongside Harun-al-Rashid and Ivan the Terrible) in *Wachsfigurenkabinett/Waxworks* (Germany, 1924) but simply as a nightmare bogeyman, chasing but not killing his quarry.

16. Interestingly, the journal of the real Jack the Ripper, if it is genuine (and on a fantasy level, if it is forged), points to a slightly different etiology for the crimes. His 1888 killing spree, not directly sexual in origin, is undertaken to punish his wife, the mother of his dearly loved young children, for being unfaithful, not so much for betraying him but for *confusing the categories of the sexual and the maternal.* The whores he kills stand in for the "whore" Florie, his wife: "A whores whim / caused Sir Jim, / to cut deeper, deeper and deeper / All did go, / As I did so, / back to the whoring mother." Eventually his hostility and megalomania grow to the extent that he fantasizes wiping all prostitutes from the face of the earth: "All who sell their dirty wares shall pay, of that I have no doubt," "I am convinced God placed me here to kill all whores, for he must have done so, am I still not here." Shirley Harrison, ed., *The Diary of Jack the Ripper* (London: Smith Gryphon, 1993), 285, 273, 283. Paul H. Feldman makes a strong case for the authenticity of the journal — and hence for the culpability of its author, James Maybrick — in *Jack the Ripper: The Final Chapter* (London: Virgin, 1997).

17. There are numerous films taking as their point of departure Robert Louis Stevenson's *The Strange Case of Dr. Jekyll and Mr. Hyde* (1886). More or less straight versions of the story include *The Modern Dr. Jekyll* (USA, 1908), *Dr. Jekyll and Mr. Hyde* (Denmark, 1910), *Dr. Jekyll and Mr. Hyde* (USA, 1912), *Dr. Jekyll and Mr. Hyde* (USA, 1913), *Dr. Jekyll and Mr. Hyde* (USA, 1920, directed by John S. Robertson), *Dr. Jekyll and Mr. Hyde* (USA, 1920, directed by J. Charles Haydon), *Dr. Jekyll and Mr. Hyde* (USA, 1931), *Dr. Jekyll and Mr. Hyde* (USA, 1941), *The Two Faces of Dr. Jekyll* (UK, 1960), and *Dr. Jekyll and Mr. Hyde* (USA, 2002). Among the spin-offs are *The Son of Dr. Jekyll* (USA, 1951), *El secreto del Dr. Orloff / Brides of Dr. Jekyll* (Spain/Austria/France, 1964), *Dr. Jekyll and Sister Hyde* (UK, 1971), *Dr. Jekyll y el Hombre Lobo / Doctor Jekyll and the Werewolf* (Spain, 1972), *The Man with Two Heads / Dr. Jekyll and Mr. Blood* (USA, 1972), *Dr. Black, Mr. Hyde* (USA, 1976), *Docteur Jekyll et les femmes / The Blood of Doctor Jekyll* (France/West Germany, 1981), *Dr. Jekyll's Dungeon of Death* (USA, 1982), *Jekyll & Hyde . . . Together Again* (USA, 1982), and *Mary Reilly* (USA, 1996). There are also many TV adaptations, and comedy and musical versions.

Jack the Ripper is an elusive presence in *The Lodger* (UK, 1926) and later adaptations of the novel by Marie Belloc Lowndes including *The Lodger* (UK, 1932), *The Lodger* (USA, 1944), and *The Man in the Attic* (USA, 1954). A variant on the theme is offered in *Room to Let* (UK, 1950). A fully fledged Ripper narrative emerged in *Jack the Ripper* (UK, 1959), which was followed by *A Study in Terror* (UK, 1965), *Jack el destripador de Londres / Sette cadaveri per Scotland Yard / Jack the Mangler of London* (Spain/Italy, 1971), *Jack the Ripper* (West Germany/Switzerland, 1976—known as *Der Dirnenmörder von London* in a cut version), *Murder By Decree* (Canada/UK, 1979), the television miniseries *Jack the Ripper* (UK, 1988), and *From Hell* (Czech Republic/USA, 2001). Variants include *Hands of the Ripper* (UK, 1971), in which the killer is Jack's daughter; *Das Ungeheuer von London City / The Monster of London City* (West Germany, 1964) and *Lulú de noche / Lulu By Night* (Spain, 1985), both of which involve the production of a stage play about Jack the Ripper; *The Ripper* (USA, 1985), featuring a college professor (giving a course on famous crimes in the cinema—what else?) possessed by the evil in Jack the Ripper's ring; and *Jack's Back* (USA, 1988), which showcases copycat murders marking the 100th anniversary of the originals.

There is considerable convergence in the two myths: it is noteworthy, for example, that the only woman hurt in Stevenson's story is a match girl who is run over, and it is only later that Hyde becomes a killer of whores, while there are frequent suggestions that Jack the Ripper, like Jekyll, is a doctor. In *Preposterous Violence: Fables of Aggression in Modern Culture* (New York: Oxford University Press, 1989), James B. Twitchell notes: "In each movie version, Hyde has become progressively more violent, more independent of Jekyll's repressive codes, and more willing to strike out on his own" (202).

18. Klaus Theweleit, *Male Fantasies, I: Women, Floods, Bodies, History* (Cambridge: Polity, 1987), 191.

19. Geoffrey Nowell-Smith, *Luchino Visconti* (London: Secker & Warburg, 1967), 176.

20. Claretta Tonetti, *Luchino Visconti* (London: Columbus, 1987), 90.

21. Sam Rohdie, *Rocco and His Brothers (Rocco e i suoi fratelli)* (London: BFI, 1992).

22. Ibid., 66, 25, 15.

23. Ibid., 70.

24. Ibid., 52, 15.

25. Ibid., 66.

26. The client is played by film director Werner Herzog.

27. Anneke Smelik, "And the Mirror Cracked: Metaphors of Violence in the Films of Marleen Gorris," *Women's Studies International Forum* 16, no. 4 (1993): 357.

20. The Paradigm and Its Challengers

1. Michelle Citron, in "Women and Film: A Discussion of Feminist Aesthetics," *New German Critique* 13 (Winter 1978): 104.

2. Roy Armes, *French Cinema Since 1946, Vol. 2: The Personal Style* (London: Zwemmer, 1970), 75.

INDEX